The State in Contemporary Islamic Thought

The State in Contemporary Islamic Thought

A Historical Survey of the Major Muslim Political Thinkers of the Modern Era

Abdelilah Belkeziz

Translated for the Centre for Arab Unity Studies by Abdullah Richard Lux

I.B.Tauris Publishers
In Association With
The Centre for Arab Unity Studies

مركز دراسات الوحدة العربية
CENTRE FOR ARAB UNITY STUDIES

مؤسسة محمد بن راشد آل مكتوم
MOHAMMED BIN RASHID
AL MAKTOUM FOUNDATION

The translation and publication of this book was made possible by the generous financial support of the Mohammed Bin Rashid Al Maktoum Foundation.

New paperback edition published in 2015 by I.B.Tauris & Co. Ltd
6 Salem Road, London W2 4BU
175 Fifth Avenue, New York NY 10010
www.ibtauris.com
Published in association with the Centre for Arab Unity Studies

Centre for Arab Unity Studies
'Beit Al-Nahda' Bldg. – Basra Street – Hamra
PO Box: 113-6001 Hamra
Beirut 2034 2407 – LEBANON
www.caus.org.lb

First published in 2009 in hardback by I.B.Tauris & Co. Ltd

ISBN: 978 1 78076 649 2
eISBN: 978 0 85773 805 9

A full CIP record for this book is available from the British Library
A full CIP record is available from the Library of Congress

Library of Congress Catalog Card Number: available

Designed and Typeset by 4word Ltd, Bristol, UK

Contents

Preface to the English Language Edition ix

Preface xix

PART ONE: From the Nation State to the State of the *Khilāfah*

1 **The State of the '*Tanẓīmāt*' or the State of Reason and *al-Shar'* (Islamic Law)** 3

The State and Reform

The Context of the Nation State in the Islamic Reformist Consciousness

Heralding the State

What is the Position of *al-Shar'* (Islamic Law)?

2 **For the Sake of the Nation State: A Criticism of Political and Religious Autocracy** 27

Introduction

The Last Cry of Reform

On the Criticism of Autocracy

– On the Criticism of Religious Justifications for Autocracy

– On Autocracy, the Destroyer of Civilization

3 **The Conditional State: The Constitutional Question in Modern Shī'ite Political *Fiqh*** 47

Introduction

Al-Imāmah (the imamate) and Authority in the 'Age of Occultation'

From 'Permission' for Illegitimate Political Authority to Theorizing Legitimate Political Authority
- On Legitimate Political Authority: From 'Infallibility' (*al-'iṣmah*) to the Constitution
- 'Constitutional *Fiqh*'

4 **From the Nation State to the State of the *Khilāfah*: Renewal of 'Islamic Legal Politics'** 71
Introduction
On the Causes of the Return to the Idea of the *Khilāfah*
- On the Islamic Legal Causes
- On the Political Causes
On the Renewal of 'Islamic Legal Politics'
- On the Meaning of the *Khilāfah*
- On the Concept of *Ahl al-Ḥal wa al-'Aqd*
The *Khilāfah* of Necessity, the Necessity of the *Khilāfah*

5 **On the Theoretical Criticism of the *Khilāfah*** 95
The Blessed *Khilāfah*: Theoretical Tragedy and Political Impediment
A *Khilāfah* Without an Islamic Legal Origin: The Thesis of 'Abd al-Rāziq
- The Absolute Sultanate or 'Sublimity in Politics' *(al-Ta'ālī bi-l-Sīyāsah)*
- The *Khilāfah* in the Measure of Islamic Law
- Brute Force is the Basis of the *Khilāfah*
- Government in Islam is Political
Criticism of the *Khilāfah*...from Afar

PART TWO: From the Islamic State to the Religious State

6 **On the 'Islamic State' – Religious and Political Aspects** 119
The Birth of the Problematic of the 'Islamic State'
- On the Need for a State
- The Islamic State and the Religious State
The Islamic State in the Discourse of Ḥasan al-Bannā:
- Divergences in Understanding
- The State and the Constitution
- The Multiplicity of Political Parties or the Specter of Civic Strife (*al-Fitnah*)

7 **The State and *al-Sharī'ah* in the Criticism of the Secular Idea** 143
The *Sharī'ah* of the State
A Debate Against the Secular Idea

On the Subject of 'Implementation of the *Sharī'ah*'
– *Sharī'ah* and *Ijtihād*
– The Rulings of the *Sharī'ah*: Descent and Gradual Implementation

8 *Al-Shūrā* and Democracy – Connection and Disjuncture 171
On the Meaning of *al-Shūrā*
The System of *al-Shūrā*
Al-Shūrā and Democracy: on Relations of Proximity
Al-Shūrā is Religious and Democracy is Secular

9 Pseudo-Theocracy in the Rule of Allah – '*al-Ḥākimīyah*' 195
On the Destinies of the Expression 'Islamic State'
The *Jāhilī* Society and the Muslim Society
On the Concept of '*al-Ḥākimīyah*'

10 Pseudo-Theocracy: On the '*Wilāyat al-Faqīh*' 219
From 'Conditional' to the 'Imamate': The Context of Retreat
On the Renewal of Subjects of the *Fiqh* of the Imamate
– The Imamate and its Designation
– The Invalidation of *al-Shūrā*
On the '*Wilāyat al-Faqīh*'
– On the Need for Government
– On the Functions of the *Fuqahā'*
– On the Model of Islamic Government

11 On the Criticism of 'Divine Right' 241
On the Criticism of Religious Authority
On the Criticism of '*al-Ḥākimīyah*'
On the Criticism of the '*Wilāyat al-Faqīh*'

12 Is There a Contemporary Islamic Thought? 267
On the Application of the Term 'Islamic' to 'Islamic Thought'
On the Conceptual Affiliation to Contemporary 'Islamic Literature'

Epilogue 285

References 297

Index 309

Preface to the English Language Edition

Between the time of presenting this book for publication in the summer of 2001 – after having been working on it since 1994 until I finished editing it in late 1999 – and the time of publication of the first edition by the Centre for Arab Unity Studies in 2002, a drastic, dramatic change has transpired, that might have some correlation to the subject which I have addressed: namely, the events of 11 September 2001, and their major political and cultural repercussions and consequences – especially those pertinent to the relation between Islam and Muslims and the West.

The subjects of this book never encompassed the relation between Islam and the West until the attacks on New York and Washington stopped me in my tracks – imposing upon me the realization that I ought to take this subject as central to the book, or at least attempt to fill in some gaps; or support otherwise elucidated topics; or to reconstruct a given hypothesis; or enrich the text with contingent amendments or addenda imposed by current grave variables... The book embarked – in the first instance – on an explication of various conceptual methodologies in cognizance of the 'question of the state' that are implemented by two contemporary Islamist discourses: the *Islamic Reformist* discourse and the *Islamic Revivalist* one. It had to observe and analyze the methods utilized by such an Islamic consciousness for the issue of state in regard to the four main problematics that were thrust upon it, or even might have been self-engendered while contemplating the models of the nation state, the state of the *khilāfah*, the Islamic state, and the religious 'theocratic' state. Upon such observation and analysis, the book further had to trace this cognizance over a long time-span that involved five generations of Islamist intelligentsia: from the generation of al-Ṭahṭāwī up to that of 'al-Jihādīyah al-Islāmīyah' in the late twentieth century. Nonetheless, it would be almost impossible to take the events of September 11 for granted that neither the book nor its author are able to discuss their inferences; equally, it would be impossible to shun these events totally and claim that this book is a text devoted to thought and discourses rather than being an analysis of transient political circumstantialities. It is true that the Islamic Reformist discourse possesses such a sustained structure that it is capable of protecting its own intellectual identity from any politicized suspicion, but this is definitely not applicable to the Islamic Revivalist one: which is much further from thought, and rather much closer to politics. The important point, here, is that the Islamist Reformist–Revivalist discourse has become, today, in its new '*jihadist*' incarnations, even more manifest in arenas of propaganda and effective political utility – to the extent of casting all former Islamist discourses and their actions into the background of a scene that, nowadays, is dominated solely by it.

It might be possible for some who have analyzed the discourse of this book to deem it nothing but a text rife with assumptions and judgments: unsympathetic, and inconsiderate in socio-political and socio-cultural senses. Or it might have been considered a critique with limited objectivity towards Islamic Revivalist 'ideology'. It was unfairly branded as biased by many others who did not find in it justifications for their beliefs and attitudes. Some others would have even stronger reactions; however, the calamity of 9/11 brought the 'Islamist' discourse again under the microscope of critical attention[1] – or rather indictment. 'Fortunately' (if such a term may be indeed used), under such circumstances the book broke loose of defending itself against those who were now in need of exonerating themselves. Still, this 'fortune' is yet temporary and transient; however 'unfortunate' the case may be, 9/11 *did* prove many deductions already stated in the book!

Let us return, here, to five of these deductions surmised in the book and examine how the calamity of 9/11 re-emphasized them.

First, the book referred to some features and ad hoc cases of what we considered as a declining or retrograde trajectory of the Islamic reason experienced since its Reformist seminal moment in the nineteenth century up to its *salafist* (*jihadist*) one in the last quarter of the twentieth century, and passing through its Revivalist seminalist moment (of the Muslim Brotherhood) that spans over eight and a half decades,[2] The book referred to this decline by way of transition from the problematic of the nation state, to that of the state of the *khilāfah*, then to that of the Islamic state, and eventually, the problem of the religious (theocratic) state: the state of '*al-ḥākimīyah*' and that of the '*wilāyat al-faqīh*', alongside this gradual regression – that accompanied this transition – in the meaning of state, authority and politics. There was a horrendous regression in terms of knowledge and awareness of modern Islamists. And, if

i such a devolving transition means extricating politics and authority from the orbit of public right, free choice and legal, parliamentary and public accountability (in the case of the nation state);
ii and placing them in the orbit of the right of a sultan, his associates (*ahl al-ḥal wa al-ʿaqd*), the conditional pledge of allegiance (*al-bayʿah al-mashrūṭah*), and the jurisprudential accountability over the ruler (in the case of the state of the *khilāfah*);
iii subsequently, then to place these in the sphere of the right stipulated by having what is political depend on what is religious and having the latter as the religious authority (*marjaʿīyah*) in promulgating the constitution and establishing laws and running affairs of state (in the case of the Islamic state);
iv and then to the sphere of a right constrained to 'Islamic clerics' and an unconditional oath of allegiance to the authority of clerics: and their emir – or specifically – their imam (in the case of theocratic state);

then the status quo of this transition of Islamist decline – of the type of 9/11 in the USA, 16 May in Morocco, 11 March in Spain, and '*jihadist*' groups in Algeria and Saudi Arabia – is far more dangerous than the preceding ones, and, however, bears clear witness to this curve of deterioration. As the Islamist religious state is not one comprised of clerics and *fuqahā*ʿ (as was conceived by al-Mawdūdī, al-Nadawī, Sayyid Quṭb and Khomeini), but rather is one made of 'semi-*fuqahā*ʿ' and 'pseudo-*fuqahā*ʿ' from among militant Islamists who deemed the Taliban government – which emerged from amidst the darkest moments ever of the Middle Ages – a role model and a beacon of politics and power!

In parallel to this deterioration in conception of authority, state and politics and in designating the Islamist position in society and religion, there is deterioration in conception of other topics that establish distinctions and differences between what is religious and what is political in thought and politics. Islamist Reformers designated those who speak on such topics as Westernized liberals, the first Revivalists viewed them as secularists, whereas *jihadists* considered them blasphemous atheists! It did not stop at cultural designation only, but was manifested on the political ground: Reformers argued with their opponents (al-Afghānī argued Dahrīs of India and the debate between Muḥammad 'Abdūh and Faraḥ Anthon), the Revivalists boycotted their 'ignorant' secularist(s), and libeled them in their journals, then the *jihadists* fought their opponents (atheists) and shed their blood in the name of promoting virtue and preventing vice! And so, Islamists pursued an ever-narrowing path in debating their opponents among their compatriots – shifting from blame to blood in a way that stirred sedition – the wounds of which have widened more and more and are still unhealed to this very day.

The second is the deterioration of awareness in the world and time and their relevant elements and standards, among which is the Islamist perception of the location occupied by Muslims and their societies in this world. Islamist Reformers classified the world into two worlds: the world of progress, urbanization and development; and the world of decline and backwardness. They aspired to enable their own communities to keep pace with the first world. Upon this categorization, they were never distracted away or hushed by European imperialist authoritarianism, they did not get entangled in a random muddle between a civilized cultural West and an imperialistic one, and the tree of imperialism did not deter them from beholding the modern civil and cultural orchard arising from Europe. A new categorization arose with Islamist revivalism that overthrew the concepts of progress and decline and viewed the world in the eye of a secular West on the one hand, and an Islamic one on the other (al-Bannā, al-Mawdūdī, al-Nadawī, Sayyid Quṭb, Muḥammad Quṭb, 'Awdah, al-Nabahānī...), overthrowing – with such acute polarization – any threshold of communication between the two, and ousting the definition and classification of the world from the scope of politics and its terminology to the scope of culture and essence. Naturally, Islamic Revivalism would replace the question of progress with that of identity which had long preoccupied Islamists.

However, the major deterioration occurred with the rise of *jihadist* Islamism in the last three decades, especially at the end of the twentieth century. In this manner, the chasm between the worlds of Islam and (secular) West widened to a degree that they both grew two absolute entities that are separate and running in parallel lines – just as in Euclidean geometry – to the effect that it became almost impossible to delineate them culturally – as previously accomplished by the Revivalism of the Muslim Brotherhood – by saying that they are merely two distinct systems of ideologies and values. One of the tasks of the message of Islam is to rise up to play the role of guiding a secular, materialistic, urbanized Western world to the right path (the faith and values of Islam): as al-Mawdūdī, al-Nadawī, and Sayyid Quṭb tried to express it. The world was divided – according to the new *jihadist salafist* movement – into two categories (as stated by Osama bin Laden), there is that world of absolute evil represented by the atheist 'Crusader West', and there is that world of absolute goodness represented by the communities of Islam. However, this religious–moral division of the world – which resembles that of George W. Bush when he divided the world into the 'axis of evil' and 'axis of good' – does not end up in the same place reached by (moderate) Islamic Revivalism, that is, the revival of Muslims' duty to 'save' the West from its atheism and materialism. Indeed, it goes further in defending the necessity of confrontation with it (the West) in a battle of survival or extinction, in which there is no place for middle ground. Henceforth, from politics to economy to culture, from these to ethics and religious mythology (I don't mean religion), and then from dialogue to boycott and ultimately war ...thus meanders the journey of Islamic reason's retrogression in understanding the world, and hits rock bottom without caring for the doom awaiting its Islamic communities!

Third is the deteriorating cognizance of Islamist intelligentsia in the West – as a topic for assimilation and knowledge – for almost nine decades. Reformers came to grips with the West via synthetic reasoning along with the latter's distinction, variation and controversial aspects; they could have, though, vilified and defamed colonialism, turning public opinion against it, in fact this is exactly what al-Afghānī did as no one ever did before him (or after); however, they acquired an awareness of the relatively limited phenomenon of colonialism and how to avoid mixing it with the overall outcome of the West under one rubric. Because of this discernment between a cultural-civilized West and an imperialist-political one, they did not hesitate to get involved in dialogue with it (with Orientalism): this dialogue was so profound and deep that it represented a turning point in the history of Arab thought. As for Revivalists, the differences between the cultural-civilized West and the imperialistic one waned in a way that the term 'West' briefed all its variety and differentiations, and implied synonymous inferences – in the Islamic Reformist imagination – such as: anti-Islamism, dominion, authoritarianism, alienation, and cultural hybridization...And so the openness to Western knowledge – initiated by Islamist Reformism – came to an end, and was replaced by introversion and reliance on an inherited collective of Islamic thought and values rendering it the only open link to Western knowledge.

Isolation from the West increased with the rise of the second '*jihadist*' generation of Islamic Fundamentalism. From this view, the West is no longer designated politically as the colonizer and arrogant menace that jeopardizes the core identity and civilized character of the *ummah*, as had already been conceived by Revivalism. Neither is it a world with which it is possible to engage in dialogue or to even make use of its intellectual, political and civilizational products as was the case with Reformism. In fact, this West became designated culturally and religiously in a single, monolithic conceptual entity summarized by the idiom of the 'Crusaders'. The Crusader West versus '*jihadist*' Islam; for Muslims, the Crusaders were nothing but a horde of barbarians that launched an aggression against their sanctuaries, throughout history the only means of dialogue with them was that of the sword and bloodshed. And here are today's '*jihadists*' resuming their 'dialogue' in light of the examples of 'New York's and Washington's conquests'.[3] They never stopped at this point, nor did they question whether they really represent Islam or not; their only concern was: how to strike the 'Crusaders' in their own lands, and inflict damage on their own military, economy and peoples. There is no need to differentiate between a general and a child; all of them 'came from wombs of infidels', and it is an 'Armageddon'; and there is no need to inquire into trivial things!

Fourth is the ongoing retreat in the political content of contemporary *salafist* movements since their initial nationalist moment up until their latest one (*jihadist*). Nationalist Salafism (al-Afghānī, Ibn Bādīs, Rashīd Riḍā, al-Fāsī) had an anti-colonialist political approach, its discourse succeeded in mobilization of the public for the cause of struggle for liberation and independence. In fact, Salafism led to further production of nationalist movements in some Arab countries as was the case in the Arab Maghreb in which the Algerian Nationalist movement 'Ḥizb al-Sha'b'[4] emerged out of 'Jam'īyat 'Ulamā' al-Muslimīn' and the thoughts of Ibn Bādīs. Similarly, the Moroccan Nationalist[5] movement emerged from the womb of the *salafist* movement in 'al-Qurawīyīn' and the thoughts of its major sheikhs (such as Muḥammad bil-'Arabī and al-Dakkālī) and its new clerics (al-Fāsī and al-Wazzānī). Islamic Reformism with its two major tributaries: the Muslim Brotherhood and 'Ḥizb al-Taḥrīr' might have restored some of these nationalist trends in the Palestine War in 1948, the Suez Canal War of 1956, and the recent example of Islamic resistance (with Ḥamās and Islamic Jihad – al-Jihād al-Islāmī). However, this political content has changed alongside '*jihadist*' Salafism since the second half of the 1970s.

The political content of '*jihadist*' Salafism replaced nationalism with '*jihad*', this kind of *jihad* is not derived, however, from its textual and historic Islamic sense[6] as being a duty to defend (*dār al-Islām*) or even as being a 'holy war' in non-Muslim domains (*dār al-kufr*, *dār al-ḥarb*), but rather as war against a state and community that are branded as infidels in Islamists' view. Thus relocating *jihad* from *dār al-kufr* to *dār al-Islām* and opening the gates toward uncharted terrains of strife. And, if such a '*jihadist*' war within (*dār al-Islām*) or against Muslims had started before 9/11, in which Egypt and Algeria were the main battlefields, then the post-9/11 repercussions were even darker and graver, spreading to new and untouched grounds: besides the non-stopping attacks of 'al-Jamā'ah al-Salafīyah li-al-Da'wah wa al-Qitāl' in Algeria against the project of 'al-Wi'ām al-Madanī', al-Qā'idah targeted Saudi Arabia more than once. Similar organizations ('al-Salafīyah al-Jihādīyah, 'al-Takfīr wa al-Hijrah', and 'al-Ṣirāt al-Mustaqīm') targeted Morocco on 16 May 2003; and what '*jihadist* Islamism' is yet to unfold is likely to be even greater.

Fifth, is the deterioration and decline that Islamic culture has revealed since its Reformist start in the nineteenth century and its fundamentalist outcomes at the beginning of the twenty-first century. Islamic Reformism contributed thought, whereas Islamic Revivalism offered propaganda; '*jihadism*' on the other hand offered partisan takfīrī ideology. Islamic Reformism implemented theses and literature; Revivalism utilized rhetoric and rubrics; *jihadism* used political *fatwās* (not jurisprudential) and military directives! And so, on goes the story, from intellectuals down to apologists and eventually militants, thus contemporary Islamic discourse hit a near fathomless rock bottom with a daunting increase in the enrollment of half-educated individuals to Islamism. Reformers were once categorized as the sophisticated high-class elite. Then Revivalists emerged out of rising bourgeoisie even though their education and knowledge were inferior to Reformers. As for the *fuqahā'* (jurists) of *jihadism*, they are less informed, less educated, and most of them never finished school; the majority of their supporters are among those who discontinued their undergraduate education. The 9/11 attacks and the ones that ensued in Saudi Arabia and Morocco proved the capability manifested by Islamist leaders in recruiting their enthusiasts who are mostly socially-marginalized, passive individuals; indeed, they are recruited without much effort by those princes of 'jihad' who know well how to exploit those weak subjects.

These were the conclusions that the book surmised and were further confirmed by the 9/11 attacks and its repercussions, it was necessary to recollect them, moreover, to re-read them in light of the quake of that day and its consequences. However, other features were drawn in this concern which were mainly dictated by events that took place in the interval between finishing this book in late 1999 and writing this second edition preface that show some retreat in the fervor for 'theocracy' in state, authority and politics. During this period, the religious government of the Taliban[7] in Afghanistan fell, which was a government that subjugated politics to religion in the extreme, empowered absolute authorities of its men, and almost exterminated every aspect of civil society in its community, shrouding every corner of it with a mantle of prohibition.[8] Meanwhile, another religious government took control in the Sudan under American pressures, after eliminating each other and the discord with one of its major partners (the apprehension of al-Turābī).

The Iranian state of the *wilāyat al-faqīh* also faced a growing wave of domestic political rivalry from an Islamic reform movement and other liberal and secular ones, some authoritative references reconsidered the issue of '*wilāyat al-faqīh*' (Muntaẓirī).[9] Some reconciliation was made between the Egyptian government and various militant religious groups which led the latter to think twice about the option of violence and extremism; similar reconciliation was made between the Saudi government and its religious opposition rendering it a moderate reformism. Participation of the Islamic movement steadily increased in political and parliamentary arenas in some Arab countries – such as Morocco, Jordan and Bahrain, after continual objection in order not to get 'polluted' by politics and institutions. Waves of fanaticism, violence, *takfīr*, and *jihad* for the sake of the religious state did not stop – so as to avoid saying that they 'escalated'; however, other incidents opposing these trends – such as the ones cited above – occurred in the last five years, and they indicate that the tone of Islamism's evolution shall not be monotonous, it will rather be subject to long-lasting tensions and debates.

If this acute depression in rates of knowledge, openness, and tolerance in Islamic reasoning and its concomitant tangible reflection in phenomena such as fanaticism, violence, *takfīr*, and *jihad* continues against Muslims, which endangers the Arab socio-political structure (and civil community) with havoc and desertification, then academic fidelity requires further urgent examination of the phenomenon of '*jihadist*' Islamism with sociological analysis to grasp reasons that led it to demolish all that it had constructed previously. Although this preface is not a proper place to analyze this issue,[10] at least notice should be given here that the violence of jihadist princes did not just fall from the sky or come out of religious text, but in fact it was conceived within a nest of a local and international milieu that conferred upon it its own entity. It emerged within a socio-political framework produced by foreign aggression against Arab and Islamic lands, the intensity of such violence was amplified after the rise of the conservative Republican Party to power in the White House in 2001, and the domestic violence that restrained limits and shut doors in the face of political freedoms for these radical political groups. The problem is that policies of containing Islamic confrontationalism have continued to utilize strategies and dubious instruments (of security extirpation), this will in turn increase the inclination towards confrontation and make these groups seek more extremist options; in this case, radical reconsideration of this security approach is demanded.[11]

Hence, this book was a research into contemporary Islamic thought and the problem of the state in this culture. The logic or research, however, led the book to collide in a moment with this 'thought', which is no longer a thought, but rather a partisan and militant philosophy, and if this book primarily explored political phenomena rather than ideological ones, it was due to the fact that we are no longer able to identify features of ideology amid this blood bath – 'language of swords has triumphed over the language of books' (Abū Tammām, d. CE 850).

Notes

1. Al-Sayyid, Raḍwān, *Al-Ṣirāʿ ʿalā al-Islām: al-ʾUṣūlīyah wa al-Iṣlāḥ wa al-Sīyāsāt al-Dawlīyah* (Beirut: Dār al-Kitāb al-ʿArabī, 2004).
2. Belkeziz, Abdelilah, *Al-Islām wa al-Sīyāsah: Dawr al-Ḥarakah al-Islāmīyah fi Ṣawgh al-Majāl al-Sīyāsī* (Beirut: al-Markaz al-Thaqāfī al-ʿArabī, 2001).
3. Roy, Olivier, *Les Illusions du 11 Septembre: Le Débat Stratégique Face au Terrorisme* (Paris: Seuil, 2002).
4. Al-Fāsī, ʿAllāl, *al-Ḥarakāt al-Istiqlālīyah fi al-Maghrib al-ʿArabī* (Tangier: ʿAbd al-Salām Jasūs, 1948), and Merad, Ali, *Le Réformisme musulman en Algérie de 1925 à 1940: Essai d'histoire religieuse et sociale,* Collection du Monde Musulman, 2nd edn (Algiers: Editions el Hikma, 1999).
5. Belkeziz, Abdelilah, *al-Khiṭāb al-Iṣlāḥī fi al-Maghrib: al-Takwīn wa al-Maṣādir (1844–1918),* Fikr ʿArabī Muʿāṣir (Beirut: Dār al-Muntakhab al-ʿArabī, 1997), and Laroui, Abdallah, *Les Origines Socials et Culturelles du Nationalisme Marocain, 1830–1912,* 2nd ed. (Casablanca: Publications du Centre Culturel Arabe, 2001).
6. Redissi, Hamadi, *L'Exception Islamique, La Couleur des Idées* (Paris: Seuil, 2004), pp. 84–92.
7. Overthrowing the Taliban by US invasion is by no means legitimate; conversely, it would have been more than legitimate if it had been overthrown by the free will of Afghani people.
8. Forbidding women to work, forbidding music, shaving beards, destroying statues etc.
9. For many years Muntaẓīrī criticized the concept of '*wilāyat al-faqīh*', and he escalated his attack upon the lifting of his house-arrest sentence.

10. This issue was partly analyzed in the introduction of: Belkeziz, Abdelilah, *Al-Islām wa al-Sīyāsah: Dawr al-Ḥarakah al-Islāmīyah fi Ṣawgh al-Majāl al-Sīyāsī.*

11. Belkeziz, Abdelilah, *Al-'Unf wa al-Dīmuqraṭīyah*, 2nd edn (Beirut: Dār al-Kunūz al-Adabīyah, 2000).

Preface

– 1 –

This study addresses a pivotal problem in the field of theoretical and political thought: the nexus between the religious and the political in the consciousness of contemporary and modern Islamic intellectual elites: how did this consciousness represent them, how did this thought express these elites for more than a century and a half; this problem became even more theoretically intense over the question of state in this consciousness, which would then develop – from the European invasion of Muslim lands in the 19th century – into an entanglement, in which all problems pertaining to social, political and religious issues in both the Islamic and Arab world would become enmeshed.

This problematic has *asbāb al-nuzūl* (occasions of revelation) in the consciousness of these elites: the defeat of Muslims before a triumphant European invasion, and an urgent need to grasp the reasons and factors of such a defeat. Even if such a problematic paved the way – to a great extent – to the phenomenon of preoccupation with the question of politics within the consciousness of the elites, and its eventual transformation into a pivotal intellectual theme of their writings, it still did not justify, however, why such preoccupation dominated Islamic and Arab production in subsequent times to a degree that it imposed itself on our modern and contemporary thought as political ideology – in the most generalized sense! It was not surprising that various classes of intellects embarked on a sojourn of examining the question of politics in their researches and studies: theoretical (philosophical) studies – producing theoretical knowledges, *fuqahā'*, clerics, apologists, historians, politicians, statesmen, chroniclers of travels...etc. In this context of the increasing size of the dimension in political thought, the political question exited from its natural theoretical context, political science, and it became a 'public affair' capable of being addressed by any writer!

For this reason, it also had a massive impact in regard to Arab-Islamic conceptual production; it was copious in quantity, impoverished in quality to an unprecedented degree that led to the production of ideological babble in intractable matters by people who are unqualified or who did not meet criteria for examination and investigation! The reader cannot discern amid such overabundance of texts – especially the most recent ones – between what is valuable and what is worthless, either due to scarcity of reliable and worthy writings, or due to interpolation of ideas and ideological disparity in a single text. If we exclude works of Islamic Reformers in the nineteenth century and the beginning of the twentieth century – which possessed intellectual content worthy of consideration – then the rest of what has been produced throughout 70 years does not gain in political thought any status except for truncated bits and pieces that are still waiting to be swept away by intellectual history.

We tried – with difficulty – to find among all these contemporary Islamic texts that which merits scrutiny in order to address the ambiguities of position therein in the question of the state. We admit – at the outset – that such endeavor was incomplete due to the difficulty in locating 'all' the relevant texts that potentially deserved to be considered in this matter. The excuse is that we wanted texts that were sufficiently representative, and to, at the same time, avoid being accused of selectivity; rather, in pursuit of an integrated intellectual material, that is capable of accepting *aḥkām* and generalizations, and aids in constructing subjects and deriving conclusions in the subject of the study.

– 2 –

The study covered a period of over little more than a century and a half, a period that extends from: *Takhlīṣ al-Ibrīz fī Talkhīṣ Bārīz* by al-Ṭahṭāwī to: *al-Sīyasah al-Shar'īyah*. by al-Qaraḍāwī (1998). It addressed five generations of Islamic intellectuals who had dealt with the political question in Islam, and the problem of state, in particular; these texts were the main subject of this study. These generations were as follows: the first Reformist generation: al-Ṭahṭāwī, Ibn Abī al-Ḍayyāf, Khayr al-Dīn al-Tūnsī, Jamāl al-Dīn al-Afghānī, and Muḥammad 'Abdūh (even if he belonged to more than one epoch), then the late Reformist generation: al-Kawākibī, Rashīd Riḍā, and al-Nā'īnī. The third generation was that of: Ibn Bādīs, 'Alī 'Abd al-Rāziq, Ḥasan al-Bannā, al-Mawdūdī, al-Nadawī and al-Khomeini stretches to include 'Allāl al-Fāsī, al-Ghazālī and al-Huḍaybī. The fourth generation is the one of Sayyid Quṭb, Muḥammad Quṭb, al-Qaraḍāwī and al-Sibā'ī, and it expands to include 'Abd al-Salām Yāsīn. As for the fifth generation, it is that of Fatḥī Yakan, 'Abd al-Salām Faraj, Rāshid al-Ghanūshī, al-Turābī (a pioneer), Fahmī Huwaydī and Muḥammad 'Amārah...etc.

We mentioned the above names on the basis of categorization and significance, and it is not restricted to only these. However, it was the most influential and productive over the masses of people in Islamic thought. Obviously, this categorization of thought into generations is a chronological categorization, not a classification of essays. Except for the first two generations – their texts shared a tight intellectual relationship rendering it a unified and harmonious discourse (which is not seen in late writings of Rashīd Riḍā) – all remaining generations manifested internal intellectual divisions distributing their intellects into movements, the generation of Ḥasan al-Bannā, for instance, was not totally a 'Muslim Brotherhood' generation: many of its late members were Reformers like 'Abd al-Rāziq, Ibn Bādīs, and 'Allāl al-Fāsī, similarly, it had some extremist members such as al-Mawdūdī, al-Nadawī and al-Khomeini. This is also true of the fourth generation where we may find repulsion between Quṭb and al-Sibā'ī; the fifth generation is no exception, as is represented in the astronomical distance between 'Abbūd al-Zamur, Shukrī Muṣṭafā, 'Abd al-Salām Faraj and Rāshid al-Ghanūshī, or Muḥammad 'Amārah or Muḥammad Salīm al-'Awā.

This overlapping between various movements within one generation – after a homogenous Reform moment – is not a good reason to deny the phenomenon of coincidence between the temporal moment (the generation) and the typology of Islamic 'knowledge' dominating it. Every generation was rife with a dominant intellectual trend that shaped all its affiliates; the presence of theses that went against the current did not alter its dominant nature, as these theses were few, according to these results – in the context of an exception that refutes a rule. No one today can deny that Ibn Bādīs and 'Abd al-Rāziq were exceptions in their own generation; similarly, no one can deny that al-Sibā'ī was an exception in his own generation just as al-Ghanūshī is an exception – today – in the generation of *jihad*! This remark leads us to state that categorization is likely coming closer to classification of a typology of Islamic intellectual elites that have followed successively one after another through this long period of time. This, in particular, compelled us in this study to undertake the method of the problematic of categorization, or say, categorizing of thought into problematics – bearing in mind that there is some kind of correlation for each problematic to a given intellectual generation among these generations.

Upon reading texts of Islamic thought, modern and contemporary, we have surmised four conceptual problematics about the state that these five generations have utilized. The problematic of the nation state for Islamic Reformism in its first and second generations; the problematic of the state of *al-khilāfah* for Rashīd Riḍā (which al-Azhar *'ulamā'* had defended in their battle against 'Alī 'Abd al-Rāziq), then the problematic of the Islamic state according to al-Bannā and the Muslim Brotherhood: at the level of the political party as well as at the conceptual; and lastly the problematic of theocratic state as viewed by al-Mawdūdī, Quṭb and Khomeini, and subsequently the jihadist *takfīrī* movement. These problematics produced the four primary discourses in modern and contemporary Islamic thought: Reformist discourse, *salafist shar'ī* discourse, Muslim Brotherhood discourse, and then theocratic discourse: discourse of '*al-ḥākimīyah*', '*wilāyat al-faqīh*' and *jihad* within the '*dār al-Islām*'.

Every generation experienced the problematic of the state in a distinct fashion, and produced a discourse addressing it, however, that did not mean, absolutely, that there had been a total break between these problematics and these discourses, in fact, there were signs of communication between them, especially after the emergence of the problematic of the Islamic state and the Muslim Brotherhood discourse. The important point is that the epistemological time for each of these problematics was not always congruent with the time of the generation that founded and addressed it. The problem of the nation state did not end with the absence of Muḥammad 'Abdūh and al-Kawākibī and Rashīd Riḍā's overthrow of it; it was renewed with 'Alī 'Abd al-Rāziq, Khālid Muḥammad Khālid, 'Allāl al-Fāsī, Muḥammad 'Amārah and Raḍwān al-Sayyid....etc. Similarly, the problematic of the Islamic state did not disappear after the disintegration of its first generation: that of al-Bannā and 'Abd al-Qādir 'Awdah, rather it was renewed with al-Qaraḍāwī, 'Abd al-Salām Yāsīn, Fahmī Huwaydī and Muḥammad Salīm al-'Awā....etc. It remained though a defensive renewal against invasion of other intellectual theses which were rampant, additionally, this renewal did not add to the foundational subjects a new intellectual horizon that enriched its theoretical position, in fact this renewal simply revived it. This was – exactly – what led us to say that the history of modern Islamic thought is a declining and diminishing one.

– 3 –

We also endeavored in this study to address modern Islamic thought *in toto*, in its two manifestations: Sunni and Shīʿite, we attempted to cover the dire need for knowledge about the spread of intellectual Shīʿite *fiqh* and accord it the position it deserves in modern Islamic intellectual thought after a period of negligence by non-*bayʿah* Muslim authors and writers. Our initiative for this was not only as a result of contemporary events that have proved the vitality of *bayʿah* political thought socially and politically, but also due to our pointed realization that any academic study of Islamic thought would remain incomplete and truncated if we excluded the *bayʿah* intellectual legacy, or even it would have ended – unawares – in a certain form of sectarian and denominational fanaticism and a dogmatic–ideological partisanship! True, we have no doubt, that attention was driven to Shīʿite Islamic thought to a certain degree in the field of the history of ideas and cultural studies in the last two decades, it brought to an end a long period of ideological exclusion, however, in general, the majority of this attention was directed towards the Medieval Shīʿite legacy and it did not take any – or took only very little – modern Shīʿite writing into consideration. If we rule out studies undertaken by Shīʿite scholars (many of which, unfortunately, were cast aside too), very few non-Shīʿite writers have been concerned about these modern writings!

Although we did not give this legacy its full due in this study and research, we dedicated part of this endeavor to address three contemporary stations in it: the constitutional intellectual moment in the beginning of the century with al-Nāʾīnī; the 'universal' intellectual moment with the theory of '*wilāyat al-faqīh*', in its new formula in the 1960s, and then the critical intellectual moment, in which Shīʿite political *fiqh* reason reconsidered central assumptions of the *wilāyat al-faqīh* – in this way re-establishing connections with the first moment. We assume that inclusion of representative intellectual texts studied of Shīʿite thought in the twentieth century may lessen the imbalance – in research – between bayʿah and Sunni literature. Also what apparently seems as Islamic Sunni thought, is not so in reality of Sunni *fiqh*; some of which, especially the concept of *al-ḥākimīyah* and its conceptual basis was nearer to Shīʿism than to Sunni antecedents! This is not applicable to Shīʿite thought, which presents itself with this description, even if it inclined to renewal.

What captured our attention in the analytical presentation of modern Shīʿite intellectual discourse regarding the state, especially the open critical discourse, that is relatively free from the fetters of the *imāmah* and, specifically, those of the *wilāyat al-faqīh*, is that this discourse provided huge incentives for openness to the Sunni legacy, to examining its topics, this was a good reason for establishment of the critical distance in it with the original authenticity of the Shīʿite *fiqh* thesis. Therefore, it is not surprising to find the concept of *al-shūrā* in its discourse, at a time it is considered unfavorable due to its opposition to the central principles of *al-taʿyīn* (instatement) and *al-waṣīyah* (appointment), also due to its opposition to the principle of *ʿiṣmah* (infallibility) which is the reason for having the *ummah* take full charge of the *wilāyah* over itself, and that is not acceptable due to the fact that *ummah* lacks *iṣmah*, and that is not achieved by *ijmāʿ* or by *al-shūrā* of the *ahl al-ḥal wa al-ʿaqd*. As it is a divine boon! Interestingly, this Shīʿite openness to the Sunni legacy produced a critical thesis rich with theocracy (the government of God), *al-ḥukūmah al-ilāhīyah*, whereas the Sunni openness to the Shīʿite legacy – on the part of al-Mawdūdī, Quṭb and *takfīrī*-oriented thinkers and groups produced transformation of Sunni conceptualization of the state, and resulted in projecting *al-shūrā* and *iḥtisāb* on the ruler, and led the Sunni reason – for the first time – to transform the *imāmah* from its classification among the *furūʿ* (derivative categories, lit., 'branches') to the *uṣūl* (primary sources, lit. 'roots'), and from *fiqh* (jurisprudence) to *ʿaqīdah* (creed), which paved the way for claiming a theocratic state to achieve the Islamic concept of rule!

We are convinced that this 'silent dialogue' between Shīʿite and Sunni discourses, which produced a Shīʿite critical thesis and a Sunni 'universalist' one, represents the first exchange of ideas between the two thoughts even though its results were unfair and unbalanced! What is more important here, is that it filled the gap between the two to a degree that it overthrew dichotomies or traditional equations on the basis that Shīʿite conceptualization of politics possibly might not lead to a closed political system, and that its counterpart is capable of producing a conception for an open system of rule (due to its adoption of *al-shūrā* and *ʿaqd al-mubāyaʿah* (contracting of the pledge of the *bayʿah*); we saw how a Shīʿite intellect like al-Nāʾīnī or Muḥammad Mahdī Shams al-Dīn can view the constitutional system and the trusteeship of the *ummah* over itself (*wilāyat al-ummah ʿalā nafsihā*), just in the same way, we saw how Sunni intellects such as Sayyid Quṭb or Fatḥī Yakan or Saʿīd al-Ḥawā, can view a political system predicated upon a religious clergy! This means, also, that reasoning in modern Islamist discourse, is no more acceptable from a perspective of *fiqh* dichotomies, whether among Sunnis or Shīʿah; rather its occurrence is demanded within new political–intellectual dichotomies:

relativity, absoluteness in reasoning; realism (*ṭawbāwīyah*) in politics; and to be manifested in the dichotomy of the civil system versus the theocratic one.

– 4 –

We attempted in modest ways, to shift this study of modern Islamic thought in the Arab world to the wider Islamic world, upon consideration of the unity of this thought, however diverse its national and cultural sources were, and in consideration of the impossibility of understanding many givens of this thought – in the Arab circle itself – without casting some light on some of its orientations and movements in the Islamic milieu, especially in the post-Second World War period in which the relationship between Arab Islamic thought would strengthen with non-Arab Islamic thought. Although we did not address this thought in many major Islamic regions such as Turkey, Indonesia or Malaysia, or smaller ones such as (Africa) – which we admit as a major academic gap that needs to be addressed by us or others, we, however, presented other Islamic texts (especially Iranian ones) and to a lesser degree Indian and Pakistani, to break the rule of confinement to Arab-Islamic thought only: which is the case in many Islamic intellectual studies in Arab world.

We implemented texts concerning 'Indian Islam' and 'Pakistani Islam' (those of al-Nadawī and al-Mawdūdī specially) in this study to cast light on the context of emergence of an extremist Arab-Islamic discourse in politics – the discourse of *al-ḥākimīyah*, *al-jāhilīyah* and *takfīr*, so if we utilized texts of 'Iranian Islam' it was for the purpose of analyzing Islamic Shīʿite discourse in one of its major modern centers, and not for the purpose of ascertaining its impact on Arab-Islamic thought only. It is obvious for us that the Iranian scope is very important in the context of intellectual participation in the larger Islamic world, which has just as much value as the Arab scope. If we add the fact of geographical proximity between the Arab world and Iran, the mutual historical experience, and the mutual intellectual *fiqh* repercussions (the Shīʿite extension in Iraq, the Gulf, the Levant and the Sunni extension in Arabstan and other regions in Iran), we may have other reasons to think that we are in need of raising interest in Iranian intellectual production, especially the Islamist one, bearing in mind that some of this is written in Arabic, moreover many of those originally written in Farsi have been translated to Arabic and published in Iran, Lebanon and Iraq.

– 5 –

Lastly, we allowed texts to speak by themselves without boundaries, we did not present citations only for the need of including them in this study, and we were concerned in presenting the largest amount of material possible to speak for itself. Thus, we endeavored to present the unified Islamic discourse and critical discourse from an Islamic intellectual perspective. Not to avoid including our critical attitude by saying, for instance, that it is biased against intellectual material, or to avoid presenting other attitudes just because it is 'outsider' or extrinsic Islamic reasoning, or secular or other common allegations in ideological clashes of the present...rather we did so to address mechanisms of evolution, self-renewal and correction operating within Islamic thought. This choice was made due to the approach we implemented in analyzing the process of Islamic intellectual accumulation: modern and contemporary concerning the issue of state; being carried out by Islamic intellects, it is only natural to stop at its two seminal intellectual moments: the moment of construction and the moment of criticism.

This does not mean that we totally shunned critical intervention in the context; our objective was not only history but also analysis and criticism. Our intention was that this intervention be according to the measure that does not nullify the need to criticize that thought from within. It is a need that can only be fulfilled by Islamic thought itself. It is not meant here that we chose to practice this criticism through an intermediary and indirectly, as its moral cost was less than some might have thought. This is because we were not biased, except to the extent of certain objective limits, or what we considered to be objective limits, in addition – which is more important – we have exposed this criticism to a new form of criticism to expose its limits or to reveal its similarities with the critiqued text or to discern the ideological aspects in it. In any case, we stood as the analyzer who is impartial and objective, we also did not shift from the theoretical framework from which we departed which is the unity of Islamic discourse in its various manifestations, including the critical one. And as we did not utilize epistemological tools of approach for this thought, we did not consider the concept of unity of discourse as an intellectual pretext to combine what cannot be put together (or reduced) into a single negative and absolute statement, we were careful to examine the matter with a relative and historical eye when traversing the topography of this unity to discover the varied landscapes within in it...which are abundant.

Abdelilah Belkeziz, Rabat, 28 December 1999

PART ONE

From the Nation State to the State of the *Khilāfah*

Chapter 1

The State of the '*Tanẓīmāt*' or the State of Reason and *al-Shar*ʿ (Islamic Law)

What they term 'freedom' and what they connote by it is precisely what we term 'justice' and 'equity'.

al-Ṭahṭāwī

As for everyone who holds firmly to a religion, if he sees that other than he is straying from his religion, this does not prohibit him from calling for what is for the good – both within himself and in his works that pertain to worldly interests as is done in the European community.

Khayr al-Dīn al-Tunsī

The State and Reform

The idea of the state (*al-dawlah*) – in modern political thought – gestated in the idea of Reform (*al-iṣlāḥ*), and it was among its theoretical fruits. It was not put forth – in the consciousness of the Reformers (*al-iṣlāḥīyūn*) – as being an independent conceptual matter, but rather it was carried along in tandem with thinking about the sum total of causes that had led Arab and Islamic societies to a state of manifold delay: lagging behind the age, and lagging behind referential past; just as it was carried along with thinking about the sum total of possible means of attaining to the causes of advancement and renaissance, and positive entry into modern civilization. In every case, it was Islamic Reformism (*al-iṣlāḥīyah*) which first formulated a thesis about the state (*al-dawlah*) and the political question since the locking of the gates of discussion for subjects of 'Islamic legal politics' (*al-sīyāsah al-sharʿīyah*) in the Islamic Middle Ages, consecrating itself as the sole repository of knowledge on the subject for successive generations of *fuqahāʾ*.

The value of Islamic Reformist participation in the subject might be that it carved out a niche defensively – sometimes explicit and at others more tentatively – about the idea of the 'nation state' (*al-dawlah al-waṭanīyah*) and its model, and in this its progenitor and audacity is concealed if we don't take into account that defense that does not belong – objectively – to the total of what might be defensible among the Islamic inheritance: if this state is not among the sum of its parts or aspects. If this means, at a primary level, that this new participation is not a repetition or something moving according to the dictates of a familiar concept, it signifies at a secondary level that the catalyst for it was nothing more than a confluence of reality and need: the reality of a new age that imposed its facts in draconian fashion on other societies and cultures, and the need to adjust to this – defensively in regard to the harmful, and advantageously with regard to the beneficial.

This realization drives us to discuss the conditions of the birth of the idea of the nation state in Islamic Reformist consciousness. The conditions are historical–political in the first instance, and discursive by way of emergence in the second: the effect of Napoleon Bonaparte's invasion of Egypt at the end of the eighteenth century. In strict terms, the causes of such a huge inversion were sought in Napoleon's invasion, in hypotheses by political historians and those of thought. It was a tremendous reversal of affairs that opened up the permissibility of accessing the inherited Islamic conceptual criterion, rammed into the consciousness of the elites in the crucible of modern conceptual orders arriving with the convoys of the European invasion – both material and cultural – of Islamic societies. While it is difficult to resist the supposition of a correlation between that invasion and the gestation of the concept of the nation state, it is not at all difficult to come across certain previous aspects of renewal (*al-tajdīd*) in this consciousness, from the standpoint of the epoch. We incline towards Al-Sayyid's assertion that:

> The Napoleonic entrance into Modernity, through which new states and elites would be precipitated, does not imply that we ought to ignore domestic movements for renewal and renaissance in the eighteenth and nineteenth centuries, meaning that this realization suffices to acquaint us with the phenomena and contexts which defy interpretation solely through the Napoleonic or Western invasion.[1]

That same movement for reform presented itself through the reformism of the Wahhābīs in the Najd, and the Sanūsīyah in Libya and North Africa, and the Mahdīyah (Mahdīsim) in the Sudan and the movement for jurisprudential (*fiqh*) reform in Yemen as led by Al-Ṣan'ānī and al-Shawkānī.

True, it is possible to assert that these movements came into existence on the fringes of the Arab-Islamic world and not in its centers such as those of Turkey, the Levant or Egypt; rather, these were regional movements defending local interest in the first instance,[2] not that this is a reason to ignore a phenomenon worthy of consideration which is the coincidence and succession of the movements within a limited historical timeframe. 'It is conspicuous when we find numbers, such as these, of reformers appearing in closely related periods of time in the countries of the Muslims, and we consider ourselves before a reformist wave engendered by the Islamic environment in every region.'[3] Yet, does this imply that this reformist 'wave' contains within itself the possibility of producing the idea of the nation state? Decisively, the answer is no. However, is it not possible to assume that its persistence in these historical circumstances connotes something of a relation to our subject: is it not permissible to suppose that its espousal of the principles of renewal and *ijtihād* and reform paved the way for a conceptual, political and spiritual climate open to other forms of renewal and reform outside of those encompassed by the traditional Islamic system? Is it not an epistemological duty to reconsider, when we read from this period of Islamic thought, to turn towards the law of knowledge and conceptual accumulation? Did not Ḥasan al-'Aṭṭār engender the rise of al-Ṭahṭāwī? Did not 'Moroccan Wahhābism' at the beginning of the nineteenth century during the reign of Sultan Sulaymān give rise to Reformist thought at the end of the same century?[4] And what of the correlation to al-Ḥajawī and al-Sulaymānī and others?

We are certain that modern Islamic Reformism is not a spontaneous extension of Wahhābī, Sanūsī or Madhist heritage because its problematic is essentially different from the problematic of these others;[5] even if the general mood was conducive to reform in the middle of the nineteenth century – due to the precursors of the call for *ijtihād*, and for the return of an Islam of the *uṣūl* (original fundamental principles) when these were among the results of the reformism of the outlying regions. It was to the same extent, perhaps, that the effect of the European threat on the consciousness of Islamic elites played an identical role in the inception of the Reformist idea in that consciousness. In any case, if Islamic Reformism precipitated a break with all that had preceded it (e.g., the Wahhābi variation) along the lines of its problematic, then it was not liberated to a great degree from the obligation to found the idea of reform on the basis of a return to the '*al-salaf al-ṣāliḥ*' (the pious ancestors – from which orientation the terms '*salafī*' and (the Latinized) '*salafist*' are taken) and their authoritative referential ideal according to the dictates of the famous Mālikī encomium: 'The last of this *ummah* will not be made righteous except by that which the first of it was made so'. This obtained despite the fact that modern Islamic Reformism took much from contemporary civil principles and did not find harm in considering the return to the *salaf* a 'breach of tradition'[6] while endeavoring in *ijtihād* and renewal on one side[7] and reconciliation with modern thought, as having inherited the best and most pure part of the heritage of Islam, on the other.

The question of the state, then, was conceived within the question of modern reform. It was not in the realm of possibility of the discourse of Sufi-Tawḥīdī Reform of the eighteenth century and at the beginning of the nineteenth to reach the idea of the state because its problematic was a *cultural-religious* problematic, the revival of the religion, and it was not a *political* problematic. Here, is a second aspect of the numerous separations and distinctions between the two types of reforms. However, what is most significant is that a phenomenon, demanding attention and scrutiny in examination of the history of Arab and Islamic thought, be indicated and that is the dominance of the *political* problematic in its relation to other problematics. This conceptual preoccupation with the question of the state, from the *Takhlīṣ al-Ibrīz fī Talkhīṣ Bārīz* at the beginning of the second quarter of the nineteenth century to *Al-Khilāfah aw al-Imāmah al-'Uzmah* (*The Khilāfah or the Grand Imāmah*) of Rashīd Riḍā at the end of the first quarter of the twentieth century, is nothing but material evidence of this.

The dense presence of the political question in modern Islamic conscience belongs to the elite's general consideration that the failures that afflicted the members of Islamic societies and its civilization in general could be traced back to political factors[8] in the first instance – to their countries and their *political systems* to be precise. This consideration was not coincidental in the consciousness of the *fuqahā'* and the Islamic intellectual elite, but rather, it was very ancient indeed. Perhaps, it goes back to the conditions and nebulous circumstances of the collapse of the system of the *khilāfah* and the establishment of 'biting' draconian rule (*al-ḥukm al-jabrī al-'āḍ*) or 'mordacious' rule (*al-'aḍūḍ*). None among the *fuqahā'* would doubt the soundness of the socio-cultural system or Islamic values – in any age – but aspersions and criticisms were directed towards the *political* system on account of its being the system that diverted the Qur'ān and the *shar'* (Islamic law – *al-sharī'ah*). Doubt entered into the unity of the Islamic group and led to a protracted ordeal that has not ceased to this day.

The intensity of this call increased and this criticism reached a climax with the Shī'ah and the Kharijites, and all of those who were counted among the 'Rāfīdūn' (the 'Rejectors'), and its intensity might have lessened relatively with *al-Qurr'ā'* ('Readers') for example from the standpoint of 'advice' with a segment of the *fuqahā'*, but it falls – conceptually – between a group of the scribes of the *Dīwān* and the authors of '*al-ādāb al-sulṭānīyah*' ('mirror for magistrates') genre and *fuqahā'* of the *khilāfah* and the *imāmah*, and between what publicly assailed the illegitimacy of the sultan. However, the common denominator among these, despite differences in the degree of their harshness, were sentiments of intense unease over the glaring disparity between the image of Islam and its socio-political system, in the ideal sense, and between what was the status of the political system in reality as debased and reprehensible.

Islamic Reformism inherits the selfsame supposition: the failure in the political system does not inhere in the socio-cultural system, but it does express some form of acknowledgement that the socio-cultural system is afflicted, in its turn, by that failure – without entertaining the conviction that reform of this is contingent upon the reform of the first according to the logic of a result following its cause or a branch following from its root. Perhaps this factored in the basis of the underdevelopment of *social* Reformist thought with the third generation of Reformers,[9] that is, after what was more than a half century of the crystallization of the Reformist *political* thesis; rather, it perhaps explains the very substantial accumulation of Arab-Islamic thought in this field, and perhaps it is not permissible to compare it to knowledge produced in relation to the political question!

Despite the fact that this (modern) Reformism inherited this supposition – contributing to it what it did – it persisted in a way that was more catastrophic than its predecessor in a conceptual discourse rooted in the Medieval Arab-Islamic conceptual realm; it perceived the magnitude of the failure according to the implications of two facts that were entirely new in the history of Islam. The first was that this modern (Islamic) political system was lagging behind its predecessor of the Medieval period, and it had reverted to an even worse decline – however tenuous its legitimacy might be – after once having been strong (even if only in confronting external enemies). The second of these was that it was lagging behind the modern political age and unable to keep pace with it in strength or competition without an ability to detach from itself and seek or take whatever means might rectify its situation. It is of no doubt that this tragic consciousness of the dual nature of this backwardness of the political system – in the modern Islamic Reformist discourse – justifies to a large extent that clear conceptual preoccupation with the political question; rather, that the ideological megalith in the appraisal of it as being the mother of all questions of society and the cornerstone in the initiative for triumphing over the underdevelopment of the Muslims and for victory in the case of the advancement of them.

Regardless of however we might struggle to interpret the causes for the hegemony of the political question in modern Islamic thought, we are not able to ignore the objective historical conditions that imposed themselves, in the nineteenth century, on the Reformers, and colored through their deductions, the particular focal points of their attention and their questions which, in effect, conditioned their consciousness along these lines or that. They are, *in toto*, the conditions of increasing European expansionism and encroachment on Arab and Islamic countries – either in the form of occupation – which began early in Egypt, Algeria and India – or in a fashion that would exert pressure to facilitate a stage which would eventually transform into occupation such as was the case with most of the protectorates of the Ottoman State, Iran, Morocco and Yemen. True, the threat *was* cultural in the consciousness of the elite intelligentsia and its themes ran the gamut between threatening the creed and corrupting morals and values. Despite that, Islamic Reformism perceived it as a *political* threat – in the first instance – and confirmed that defense against its harms of the creed, the culture and values were not possible without a *political* response to it. This implied that modern Islamic Reformism, from the middle of the nineteenth century, did not present itself as being a movement of religious revival and a resurrector of civilization, but rather as being a movement of political, social and conceptual reform – even if questions of intrinsic essence and Islamic identity were among the sum total concerns of its thought and among the paragraphs of its reformist texts.

In this sense, the excessiveness of the political question in the Reformist conscience is a spontaneous reaction to a threat that was, in essence, political. Thus, the Reformers attributed the advancement of Europe and its superiority to the strength of its political system (a strong army, effective administration, institutions of justice, advanced fiscal regulation) and they attributed the underdevelopment of their societies, by comparison, to the 'backwardness' of the traditional political system. Similarly what was at the basis of the crystallization of a modern Reformist thesis in the Islamic consciousness was an objective scope for hypothesizing and dealing with the question of state as being the mother of all political questions and the primordial basis of reform.

The Context of the Nation State in the Islamic Reformist Consciousness

This context began as a political one, in the early stages, before an amalgam of political and cultural factors in the second half of the nineteenth century, after some Reformers had forged a connection to the Liberal conceptual order. We digress briefly to discuss this context – the crystallization of the concept of state for modern Islamic Reformism in three seminal moments:

The European model of the modern nation state represented the first moment. The Muslim Reformers did not acknowledge this state directly through European Liberal thought and its political theoretical order, but rather, they acknowledged it in a political context which was foreign pressure, occupation and colonial administration; that is, according to the significance of its political model in the Islamic lands that had fallen into the grip of colonialism. There is no doubt that this acknowledgement was obtained through observation of Europe at its epicenter and observation of its countries; that is, that these observations were obtained through travel and tours[10] of the sort taken by al-Ṭahṭāwī, and Aḥmad Fāris al-Shidyāq, and al-Ṣaffār[11] to Europe in the first half of the nineteenth century, and with that the threat of this state as being a colonizing state. This was more manifest in effect on the consciousness of these Reformers than others because it was the threat that drew attention to the epicenter of power in Europe: its modern state. There is no doubt that this 'discovery' of the modern state via this direct historical conduit, and not through the Liberal conceptual order, would play the most decisive and far-reaching of roles in branding the Islamic Reformist legacy with the mark of weakness in grasping its theoretical subjects: the brand of epistemological poverty that characterized its conceptual production in the matter of the political question, and in particular, the question of the nation state.

The second seminal moment is the experience of reforms engaged in by Muḥammad ʿAlī in Egypt during the era of the French aggression against it, and in the extent of his rebellion against the 'Sublime Porte' and his looking forward to constructing and forging a strong center for Egypt independent of the Ottoman state.[12] Its reform programs included modernization and strengthening of the institution of the army. The program itself revolved, practically speaking, around this goal in particular: developing the educational system and dispatching delegations to Europe with the intention of developing this sphere from the construction of munitions factories and textile mills to the development of the agricultural system and land-ownership. However this program, which almost became an archetypal program for reforms in Islamic countries thereafter,[13] did not contain within it a lesson of the modern state other than that on the side of material force. Despite this, who would deny today that this pioneering attempt of Muḥammad ʿAlī was a course charted by the idea of the modern state in the consciousness of Islamic Reform, and that this was understood later on as being the political experiment that anticipated the empowering of a center among the centers of the Islamic countries that would be as a thorn to repel the greedy aspirations of those with hostile designs on them? It is sufficient that we are still, up until today, historicizing the project of political modernity in the modern Arab-Islamic countries according to this experiment of Muḥammad ʿAlī!

As for the third seminal moment it was the experiment of the Tanẓīmāt (reforms) that the Ottoman State undertook in the nineteenth century (political, military and administrative); and it is an experiment that had analogs in Tunisia and the Maghreb in the same epoch. In general, its significance, besides its political results, is in that it reinforced the centrality of the Reformist idea – which the elite endorsed, and provided an impetus for the idea of the modern state. More than that, this experiment – in Egypt, Turkey, Tunisia and the Maghreb – created, objectively, a need for a Reformist thought that would justify it and accord to it religious legitimacy. This is what explains the phenomenon of the increasing demands upon the Reformist elite by the state, and the connection of some of its symbols with the sultan.

This context was objective, and among the things which came in tandem with it were pressuring realities that made them objectionable in relation to the Reformers, the elite and the traditional institutions (such as al-Azhar). Generally the prevailing consciousness was that modern European civilization imposed its rhythm on the world, and it did not leave much of a margin for escape from its laws. When Khayr al-Dīn al-Tunsī wrote:

> ...verily European civilization has overspilled the earth and nothing opposes it except its own power of continuous flooding; and it is feared for the kingdoms surrounding Europe due to this flood, unless they imitate and take the

> path it took in worldly systemizations (tanẓīmāt), which may save them from drowning,[14]

This was not an individual cry as much as it was speaking in the name of an elite that had taken its first lesson in the realities of the new world. In some sense, this lesson was absorbed and memorized as a form of introduction to this world of the modern state from the standpoint of its being one of its manifestations.

Heralding the State

The first of the Reformist subjects about the state began with al-Ṭahṭāwī and Khayr al-Dīn al-Tunsī who took the greatest care with the question, and most of what they wrote is in relation to it. Even though other Reformers of their generation, or those coming after them, were concerned with the nation state or the modern state, and they made a valuable contribution to the defense of it, the uniqueness of al-Ṭahṭāwī and al-Tunsī underlying their boldness was in defending this state *as an idea*, and even more, its model in Europe. From this they proceeded to a detailed definition of this typology that did not rebuff objective neutrality and was not timid in their declaration of support for it.

When we revisit today the texts of the first generation of the proponents of the *Nahḍah* on the subject, almost a century and a half since they were penned, and attempt to understand the reasons for their preoccupation with the modern state, we find that among the most important is the formation of that state – in their view – according to the dictates of justice (*al-'adl*). Al-Tunsī says:

> The current situation in the kingdoms of Europe has not been the same since ancient times...and it should not be fancied that their people arrived at that which they have due to the increased fertility [of their lands] or the moderate [temperatures] of their territories...or that that is of the effects of their religion...verily they have reached these goals and advancement in sciences and industry through systemizations (*tanẓīmāt*) based on political justice.[15]

If that progress were the result of nature or the fruits of Christianity, it would also have been ancient because nature is fixed and Christianity is very old in Europe. Thus, there is no significance to its newness except that it is a *manufactured* advance, which Europe manufactured through its systemizations (*tanẓīmāt*) based on the dictates of justice.

Where does this justice manifest itself in the view of the Reformers?

It manifests in the law whereby the matters of politics and state are regulated: it is at this point where this principle becomes clear. Al-Ṭahṭāwī describes, in effusive terms, the institutions of the French political system and he concludes, to the benefit of the reader, by saying:

> the law according to which the French operate, which they take as a basis for their politics, is the law that has been promulgated for them by their king known as Louis XVIII, and it is still followed by them in satisfaction, and in it are matters that any reasonable person cannot deny are based on justice.[16]

Al-Ṭahṭāwī warns that 'most of what is in it is not in the Book of Allah (i.e., the Qur'ān) and the *sunnah* (normative practice) of His Messenger' – absolved of any blame and transcending any doubt; he justifies the reason for his citation of this so the Muslim reader may know:

> how the fact that their minds have been governed by the idea that justice and equality are among the reasons for the perpetuation of dynasties and the respite of people; and how rulers and subjects have been driven to this so that their countries have prospered long, their knowledges have multiplied, their wealth has accumulated and their hearts have found respite; you do not ever hear any among them who is complaining about *injustice*

repeating the reminder to his addressees of the maxim influential among all Reformists – ancient and modern – that 'justice is the basis of civilization (*al-'umrān*)'[17] just as its destruction lies in wrongdoing and injustice. This law, as the Reformers realized, is written in a book and it is the authoritative referent of the state and its basis in the promulgation of laws. It is the constitution. The Reformers express it in various terms from the standpoint of the 'guarantor of the proviso' *(qabīl al-sharṭah)*[18] or *'la constitution';*[19] however they all concurred that for the countries that have taken it (as a system), their people have gained much with which to establish civilization.[20] Al-Ṭahṭāwī, for example, made an effort to define for his people this constitution (*al-sharṭah*), and engaged in translating the articles of the French Constitution completely in his book *Takhlīṣ al-Ibrīz,*[21] giving pause before the first fifteen articles to explain and detail clearly in its context how the affairs of the state and the people are regulated according to what justice dictates of laws.

However, the Reformers found an analog also between the meaning of justice and the meaning of freedom. Despite the fact that they were able to find in their Islamic heritage much of what might assist in defining 'justice' and delimiting its meaning, the matter that did not correlate to an understanding of what was 'freedom', which had no roots in the Islamic heritage[22] and which was on the same footing for others as invention or innovation[23] in the worst of cases, or which might prompt a traditional understanding of it[24] in the best cases...(Despite that) they did not hesitate to find correspondence between the two meanings. Al-Ṭahṭāwī, for example, says in the exposition of his definition for it:

> and what they term 'freedom' and what they connote by it is precisely what we term 'justice' and 'equity', and that is because the meaning of rule by freedom is establishing equity in rules and laws where the ruler does not behave unjustly towards any human being. Rather, the laws are decisive and taken into account.[25]

Perhaps this definition implies that the meaning of freedom is restricted: political freedom is indicated which agrees with – by right – the meaning of justice.

The Reformers were not ignorant of the levels of freedom or of its various connotations. They were well aware of these, and they posited categories which were appropriate to them.[26] However, they were impelled, by force, to devote special attention to political freedom in particular from the standpoint that it was the freedom guaranteeing the natural rights of people[27] and guaranteeing public rights and, at the forefront of these, their right to political participation.[28] That is, from the standpoint that it is an analog for the meaning of justice.

What does it mean for the modern state to exist on the principle of justice, and to translate this principle into a basic law (that is, the constitution), that is surrounded by the dictates of its laws and protects the freedom of the individual and the group?

It means to reconsider the relation of the rulers to the ruled, along the lines that delimits the powers of the first and the operation of ruling of necessary restraints on them, where the others enjoy powers that were in ancient times the exclusive domains of the ruler. Arab and Muslim Reformers paused long before this new thing descended onto the scene of the sultanate in their history – before the concept of the restraint of the authority of the ruler, they attributed to it the secret of the progress of the political system in Europe and its civilization. These Khayr al-Din al-Tunsī exhibits as 'the origins of their political systemizations (*tanẓīmāt*) which are the basis of the civilization,' and he says:

> know that the European nations has not been confirmed for them through experiment that the unfettering of the hands of the kings and the men of their

> states to behave in the politics of the kingdom without restraint, brings injustice that leads to the destruction of kingdoms...asserting authoritatively the necessity of the participation of the *ahl al-ḥal wa al-ʿaqd*...in all spheres of politics, along with putting the responsibility for the administration of the kingdom directly on the ministers...[29]

Restraining here occurs in two regards: the sphere of parliamentary representation (the *ahl al-ḥal wa al-ʿaqd*) and the sphere of delegation of authority (to the ministers). The absolute ruler who enjoyed all powers became called upon – in this modern state – to relinquish a portion of his or her powers to the subjects or, in other words, to whoever might represent them[30] and it is a call for the government to enjoy real executive powers. This, precisely, is what instigated the attention of al-Ṭahṭāwī when he wrote '...The king of France does not have absolute freedom of conduct and French politics is a law of restraints, from the standpoint that the ruler is the King on condition that he operates according to what is mentioned in the laws...'[31]

Ibn Abī al-Ḍayyāf pushes the issue to the furthest limit of category and theorizing, being influenced by Ibn Khaldūn who divided rule into three categories: absolute rule, republican rule, and rule restricted by law. The possessor of 'absolute rule' 'drives people with his rod to what he desires from them and according to his interpretation of interest...and the bodies of humans are driven and corralled like cattle...fearing from his garrison which he made into an instrument of his domination and incontrovertible force.' His matter with the subjects is his matter with his ministers, these in the end are no more than 'ministers to execute the goals of their kings'. Because the kings are their own providers, 'they have no power to oppose them in a fashion that necessitates sheathing the sword of appetitive desire because they are between the fangs of the lion and its claws, he sees them as domestic animals of his house who were fed on his food and he does not see in their hands wealth other than his wealth and all of them are servants and clients.'[32]

Ibn Abī al-Ḍayyāf notices that this mode of draconian rule is extinct[33] and 'it has ceased by the goodness of Allah in most of the kingdom of Islam' except in the case of 'the noble Ḥassanid Alawite Sultanate in Fez and Marrakech.'[34] And he supposes that this was in relation to the people of Morocco 'the greatest of reasons for their underdevelopment *vis-à-vis* this temporary civilization.'[35] The historian of modern Tunisia considers this draconian rule as illegitimate from the religious standpoint because it 'behaves in regards to the slaves of Allah (i.e., human beings) and his lands according to whim' whereas *al-sharī'ah* 'came to extricate the culpable person (*al-mukallaf*) from the entreaties of his whims',[36] and he concludes with a reiteration of the explanation of Ibn Khaldūn for the collapse of civilization on account of 'the injustice of the kings is the strongest cause in demolishing countries, destroying civilization and rendering nations extinct.'[37]

Ibn Abī al-Ḍayyāf defines this category of rule as being on the basis that the people:

> provide a man from among them by choice, who tends to their politics and their interests for a specified period, and when this period is over, they appoint other than him through their choice...and one of them or another might have an outstanding record [during his tenure] so they might ask him to increase his term. They do not confer on this position anything of the pomp of the king or his insignia; rather he is one of them executing what agrees with the opinion of the people of consultation (*ahl al-mushūrah*). And they have in that, laws which they respect with the same respect accorded to holy laws (*al-sharā'i' al-muqaddasah*) and they stop at its limits.[38]

The prevailing system, then, is on four bases: it is not a system of inheritance like the system of domination by absolute incontrovertible force; it persists on the basis of election of the ruler; the ruler is not absolutely free of conduct, but rather is called upon to execute what is agreed upon by the '*ahl al-mushūrah*' – that is the council/parliament (*majlis*) of representatives; and lastly, it is a system that respects the constitution to the degree of holy sanctity. It is the *just* system (*al-niẓām al-'ādil*).

Ibn Abī al-Ḍayyāf, however, is a Muslim thinker who does not find a reason to abandon his heritage of belief in the subject of the *imāmah* (imamate) and the *khilāfah* (caliphate), even if he is fascinated with this system from afar. Thus, when he defines – objectively – according to this category of rule, and in his observance of the principle of *al-shūrā* (and this is the basis of just rule according to him), he attempts to assess the necessary Islamic legal distance with it, and that is by noticing that 'the principles of the Islamic *millah* (denomination – in Ottoman parlance: *millet*) do not specify this republican category, because the position of the *imāmah* is obligatory for the *ummah* according to Islamic law and they incur sin if they abandon it...'.[39] Thus, Ibn Abī al-Ḍayyāf inclines towards the third mode of rule that he terms 'rule restricted by law' (*al-mulk al-muqayad bi-qānūn*), when this rule is compatible with Islam, in what he surmises, because its axis is reason (*al-'aql*) and law (*al-shar'*), and the holder [of the office] conducts [affairs] by law which he does not transgress, and if he does, then the *bay'ah* (i.e., the pledge of allegiance – to obey him) is nullified.[40] The Muslims witnessed this form of restricted rule in the period of the Rāshidūn Caliphs.[41]

The truth is that there is nothing in this demonstration which is strange. Ibn Abī al-Ḍayyāf is like all Muslim Reformers, he pays close attention to undertaking a clarification of the principle of justice in the system of rule in Islam and draws on the precedent for this system. When justice in Islam proceeds according to the dictates of *al-shar'* (Islamic law) before reason (*al-'aql*), then defense of 'republican rule' cannot be rectified Islamically, so long as its axis remains reason alone. Thus, 'restricted rule', the axis of which is justice expressed in law[42] – is in contradistinction to rule by force which is in want of reason; and when republican rule is not supported in the *shar'*, then justice is not realized except in the confluence of reason (*al-'aql*) and Islamic law (*al-shar'*), and the one system of *just* rule is the 'rule restricted by law'.

This category resembles the category of 'Abd al-Raḥmān bin Khaldūn for the modes of rule (natural rule, political rule, and the *khilāfah*)[43] with minor modifications. Despite the fact that the effect of it was apparent to all Muslim Reformers in the nineteenth century, perhaps 'Abdullah Laroui was correct when he noticed that 'all the authors in the middle of the last century (i.e., the nineteenth) dwelled long on justice (*al-'adl*), making it into an analog of reform.' The secret of the Reformers' attention to Ibn Khaldūn is linked to their being busy with the matter of justice,[44] and his political writings were among the most vital in sating the need of the Reformists for perceiving the contribution of Islamic thought, in the Medieval period, in dealing with the question of state. It is a need that exerted pressure on them when they were observing the progress of Europe in building the state and founding its theories in apposition to what appeared to them as glaring Islamic epistemological poverty in the field.

Justice, then, is the secret of European progress because it is the basis of its modern political system. When the matter of this system was as such, a defense of it could be formulated without reservation, trepidation or fear of castigation or reprisal because *justice* was *among the dictates of the system in Islam*, and heralding it is among the rules of wisdom and 'that for which the believer seeks' which is not permissible to oppose – even if those operating according to it are people who are not from among the believers in the creed of Islam. Just as Ibn Rushd defended the obligation to borrow from the 'ancients' – that is, the Greeks – in their philosophy and their logic despite what was a matter of contention between them and the

Muslims in matters of creed[45] 700 years before the age of the Reformers so did the Muslim Reformers do in the nineteenth century when they were championing the model of the prevailing modern nation state in Europe and shunning concern for the religious chasm that separated them from Europe.

When Khayr al-Dīn al-Tunsī was in the process of justifying the reasons for writing his book: *Aqwam al-Masālik fī Ma'rifat Aḥwāl al-Mamālak* (*The Surest Means for Knowledge of the Conditions of Kingdoms*) two reasons impelled him. The first was: 'enticing those with resolution and determination among the men of politics and science to perceive what they are able among the means of arriving at the best state [i.e., condition] for the Islamic *ummah* and propagating causes for its civilization...' The second, which is more important for us here is:

> warning those who are oblivious among the general population of Muslims about their persistence in turning away from what is praiseworthy in the [practice and] progress of others and in agreement with our *shar'* (Islamic law), only for the idea stuck in their heads that all of that by which non-Muslims proceed and order their affairs ought to be cast out, and that their writings in those matters should be flung aside and not mentioned...the point is that if something is published by other than us and if it is correct in its positions in a number of indications...then there is no grounds for denying it. Rather, it is *obligatory* to have recourse to it and to employ it. As for every person who clings tightly to a religion, when he sees another straying in his religion, that does not prohibit him from calling for what is better for himself among his works attaching to worldly interest just as is done in the European nations.[46]

It is clear that the matter does not pertain, in this Reformist exposition of the model of the (modern) nation state, to only the historical benefit or a neutral realistic assessment but rather it pertains to the Renaissance message [of the *Nahḍah*] or to furthering its goal of promoting concern for acquiring the catalysts that drove Europe decisively to build its strong modern civilization. Thus, when 'the civilization of the nation is an expression of obtaining of what is necessary for the people of civilization among necessary tools in order to improve their circumstances physically and spiritually,' as al-Ṭahṭāwī says[47] then 'what is necessary' is nothing other than the *tanẓīmāt*, that is, the sum total of the Reformist procedures that may be of benefit from the European experiment in building the nation state and which the Reformers presented as a meritorious goal expressed by Khayr al-Dīn al-Tunsī when he said, 'the order of the indicated systemizations (*tanẓīmāt*) is among the necessary things of our time'.[48] Is this audacity? There is no doubt that we should take into consideration the historical circumstances – political and social – that were finding expression in these contexts. However, it was a justification and a concept at the same time, as we shall see later in this first chapter.

What is the Position of al-Shar' (Islamic Law)?

The objective question in defense of the Islamic Reformers' model of the modern state and the excellences of the *tanẓīmāt* connected to it remains: what is the position of Islam with regard to these *tanẓīmāt* – derived from another, alternate and different authoritative source of reference (*marja'īyah*)? Do they enter into the category of reform decreed to be obligatory by the rulings of the *shar'*, or do they belong to a class of blameworthy innovations delving into which is proscribed? In a word, do these *tanẓīmāt* conflict with the *sharī'ah*?

To be honest, the assertion that the first generation of Reformers – the generation of al-Ṭahṭāwī and al-Tunsī – did not devote as much attention to the *fiqh* aspects of this question as for example, Muḥammad 'Abdūh would do later on, is not necessarily correct. Rather the question was focused on the legitimacy of Reform in the view of Islam and in relating Reform to *renewal* (*al-tajdīd*) and innovations (*al-ibdā'*) and inventions (*al-iḥdāth*) in religion, and [other] innovation, in a question that was more realistic and pragmatic: 'Do the *tanẓīmāt* conflict with the dictates of *al-sharī'ah*?' To be fair, it should also be acknowledged that the response of the Reformers to the question did not always reach the same degree of clarity and boldness, even if the intent, in the end, was the same. Al-Ṭahṭāwī answered, for example, by calling attention to the fact that most of what was transmitted in the French Constitution 'is not in the Book of Allah the Almighty and not in the *sunnah* of his Messenger',[49] without denying that its matter rested on the dictates of reason (*al-'aql*) that does not contravene the dictates of the *sharī'ah*. Whereas, on the other hand, Khayr al-Dīn al-Tunsī did not transcend the principle of comparison in the first case and focuses directly on the common denominator, declaring in decisive language: 'The *sharī'ah* does not proscribe setting up political systemizations (*tanẓīmāt*) for the purposes of civilization and the growth of it.'[50]

If al-Tunsī does that without hesitation, those who tested the pretext against the *sharī'ah* in order to *resist* the *tanẓīmāt* and Reform raised a challenge before him! These, to the exclusion of all others, were the ones who objected to the *tanẓīmāt* and not the *sharī'ah*. This objection of theirs has no connection to any defensive position assumed of the *sharī'ah*, but rather in essence – is a political objection impelled by their fear that the setting up of the *tanẓīmāt* and the putting in motion of reforms would detract from their central positions in authority and would adversely affect vested interests that they had formulated in the absence of legitimate accountability and laws to restrain them. *This* was the matter which was actually negatively impacted by these *tanẓīmāt*.[51]

The problem is that this opposition, in the name of the *sharī'ah*, to the *tanẓīmāt* did not remain restricted to the narrow circle of those who had vested interests among the elite in resisting reform. Rather it widened its scope to embrace the masses as well. Al-Tunsī registers despair when he says, 'The masses in the principle of the matter have rejected these *tanẓīmāt* entirely, even to the extent that in some of the reaches of the kingdom, there have been strikes.' He knows well that they did not do that spontaneously and that they did not take a hostile position towards reform, but rather that:

> the reason for that is that the agents of these factions and other than they who had vested interest in conducting their affairs without restraint or accountability – when they became convinced that conducting administration and laws according to the dictates of the *tanẓīmāt* would hinder their personal ambitions – they sought to mislead the masses through false pretexts and subterfuge to adversely dispose them [towards these reforms] according to the like of their slogan: 'This new *shar'* (law) contradicts the *sharī'ah* of Islam.[52]

There was no doubt, then, about the necessity of undertaking the defense of the *tanẓīmāt* and of convincing the 'masses' that it did *not* contravene the *sharī'ah* but rather that it was actually an *expression of the (legal) intents* of the *sharī'ah* for the preservation of rights and the establishment of civilization. How ought this be undertaken? This was to be achieved by co-opting the *fuqahā'* (jurisprudents) and the *'ulamā'* (scholars) into the ranks of Reform in order to promote the centrality of the Reformist idea and to impart the legitimacy of the *sharī'ah* to the *tanẓīmāt*. If this were the case, then there was no way to win the battle of modernization and reform without the support of the 'religious establishment', which would formulate a context for these and lift the pressures of the prohibitive measures that were being undertaken in the name of religion. However, Khayr al-Dīn al-Tūnsī did not desire that satisfaction for the sake of the *fuqahā'*, rather he wanted the rule of the *fuqahā'* to operate according to the dictates of a strong conviction that the endeavor of the *tanẓīmāt* was not a *political* goal only, but rather that it was also an *Islamic legal obligation*, and it was a realization nourished by the background basis of Islamic culture from one angle and his belief that 'European civilization' itself did not evolve except through the borrowing by Europe from Islam, on the other.

Khayr al-Dīn al-Tūnsī did not experience great difficulty in searching for a means to enlist the elite of the *'ulamā'* in his Reformist effort. They saw it in the form of an alliance and a 'conspiracy' between the men of politics and between these *'ulamā'*. We read what he says in this regard:

> Thus, verily when the Islamic *ummah* was restrained in its religious and worldly actions by the heavenly *shar'* and the Divine limits (*al-ḥudūd*)...and there was a good pertaining to a need for it, rather the descent of a new necessity...then things proceeded according to the dictates of the interest of the *ummah*, and working according to it until their conditions improved, and taking the lead in the race for progress which rests on the society and a coalition of a faction from among the *ummah* well versed in the strictures of the *sharī'ah* and men who know policies and the interest of the *ummah* ...and these cooperate for the benefit of the *ummah* and they facilitate what is to its good interest and repel what is corrupting of it...and you, if you have taken a lesson from what we have iterated, will know that mixing the *'ulamā'* with the men of politics for the purpose of cooperation for the aforementioned intention, is among the most important obligations in terms of Islamic law for the general welfare.[53]

This is not what al-Tūnsī *wants*, this is what is dictated by the *tanẓīmāt*. They rest on 'the men who know policies', that is, worldly affairs, because they follow according to the dictates of laws – upon which the 'European kingdoms' are established, and the laws are these 'rational laws based on tending to the worldly objective'.[54] Similarly, they rest upon the *'ulamā'* and those who know the affairs of the *sharī'ah*, and will ensure the satisfaction of the Muslim masses. If al-Tunsī manifests feelings of jubilation over the position of some of the *'ulamā'* who provided support for the *tanẓīmāt*,[55] he also emphasizes his strong warning that the political-religious alliance (between the men of the state and the *'ulamā'*) is an obligation for delving into the challenge without the ongoing cacophonous clamor – in the name of Islam – affirming that 'among the most important obligations of the emirs of Islam and their ministers and the *'ulamā'* of the *sharī'ah* is unity in setting up institutional organizations for supporting justice and consultation...despite the expression of some opposed to this that these *tanẓīmāt* are not commensurate with the condition of the Islamic *ummah*'.[56]

Previously, we explored how the term 'justice' was defined, and it is the analog of reform in the consciousness of Arab Reformism because it is the result of the conjunction of *al-shar'* (Islamic law) and reason (*al-'aql*), on the basis of their mutual correspondence and lack of contradiction in intent. This is what confirms that here is the Renaissance thesis (of the *Nahḍah*) on the modern state and the '*tanẓīmāt*' for al-Ṭahṭāwī and al-Tunsī as well as Ibn Abī al-Ḍayyāf. Thus, we are convinced of the relation between the concept of reform with these proponents of the *Nahḍah*, despite their participation to varying degrees in drawing from the European experiment and their borrowing tools and implements from it, or rather, *ideas* to be employed in winning the battle of reform in their countries. They never entertained the idea that their call for reform, the *tanẓīmāt*, justice and modern states was among the original content of Islam and among the details of its rulings (which sought reform and renewal [*al-tajdīd*]); but rather that these were according to the dictates of operating by the *uṣūlī* principle in them which was *ijtihād* [57] and not some alien extrinsic act or some sort of cultural pilfering to be defended against and that would lead to an infatuation with the civilization of the West. Thus, a result radiating from that – an early warning – is that these Reformers were not, in undertaking the practice of defining the contours of the model of the nation state, championing it when they advocated it, on the basis of it being an alien model ('pilfered' in the Islamic language of the twentieth century); but they were joining the call for erecting the modern state on the debris of the sultanate state: a state that would intersect in its nature with what was known in the West and would be integrated with the principles of the *sharī'ah* and be decreed as 'a state of reason (*al-'aql*) and Islamic law (*al-shar'*).

Notes

1. Al-Sayyid, Raḍwān, *Sīyāsāt al-Islām al-Mu'āṣir: Murāja'āt wa Mutāba'āt* (Beirut: Dār al-Kitāb al-'Arabī, 1997), p. 17.

2. 'Azīz Al-'Aẓmah did not credit, for instance, their intellectual merits such as their banishment of backward traditional mentality and their openness to *ijtidhād* (interpretation) in the issue of *tawḥīd* (monotheism) in order to confront new (transient) paganism, he – in fact – did not recognize them except as being 'movements that sought to re-emphasize obsolete social configurations and economical nexuses, videlicet, their defending tribalism and the pursuit to shield their networks with religion as were the case with Sanūsīyah; or reclamation of such a religion-shielded tribalism for the

purpose of preserving the centricity and sovereignty of Najd which was governed by its strategic location in the international market, as in Wahhābism; or even investment of this kind of tribalism to safeguard slavery trading routes and their associated social and political networks, which was true to the Sudanese Mahdīyah'. Available in: Al-'Aẓmah, 'Azīz, *Al-'Ilmānīyah min Manẓūr Mukhtalif* (Beirut: Center of Arab Unity studies, 1992), p. 78.

3. Al-Bishrī, Ṭāriq, *Al-Malāmiḥ al-'Āmah li-al-Fikr al-Sīyāsī al-Islāmī fī al-Tārīkh al-Mu'āṣir, fī al-Mas'alah al-Islāmīyah al-Mu'āṣirah* (Cairo; Beirut: Dār al-Shurūq, 1996), p. 52.

4. Belkeziz, Abdelilah, *al-Khiṭāb al-Iṣlāḥī fī al-Maghrib: al-Takwīn wa al-Maṣādir (1844–1918),* Fikr 'Arabī Mu'āṣir (Beirut: Dār al-Muntakhab al-'Arabī, 1997).

5. The problem of Wahhābism, and similar movements, is its renouncement of backward tradition and consecration for the creed of *al-tawḥīd* (i.e., the absolute 'unicity' of Allah in 'Islamic monotheism') whereas the problem of Islamist Reformism is development or renaissance and the urge to seek their reasons.

6 To overlook tradition here means, according to 'Alī Omlīl, the reaction of social Islam (historical Islam) towards normative Islam: Islam of fundamentals. Available in: Omlīl, 'Alī, *Al-Iṣlāḥīyah al-'Arabīyah wa al-Dawlah al-Waṭanīyah* (Casablanca: al-Markaz al-Thaqāfī al-'Arabī; Beirut: Dār al-Tanwīr, 1985), pp. 13–15.

7. Almost all Islamic researchers agree upon the idea that every renewal movement must needs be *salafist*, that is, return to the Islam of fundamentals, as maintained by Rāshid Al-Ghanūshī. Available in: Darwīsh, Ṣāliḥ Q., *Rāshid al-Ghanūshī*, Silsilat al-Ḥiwār (Casablanca: Manshūrat al-Furqān, 1993), p. 42.

8. Omlīl, *Al-Iṣlāḥīyah al-'Arabīyah*, p. 24.

9. Especially with Qāsim Amīn and Ḥussayn al-Murṣufī.

10. See examples for travels to al-Maghreb: Al-'Alawī, Sa'īd bin-Sa'īd, *Uruppa fī Mir'āt al-Riḥlah: Ṣūrat al-Ākhar fī Adab al-Riḥlah al-Maghribīyah al-Mu'āṣirah*, Silsilat Buḥūth wa Dirāsāt no.12 (Rabat: Kullīyat al-Ādāb wa al-'Ulūm al-Insānīyah, 1995).

11. We addressed this travel analytically in: Belkeziz, Abdelilah, *al-Khiṭāb al-Iṣlāḥī*, pp. 81–100.

12. We do not share Ṭāriq Al-Bishrī's opinion which takes the position that Muḥammad 'Alī's reforms and policies were meant to 'serve the higher purposes of the Ottoman Empire', just because he eliminated the Mamluks and mustered a campaign to liquidate Wahhābīs in 1811 under a direct commission from the Topkapi; and intended to extend the Ottoman rule over Arabia and to stifle the Greek Revolution in 1827 in order to bolster Ottoman authority over the lands of Rumeli, for this opinion ignores the military clash that started in 1831 between Muḥammad 'Alī and his son Ibrāhīm Pāshā against the Ottoman army which led eventually to his triumph and control over the Levant, first, and even further aspirations to take over Istanbul. Available in: Al-Bishrī, Ṭāriq, *Al-Ḥiwār al-Islāmī al-'Ilmānī, fī al-Mas'alah al-Islāmīyah al-Mu'āṣirah* (Cairo; Beirut: Dār al-Shurūq, 1996), p. 10.

13. Laroui, Abdallah, *La Crise des intellectuels Arabes, traditionalisme ou historicisme?*, textes à l'appui'. Série Philosophie (Paris: Maspéro, 1978), p. 143.

14. Al-Tūnisī, Khayr al-Dīn, *Aqwam al-Masālik fī Ma'rifat Aḥwāl al-Mamalik*, edited by Munṣif al-Shūfī, 2nd edn (Tunis: Al-Dār al-Tūnisīyah li-l-Nashr; Algeria: al-Mu'asasah al-Waṭanīyah li-al-Kitāb, 1972), p. 166.

15. Al-Tūnisī, *Aqwam al-Masālik*, pp. 96–8.

16. Al-Ṭahṭāwī, Rufā'ah Rāfi', 'Takhlīṣ al-Ibrīz fī Talkhīṣ Bārīz', *in: Rufā'ah Rāfi al-Ṭahṭāwī, al-A'māl al-Kāmilah li-Rufā'ah Rāfi al-Ṭahṭāwī,* by Muḥammad 'Amārah

(Beirut: al-Mu'asasah al-'Arabīyah li-al-Dirāsāt wa al-Nashr, [1973–7]), vol. 2, p. 95.

17. Al-Ṭahṭāwī, *Takhlīṣ*, p. 95.

18. Al-Ṭahṭāwī, *Takhlīṣ*, p. 95.

19. Al-Tūnisī, *Aqwam al-Masālik*, p. 210.

20. Al-Tūnisī, *Aqwam al-Masālik*, p. 210.

21. Al-Ṭahṭāwī, *Takhlīṣ*, p. 102.

22. About the concept of freedom, 'Abdullah Laroui maintains in his valuable research, that the medieval Arab-Islamic community did not experience a state of 'freedom' and for this reason the Arab lexicon had no reference to that word then, nor did the Islamic *fiqh* and Scholastic Theology. Available in: Al-'Arawī, 'Abdullah, *Mafhūm al-Ḥurīyah* (Casablanca: al-Markaz al-Thaqāfī al-'Arabī, 1981), pp. 13–17.

23. Aḥmad bin Khālid al-Nāṣirī, the Moroccan historian, states as he monitored the European pressures on the Moroccan state (during the nineteenth century) to deliver freedom (among which is the emancipation of Moroccan Jews): 'I know for sure that this freedom brought about by the *Franj* during these years is indeed devised by heretics, as it necessitates overthrowing God's rights, parents' rights, and those of humanity at once...'. Available in: Al-Nāṣirī, Abū al-'Abbās Aḥmad bin Khālid, *Al-Istiqṣā' li-Akhbār Duwal al-Maghrib al-'Arabī*, edited by Ja'far al-Nāṣirī and Muḥammad al-Nāṣirī (Casablanca: Dār al-Kitāb, 1954–6), vol. 9, pp. 114–15.

24. Although the Moroccan historian, al-Sulaymānī, admits in a book he edited in 1911 that 'Freedom might be presented to be the contrary of tyranny, or what used to be known by the time of *al-salaf al-ṣāliḥ* as *al-shūrā*, unfortunately, it is obvious that 'people have overused – in our time – the utterances of freedom and citizenship, masticating the twain with their tongues, indiscriminately and inexplicably in eulogy and censure', this in turn led him to redefine the meaning of freedom in accordance with the requisites of his own cultural apparatus, so he defines it as: 'the freedom that every sane self craves is the one in which man is free in choosing his faith and right creed, unquestioned about his ritual practices, free in his sacrosanct familial abode..., free in his money..., states what is right in his mind whenever he knows it, fears not the control of a tyrant, free in his body and never assigned a task unless he gets paid for it...'. Available in: Al-Sulaymānī, Abū 'Abdullah (al-A'raj), *al-Lisān al-Mu'rib 'an Tahāfut al-Ajnabī ḥawla al-Maghrib* ([n.p.]: [n.pb], [n.d.]), pp. 167–8.

25. Al-Ṭahṭāwī, *Takhlīṣ*, p. 102.

26. Al-Tūnsī classified it into two categories: personal freedom (*al-ḥurīyah al-shakhṣīyah*) and political freedom (*al-ḥurīyah al-sīyāsīyah*). Available in: Al-Tūnsī, *Aqwam al-Masālik*, p. 270. While al-Ṭahṭāwī classified it into five categories: natural freedom, freedom of conduct, religious freedom, civil freedom, and political freedom. (*ḥurīyah ṭabī'īyah, ḥurīyah sulūkīyah, ḥurīyah dīnīyah, ḥurīyah madanīyah*, and *ḥurīyah sīyāsīyah*). Available in: Al-Ṭahṭāwī, *Al-Murshid al-Amīn li-al-Banāt wa al-Banīn, in: Rufā'ah Rāfi al-Ṭahṭāwī, al-A'māl al-Kāmilah li-Rufā'ah Rāfi al-Ṭahṭāwī*, vol. 2, p. 473.

27. Political Freedom (*al-ḥurīyah al-sīyāsīyah*), that is the 'state freedom' (in relation to the state), is the act in which the state entrusts each of its citizens with his/her legitimate assets, and to have the citizen enjoy his/her natural freedom without any act of transgression from it. Available in: Al-Ṭahṭāwī, *Al-Murshid al-Amīn*, p. 474.

28. Political Freedom, according to al-Tūnsī's definition, is: 'having citizens involved in the royal policies, and to confer about what is best for the monarchy...'. Available in: Al-Tūnsī, *Aqwam al-Masālik*, p. 207.

29. Al-Tūnsī, *Aqwam al-Masālik*, pp. 217–18.

30. 'Once bestowing freedom...to all people was a focus of dispersing views and stirring up confusion, it was decided to have people elect a group composed of people of knowledge and magnanimity which is known to the Europeans as House of Representatives, and to us as *ahl al-ḥal wa al-'aqd ...*'. Al-Tūnsī, *Aqwam al-Masālik*, p. 208.

31. Al-Ṭahṭāwī, *Takhlīṣ*, p. 95.

32. Ibn Abī al-Ḍayyāf, Abū Zayd Aḥmad, *Itḥāf Ahl al-Zamān bi-Akhbār Mulūk Tūnis wa 'Ahd al-Amān* (Tunis: Kitābat al-Duwal li-al-Thaqāfah wa al-Akhbār, 1963–6), vol. 1, p. 9.

33. Ibn Abī al-Ḍayyāf, *Itḥāf Ahl al-Zamān,* p. 22.

34. This note is pertinent to the nineteenth century.

35. Ibn Abī al-Ḍayyāf, *Itḥāf Ahl al-Zamān,* p. 17.

36. Ibn Abī al-Ḍayyāf, *Itḥāf Ahl al-Zamān,* p. 15.

37. Ibn Abī al-Ḍayyāf, *Itḥāf Ahl al-Zamān,* p. 27.

38. Ibn Abī al-Ḍayyāf, *Itḥāf Ahl al-Zamān,* p. 28.

39. Ibn Abī al-Ḍayyāf, *Itḥāf Ahl al-Zamān,* p. 28.

40. Ibn Abī al-Ḍayyāf, *Itḥāf Ahl al-Zamān,* p. 32.

41. Ibn Abī al-Ḍayyāf, *Itḥāf Ahl al-Zamān,* p. 34.

42. Ibn Abī al-Ḍayyāf, *Itḥāf Ahl al-Zamān,* p. 45.

43. 'Natural rule is to govern masses according to duty and whim, political rule is to govern masses according to logical reasoning to secure mundane interests and deter damages. Caliphal rule is to govern masses according to legitimate reasoning of their interests pertinent to this life and the one beyond...' Ibn Khaldūn, *al-Muqadimah* (Beirut: Dār al-Kitāb al-'Arabī, 1996), p. 185.

44. Al-'Arawī, *Mafhūm al-Dawlah* (Casablanca: al-Markaz al-Thaqāfī al-'Arabī, 1983), p. 133.

45. When Ibn Rushd faced the problem of '*al-faḥṣ*' (examination) in syllogism (logic) and its subtypes bearing in mind that it is a condition in philosophical inspection, he did not hesitate to state openly the need to acquire knowledge from '*al-awalīn*' (ancient civilizations) due to their experience. So he wrote: 'others did investigate that, they demonstrated how we are in need of knowledge obtained from ancient civilizations in matters we are trying to find solutions for, and whether those others, shared with us in *millah* (denomination) or not, then the instrument that establishes *tazkīyah* (recommendation) is not measured by its affiliation to us or those others. If it meets criteria of correctness. I mean by those who do not share with us in *millah* those who lived before Islam.'

Ibn Rushd, Abū al-Walīd Muḥammad bin Aḥmad, *Faṣl al-Maqāl fi Taqrīr mā bayn al-Sharī'ah wa al-Ḥikmah min Itiṣāl aw Wujūb al-Naẓar al-'Aqlī wa Ḥudūd al-Ta'wīl (al-Dīn wa al-Mujtama')*, edited by Mohammed Ābed al-Jabri, Silsilat al-Turāth al-Falsafī al-'Arabī, Mu'alafāt Ibn Rushd, (Beirut: Centre for Arab Unity Studies, 1997) vol. 1, p. 91.

46. Al-Tūnisī, *Aqwam al-Masālik*, pp. 89–90.

47. Al-Ṭahṭāwī, *Al-Murshid al-Amīn*, p. 469.

48. Al-Tūnisī, *Aqwam al-Masālik*, p. 228.

49. Al-Ṭahṭāwī,*Takhlīṣ*, p. 95.

50. Al-Tūnisī, *Aqwam al-Masālik*, p. 165.

51. A major impasse in the functioning of the Tanẓīmāt was intervention of some of its affiliates, for their own personal interests, into its foundational and procedural aspects and that impeded its function, they manipulated its plans uninhibitedly. Available in: Al-Tūnisī, *Aqwam al-Masālik*, p. 151.

52. Al-Tūnisī, *Aqwam al-Masālik*, p. 141.
53. Al-Tūnisī, *Aqwam al-Masālik*, pp. 151–2.
54. Al-Tūnisī, *Aqwam al-Masālik*, p. 224.
55. Al-Tūnisī, *Aqwam al-Masālik*, pp. 142–3.
56. Al-Tūnisī, *Aqwam al-Masālik*, pp. 156–7.
57. Belkeziz, *Al-Khiṭāb al-Iṣlāḥī*, in: Chapter One, and al-'Alawī, Sa'īd bin-Sa'īd *al-Ijtihād wa al-Taḥdīth: Dirāsah fī Uṣūl al-Fikr al-Salafī fī al-Maghrib*, Silsilat al-Fikr al-Islāmī al-Mu'āṣir; 3 (Malta: Centre for Muslim World Studies, 1992), pp. 15–20.

Chapter 2

For the Sake of the Nation State: A Criticism of Political and Religious Autocracy

> In Islam, there is no religious authority except the authority of righteous preaching and the call to do good and abstain from evil.
>
> Muḥammad ʿAbdūh

> The *ummah* that does not perceive entirely, or mostly, the pains of autocracy does not deserve freedom.
>
> al-Kawākibī

Introduction

The axis of the thought of al-Ṭahṭāwī and al-Tūnsī is the defense of the concept of the nation state. However, this conceptual and formal convergence does not nullify certain differences between the two: especially at the level of their personal loyalties. Khayr al-Dīn al-Tūnsī was Ottoman in his orientation, not only because he was from Tunis which was a territory of the Ottoman state, but rather because he was convinced of the Tanẓīmāt initiatives which had entered into the Ottoman state during the reigns of Salīm III and Maḥmūd II (at the end of whose reign Khayr al-Dīn came into adolescence) as well as during the reigns of ʿAbd al-Majīd I, ʿAbd al-ʿAzīz, and Murād V.[1] Al-Tūnsī was among those who were most favorably disposed towards the Tanẓīmāt among the Islamic Reformers of his age. As for al-Ṭahṭāwī, he was an Egyptian who was fanatically devoted to his nation; his consciousness was delimited by the idea of the nation and the central position of the state in the scope that was defined by the nation.[2] There is nothing strange in this as al-Ṭahṭāwī was born[3] and grew into adolescence in an Egyptian entity that was independent from the Ottoman state whereas al-Tūnsī was calling for taking the caliphate into consideration with regard to discussions about reform; and moreover, he had long been interested in the question of the relation between *al-sharī'ah* and the Tanẓīmāt, whereas al-Ṭahṭāwī was not concerned with any of this due to the differing Egyptian conditions.

It is not appropriate to understand from this that the latitude of al-Ṭahṭāwī was wider than that which was to be found in the *ḥawzah* (seminary) of al-Tūnsī, and that the reform horizons of the first were more extensive than that of the second. The Tunisian Reformist culture was deeper beyond comparison than the culture of al-Ṭahṭāwī whose jurisprudential shortcomings in *fiqh* are strongly manifest in what he wrote despite his pioneering reform role[4] which we are unable to deny. The position of al-Tūnsī in regard to (political) authority (*al-sulṭah*) – in Tunis just as in Istanbul – and the opportunities which were afforded him to travel and observe the experiences of progress and renaissance in Europe,[5] are among that which explain a significant measure of his Reformist view.

If the viewpoint of the two men was defense of the idea of the nation state, as we have suggested, then this defense could not be effected only by means of heralding models of it (as realized in Europe), but rather it needed to be – in order to be correctly defended – a criticism of the existing state: the sultanate state (*al-dawlah al-sulṭānīyah*) which presented itself – or which its *fuqahā'* presented – to its subjects as being a caliphate (*khilāfah*). That is, the call alone for a modern state: the state of *justice* – meant, objectively, that the existing state did not provide such – *a just modern state.* Nevertheless, the discourse of al-Ṭahṭāwī and al-Tūnsī remains entirely silent on the matter.

For this reason, we may surmise that two matters justify their silence: the first is that al-Ṭahṭāwī and Khayr al-Dīn were part of the political system and affiliates of it; and the second is that they were among the throngs of the initiators for reforms in Egypt and Tunis. In both situations, there was nothing that called them to criticize the existing state, but rather the opposite – they were pushed, objectively, to defend it precisely because *it* implemented the reforms[6] and created the conditions for transforming it into a nation state, along the lines of what they were demanding and what they were observing. Thus, they moved to produce a positive discourse in regard to the modern state – contesting the practice of any criticism of the sultanate state.[7]

This was not the case with Jamāl al-Dīn al-Afghānī, Muḥammad 'Abdūh, or 'Abd al-Raḥmān al-Kawākibī. These were opponents of the sultanate (*al-salṭanah*) – especially al-Afghānī and al-Kawākibī – and, they were living in circumstances of the failure of the reform initiatives and the reversion of the Ottoman state – particularly during the reign of Sultan ʿAbd al-Ḥamīd II – to its political autocratic nucleus. This explains that unrestrained tendency to produce biting criticism of the sultanate (*al-salṭanah*) and its autocratic system of rule where this was an analog of defending the modern state: the state of justice, the defense of which was the common denominator among various Reformists.

The Last Cry of Reform

Perhaps, among that which is dictated by academic scrupulousness is the assertion that some of the Muslim Reformers did not blindly rush into the attack on the *khilāfah* (the sultanate) and vilification of it only out of their desire to see a system of the modern state come into existence in the Islamic countries but rather out of an earnest craving to see their own unity and the unity of their lands in confronting increasing colonial aspirations. If this observation is correct, particularly in regard to *sayyid* Jamāl al-Dīn al-Afghānī,[8] then its implications do not attain to their far reaching importance if we do not take into account what is known about him of his radical, revolutionary political and ideological objective that distinguished him from his predecessors, contemporaries and those who would succeed him among fellow Reformers; or if subsequently, we fail to consider what is known about him as the master (*ustādh*) of the modern generation of the *Nahḍah*[9] as one for whom the gravity of his Reformist positions and the expansiveness of their horizons was impossible to surpass. We are not in need, here, of undertaking to clarify the intense interest of al-Afghānī in the *khilāfah* and the sultanate; and it was not an interest for him in a political system – which he did not hesitate to disavow harshly – rather he was profoundly interested in Islamic unity that began its tenure in dispersion under the violent blows of oppression of colonialism in India, Egypt, Tunisia and, before it, Algeria.[10] Rather, that it explains his intrepid defense of the idea of the 'Islamic group' (*al-jamāʿah al-islāmīyah*) and his arduous endeavor to bridge the chasm between the Arabs and the Turks,[11] and that between these and the Persians and the Afghans, and subsequently to call the attention of all these peoples to the circumstances of the Muslims in India:[12] admonishing and reminding them of their obligation to provide assistance.

Al-Afghānī was a critic of the state of affairs of the Sultanate, and one who held the strongest of grudges against it. Despite that, he never squandered any realistic opportunity to transform his grudge into a plan of salvation to set aright whatever crack might be mended in the edifice of the regime of that sultanate. Hope for the Ottoman state had been brought down and diminished but had not yet completely vanished. Therefore, he did not hesitate, while benefiting from his relationship to the 'Sublime Porte', to tender the Islamic-legal advice sought from him, and to present a political initiative to Sultan 'Abd al-Ḥamīd II for the reform of the state of affairs of the Sultanate. It is sufficient to review the 'articles' of that initiative[13] and to ascertain the positive spirit in engaging in the matter of reform and recommendations taken from the ruling elite of the Sultanate in Istanbul. True, 'support of the rule of Sultan 'Abd al-Ḥamīd that al-Afghānī expressed as unconditional support' as Fahmī Jad'ān correctly notes:

> was tied to a number of essential Reformist demands connected to decentralization and the representative rule of *al-shūrā*, and to moving along the path of freedom in the mitigation of autocracy, in addition to the 'Arabization' of the state, or, at least, if this Arabization were not possible, to enlist Arabs in actual participation in rule.[14]

The meaning of this is that al-Afghānī did not present himself as being an intellect in the service of the sultan, but rather as the bearer of a message in the service of the *ummah*. Despite all the expressions of deference and reverence that issued from him in regard to Sultan 'Abd al-Ḥamīd II,[15] he did not hesitate to boldly confront him critically with terms that were so direct as to suggest the like of someone asking to be executed.[16]

This was the positive spirit – intent on the unity of Muslims, their progress and elevating their countries – in which he addressed all the Muslim rulers; a forthright and truthful address. We read this in a letter that he sent to the Khedive Tawfīq after his assuming control over Egypt;[17] then again, this is what we find to a greater extent in another letter dispatched to Shāh Nāṣir al-Dīn;[18] similarly we perceive the like of it in all that he wrote about Egypt, the Sudan, India and Afghanistan as well as the rest of the Islamic countries.

Was al-Afghānī deluded and was he intent on 'saving that which was unsalvageable'? No. He was not deluded in aught. He knew the measure of what he was confronting in terms of sources of resistance, and he was certain to the utmost extent that he was attempting the impossible in all that for which he was calling. In any case, he did not go public with his initiative: he acknowledged that 'Our brothers, the Turks, are not proficient in any of the work of the world except "war", and they are in all else, and in what pertains especially to the matters of building, more deficient in vision and work than others'.[19] He acknowledged that the government in Iran 'oppressed the (Islamic) *shar'* to the limit of extermination, it suppressed the civil system and discarded it, and despised the code of reasoning and *fiṭrah* (innate human nature) to the degree of expunging it altogether'.[20] So, what was it that drove him to attempt the impossible and to 'beat a dead horse' in vain?

One of the reasons was that while he was entirely distraught over the ruling elites, despite everything, he was not despondent of the people. The second, and more important, was that he was caught up more in the primacy of the matter of the external contradiction with colonialism than he was with the internal contradiction with the ruling elite of the Sultanate. Thus, it might be inferred that al-Afghānī was not concerned with the matter of the state, or at least not its *content* as a nation state or its constitution to the extent that he was concerned with its *form* as a *unified* state. This is what might seem apparent upon first glance or at a relatively shallow level of understanding; however the truth of the matter is that al-Afghānī realized early on that winning the battle with the external enemy was contingent upon the success of root-level internal reforms: at the center and in the far reaches of the territories of the khedives, as well as in the army and in the administration. And, that, at least, is what is uncovered in his Reformist initiative that he presented to Sultan 'Abd al-Ḥamīd II, and the rest of what he wrote about the subjects of *al-shūrā*, the constitution and freedom; over and above his sharp unprecedented and never subsequently equaled criticism of the Sultan and the model of the sultanate state. If al-Afghānī let out the last cry of warning in the face of this state before reality came crashing down and turned it towards extinction, then he opened the door wide before criticism of the basis upon which this state persisted and its intrinsic crisis – that of *autocracy*.

On the Criticism of Autocracy

Al-Afghānī sent an early warning that:

> The *ummah* (community) which does not have in its affairs *ḥall* (the power to dissolve [pacts]) and *'aqd* (the power to contract [pacts]), and has none to indicate its welfare, and is one whose will has no effect on its general interests, and which is subject to the rule of a single person whose desire is law and whose will is a regime, who rules as he wills and does what he wants; that *ummah*, will not be stable in any regard and its course will not be rectified...[21]

This warning is useful in specifying the point of defect in modern Islamic society: the nature of the prevailing political system and the mode of administration of authority in it. Al-Afghānī knows well that this flaw is ancient having afflicted the countries of Islam since the dissolution of the *khilāfah* and its transformation into a 'mordacious monarchy'. However, he does not stop at this initial foray into explaining the backwardness of the modern political system; rather, he provides what is almost the pronunciation of a verdict on its presence, from the standpoint that it is a contemporary system, not in terms of its legacy or original malady. Thus, he moves, in a more positive way, from repeating a *fiqh* position to producing a modern political discourse on the political question. We have no doubt that al-Afghānī was the first to produce, in systematic fashion, a modern, critical political thesis on autocracy (*al-istibdād*),[22] and to open the way to political writings that would deal fiercely with the subject and focus on it intently.

There are two seminal moments in the criticism of autocracy in modern Islamic Reformist thought. In the first, attention was paid to exposing the roots of this autocracy in the supposition of 'divine right' upon which the idea of religious authority had persisted in Islam and which had served as a pretext used by the rulers to cast their hand over the state and the rights of its subjects. As for the second moment, there was an effort to apprehend the various forms of political autocracy and to expose its systems or the mode of the operation of its machinery (to use our contemporary parlance).

On the Criticism of Religious Justifications for Autocracy

It is often said successively about the history of the sultanate state in the countries of Islam that a political and *fiqh* heritage carved out a place for the idea of religious authority for the masses. What people witnessed in the behavior of sultans and princes, and in their assuming power in the name of religion, engendered in their consciousness a distinction between their *temporal* authority and their *spiritual* authority. Subsequently, the *fiqh* of the sultan assisted in disseminating this belief, through the efforts of generations of *fuqahā'* who sought to foist Islamic legitimacy on the behavior of the sultan and to cast him in religious guise.

Similarly, rebellion against the *khalīfah* and the sultan was analogous to apostasy from the religion and tantamount to threatening the unity of the group and the purity of Islam for Muslims throughout all the ages of autocracy. Thus, progress in the domains of Islam was held captive to a decoupling of the relation between the religious and the temporal – between the Islamic *shar*ʿ and the sultan – for most of those who have dealt with Islamic history among Orientalists over the past century in research and investigation.

When Muḥammad ʿAbdūh debated against the idea of the existence of religious authority in Islam, Orientalists (such as Renan and Hanoteau) were not able to keep pace, nor were they even when he contended with them about their own argument. Rather, he directed towards these a discourse of those who used the matter as a pretext to establish an autocratic form of political rule, on the basis of their assertion that Islam did not distinguish between the worldly and the spiritual, between the temporal and the religious. Muḥammad ʿAbdūh not only rejected 'the gathering together of the two authorities in a single person': that is, temporal authority and religious authority, but he went further than that. He took the position that it was a certainty that in Islam, there was not 'that authority that was possessed by the pope for the Christian communities whereby he could remove kings, excommunicate princes, ordain taxes on kingdoms and promulgate divine laws for them…'.[23]

The system in Islam is *civil* (*madanī*), according to imam Muḥammad ʿAbdūh, and what might *appear* to be religious authority is nothing more than an aspect of ethical behavior and commanding what is just (*al-amr bi-l-maʿrūf*); this is not the monopoly of any but it applies jointly and severally over all Muslims across their different stations,[24] because it is at the core of culpability (*al-taklīf*) and Islamic-legal obligation. As for attempts to restrict this to the scope of the comprehensive powers of the authority, this has no function other than to produce a hierarchical clergy which is disavowed and utterly rejected by Islam; that is, the establishing of a religious authority within it, and among the *uṣūl* (source principles) of Islam is 'the overturning of religious authority and the performance of it is among its principles' because it is an authority which can end only in two results which contradict the nature of Islamic creed.

The first result that is implied is the establishment of the matter of the state and the political system according to the dictates of the idea of religious authority and its principles, and these are the interpolation of an intermediary between Allah and his slaves (i.e., human beings), between revelation (*al-waḥīy*) and the believers (or the society). This is a form of invention or innovation in the religion from the standpoint that there is no monasticism in Islam and there is no intercession in it, nor is there anything in it to support the concept of an intermediary that shatters the fundamental principle of a direct relationship between the religion and innate human nature (*al-fiṭrah*) – between revelation and willful submission (*al-talaqqī*).[25] This is, *in toto*, among the most specific of distinctions and unique features of Islam in comparison to other religions, and especially to the Christian religion which produced, during its history, the system of the Church and the papal clergy, towards which ʿAbdūh and the Muslim Reformers directed the most scathing criticism.

As for the second result of that, it is the idea that laid the foundation for subservience to the sultan, which interpreted it and turned it into a competitor (with Allah) in the creed of *al-tawḥīd*, and the case is that Islam 'destroys...constructing this (religious) authority and erases its very trace – even to the extent that, for the masses, nothing remains of its people – neither name nor form, and none would claim... for another, after Allah and His Messenger, any power over the creed of anyone or control of his faith'.[26] Worship or servitude (*al-ʿubūdīyah*) of any except of Allah is utterly rejected as it is at the core of the most important contentions of creed: *al-wiḥdānīyah* (the unicity of Allah) without which the Islam of the Muslim is not rectified – except by faith in it – that is, only through exclusive worship, servitude and submission to Allah alone.

There is no way, then, of avoiding a return to the origin in order to break the religious monopoly, and from there the monopoly of the understanding of the text and its interpretation, and subsequently to the liberation of the creed from the act of political exploitation. This return to the origin, in the view of Muḥammad ʿAbdūh, is nothing more than *faith*: faith in Allah, that is that 'Faith in Allah', says ʿAbdūh:

> suspends submission and servitude to leaders who disparage humanity through religious authority which is a claim to holiness and to be intercessors with Allah, and a claim to legislate and to say about Allah that for which Allah has not given permission; or temporal power and that is the power of the king and autocracy...the believer cannot allow himself to be a slave to another human being like himself – regardless of religious or temporal title...verily, the communities of the religion – whom the law of Allah has reached – and the communities of the world carrying out the rulings of Allah are pleased only with religious submission to Allah and His law and not to persons whatever their titles might be.[27]

We, then, are at the core of the idea of the civil nature of authority in Islam. And it is an idea which Muḥammad ʿAbdūh split off, repeating and defending it in the course of his endeavor to sever the illegitimate relation between temporal authority and religious authority in Islam, and to divest autocratic rule of any religious legitimacy whereby it might argue in order to execute its draconian political laws. ʿAbdūh knows that there are those who will take his argument to task and oppose it and who will assert that divesting the *khalīfah* of religious power is not a reason to bring down this attribute and divest this authority from judges, muftis or the sheikhs of Islam. He anticipates that stopping at this realization will transform into an argument against breaking the connection between the two types of authority; and thus, he does not find it sufficient to declare that the *khalīfah* 'is a civil ruler in all regards'[28] only, but rather he follows that up with the assertion that 'Islam does not create for these people (he means the judges, muftis and sheikhs of Islam) even the smallest measure of civil authority, and it does not accord them the right to claim authority over the faith of anyone or over his servitude to Allah or to target him for his point of view...'[29] All of these are equal before two facts: before the fact that the imams (i.e., the men of religion) are not more than conveyors (of the message) who have no religious authority; and before the fact that the rulers are nothing more than executors of the *sharīʿah* of Allah and that their guardianship (*walāʾ*) is nothing more than the guardianship of the *sharīʿah* and nothing else.

In whose name, then, do the rulers rule if not in the name of Allah?

Sheikh Muḥammad ʿAbdūh knows in the discernment of the Muslim and the cognizance of the *salafī* Reformer, that the question demands answers. It is not easy to say that the religion is without relation to the subject and to the Islamic legitimacy of the rule of the ruler as that leads to a logically unacceptable conclusion: that there is *no* relation of the *sharīʿah* to authority! However, he is also not able to simply assert that Islam is the basis of rule and its legitimacy, because in that case, he will again fall into the conundrum from which he is struggling to effect an exit: conferring legitimacy on the concept of 'divine right'! So what is to be done in the face of this problematic?

Muḥammad ʿAbdūh is not about to be easily or quickly lost in the wilderness of this ambiguity; and thus he does not find great difficulty in formulating an equation for this relation between the two poles of the question, and what he formulated was to remain the referential conceptual equation for all those who would 'weave on his loom' among Muslim thinkers for a century. The basis of the thesis is two principles: that the rulings (*aḥkām*) of Islamic *sharīʿah* are the primary source for legislation (*li-l-tashrīʿ*) and that the Islamic legitimacy of any sultan radiates from the excellence of his loyalty to this fundamental principle and his respect for working according to its rulings; the second is that the *ummah* is the source of authority, and reserved to it is the right to appoint the ruler, to take him to account and to remove him upon adjudication[30] because authority is a *civil* right to which recourse may be had in systemizing its affairs (i.e., the affairs of the *ummah*) and realizing its interests and guaranteeing its rights.

When the *ummah* is the source of authority, this represents the highest form of forthright expression of the idea of the civil character of authority and the political system. There is no doubt that this consciousness is what led imam 'Abdūh to defend the parliamentary representational system, and to count it as the single Islamic legal political form (of rule) capable of realizing the principle of the *ummah* exercising its sovereignty and its right to *wilāyah* (trusteeship) over itself. Like every *salafī* Reformer, he is not able, in his description of the parliamentary representational system, to dispense with the weight of the effect of the ancient Islamic legal terminology: '*ahl al-ḥal wa al-'aqd*' (people of authority); and '*ulīy al-amr*' ('those given the matter/command').[31] However, this does not prevent him from formulating for this system or from presenting the best Islamic legal justification for it in modern Islamic thought. It has been previously asserted that Muḥammad 'Abdūh devised the authoritative referential conceptual equation for modern Islamic discourse, and the fact is that it was and still is today the basis and pivot point of all making assertions in the affairs of Islam – Arab and Muslim – and is the criterion by which the degree of success or failure of any such assertion is measured.[32]

The moment of the criticism of the crisis of religious authority was necessary – from the conceptual standpoint – to open the way for criticism of political autocracy on account of its being part of the foundation on which its edifice rested. When that criticism ushered forth from a person the like of Muḥammad 'Abdūh, being who he was in the field, there was no doubt that it would cause uproar. And this, without doubt, is what happened in the twilight of the nineteenth century and at the dawn of the twentieth: the degree of ferocity in the discourse of that criticism increased; there no longer remained the slightest obstacle to making it public except for the watchful eye of the Sultan, and this was no less frightening than the opposition of the masses of believers. What factored into the increasing ferocity of that criticism was the seizing of political power – after the political failure of the Reform – and the inclination towards centralization and increased control, and, moreover, the triumph of its hostile instincts in expanding all of that in every sphere.

On Autocracy, the Destroyer of Civilization

It is an exaggeration to assert that the criticism of autocracy has a history in the Medieval Islamic political *fiqh* culture, not because what was dominant in this culture was legislating for the sultanate state and the draconian king (along the lines of what we find in the 'mirror for magistrates' [*al-ādāb al-sulṭānīyah*] genre of literature in some of the 'Islamic-legal politics'),[33] but rather it is because autocracy is a complete political system that has an internal logic and instruments of operation. It is not only political practices deviating from the path of the *sharī'ah* and in the surmise that the *fuqahā'* of general matters were not, objectively, able to attain to consciousness of this system outside the supposition of the sultan not being able to provide justice in leading people and directing politics of the world. True, the ancients spoke much about wrong and injustice and violent oppressive force, and collectively these might appear to be synonymous with the connotations of autocracy – and, indeed, they posited all of these meanings in apposition to justice; however it was only their defense of the system of the *khilāfah* that put them directly in the position of defending a political system which persisted on the basis of the principle of autocracy.[34]

There is no doubt that whoever confronted the criticism of the system of political autocracy at the beginning of the twentieth century – and at the head of these were 'Abd al-Raḥmān al-Kawākibī and Muḥammad Ḥussayn al-Nā'īnī – was before a rich legacy of the thoughts of the ancients about justice and resisting injustice; there was no way for one studying it to deny its value. However, they were able, according to the measure of what they drew from it, to achieve some benefit from the tools of approach and the problematic of the study from European thought. This precluded the possibility of their being able to deal with the question of autocracy in isolation from the matter of the *constitution*: (and it is an entirely modern questioning in their political consciousness – new to the order of their thought) and that is because of the inherent correlation between the constitution and surmounting autocracy. Al-Kawākibī knew well this relation when he wrote in the preface to his book[35] *Ṭabā'i' al-Istibdād wa Maṣāri' al-Isti'bād'* (The Hallmarks of Autocracy and the Struggles of Enslavement):[36] 'I am convinced that the diagnosis of this malady (i.e., this deterioration) is political autocracy and the cure to be administered is constitutional *shūrā*'.[37] He did not say that its cure was *al-shūrā* only, as if he were to do that, he would not, be doing anything more than repeating the thoughts of the *fuqahā'* about justice that were the basis of *al-shūrā*; nor did he simply assert *al-shūrā* on account of its being a guarantee of the subjects and the '*ahl al-ḥal wa al-'aqd*' against the solitude of the imam in the matter (of rule); but rather, he added to that and described it as being 'constitutional' – identifying it with the system of the nation state.

What does 'autocracy' mean in the discourse of Islamic Reformism?

Al-Kawākibī ponders the concept of 'autocracy' at length, endeavoring to define it comprehensively, moving from dictionaries of language to dictionaries of politics and law. We can select three definitions as being the most characteristically representative:

In the first definition, al-Kawākibī attempts to posit the phenomenon of autocracy in the scope of the conceptual discipline that specializes in its study – political science – and he says: 'When the definition of political science is that it is "administration of mutual affairs according to the dictates of wisdom", it is, in the first instance, a political inquiry and one of its most important inquiries is 'autocracy', that is, conduct in matters of shared concerned according to the dictates of whim (*al-hawā*)'[38]

We glean two conclusions of this definition: the first is that political science inquires into affairs of mutual concern (what we term in our parlance today as 'public affairs') from the standpoint that its administration falls under the reasonable or the rational – 'according to the dictates of wisdom', and that autocracy is among the forms of administrating these 'matters of mutual concern'; however, this is along the lines of what is irrational 'according to the dictates of whim'. The second conclusion is that rational politics is the administration of matters of mutual concern; as for autocracy, it is conduct in them; and *conduct*, here, implies that it is attached to *private* property and a *private* sphere. This is the first signification of autocracy: conduct on the basis of mood in a matter which does not persist except on the basis of reason, and the preservation of public good/general welfare.

For the second definition, we read: 'Autocracy, in language, is the man who is selfish in his opinions and condescends to accept advice…and the intended meaning of 'autocracy' when it is applied (in general) denotes specifically the autocracy of governments.'[39] Al-Kawākibī specifies that the meaning indicated here, linguistically, of 'autocracy' is 'monopoly of opinion', but he endeavors to transcend this narrow scope of the individual, to derive a clarification of its import with regard to 'political autocracy'.[40] He develops this meaning in the third definition when he writes: 'Autocracy, in the lexicon of politicians, is the conduct of an individual or a group in rights of a people according to whim and without fear of liability', and thus, 'it is an attribute of absolute government selfish in fact or rule that behaves in the affairs of its subjects as it wills without fear of being taken to account or repercussions of legalists...'.[41]

Political autocracy, then, is the autocracy of a system (of government) not the autocracy of an individual in it. And its cause is consciousness of the rulers of public rights as their being private/particular rights, and if not, then conduct in regard to them would not be on the basis of the dictates of will (that is, mood unfettered by wisdom or principle), and without fear of being questioned or taken to account by 'the subjects' or those represented.

This autocracy is of various types, but 'the most severe degree of autocracy is, and refuge is sought from Satan, the government of the absolutist individual, the inheritor of the throne, the commander of the army, the possessor of religious authority.'[42] Al-Kawākibī attributes this warning to the danger of claiming the combination of religious and temporal authority, along the lines of what Muḥammad ʿAbdūh did before him, and that reinforces the reconfirmation of the civil character of authority which he shares with ʿAbdūh and the rest of the partisans of the *Nahḍah*, coming close to almost partaking of the matter of the sources of 'Islamic legal politics': religious legitimacy, familial (inherited) legitimacy, and the legitimacy of force – in order to imply that the sole legitimacy for rule – which extirpates the roots of autocracy – is *constitutional* legitimacy upon which persists a political system that believes in guarantees against autocracy and through its specification of principles of strict accountability. This is what we glean from his assertions such as: 'Government, of any type, is not outside the category of autocracy if it is not under strict censorship and accountability that is not permitted in it.'[43] This censorship does not persist except through institutions where, '...those executing [policy] are responsible to the legalists who are in turn responsible to the *ummah*...'[44]

We, along with al-Kawākibī, are in the heart of the constitutional matter. However he, despite that, did not consider the matter of autocracy to be an easy one, and he was not, in spite of his defense of a constitutional political system, about to censure, take to account or distribute powers in a balanced fashion, or able to conceive of the constitution as being a magical panacea for its plague. He acknowledges that autocracy might also proceed along a system based on elections or a government supported by a constitution;[45] and thus, he goes to the limit of asserting that autocracy is not only a system, but rather it is a general socio-political culture. We read this text:

> Autocratic government is, naturally, autocratic in all its branches from supreme autocracy to the policeman, to the painter, to the street sweeper – not every category only of the lowest people of its class in ethics, because the lowest, naturally, do not care anything about dignity and good reputation, the goal of their endeavors is to prove to the one whom they serve that they are like him and the proponents of the state.[46]

Authority, then, does not only produce autocracy, rather it distributes it across the social group as well. This reproduces anew in all the manifestations of social activity.

This matter has tremendous, costly ethical consequences for the system prevailing in this society, and the human essence of individuals; when fear is necessary for those upon whom autocracy falls as this last 'harms people in permitting lies and deception and cheating and hypocrisy, and self-subservience and the repression of feeling and the killing of the spirit and the discarding of seriousness and the abandoning of work…' And the result? 'Autocracy, by its nature, takes control of the upbringing/education of people according to these accursed traits,'[47] and they are transformed into slaves of the authority and into an unproductive human quantity akin to cattle.[48]

If we leave aside the aspect of the political dimension of the matter for al-Kawākibī, and it is never separate from its ethical dimension,[49] and we proceed with the educational and cultural dimension, we find that the measure of resistance to autocracy is education and culture *not* revolution or political change; then, autocracy, as far as al-Kawākibī is concerned, 'is not resisted by force, but it is resisted by wisdom and gradualism.' If it is important that a person deduce from this that man ought discard the means of violence[50] in order to obtain the goal of abolishing autocracy, then it is more important that he direct his approach towards calling for a cultural solution, or rather, say, towards a cultural revolution which extirpates its roots. We read that, for example, in his assertion that: 'The one effective means of severing the root of autocracy is the advancement of the *ummah* in awareness and perception, and this does not come about except through education and motivation.'[51] Why? Because extirpating it from politics and the state depends on extirpating it from thoughts and people's selves.

Al-Kawākibī, however, is not the first Muslim Reformer who counted on educational and cultural reform as a segue into renaissance and progress. He was preceded in that by Muḥammad 'Abdūh; however, he was, decisively, the first to warn that tearing down autocracy and building the nation state was not possible only by putting reforms into effect (as in the case of the Tanẓīmāt), along the lines of what Khayr al-Dīn al-Tūnsī posited, nor by revolution against the prevailing system as Jamal al-Dīn al-Afghānī imagined, and not even through the establishment of constitutional rule as he himself prescribed, but that bringing down autocracy occurs only if political awareness is procured in 'public opinion'[52] and not only among the elite. Perhaps in that is another indication that the consciousness of al-Kawākibī in the matter of autocracy was not a product of the assimilation of traditional Islamic *fiqh* and conceptual subjects about wrong, and injustice and their opposite – justice; rather, it was, in addition to that, the result of embodying modern, liberal political thought. Sufficient indication of this is that he demonstrated for the characteristics of autocracy 25 researches to examine and scrutinize – borrowing these from his reading of Western thought, the axes of which were the questions of the *ummah*, government, public rights, justice, law and distinction between (different types of) authority.[53]

The Reformist discourse moves from a compulsory 'anointing' of the Ottoman '*khilāfah*' – under the pressure of sensing a need for it to persist despite its drawbacks, only because that was the way to preserve Islamic unity and to protect the lands of Islam from colonial encroachment, to its demands for putting into effect genuine reforms that would touch upon the sphere of politics; then to its sharp critique after the impossibility of depending upon it was made clear. The first result of that move is the occurrence of a shift in viewing it as being a *khilāfah* to viewing it as a sultanate state, and naturally, dealing with it as such. The Reformers – and al-Afghānī in particular – were not the victims of a delusion or a deception that it was a *khilāfah*. However, the conditions of external disintegration as well as internal disintegration pushed them to overlook its character as a sultanate, considering that the unity of the *ummah* took precedence – both according to the criterion of creed and that of politics – from the consideration of the matter of the nature of authority and the extent to which it enjoys legitimacy. Among the ironies of history is that what happened to them is the like of what had befallen the ancient *fuqahā'* after the disintegration of the *khilāfah* and its transformation into dominion/monarchy, when they found themselves pushed by force of reality, to apprehend the legitimacy of the draconian sultanate state only due to the need for it in order to safeguard the unity of the group,[54] and after that, to ensure the protection of the unity of the creed.

Al-Afghānī himself was the first to inaugurate that sharp criticism of the sultanate state on the basis of the collapse of his hopes for the rectification of the circumstances of the sultanate through reform; and the bridging of that enmity between Iran and the Ottoman state. Even if that critique of his had provided the appropriate fertile ground for cultivating new reformist thoughts in the category of defending the modern nation state, in a more primary sense, it is an acknowledgement that this defense is not new to al-Afghānī, but rather that it was deferred – to be more precise. However, appraising the cause of the deferment opens the door before a new political thesis in the matter of which ʿAbdūh and al-Kawākibī were among the greatest exponents. It is a thesis that was further commended because the Ottoman state not only failed to accomplish political and constitutional reforms but also it inclined even further towards the far reaches of brute force and autocracy. Therefore, the critique of this autocracy was the axis of this new Reformist thesis; it was the new political-conceptual form for defending a new nation state persisting on the debris of the extinct sultanate state.[55]

We conclude from the foregoing context and the givens presented in these first two chapters the following: Modern Islamic Reformism defended the state of justice, heralding the model of the modern nation state, with which it had become acquainted in Europe; it defended the Tanẓīmāt (Reforms) when the Ottoman state was occupied in undertaking them; and it transitioned to the defense of the sultanate and Islamic unity (the Islamic group) in tandem with the demand for reform of the status quo of the *khilāfah*. Subsequently, it moved to critiquing the sultanate state after the failure of reforms, the further dissemination of autocracy and the fall of the Ottoman Arab *wilāyāt* under occupation. At precisely this juncture the form of the call for the nation state came to its completion in the Islamic Reformist discourse: detaching the relation between political authority and the presumption of 'divine right' and liberating the political field from religious exploitation, then critiquing the system of political autocracy and calling outright for the constitution and cultural revolution.

Our previous discussion about the question of the nation state in the Islamic Reformist discourse is linked to the Islamic conceptual realm: the Arab and Turkish[56] in particular. And, the situation is that the subjects and preoccupations imposed themselves on another Islamic conceptual field – the Iranian. They led to the production of an analogous Islamic Reformist thesis in the matter of the nation state. In other words, Islamic Reformism of Sunni *madhāhib* inclination was not alone in finding a way to the production of this thesis; but rather, it was accompanied and rivaled by an Islamic reformism drawn from a Shīʿite *madhab marjaʿīyah*, and this is the subject of the third chapter.

Notes

1. Dumont, Paul, Le Période des Tanzimat, in: *Histoire de l'Empire Ottoman*, Robert Mantran, ed., translated by Bashīr al-Sibā'ī (Cairo: Dār al-Fikr, 1992–3), vol. 2, pp. 63–4 and 84–104.

2. Al-Ṭahṭāwī says: 'The one and only God's will has it that sons of a given nation always share one language, live under the patronage of one king, follow one *sharī'ah* and one policy.' For this reason, anyone's affiliation to a nation means 'to enjoy the rights of his country, the greatest of these rights is the absolute freedom in the "*jam'īyah ta'anasīyah*". The patriot does not acquire the epithet of freedom unless he be led by law and be determined to implement it, as his following of the rules of his country implicitly demands the latter to guarantee for him his civil rights.' Available in: Al-Ṭahṭāwī, Rufā'ah Rāfi', *Al-Murshid al-Amīn li-al-Banāt wa al-Banīn*, in: *Rufā'ah Rāfi al-Ṭahṭāwī, al-A'māl al-Kāmilah li-Rufā'ah Rāfi al-Ṭahṭāwī*, edited by Muḥammad 'Amārah (Beirut: al-Mu'asasah al-'Arabīyah li-al-Dirāsāt wa al-Nashr, [1973–7]), p. 433.

3. One of the coincidences is that Al-Ṭahṭāwī's birthday is 15 October 1801 which coincides with the day of the withdrawal of Bonaparte's army from Egypt.

4. When 'Amārah presented the critical biography of al-Ṭahṭāwī, he was very accurate and precise when he said that this *faqīh* (jurist) who was sent on an Egyptian expedition to Paris 'to recite the Qur'ān, preach to pupils and serve as their imam in prayers returned from it as a translator of the European civilization and art, he became the imam of the East and the Muslim world in pursuit of emerging from the Dark Ages and enter into the Age of Enlightenment'. Available in: Al-Ṭahṭāwī, Rufā'ah Rāfi', *Al-Murshid al-Amīn*, vol. 1: al-Tamaddun wa al-Ḥaḍārah wa al-'Umrān, pp. 29–30.

5. Khayr al-Dīn al-Tūnsī traveled to France, Germany, England, Austria, Italy, the Netherlands (Holland), Sweden, Denmark, and Belgium in special expeditions sent by the Bey of Tunisia. Available in: Amīn, Aḥmad, *Zu'amā' al-Iṣlaḥ fī al-'Aṣr al-Ḥadīth* (Cairo: Maktabat al-Nahḍah al-Miṣrīyah, [n.d]), pp. 167–72.

6. Khayr al-Dīn al-Tūnsī's attack against the opponents of the Tanẓīmāt, especially 'the official employees' was not an attack against the state but rather in defense of the Reformist project of its political elite.

7. There is no doubt that al-Tūnsī unlike al-Ṭahṭāwī, was in favor of the caliphate, and he was pro-Ottoman in tendency. However, he ignored the issue of criticizing the caliphate for a reasonable cause: the implementation of the Tanẓīmāt by the Ottoman Empire.

8. The most important thing that preoccupied al-Afghānī, and in turn made people preoccupied with him, was the 'unity of Muslims', to allow them to face the European interests that threatened them. Available in: Al-Bishrī, Ṭāriq, *al-Malāmiḥ al-'Āmah li-al-Fikr al-Siyāsī al-Islāmī fī al-Tārīkh al-Mu'āṣir, fī al-Mas'alah al-Islāmīyah al-Mu'āṣirah* (Cairo; Beirut: Dār al-Shurūq, 1996), p. 14.

9. 'Most probably he was the first to consider that the East and West are two contradictory historical entities, and most definitely Muḥammad 'Abdūh acquired from him means for understanding issues of the future in Cairo. Also Luṭfī al-Sayyid mentioned soon after him the two expressions, constitution and democracy, in Istanbul, and Salāmah Mūsā was able to take from him his favorite expression "industry, science, progress".' Available in: Laroui, Abdallah, *L'idéologie Arabe contemporaine*, preface by Maxime Rodinson, Les fondations (Paris: Maspéro, 1982), p. 30.

10. For details see: Al-Afghānī, Jamāl al-Dīn, *al-A'māl al-Kāmilah*, edited by Muḥammad 'Amārah (Beirut: al-Mu'asasah al-'Arabīyah li-al-Dirāsāt wa al-Nashr, 1981), vol. 2, pp. 25–9 and 71–95.

11. Al-Afghānī, *al-Aʿmāl al-Kāmilah*, vol. 2, pp. 9–24 and 319–22.

12. Al-Afghānī, *al-Aʿmāl al-Kāmilah,* vol. 2, pp. 289–308.

13. See the whole text of 'al-mas'alah al-sharqīyah' in: Al-Afghānī, *al-Aʿmāl al-Kāmilah,* vol. 2, pp. 9–12.

14. Jadʿān, Fahmī, *Usus al-Taqqadum 'inda Muffakirī al-Islām fī al-ʿĀlam al-ʿArabī al-Ḥadīth* (Beirut: al-Mu'asasah al-ʿArabīyah li-al-Dirāsāt wa al-Nashr, 1979), p. 256.

15. Al-Afghānī, *al-Aʿmāl al-Kāmilah,* vol. 2, p. 21.

16. Al-Afghānī addresses the Ottoman Sultan 'Abd al-Ḥamīd II and says: '...his majesty plays with the lives of millions of our *ummah* according to his whim, there is no one to object to that. Does not Jamāl al-Dīn have the right to play with his prayer beads as he wills?!! I came to plead with your majesty to release me from my *bayʿah* (pledge of allegiance) to you, as I have retracted it...yes...I took oath of allegiance to your caliphate, yet no Caliph should break his promise. In your majesty's hands is *al-ḥal wa al-ʿaqd*, and it is in your capacity to not promise at all, but if you do promise then you must fulfill it, and I took plea of a certain issue, you promised to fulfill it, yet you did not.' Available in: Al-Afghānī, *al-Aʿmāl al-Kāmilah,* vol. 2, pp. 23–4.

17. The text of the letter: 'May your highness give me permission to state with freedom and loyalty that: the Egyptian people – like the rest – are not free from sloth and ignorance among them, yet they are also not deprived of scholars and reasonable people. Thus, in the way you look upon your people, your people will look upon your highness similarly, so if you accept my advice in making the *ummah* participate in ruling the country by means of *al-shūrā,* so that you give your orders to hold elections to choose deputies from people to set out rules and function by your name and will, then that will give your throne strength and longevity.' Available in: Al-Afghānī, *al-Aʿmāl al-Kāmilah,* vol. 2, p. 300.

18. 'You have to know *ḥaḍrat* Shah, that with constitutional rule, your crown and authority shall be stronger and greater than the *status quo*...undoubtedly, O Shāh, you have read and known about a nation that survived without having a king. Yet have you ever known a king to survive without a nation or people?!'; and, in a reference to his rejection of Shāh Nāṣir al-Dīn's offer in appointing him (al-Afghānī) as prime minister, he clearly states: 'I never demanded and will never ask for the prime ministry, and I do not want and never did want anything but to educate Muslims and see my country flourish, and I do not say but what I deem worthy of saying and obligatory, let the Shāh and intelligent people of the country reconsider what I am saying very well, then decide what they see appropriate, and see it executed.' Available in: Al-Afghānī, *al-Aʿmāl al-Kāmilah,* vol. 2, p. 283.

19. Al-Afghānī, *al-Aʿmāl al-Kāmilah,* vol. 2, p. 16.

20. Al-Afghānī, *al-Aʿmāl al-Kāmilah,* vol. 2, p. 281.

21. Al-Afghānī, *al-Aʿmāl al-Kāmilah,* vol. 2, p. 329.

22. Aḥmad bin Abī al-Ḍayyāf did this also, however his predilections for Ibn Khaldūn prevented him from developing a modern prospect for the issue of autocracy.

23. 'Abdūh, Muḥammad, *al-Aʿmāl al-Kāmilah*, edited by Muḥammad 'Amārah (Beirut: al-Mu'asasah al-ʿArabīyah li-al-Dirāsāt wa al-Nashr, 1972–3), vol. 3: al-Iṣlāḥ al-Fikrī wa al-Tarbawī wa al-Ilāhīyāt, p. 233.

24. 'There is no religious authority in Islam but that of good advice, promotion of goodness and prevention of vice. And this authority is given by Allah to even the lowest of Muslims to hold anyone above him accountable and vice versa.' Available in: 'Abdūh, *al-Aʿmāl al-Kāmilah*, vol. 3, p. 285.

25. 'Every Muslim has the right to know about Allah from Allah's holy book, about his Prophet from his Prophet's words, without there being any intermediary, whether

a predecessor or a successor; instead he has to attain what makes him perceive these means properly beforehand...so in any case, there is no such thing as religious authority in Islam...'. Available in: 'Abdūh, *al-A'māl al-Kāmilah*, vol. 3, p. 288.

26. 'Abdūh, *al-A'māl al-Kāmilah*, vol. 3, p. 285.

27. 'Abdūh, *al-A'māl al-Kāmilah*, vol. 4: fī Tafsīr al-Qur'ān, p. 430.

28. 'Abdūh, *al-A'māl al-Kāmilah*, vol. 3, p. 288.

29. 'Abdūh, *al-A'māl al-Kāmilah*, vol. 3, p. 289.

30. 'The *ummah* or the deputy of *ummah* is the authority that instates the ruler, and the *ummah* has the right to control him or depose him whenever it sees that suited to its own interest.' Available in: 'Abdūh, *al-A'māl al-Kāmilah*, vol. 3, p. 287.

31. 'Justice in having the *ummah in toto*, free and independent in running its affairs... so that no one can control its public affairs unless he is someone trusted from among *ahl al-ḥal wa al-'aqd*, whom the Qur'ān calls *ulīy al-amr...*'. Available in: 'Abdūh, *al-A'māl al-Kāmilah*, vol. 5: fī Tafsīr al-Qur'ān. p. 285.

32. 'The more that we move away from the time of 'Abdūh, the more he appears closer and more modern to us and even replies to our anxious questions. In return, we find ourselves – objectively – obliged to re-read him and give him his just due.' Available in: Al-'Arawī, 'Abdullah, *Mafhūm al-'Aql: Maqālah fī al-Mufāraqāt* (Beirut: Casablanca: al-Markaz al-Thaqāfī al-'Arabī, 1997), in: chapter 1.

33. 'Abd al-Laṭīf, Kamāl, *fī Tashrīḥ Uṣūl al-Istibdād: Qirā'ah fī Niẓām al-Ādāb al-Sulṭānīyah* (Beirut: Dār al-Ṭalī'ah, 1999).

34. We will discuss the justifications of this note in details later on when we present 'Alī 'Abd al-Rāziq's critique of the system of *khilāfah*.

35. He wrote it in 1901.

36. Al-Kawākibī,'Abd al-Raḥmān, *Ṭabā'i' al-Istibdād wa Maṣāri' al-Isti'bād*, in: *'Abd al-Raḥmān Al-Kawākibī, al-A'mal al-Kāmilah li-al-Kawākibī*, Silsilat al-Turāth al-Qawmī (Beirut: Centre for Arab Unity Studies, 1995), p. 430.

37. This clear distinction for al-Kawākibī is not taken in the sense that Muslim Reformists did not stumble on the obstacle of confusion between concepts of the *shar'* system and that of modern Liberalism. In fact, this confusion became concomitant with Reformist writings for a long time.

38. Al-Kawākibī, *Ṭabā'i' al-Istibdād*, p. 435.

39. Al-Kawākibī, *Ṭabā'i' al-Istibdād*, p. 437.

40. 'Other connotations may appear for the Reformist sense of the word *istibdād* such as: *isti'bād, i'tisāf, tasalluṭ, taḥakkum*...and many synonyms for *mustabbid* such as: *ṭāghyah, ḥākim bi-amrih ḥākim muṭlaq*...'. Available in: Al-Kawākibī, *Ṭabā'i' al-Istibdād*, p. 437.

41. Al-Kawākibī, *Ṭabā'i' al-Istibdād*, p. 437.

42. Al-Kawākibī, *Ṭabā'i' al-Istibdād*, p. 438.

43. Al-Kawākibī, *Ṭabā'i' al-Istibdād*, p. 438.

44. Al-Kawākibī, *Ṭabā'i' al-Istibdād*, p. 438.

45. '...the description of autocracy in addition to including the single absolute ruler's government in which he took charge by force or inheritance, also includes the elected restrained ruler's government in which he is irresponsible, also includes the government of the group even if elected, because participation in opinion does not support autocracy...it includes constitutional government in which the power of legislation and that of execution are separated from censorship...'. Available in: Al-Kawākibī, *Ṭabā'i' al-Istibdād*, p. 438.

46. Al-Kawākibī, *Ṭabā'i' al-Istibdād*, p. 470.

47. Al-Kawākibī, *Ṭabā'i' al-Istibdād*, p. 499.

48. Al-Kawākibī, *Ṭabā'i' al-Istibdād*, p. 500.

49. Al-Kawākibī considers any *ummah* 'that never feels the pains of autocracy does not deserve freedom', the explanation is that '...if it falls into humiliation...it becomes inferior in its behavior...just like beasts, or even lower, never seeks freedom or justice, never knows the value of independence or merit of order, even it adopts no function but to be a minion of the oppressor...'. Available in: Al-Kawākibī, *Ṭabā'i' al-Istibdād*, p. 529.

50. 'Autocracy shouldn't be fought by violence, in order not to ignite sedition that might cut down people like crops...'. Available in: Al-Kawākibī, *Ṭabā'i' al-Istibdād*', p. 532.

51. Al-Kawākibī, *Ṭabā'i' al-Istibdād*', p. 531.

52. Al-Kawākibī, *Ṭabā'i' al-Istibdād*', p. 533. We think he is the very first Arab and Islamic intellect to use the term 'public opinion'.

53. Al-Kawākibī, *Ṭabā'i' al-Istibdād*', pp. 525–9.

54. The same reasons: 'unity of *ummah*, the foreign danger...' are still compelling contemporary Arab intelligentsia to give the national and Pan-Arab case priority over the democratic one, or to perceive the latter according to the rules and norms of the former.

55. There is another factor that should not be overlooked: al-Kawākibī and 'Abdūh's criticism focusing on political and religious autocracy in a circumstantial function, whereupon Ottoman states started to fall under imperial occupation such as Egypt and Tunisia. This implied that the foreign danger was already extant so that changing priorities would be in vain.

56. Jamāl al-Dīn al-Afghānī was Iranian; however, his attachment to the Arab-Turkish world almost outweighed his lineage or even his sect.

Chapter 3

The Conditional State: The Constitutional Question in Modern Shī'ite Political *Fiqh*

> The *ummah* has the right to censure, supervise and take into account any opponent of *al-wilāyah* (the trusteeship).
>
> al-Nā'īnī

Introduction

Modern Shī'ite political *fiqh* made a major conceptual contribution to apprehending the constitutional question and in formulating a contemporary opinion about the constitutional political system. It is a contribution which appears natural in consideration of the political context from which it originated and which was stamped by the increasing fierceness of the constitutional battle that was being waged in Iran at the beginning of the twentieth century that ultimately led to the declaration of a constitution in 1906. But, it does not appear 'natural', in consideration of the general conceptual context and the axioms that governed the view of the Shī'ite *fuqahā'* in the matter of authority[1] of the Imams (*al-sulṭah al-imāmīyah*). Rather, the opposite seems to have been the case as though it represents an unprecedented turn in Shī'ite jurisprudential interaction with the subject. Despite the fact that history records for many of the modern Iranian Shī'ite *fuqahā'* a confirmed position of support for the constitutional struggle which the country witnessed,[2] and even if this support pertained to a national and political position taken by the Iraqi *al-ḥawzah al-'ilmīyah* (religious seminaries and centers of learning) of al-Najaf[3] more than it pertained to a particular Shī'ite *fiqh* position in the matter.

The treatise of *Tanbīh al-Ummah wa Tanzīh al-Millah* (*Warning to the Ummah and Admonition to the Denomination*)[4] of Muḥammad Ḥussayn al-Nā'īnī represents a unique conceptual *fiqh* text in apprehending the matter of autocracy (*al-istibdād*),[5] and in the victory of the constitutional idea in the Shī'ite conceptual context. The author of the treatise[6] was one of the greatest Shī'ite *mujtahids* of the modern age. He studied under the most prominent authorities such as al-Mirzā al-Shīrāzī (author of the famous *fatwā* [legal opinion] which forbade working in and involvement with tobacco – using, selling or buying it) as well as grand ayatollah al-Ākhūnd Muḥammad Kāẓim al-Khurāsānī;[7] and, similarly, hundreds of *'ulamā'* graduated under him – the most important of them being *al-sayyid* Muḥsin al-Ḥakīm who came to hold the supreme *al-marja'īyah*[8] until the beginning of the 1970s as well as *al-sayyid* Abū al-Qāsim al-Khoei who came to have the greatest *al-marja'īyah* upon the death of al-Ḥakīm.[9] Similarly, his positions would ignite the passions of a new generation of *fuqahā'* who would have pivotal roles in some of the chapters of the Iranian Revolution. Ayatollah al-Ṭālqānī, one of the leaders of the Revolution describes him in his preface to the treatise *Tanbīh al-Ummah wa Tanzīh al-Millah* as follows: 'He was one of the greatest Shī'ite *'ulamā'* and one of the most prominent of the *marja' al-taqlīd* possessed of opinion and insight in recent centuries.' As for his treatise, grand ayatollah al-Khurāsānī lauded it by saying it 'is beyond all praise', just as grand ayatollah al-Māzindarānī commended it in similarly exceptional terms.[10]

Al-Nā'īnī's book *Tanbīh al-Ummah wa Tanzīh al-Millah* takes on a vital conceptual *fiqh* task of tremendous importance and consequence: it produces a formulation that would vindicate the modern constitutional system from within the establishment of Shī'ite *fiqh*, and rests for support on objective arguments which were imposed by the new political context upon Iran at the end of the nineteenth century. The importance of the writing of this treatise does not require qualification. Iran had witnessed an epoch of extensive autocracy during the reign of Nāṣir al-Dīn Shāh (the fourth shah of the Qajār Dynasty), who ruled from 1848 to 1896, and then in the reign of Muẓaffar al-Dīn who succeeded him.[11] There was no doubt that social and religious denial would express itself, especially in view of the fact that something similar had transpired in Turkey and Egypt. As for the nature of its boldness, it was a pioneering treatise of its kind, unprecedented and not based on any previous work of *fiqh* – neither ancient nor modern. Ayatollah al-Ṭaliqānī acknowledged in his preface to the book[12] that the idea of constitutional government (specified)[13] 'did not crystallize…in an Islamic quarter, rather it was delegated to us from the outside, and the *'ulamā'* of Islam found it beneficial, so they built upon it and commended the ranks of those calling for implementation of it.'[14]

The value of al-Nā'īnī's book cannot be realized except by putting it back into the context of Shī'ite political *fiqh*. Outside of this context, it might appear ordinary to whomever has looked over *Ṭabā'i' al-Istibdād* (*The Hallmarks of Tyranny*) of al-Kawākibī, for example, and it is not entirely far-fetched that Muḥammad Ḥussayn al-Nā'īnī wrote it under the influence of al-Kawākibī; there are many indications in the text of that, some of which we shall indicate at the proper time. What concerns us now is to recall the subjects of concern for Shī'ite *fiqh* in regard to political matters: the matter of the imamate and the situation of *al-sharī'ah* in regard to political authority after the 'occultation' (*ghaybah*) of the infallible Imam (*al-ma'ṣūm*), which will shed light on many aspects of the importance and value which pertain to the treatise of al-Nā'īnī.

Al-Imāmah (the imamate) and Authority[15] in the 'Age of Occultation'

The partisanship (*al-tashayyu'*) of the *āl al-bayt* (lit., 'people of the house' – descendents of the Prophet through the line of his daughter Fāṭimah and cousin and son-in-law 'Alī bin Abī Ṭālib) began with the crisis of the struggle over political power between 'Alī and Mu'āwīyah. That was a chapter among chapters of the previous struggle which began with the death of the Prophet about which the imamate and the right to rule would revolve;[16] but the origin of the Shī'ah as a creed and as a *madhāhb* would occur after Yazīd bin Mu'āwīyah's seizure of power following the killing of al-Ḥussayn bin 'Alī in the slaughter of Karbalā'. During the intervening period between the middle of the first century after the *Hijrah* (the date of the killing of al-Ḥussayn) and the end of first quarter of the fourth century of the *Hijrah* with the 'occultation' of the Twelfth Imam, Muḥammad bin al-Ḥasan al-Mahdī in 329 of the *Hijrah*, the *fuqahā'* and the *mutakallimūn* (theologians) of the Shī'ah directed their attention to one concern: confirmation of the Islamic legal right of the imams of the *āl al-bayt* to be considered imams and caliphs – and disavowal of the Islamic legality of usurped governance and the crimes in which the Umayyads engaged by way of the sword. With the 'occultation' some modifications transpired in regard to the nature of the matter: so long as among the primary matters of consideration was the confirmation of the impossibility of establishing an Islamic legal state (*al-dawlah al-shar'īyah*) except in the time of the 'return' of the awaited Imam. That was what opened the door to the concept of 'waiting' (*al-intiẓār*) in Shīʿite *fiqh*. The subsequent result was that operation according to the constraints of the principle of 'waiting for the emergence [of the Imam]' (*intiẓār al-faraj*) transformed this principle practically into 'an effective tool for establishing new means for exiting [from this dilemma], which then transformed into practical operational rules for *fiqh* thinking in regard to politics. Along with proceeding from the existence of the occultation of the Imam al-Mahdī is an expression of the impossibility of establishing an Islamically-legal state that led the *fuqahā'* to deactivate the rules which were needed for the establishment of Islamically-legal authority.'[17]

This, however, posed new problems branching from the original conundrum, and most important of these was that the disabling of these *aḥkām* (rulings) meant leaving the Shīʿite Muslims under the control of the rules of the unjust system (*niẓām al-jawr*) and the freezing up of the requirements of the religion for the group, and bewilderment without regulation of the matters of their life that could only be achieved through a political authority (*sulṭah*), and so on. The fact of the matter is that the points of contention become clearer when we return to the original problematic question of the state in Shīʿite *fiqh* in the age of occultation. The basis of this is that the Imam – 'who is charged (*al-mukallaf*) by Allah' in the position of leadership, is absent, and his rule is usurped by unjust political authority, and the people of the *madhab* (i.e., the Shīʿah) cannot aspire to political authority because in that there is an implicit competition which is not legally mandated with those who possess Islamic legitimacy (the imams)...but, do not people need an authority that will regulate their affairs, and if so, what ought to be done?

There is no way out of this paradox except by designating someone who will represent the imam during his occultation, and in some sort of cooperation under compulsion with the existing political authority in certain matters – despite its usurpation of the rule of the imams. But the question remains: is the deputy representative (*nā'ib*) of the Imam in a particular station with regard to the Imam? That is, does he possess the same powers that the Imam enjoys? Also, is it possible to cooperate with the existing political authority – despite necessary needs which call for that – when this is not legally mandated Islamically?[18]

Later on, Shīʿite *fiqh* answer the first question – by specifying the principle of the obligation to set up a deputy representative of the Imam (*nā'ib li-l-imām*) – from among all the *fuqahā'* who possess the qualifications of religious *marjaʿīyah* – with the delimiting of their authority to what is not (reserved to) the authority of the (infallible – *ma'ṣūm*) Imam. There is also the stipulation which allows them to assume the performance of managerial duties that are in the scope of what is known as *wilāyat al-faqīh al-khāṣ* (the particular/special trusteeship of the *faqīh*)[19] according to some of the *fuqahā'*, whereas some others took the position that it is necessary to establish the position of the Imam in regard to *all* his powers and authority,[20] and that is in the scope of *wilāyat al-faqīh al-'āmah* (the general trusteeship of the *faqīh*).[21] As for the second question it was answered in stages along the following lines:

In the first stage, distinction was made between the Islamic legality of the usurping and unjust political authority – and this was not provided for – and between the legality of working with it:

> Deemed possible was cooperating with it according to particular limits, and proceeding from the point of necessity (the need of people to cooperate with it) and sometimes on the basis of the obligation to command what is right and to forbid what is unjust (*al-amr bi-l-ma'rūf wa al-nahīy 'an al-munkar*) and the establishment of legal culpability (*al-takālīf*) which is not possible without the establishment of an authority (*sulṭah*).[22]

Previously, Muḥammad Bāqir al-Sabzuwārī justified that by arguing against 'the impossibility of relinquishing the rights of the people through refusal to cooperate with the sultan.'[23] If we fail to take into consideration the fact that Shī'ite *fiqh* was typically disinclined to provoke the unjust political authority in the age of occultation[24] in order for that not to become a rationalization – in the [Shī'ite] *madhab* – for a renewed illegal endeavor to usurp the rule of the Imam after the unjust political authority's usurpation of it, we realize that considering (compulsory) cooperation, was not beyond the realm of possibility despite the general conception of the imamate and the Ja'farī *madhab* as a group of 'rejectors' (*rāfiḍah*) and a closed *madhab*.

In the second stage, there occurred a development in *fiqh* in the matter of cooperating with the existing political authority, reaching a degree that imparted some religious legitimacy: not only with regard to that cooperation, but also, that political authority (*sulṭah*) itself. The fact is that the understanding of this new point of *fiqh*, attaching to the matter of legitimacy of cooperation with the usurping political authority, is based on a return to the givens of the response of Shī'ite *fiqh* to the original question pertaining to the possibility of setting up someone who would serve as the deputy representative of the Imam in his heading and leading the Muslims during the Age of Occultation, in the consideration that it was a matter logically connected and in *fiqh* to the following: the question of cooperating with the political authority and the legality of that cooperation, as previously mentioned.

It did not suffice the Shīʿite fuqahāʾ to solve the matter of the occultation and its *aḥkām* (rulings) – and among these were the doctrines of 'deactivation' (*al-taʿṭīl*) and 'waiting' ('*al-intiẓār*') through positing the permissibility of establishing deputies for the Imam (from among the *mujtahids* of the *fuqahāʾ*) and their entrusting them with the powers of command of the imamate in the period of occultation only. Rather, they went so far as to assert the viability of 'permission' – *al-idhn*: permitting a *faqīh* possessed of all the requisite qualifications of a *marjaʿ* to govern through the entrusting of authority, and naturally on the basis of the trustworthiness of the *faqīh* to rule with requisite piety and justice. This was the case, despite the fact that this entailed entering the *fuqahāʾ* into the realm of necessitating the establishment of leadership (*al-riʾāsah*) in society – even if it rested for support on a corrupt person (*fāsiq*)[25] – if the domains of Islam were not threatened from the outside; except that 'permission' (*al-idhn*) would then be, by force of material facts, a form of religious sanctification of the political authority (*sulṭah*) stripped of its legitimacy, and especially when that political authority has succeeded in benefiting from the glorification of its image among the masses, whether the permission is general or limited.[26] Probably the treatise of al-Sharīf al-Murtaḍā, *Masʾalah fi-l-ʿAmal maʿa al-Sulṭān* (*A Matter of Dealing with the Sultan*) is the best early Shīʿite assessment of the problems of cooperating with political authority,[27] and it opened a chapter, in what followed, on the *fiqh* 'theory' of 'permission' (*al-idhn*) for the sultan and the entrusting of general command according to the limits of acceptance and obedience.[28]

This was the context and the result of the Shīʿite *fiqh* view of the matter of the imamate and political authority, and the Islamic legality of this, in the period of occultation. From the standpoint of trustworthiness: historically and scientifically, the assertion that the heritage of *fiqh* – actually in itself – assisted al-Nāʾīnī in formulating his modern thesis on the political issue, and in his liberation – to a great degree – from the fetters of Shīʿite *uṣūlī* and *fiqh* discourse around the impermissibility of thinking about political authority outside the supposition of the one, single Islamically-legal right of the infallible imams of the *āl al-bayt*. Similarly, it distanced him from assertions about the necessity of abiding by the line of 'waiting' (*al-intiẓār*) until the time of the re-emergence of the absent Imam. Trustworthiness itself dictated that he transcend the temporary solutions arrived at by the political reason of Shīʿite *fiqh*: according the functions of the imamate temporarily to the deputies of the imam, that is, on the *fuqahā'*, and facilitating a device in *fiqh* – by means of the jurisprudential concept of 'permission' (*al-idhn*) for the matter of cooperating with the usurping political authority. That not only was a transcendence of and breaking from the creed of 'waiting' (*al-intiẓār*), but a thesis of that itself which cast the matter of 'permission' along the lines of an assertion of legitimate political authority, and how an alternative to the extant unjust political authority might be effected.

From 'Permission' for Illegitimate Political Authority to Theorizing Legitimate Political Authority

In the treatise *Tanbīh al-Ummah*, Muḥammad Ḥussayn al-Gharawī al-Nā'īnī offers a strongly reasoned argument for the defense of legitimate political authority effecting liberation from the tethers of (the doctrine of) 'waiting' (*al-intiẓār*), and shunning the principle of 'permission' (*al-idhn*) at one and the same time: that is, it decoupled the relation between the Islamic legality of political authority and the return of the absent Imam, and it refused to allow the unjust sultan to enjoy religious legitimacy through the means of a *fiqh* 'permissibility' of entrusting general political matters to him. The significance of this is that the road to establishing this Islamic legitimacy – in the view of al-Nā'īnī – is feasible *without* submitting to the theory of the imamate or the theory of the legality of cooperating with the usurping political authority. This type of view of the matter of the state (*al-dawlah*) is new to Shīʿite political *fiqh*, and it is what created for it a new basis as regards to the political question in Shīʿite Islamic thought.

Why is this thinking about legitimate authority new?

This question branches into two seminal questions – the first of which is the question about the need for authority – any or which authority – and the second is the question on the origin of this authority.

Concerning the first question: al-Nā'īnī reiterated what those previous to him among the Shīʿah and others had done when they had often repeated the necessity of the state (*al-dawlah*) for human society in general and for Islamic society in particular, the means of this and its prerequisites aside; if it is the case that 'there is no difference in acknowledging the need for authority between those who assert its being necessary for the individual or the group and between the legitimacy of its rule on the consideration of its arrival at the center of power by way of elections or by way of inheritance or by domination or coercion'.[29] So long as there is this principle of necessity, of need for 'rectification of the general order and regulation of the life of the human being'. However, the more capable power in providing the best response to this necessity is the subject of the second question and that is the power that 'springs from itself' (the *ummah*) – expressing its culture and identity, preserving and defending it.[30] This merits the safeguarding of the dignity of the country and its independence and the holding of the *ummah* together that preserves its identity. Among the functions of authority is 'the preservation of the internal order of the country and the development of society' and the establishment of justice and 'to be cautious of foreign intervention in the country'; and the protection of its independence: these are what are conveyed by the meaning among 'legalists' of the maxim 'protecting the purity of Islam' (*ḥifẓ bayḍat al-Islām*) or as according to others 'preservation of the nation'.[31] And, if this is sufficient to prove the original source principle for establishing authority – the rectitude of the system – then it is also sufficient to prove that taking up this task is predicated upon setting up an authority that enjoys national legitimacy springing from society.

On Legitimate Political Authority: from 'Infallibility' (al-'iṣmah) *to the Constitution*

Political authority – in the view of al-Nā'īnī – does not exceed one of two types: royal authority (*sulṭah tamlīkīyah*) or entrusted authority (*sulṭah wilāyātīyah*). The difference between them is in their nature: in the means for the establishment of each, in their typologies, and in the form of governance within them. That distinction is successive and ensuing from it is a second distinction between the two types of governance permitting the attribution to them of one of two types: the rule of injustice (*ḥukm al-jawr*), and the rule of justice (*ḥukm al-'adl*).

As for the rule of injustice, the 'holder of authority' (*ṣāḥib al-sulṭah*) behaves in the lands like a king in his personal dominion, without any limit or restraint. And he, if he does not abide by the sanctity of any individual or right, compels his subjects to submit to his command and to bow to his will, even if he is unaware of the necessity of preserving the lands in accordance with what responsibility as a ruler ordains![32] Along with this he is 'not ashamed from asserting himself to be absolved of error and to be sacrosanct unto himself and above any criticism or questioning.' And he, in that way 'is not lacking...in pseudo-*'ulamā'* who will create justifications for him in whatever he wills.'[33] Just as al-Kawākibī discussed the pyramidal arrangement of tyranny, wherein its valuation from highest to lowest is transformed into a generalized prevailing culture,[34] so did al-Nā'īnī in similar fashion when he described the results of action of political deviance on the social values of society.[35]

As for the rule of justice, political authority in it is a trusteeship (*wilāyah*) not a possession as it is in the first type. From that, there ensue two results: the first is that entrusting political power is for firmly establishing qualitative trustworthiness 'the goal of which is direction and use of special/personal power in the state for its goals and not for the goals of the holder of political power.' This is the matter that dictates, objectively, the diminution of absolute power of rule and the restraint of it. The second result is that the people are no longer a flock of sheep in the hands of the holder of power – the king of the state – but rather they become 'participants' in political power; and on the basis of this participation, individuals among the people possess the right 'to question politicians and to take them to account and to oppose their actions, along with their enjoying security and freedom of opinion and expression of it.'[36]

Thus, we are before a modern model of the state defended by al-Nā'īnī without considerable difficulty, even if he was only rarely inclined to indicate its Western European roots.[37] However, authority derived from this modern model requires, as he noticed, guarantees so that the rule of justice will not become transformed into the rule of injustice, and the trusteeship into dominion. Here, al-Nā'īnī needs the implements of his *fiqh* knowledge side-by-side with his modern knowledge in order to effect an exit from the problematic trap towards which it pushes the question: the guarantee of the justice of political authority and its legitimacy – in Shī'ite political culture – is infallibility (*al-'iṣmah*): the infallibility of the imam, and the assertion of this is among the *uṣūl* of the Ja'farī Imāmī *madhab*[38] which is not possible to disregard. If so, then what is the way to provide guarantees for the justice of the political authority without running into the obstacle of infallibility (*al-'iṣmah*)?

Al-Nā'īnī submits that, 'I bring up these means that might conceivably ensure these guarantees: they are (auto-) infallibility in the ruler'; but he goes beyond that quickly to the assertion that infallibility is absent (*ghā'ibah*) along with the absent Imam, and that the wise ruler combining 'perfections (*al-kamālīyāt*) in himself' does not exist,[39] and, therefore, the absence of infallibility and wisdom necessitate another alternative even if one is unable to raise the sultan to a position of infallibility; and that alternative – according to al-Nā'īnī – is none other than the constitution, then subsequent supervision (*al-riqābah*) and accountability (*al-muḥāsabah*) on their account of being the two guarantees that will protect against authority from turning into unjust authority.

Al-Nā'īnī reaches the conclusion that the constitution is 'the supreme among law and rules necessary to be incumbent upon every individual,' and 'it delimits the powers of the ruler, and acknowledges the rights of the people and their freedoms'; however, when he goes back to determine the self-evident axioms in the subject, he acknowledges that there are those among the *fuqahā'* and the masses who will demand proof of the connection of this to *fiqh*. Thus, he hastens to attribute the constitution to the sphere of politics and particular organizations among the categories of *fiqh*, expressing it in the form of an operational directive (*al-risālah al-'amalīyah*)[40] deriving its legitimacy from 'an absence of contradiction of any of its articles with the rulings of the holy *sharī'ah*.'[41] Al-Nā'īnī, however, finds in discussion of censorship and accountability a wider margin of freedom. In it, he finds a way out from the objections of opponents – among the *fuqahā'* in particular – to the assertion of the *marja'īyah* (authoritative referential status) of the constitution in the political system (side-by-side with the *marja'īyah* of the Imam or his deputy – the *faqīh* who has all the requisite qualifications for *al-marja'īyah*). He knows well enough that the compliance of the authority with the constitution is conditioned by inception of 'a body of guidance and oversight/supervision (a national *shūrā* council)' that implements the policies of the executive body under the rules of accountability and is responsible for its actions before the people;[42] implying that the establishment of such a body (for supervision and accountability) provides an opportunity for the *fuqahā'* to exercise their supervisory functions on the account of them being deputies of the Imam through their membership in the council (*majlis*) or the membership of the 'most honorable who have permission from the just *faqīh*'. And, this, in the esteem of al-Nā'īnī, is sufficient 'to bestow legitimacy upon the work of the council'[43] from the standpoint of Shī'ite *fiqh*.[44]

Al-Nā'īnī does not desist from warning that this theoretical supposition – of *fiqh* and *ijtihād* – is fraught with confrontation by the opposition from various pervasive centers, political and religious, the incentive of which was the defense of the interests of the despotic sultan and those who benefit from him – the *fuqahā'* being among them. Thus, he does not pause on many occasions to go into details to expose the vital link between religious despotism and political, but endeavors more strenuously to found his political constitutional idea from within the sphere of Shī'ite *fiqh*...as well as from external frontiers.

'*Constitutional* Fiqh'

Al-Nāʾīnī finds many reasons that justify (for him) the requisite Islamic legality to advocate the conditional system (the constitution) as well as to justify the search for the formulation to meet this demand and, at the top of the list, there are two reasons: political and religious. As for the political, it is to be found in the monstrosity of the unjust sultan and his deviance – exercising blind tyranny against the *ummah* to squander its rights and freedoms and encroach upon its sanctity and sustenance. It has been affirmed in history that autocracy 'is the gate which leads to destruction',[45] just as it has been affirmed that enjoyment by the *ummah* of its natural and legitimate rights – and freedom and equality in their distribution – is a guarantor of its ability to develop, and so on.[46] As for the religious reason, latent in the rulings of Islamic law, it is that autocracy is causing people to submit by force, and pushing them – through coercion – to proffer obeisance to the despot. If they refuse to resist that despotism – and this is an Islamic legal duty – and they are pleased with slavish worship of the idolatrously excessive ruler (*al-ḥākim al-ṭāghī*), then that is not only for them 'a wronging of themselves and a deprivation of the benefit of freedom' but also it actually becomes 'as specified by the blessed verses of the Qurʾān and the transmitted accounts of the infallible Imams: worship of *al-ṭughāh* to the degree of taking partners (*al-shirk*) in the worship of Allah the One and Only.'[47]

If so, resisting despotism is an Islamic legal obligation and not only a political need; and if it is specified, then it is a shackle on the hand of despotism and a blow to its core, then the meaning of this is, logically, the defense of it (i.e., the specified resistance to tyranny) is another Islamic legal obligation:[48] to save the *ummah* from the brutality (*baṭsh*) of the unjust sultan and to save the creed of *al-tawḥīd* from the semblance of idolatry (*al-shirk*).[49]

But what is to be done then if autocracy is able to afford itself the same pretext and absolve itself in the name of religion? Rather, what is to be done if those who oppose conditionality are enemies who reject its legitimacy and the need for it in the name of *al-sharīʿah* as well?

Al-Nāʾīnī rebuts the objection of the 'people of autocracy' (*ahl al-istibdād*) to freedom in their assumption that 'people's attaining it will incontrovertibly necessitate, the engendering of ability to liberate [themselves] from respect for the Islamic legal rulings…and secondly that the call for freedom conflicts, practically, with the call to respect the rulings of the holy *sharīʿah*'.[50] Similarly, he rebuts their opposition to the constitution by claiming that it is 'a secondary legislation (*tashrī'*) conflicting with *al-sharī'ah*' and that 'promulgating any other law in the lands of Islam is innovation (*bid'ah*) opposed to the work of the keeper of *al-sharī'ah*'.[51] Even if al-Nā'īnī does not pause long to refute the supposition of a necessary correlation between the meaning of freedom (*al-ḥurrīyah*) and the meaning of liberation (*al-taḥrīr*) from the rulings (*aḥkām*) of the *sharī'ah* – finding it sufficient to mention the *sunnah* of the Prophet and his Companions in the modality of this freedom[52] and in the assertion that is among the necessities (*ḍarūrīyāt*) of the religion;[53] he gives protracted pause before the mistaken assertion that the constitution is an innovation (*bid'ah*) – especially because the defenders of the constitution were charged with heretical innovation on three counts: in the assertion of a constitution; in the assertion that it should be respected and the necessity of this; and in the assertion of the obligation to take transgressions of it to account. Al-Nā'īnī begins his criticism by defining the meaning of innovation (*al-bid'ah*) in Shī'ite *uṣūl*, saying:

> Among the most apparent essential assumptions of Islam, and what the *'ulamā'* of the *ummah* have agreed upon, is that confrontation of prophethood, and competing with Islamic law (*al-shar'*) is among that which is transmitted in the reported accounts by the term *al-bid'ah* (innovation), and in the terminology of the *fuqahā'* by the term *al-tashrī'* (legislation). It is effected when new law is in contradiction of what has been promulgated by *al-sharī'ah*...As for the case when new law is not promulgated under the heading of *al-ja'l al-shar'ī* (the legitimate law giver), then this does not correspond to what is termed *bid'ah* just as the meaning does not apply to any injunctions to respect or necessitate the obedience of this law.[54]

In the opinion of al-Nā'īnī, that is what confirms the status of the constitution as it is 'not subsumed itself under the heading of legislation (*al-tashrī'*)' and, thus, it does not constitute legislation in conflict with the divine legislation; and there is no competition with prophethood or the authority to legislate that pertained to it. Moreover, it is 'not subsumed under the rubric of forbidden innovation (*al-bid'ah al-muḥarramah*)'.[55]

This *fiqh* refutation does not suffice for al-Nā'īnī and he takes to arguing on the basis of another *fiqh* principle distinguishing – according to what the *fuqahā'* have defined – between the two categories of obligatory (*ṣinfayn min al-wājib*): obligatory itself (*wājib bi-l-dhāt*), and 'it is what is commanded by itself', and obligatory for other than itself (*wājib li-ghayrih*)[56] which becomes obligatory on the basis of its attachment to other obligations which render it thus, that is, obligatory (*wājib*). For this, in regard to the condition of the constitution, it becomes obligatory on the basis of its attachment to other obligations (*wājibāt*) – the safeguarding of the system and the restraint of political authority.[57]

In both cases, there is no argument for rebuttals in the scales of *fiqh*. After this refutation, it is possible for the other remaining derivative objections to be brought down: from the angle of the assertion that in the convening of the council (*majlis*) of *al-shūrā*, there is an interference in the matter of the imamate and in the state in which the principle of subservience dictates the impermissibility of the *ummah* in interfering with the matter (*amr*) of the imamate;[58] or from the standpoint that electing the council on the basis of the comprehensive qualifications for the deputy of the imam because engaging in the affairs of the *ummah* is of that which enters into the category of supervisory functions (*al-waẓā'if al-ḥisbīyah*), and these are among the entrusted things which are delegated exclusively to the *fuqahā'* on the basis of their being considered deputies and are not left to the general population (*al-'ām*) and so on.[59] We mentioned that the remainder of these objections and whatever resembles them can potentially be rebutted because al-Nā'īnī succeeds in 'covering' his position both in terms of *fiqh* and politics and not simply as only a result of his success in formulating an argumentative thesis with the conservative *fuqahā'* and in pulverizing their systematized presumptions but also, and chiefly, because of his ability to put forth the subject of authority along lines different from what the (Shī'ite) *Imāmī fuqahā'* had done before him. These had proceeded, usually, from the matter of the imamate where in the discussion about *al-wilāyah*, they affirmed the legitimate inalienable right of the imams to the imamate; and when they confronted the case of the occultation of the Imam, they entrusted his functions to his deputies (i.e., the *fuqahā'*).[60] As for al-Nā'īnī, he proceeded directly from the subject of *al-wilāyah* – deciding that the supervisory functions (*al-waẓā'if al-ḥisbīyah*) were not to be dropped in the absence of the Imam or in the case of the inability of his deputies among the *fuqahā'* to exercise them, but rather that they were to be incumbent upon the rest of the *ummah*[61] because the discourse of Islamic legal culpability (*al-taklīf*) specifies the *entire ummah* and not the *fuqahā'* exclusively. Thus, it is obligatory for the *ummah* to exercise this trusteeship (*wilāyah*) *over itself*.

From reading the treatise *Tanbīh al-Ummah* of Muḥammad Ḥussayn al-Nā'īnī, a number of conclusions can be drawn with regard to what presents as a significant measure of boldness, if not to say danger, concerning the relation of the treatise to the fixed *fiqh* and creedal positions upon which Shīʿite *fiqh* had rested for a long time; and these are, in sum, five deductions.

The first deduction is that which caused the revolution in Shīʿite consciousness and *fiqh* and effected its liberation of them – from the arrested state in the rulings of the 'occultation'. It is true that there were precursors, as we have indicated, from the standpoint of the success of some movements in *ijtihād* in *Imāmī* (*fiqh*) in order to effect an exit from the debilitating tradition of the rulings and the 'waiting' (*al-intiẓār*) until the period when the occultation was lifted to formulate the context for cooperation with the usurping political authority; and *fiqh* 'permission' (*al-idhn*) for rulers to be entrusted with authority. These precursors, no doubt had their importance in forming a realistic 'political conscience' among the Shīʿah and their *fuqahā'*; however, the idea of the deputyship of the Imam in the *wilāyah*, from the standpoint of the *fuqahā'* and the *mujtahidūn* who possessed the requisite qualifications for *marjaʿīyah* (that is, what was known as the *wilāyat al-faqīh* both 'general' (*ʿāmah*) and 'particular' (*khāṣah*), did not go outside the logic of the problematic of the imamate in the era of occultation. More significant than that is that the *wilāyah* was constrained to a limited group of society, and it alone, according to the obligation of the imamate, had the right to the matter of this *wilāyah*. As for society, it did not possess that because if it did, then it would encroach upon the station of the imamate (which is specified by 'divine appointment'), and its members would end up competing with the *fuqahā'* in the legal specialization which none other than they possessed. Thus, the revolution, to which we refer, is al-Nā'īnī's defense of taking politics and authority from the rulings of the occultation and its consequences and transforming them into a 'general matter of concern' and, moreover, in his expanding the sphere of political participation to include *all* Muslims, not only the qualified *fuqahā'* among them.

The second deduction pertains to deputy representatives and representation: representation was the particular domain of the *fuqahā'* at the exclusion of all others ever since Shīʿite *fiqh* had emerged from the shock of the 'absence of the infallible one (*al-maʿṣūm*)' to attempt to find guidance in the positing of deputy representatives for the Imam in the period of his absence. The deputy representatives alone enjoyed religious legitimacy – in Shīʿite *fiqh* literature – and they were representatives of the Imam among those who could furnish the requisite qualifications to exercise the functions of *al-marjaʿīyah*. With al-Nā'īnī and his treatise, the matter differs at the root-level: we have moved from the formula of deputy representatives of the imam to the formula of representatives of the *ummah* who ultimately came to possess – in the National Shūrā Council – the right to engage in the functions of the representatives of the Imam: the supervisory functions. It is true that he did not attack the legitimacy of deputyship of the Imam – and he would not have been able to do so even if he had wished – but he transferred the functions of this deputyship in practice to the Shūrā Council; rather, he did more than that in his implicit distinction between the authority of the deputies of the Imam that was not subject to censure or accountability and the authority of the conditional state existing on the basis of these two principles.

The third deduction pertains to the previous two, specifically in regard to the question of *wilāyah* and to whom it should be accorded. Shīʿite *fiqh* had explored the formula of *wilāyat al-faqīh*[62] in every aspect except in minor branch details (*farʿīyāt*) – such as the boundaries of the *wilāyah* and whether it is 'particular' (*khāṣ*) or 'general' (*ʿām*). Al-Nāʾīnī, however, completely inverted the equation upon his defense of another form of *wilāyah*, that is, the trusteeship of the *ummah* over itself (*wilāyah al-ummah ʿalā nafsihā*), thus he goes to the limit of defending a system in which the guardianship of the *fuqahāʾ* towers above people...naturally, without colliding with them.[63]

As for the fourth deduction, it pertains to giving priority to *al-shūrā* – according to al-Nāʾīnī – over *ijtihād* as a necessary base in the establishment and functioning of a political system.[64] Consequently, he gainsays the logic of Shīʿite *fuqahāʾ* which maintains that: the *mujtahid* fulfilling the criteria of *ijtihād* ought not follow opinions of others given the status of knowledge he has already achieved,[65] he delivers an opinion that is congruent with his own thoughts in regard to the public character of the political field, the concept of nationalist political representation, and the trusteeship of the *ummah* over itself; as all of these blend harmoniously with the concepts of *al-shūrā* and opinion of the majority. Meanwhile, implementation of *ijtihād* consolidates positions of the *fuqahāʾ* and the legitimacy of their demands to monopolize the *wilāyah*. We may even conclude here that al-Nāʾīnī has shifted us from the rule of *ijtihād* to the rule of *al-shūrā*, although he never toppled *ijtihād* – being a *mujtahid* himself – but rather he re-constructed it anew so that, *ijtihād* is no longer the privilege of an elite – the *fuqahāʾ* – who speak on behalf of the public, but it became, in fact, a *public* act practiced by *ummah* as it practices its own right in *wilāyah*.

Finally, the fifth deduction is that al-Nāʾīnī deemed citizenship (*al-muwāṭanah*) and not *religion* to be the cornerstone upon which political rights of the *ummah* in an Islamic community, such as the Iranian one, are built. This is clearly stated as he says: 'The membership of the Shūrā Council is not confined to Muslims only; non-Muslim minorities have the right to be represented in the Council as well, and they have to participate in elections since their followers are compatriots in the nation and possess shares in the state's monies. Moreover, the public character of *shūrā* and elections depends on their participation.'[66] Evidently, al-Nā'īnī departs from the problematic of the traditional *dhimmī* (non-Muslim) concept to adopt the ideology of modern citizenship, which stems from a Western Liberal source.

Undoubtedly, in light of givens of the analysis above, al-Nā'īnī's treatise, *Tanbīh al-Ummah wa Tanzīh al-Millah*, represents a genuine intellectual revolution in the historical context of Shī'ite political *fiqh*: a revolution that reassessed the axioms that had constituted that *fiqh* and re-introduced new political concepts into its system: the constitution (or *al-mashrūṭah*), the Shūrā Council, representatives of the people, accountability before the people, citizenship, modern legal authority, the law and so on. Despite the fact that this review resulted in launching the effectiveness of *ijtihād* in interpreting legal texts (*ta'wīl*), as well as in legal extraction (*takhrīj*) and derivation (*istinbāṭ*); it never impugned constants such as the imamate (*imāmah*), representation of imam, and functions of the *fuqahā'* during the age of occultation (*ghaybah*). It never conceded, however, its essential pursuit: to defend the constitution (*al-mashrūṭah*) by regarding it as (the solid foundation for the well-being of *ummah*),[67] nor did it bargain over its new concepts intellectually.

Again, we have no doubt that this treatise alleviated two pressing concerns in the modern Iranian national and Islamic nation: theorization of a constitutional movement, and appeal for an escape from the Shī'ite jurisprudential impasse. As for the first demand, a hint was made previously concerning the general political milieu in which this treatise was composed, which is the circumstantionality of modern Iran's endeavors to impose a constitution in the system and form the Shūrā Council (as was actually achieved in 1906). Although the *ḥawzah al-'ilmīyah* in Najaf and elsewhere had the greatest of influence in leading this struggle through the positions of its *'ulamā'* and *marāji'*, nevertheless, this movement lacked a political ideology that was proportional to the nature of the constitutional battle; and it was impossible for this ideology but to be modern in order to address the ultimate goal of this struggle: that is, the goal of achieving a modern constitutional authority. In such a manner the treatise of al-Nā'īnī was the ideological and political '*manifesto*' that the constitutional movement needed at that time in the country. Al-Nā'īnī apprehended this need very well when he deliberately retorted the fallacies of those who stood against the Constitution and the establishment of the Shūrā Council, defending both of them while at the same time overlooking the drawbacks of this model (which would soon emerge after he completed editing his treatise).

As for the second demand, the pervasive unsung existence of which we incline to emphasize in many Shī'ite *marāji'*, its only flaw is that the concept of '*wilāyat al-faqīh*' and having *fuqahā'* carry out the functions of the imam – totally or partially – during the age of occultation (especially in regard to the *waẓā'if al-ḥisbīyah*), did not solve the problem of having a Shī'ite *fiqh* vis-à-vis an unjust authority in which *fuqahā'* are no longer capable of practicing their roles due to its injustice, especially after the collapse of settlement between them and the ruling Qajārī dynasty by the end of the nineteenth century. The quest for a constitution – as it is concomitantly a quest for restraining the ruler's powers – was fair enough for them, at least to restrain the brutality of the unjust authority and to secure a minimal margin for their political participation in the Shūrā Council. We possess two clues at least for this concern: the first is that the Iranian Shī'ite *marāji'* participated effectively and strongly in the constitutional battle without having experienced a moment of a taking a negative position towards it. The second clue is that al-Nā'īnī's treatise was received with favorable acclaim within the Shī'ite *fiqh* arena, and moreover, it garnered panegyrics from distinguished Shī'ite *marāji'* in modern times: namely, ayatollah al-Ākhawand Muḥammad Kāẓim al-Khurāsānī and ayatollah al-Māzindarānī. We hold the assumption that such panegyrics connote some sort of accepted legitimacy for the text, attainable only when the lauder concurs with the lauded.

Al-Nā'īnī's treatise not only posited a conceptual exit for the impasse of Shī'ite *fiqh*, we may maintain that it salvaged this *fiqh* from its crisis in the age of occultation and also freed all its *fuqahā'* from the crucible of the *ghaybah*!

We are left, here, with one question that poses itself to the reader of al-Nā'īnī's treatise: was that conceptual revolution prompted by the author of this treatise conceived from within or without the Shī'ite *fiqhī* reason; in that, were there predilections conducive to its emergence within the legacy of Shī'ite political *fiqh*, or did it simply crystallize from without – outside its theoretical apparatus?

It was implied earlier, that the heritage of Shī'ite *fiqh* was not devoid of some realistic moments in which it partially departed from 'the mythology of the *imāmah*'[68] towards a more realistic approach in dealing with the political question; such as permitting interaction with an unjust authority – or via legitimization of its authority by means of *fiqh* 'permission' (*al-idhn*). Definitely, al-Nā'īnī exploited these precedents and built upon them to great effect (given the extent of the involvement of *fuqahā'* in the constitutional battle). However, the conceptual framework and the political lexicon he implemented in writing his treatise, as well as the problematic he explored, all imply that he ultimately found something of his long-sought goal in epistemological system of non-Muslims, which his traditional milieu could not provide.

It is true that while we possess no indication whereby to confirm that al-Nā'īnī was somehow introduced to European thought – as was the case with al-Ṭahṭāwī, al-Tūnsī, al-Afghānī Muḥammad 'Abdūh, and al-Kawākibī, if at different levels – we can at least take into account his reference to the European breakthrough in developing a political system in light of 'principles of our Islamic *sharī'ah* as he states[69] by considering it an indication of his interest in the liberal political model in Europe if not an indicator of some knowledge of the conceptual system that established it. Indeed, al-Nā'īnī may have actually been convinced that the modern European democratic system was inspired by principles and fundamentals of Islam; and this might have led him to the astonishing thesis when addressing opponents of *al-shūrā*: 'Instead of saying of the public national *shūrā*, which the Westerners are implementing "these are our belongings returned to us",[70] we brand it – full of stubbornness and intransigence – as in contravention of Islam'.[71] He certainly understands that this *shūrā* is not within the lands of Islam (*diyār al-Islām*), but rather in European lands, and it provided those with 'power and superiority' around the globe, consequently, it is inevitable for us to learn from them, even if in a self-consoling manner, that this was our product and we might wish to retrieve it!

We did not want in the previous context to pursue a historical review of Shī'ite political *fiqh*, nor did we want to delve into roots of the concept of the *imāmah* in it or its impact on modern Shī'ite thought, this is not our topic exactly; rather, we meant to analyze a moment in modern intellectual Reformism within the Shī'ite intellectual arena, which was represented primarily by al-Nā'īnī's thesis on the constitutional question at the beginning of the twentieth century. Unfortunately, this was a solitary moment in modern Shī'ite thought, no other coincided with it, nor did any antedate or follow it[72] in defense of the constitutional idea and the subject of the nation state.

Notes

1. The Arabic root s-l-ṭ from which both the term *sulṭah* and the term *sulṭān* (which has come into English) derive has the underlying connotation of 'authority' – similarly, it may also denote power – including political power. For this reason, the term *sulṭah* might be translated as 'political authority' or 'political power' – depending on the context; however this may be, at times, too restrictive when 'authority' is more general and universal – Translator.

2. Al-Khalīlī, Ja'far, *Madkhal ilā Mawsū'at al-'Atabāt al-Muqadasah*, 2nd edn (Beirut: Mu'asasat al-A'lamī, 1987), p. 179.

3. The term *ḥawzah 'ilmīyah* (pl. *ḥawzāt*) refers to a center of learning in the Shī'ite world and, while it does carry the connotation of a seminary, the curriculum, function and overall significance are significantly broader – especially in connection to the institution of *al-marja'īyah* (see below). The most prominent of these *ḥawzāt* are historically al-Najaf in Iraq, Qom in Iran (from the Safavid period onwards) and in the region of Jabl 'Āmil in South Lebanon – Translator.

4. The full text of the letter can be found in: al-Sayf, Tawfīq, *Ḍid al-Istibdād* (Beirut; Casablanca: al-Markaz al-Thaqāfī al-'Arabī, 1999), pp. 213–369.

5. As the author will discuss, the term *istibdād* carries numerous connotations and may connote 'autocracy', 'despotism' as well as 'tyranny' – given that, often 'tyranny' and 'despotism' or 'oppression' are 'features' or associated with autocracy.

6. Born in the city of Nā'in in the vicinity of Iṣfahān, Iran (either in 1273AH/1856CE or 1277AH/1860CE and died 1355AH/1936CE), Muḥammad Ḥussayn al-Nā'īnī lived in Iran between Nā'in and Iṣfahān and was almost 30 years old before he left to settle in Iraq. He traveled between Sāmarrā' and al-Najaf until his death. For more details, see: Tawfīq, *Ḍid al-Istibdād*.

7. Al-Sayf, *Ḍid al-Istibdād*, p. 66.

8. The term *al-marja'īyah* coming from the Arabic root (r-j-') which connotes 'returning' or 'going back' denotes an 'authoritative referent' or 'point of reference' wherein a historical personage or event provides the referential basis for judgment in regard to a particular issue, problem or model. In the world of Shī'ite *fiqh*, *al-marja'īyah* has become highly institutionalized where a religious scholar or jurisprudent (*'ālim* or *faqīh* – pls.*'ulamā'* and *fuqahā'*) has attained to a rank of *marja'* where he may be consulted in matters of Islamic law and subsequently 'imitated' as an 'authoritative recourse for imitation' – *marja' al-taqlīd* – Translator.

9. Al-Sayf, *Ḍid al-Istibdād*, p. 132.

10. The foreword of al-Ṭālqānī and the panegyric of al-Khurāsānī and al-Māzindarānī for the treatise in: al-Sayf, *Ḍid al-Istibdād*, pp. 234–7.

11. Muẓaffar al-Dīn was weak, for this reason al-Ṣadr al-A'ẓam was able to spread his power and influence over the country.

12. The first edition of the book was published in 1909, whereas the edition introduced by al-Ṭaliqānī is relatively new having been published in the second half of the 1950s.

13. The Iranians called their constitution '*al-mashrūṭah*'. Al-Ṭahṭāwī, however, defined first the French term '*la charte*' (carte or carta). The model of the Iranian constitution is Belgian, so it is possible that this term means the same thing to them. The dynamics of years 1905 and 1906 gave this term the concept of conditions or limits, referring in this sense to putting conditions on the Shah, and restraining his powers). See: Al-Sayyid, Raḍwān, 'Dirāsat muqāranah li-al-mujtama' al-madanī fī kul min Īrān wa al-Waṭan al-'Arabī', paper presented at: *al-'ilāqāt al-'arabīyah-al-īrānīyah: al-itijāhāt al-rāhinah wa āfāq al-mustaqbal: buḥūth wa munāqashāt al-nadwah*

al-fikrīyah, conducted by Centre for Arab Unity Studies in cooperation with the University of Qatar (Beirut: Centre for Arab Unity Studies, 1996), p. 678.

14. Al-Sayf, *Ḍid al-Istibdād*, p. 220.

15. The first dispute that beset Muslims – after the death of their Prophet – is the one concerning the *imāmah*. See: Al-Ash'arī, Abū al-Ḥasan 'Alī bin Ismā'īl, *Maqālāt al-Islāmīyīn wa Ikhtilāf al-Muṣalīn*, edited by Muḥammad Muḥyī al-Dīn 'Abd al-Ḥamīd, 2nd edn (Beirut: Dār al-Ḥadāthah, 1985), p. 39.

16. Al-Sayf, *Ḍid al-Istibdād*, p. 173.

17. The danger and significance of this question stems from the importance of the issue of the *imāmah*, as it is – according to Shī'ites – not a secondary issue, but a fundamental pillar in religion (that is, of the *uṣūl*).

18. Al-Anṣārī, Murtaḍā, *al-makāsib*, edited by Muḥammad Klāntir (Beirut: Mu'asasat al-Nūr, 1990), p. 154.

19. Al-Narāqī, Aḥmad, *'Awā'id al-Ayām*, 3rd ed., (Qom: Maktabat Baṣīratī, 1988), p. 188.

20. We shall explain this in detail in Chapter Ten.

21. Al-Sayf, *Ḍid al-Istibdād*, p. 155.

22. 'Apparently, when the Imams knew that justice will not be fulfilled under a despotic/tyrannical ruler...and that Muslims have rights which they can only restore by solicitation and cajolery of rulers and princes, they allowed them to do so, as forbidding that would be a total forfeiture of their own rights.' In: Al-Sabzuwārī, Muḥammad Bāqir, 'Kifāyat al-Aḥkām' *in*: *al-Mu'jam al-Fiqhī* (Qom: Markaz al-'Ajam al-Fiqhī fī Al-Ḥawzah al-'Ilmīyah, [n.d.]), p. 77.

23. Al-Sayyid states that the Imams of the Shī'ites refused to persevere to restore authority a long time before the occultation of the 12th Imam (since Zayn al-'Ābidīn they stopped pursuing to restore authority via revolting against illegitimate Caliphs. The 6th Imam Ja'far al-Ṣādiq, especially, refused any support to restore his right in caliphate by force, and he forbade his followers from any revolutionary movements in the name of Imam until the awaited Imam comes and restores his own right by sword). Available in: Al-Sayyid, *al-Ummah wa al-Jamā'ah wa al-Sulṭah* (Beirut: Dār Iqra', 1984), p. 25.

24. 'Alī bin Abī Ṭālib retorted *al-khawārij* and their saying that there is no rule but God's: 'the rule is to God and there are rulers on earth, people must have whether a just leader or a tyrant, to unite the nation, decide matters, distribute rights, fight enemies, take from the strong to give to the weak, to satisfy the just ruler and make the tyrant likeable'. Al-Sayyid, *al-Jamā'ah wa al-Mujtama' wa al-Dawlah* (Beirut: Dār al-Kitāb al-'Arabī, 1997), p. 28.

25. This permission could be general in many issues, like the one given to the Safavid shāh Tahmāsp from al-Karakī, and it could be specifically utilized in defense against aggression, like the one given to Qajārī Shāh Fatḥ 'Alī Shāh from Kāshif al-Ghiṭā'. Available at: Al-Sayf, *Ḍid al-Istibdād*, pp. 170–1.

26. See profound analysis for the letter in: Al-Sayyid, *al-Ummah wa al-Jamā'ah,* pp. 243–57.

27. Al-Sayf explains this open approach in Shī'ite *fiqh* to the emergence of an interpretational current in Iraq (which is different from the *Intiẓārī* current in Qom) that favored the establishment of *fiqh* that deals with reality, influenced in this way by the *ijtihād* movement in the Sunni world, and the movement of philosophy and reasoning in the 4th *Hijri* century, and the reasoning mechanisms it produced. Available in: Al-Sayf, *Ḍid al-Istibdād*, p. 174.

28. Al-Nā'īnī, Muḥammad Ḥussayn, 'Tanbīh al-Ummah wa tanzīh al-millah', in: al-Sayf, *Ḍid al-Istibdād*, p. 245.

29. Al-Sayf, *Ḍid al-Istibdād*, p. 245.
30. Al-Sayf, *Ḍid al-Istibdād*, p. 246.
31. Al-Sayf, *Ḍid al-Istibdād*, pp. 248–9.
32. Al-Sayf, *Ḍid al-Istibdād*, p. 249.
33. Al-Sayf, *Ḍid al-Istibdād*, in: Chapter 2, p. 41
34. According to the rule (people follow the religion of their king), thus the subjugation of subjects to the tyranny of the authority and their surrender to its will, will be reproduced in the various classes of people. So that the oppressed subject will try to oppress and manipulate those who are below him in status, we may say, that every individual will try to imitate the sultan in his relationship with those who are below him. Available in: Al-Sayf, *Ḍid al-Istibdād*, p. 251.
35. Al-Sayf, *Ḍid al-Istibdād*, p. 253.
36. Upon describing this authority as limited, restrained, fair, conditional, responsible and constitutional, he admits implicitly of these fundamentals. Available at: Al-Sayf, *Ḍid al-Istibdād*, p. 254.
37. (The rule of Imam-according to Shī'ites is an infallible religious rule). Available at: Amīn, Aḥmad, *Ḍuḥā al-Islām*, 10th edn (Beirut: Dār al-Kitāb al-'Arabī, [n.d.]), p. 221; Ibn Khaldūn, *al-Muqadimah* (Beirut: Dār al-Kitāb al-'Arabī, 1996), pp. 190–1; and al-Shahristānī, Abū al-Fatḥ Muḥammad bin 'Abd al-Karīm, *al-Milal wa al-Niḥal*, edited by Muḥammad Sayyid Gaylānī (Beirut: Dār al-Ma'rifah, 2000), p. 146.
38. Al-Nā'īnī, 'Tanbīh al-Ummah', p. 256.
39. The practical dissertation for Shī'ites is a text in which the interpreting jurist presents his attitudes, *fatwas* in issues that impose themselves upon them. So that this text be a starting point for his entrance in the field of authoritative reference *marji'īyah*.
40. Al-Nā'īnī, 'Tanbīh al-Ummah', p. 257.
41. Al-Nā'īnī, 'Tanbīh al-Ummah', p. 258.
42. Al-Nā'īnī, 'Tanbīh al-Ummah', p. 259.
43. Regarding the legitimacy of the council of *Shūrā*, it belongs to the clue of *ahl al-ḥal wa al-'aqd* – according to the fundamentals of *ahl al-sunnah wa al-jamā'ah* as they see that the opinion of *ahl al-ḥal wa al-'aqd* is mandatory. Electing this body by people is the reason of giving it the title of *ahl al-ḥal wa al-'aqd*, thus we see no other excuse to search for another clue of legitimacy elsewhere. Available in: Al-Nā'īnī, 'Tanbīh al-Ummah', p. 258.
44. Al-Nā'īnī, 'Tanbīh al-Ummah', p. 260.
45. Al-Nā'īnī, 'Tanbīh al-Ummah', pp. 260–2.
46. Al-Nā'īnī, 'Tanbīh al-Ummah', p. 269.
47. This inclusive inference resembles the plain logical inference implemented by Ibn Rushd – on the basis of Aristotelian analogy – to prove the religious legality of philosophy, to retort the call of al-Ghazālī that demanded forbidding it and holding those who implement it as blasphemers, the three issues of this logical inference are as follows: *shar'* (demanded reasoning the intelligibles), wisdom (= philosophy) is reasoning, so *shar'* demanded functions of philosophical reasoning. Available in: Ibn Rushd, Abū al-Walīd Muḥammad bin Aḥmad, *Faṣl al-Maqāl fī Taqrīr mā bayn al-Sharī'ah wa al-Ḥikmah min Itiṣāl aw Wujūb al-Naẓar al-'Aqlī wa Ḥudūd al-Ta'wīl (al-Dīn wa al-Mujtama')* Introduced by Mohammed Abed al-Jabri, Silsilat al-Turāth al-Falsafī al-'Arabī, Mu'alafāt Ibn Rushd (Beirut: Centre for Arab Unity Studies, 1997).
48. 'Deliverance from mean thralldom is among the ranks of monotheism and necessities of pure monotheistic faith.' Available in: Al-Nā'īnī, 'Tanbīh al-Ummah', p. 269.
49. Al-Nā'īnī, 'Tanbīh al-Ummah', pp. 301–2.

50. Al-Nā'īnī, 'Tanbīh al-Ummah', p. 311.
51. Al-Nā'īnī, 'Tanbīh al-Ummah', p. 260–1.
52. Al-Nā'īnī, 'Tanbīh al-Ummah', p. 304.
53. Al-Nā'īnī, 'Tanbīh al-Ummah', p. 311.
54. Al-Nā'īnī, 'Tanbīh al-Ummah', p. 313.
55. Al-Nā'īnī, 'Tanbīh al-Ummah', p. 312.
56. 'The obligation to organize constitution is essential, especially in the way previously discussed, as it will restrain and limit despotism, and as far as its clauses are congruent with the fundamentals of faith. This obligation is logical due to the importance of having the regime preserved and its authority restrained…'. Available in: Al-Nā'īnī, 'Tanbīh al-Ummah', p. 313.
57. Al-Nā'īnī responds to this sarcastically by saying 'no Imam be in charge of rule in Iran, nor the time is 'Alī's in Kūfah, nor the deputies of *ummah* in the council of *Shūrā* are ordered anything except to prevent seizing power and limit unjust control'. Available at: Al-Nā'īnī, 'Tanbīh al-Ummah', p. 316.
58. Al-Nā'īnī replies to this thesis by three notes: first (*ummah* has the right of censorship and to hold anyone who opposes *wilāyah* accountable), according to the rule of *shūrā* which constitutes the authority of Islam, and which is a right that is not dropped even upon putting the *wilāyat al-faqīh* under probational tasks. Second the citizens who pay taxes to the state – which are its pillars in establishing the public interest – consequently, the state and its personnel (belong to people who pay them…and so they have the right to hold those receiving the money accountable). Third censorship and accountability is the backbone for deterring violations and preventing wrongdoing. Available in: Al-Nā'īnī, 'Tanbīh al-Ummah', pp. 317–8.
59. Al-Sayf, *Ḍid al-Istibdād*, p. 156.
60. That what we can notice when he states: 'this era in which the infallible Imam is absent, and the position of *wilāyah* is taken away from its general deputies so that they are incapable of performing their duties and they are unable of restoring it from the one who seized it, here, do we consider ourselves assigned the duty – according to *Shar'*-of working hard to restore the *wilāyah* to its original form, or at least limiting the despotic seizure as much as possible…' his letter answers this question positively: the legality of doing so. Available in: Al-Nā'īnī, 'Tanbīh al-Ummah', pp. 283 onwards.
61. The form would crystallize more, as we shall see in another chapter, in the beginning of 1970s upon the release of Ayatollah al-Khomeini's book *al-Ḥukūmah al-Islāmīyah*, which would eventually be a cornerstone in the constitution of the 'Islamic Republic' after the Iranian Revolution in 1979.
62. The letter was received with critical acclaim by the great religious authorities, that indicated that al-Nā'īnī succeeded in not raising any animosity against him in Iran (Qom) or Iraq (Najaf).
63. Al-Nā'īnī considers taking the majority's opinion in *Shūrā* as mandatory, he supports his point of view by giving the Prophet as an example since he used the majority's opinion on many occasions even though his own opinion went in contradistinction to theirs. Available in: Al-Nā'īnī, 'Tanbīh al-Ummah', pp. 322–3.
64. Al-Sayf, *Ḍid al-Istibdād*, p. 162.
65. Al-Nā'īnī, 'Tanbīh al-Ummah', p. 329.
66. Al-Nā'īnī, 'Tanbīh al-Ummah', p. 323.
67. Expression used by Dr al-Jabri in: Al-Jabri, Mohammed Abed, *al-'Aql al-Sīyāsī al-'Arabī: Muḥadidātih wa Tajallīyātih*; 3 (Casablanca: al-Markaz al-Thaqāfī al-'Arabī, 1990), pp. 283 onwards.

68. 'The rest of the world is racing in progress and they attained power and prosperity with what they have utilized from Islamic policies; what they have assimilated from its fundamentals; and what they could acquire through specialization and derivation, so that they achieved this spectacular outcome which we stand witnesses to them now. On the contrary, Muslims are declining, day after another, and we recovered some of our awareness, we began to acquire the things which had already been adopted by those who had acquired them from the rules and laws of our religion...' Available in: Al-Nā'īnī, 'Tanbīh al-Ummah', p. 299.

69. Qur'ān, '*sūrat Yūsuf*', (12:65).

70. Al-Nā'īnī, 'Tanbīh al-Ummah', p. 294.

71. Later on they were followed, in the 1950s and 1960s, by the modern radical and chauvinist ideologies of 'Alī Sharī'atī in Iran.

Chapter 4

From the Nation State to the State of the *Khilāfah*: Renewal of 'Islamic Legal Politics'

> The *imāmah* is the matter of the Prophetic *khilāfah* in safeguarding the religion and the politics of the world.
>
> al-Mawardī

> There was silence on the question of the *khilāfah,* then the Turkish revolution made it...the mother of all questions subject to research.
>
> Rashīd Riḍā

Introduction

The 1920s would bear something new in regard to consciousness of the question of the state and authority in modern Islamic thought: among which the idea of the nation state would witness a revival with the liberal movement in Egypt, especially in the writings of Luṭfī al-Sayyid, and it would come to know a parallel decline in the Islamic discourse that reflected a complete reversal that would be experienced by the Islamic Revival as a whole, conceptually, symbolically and among the masses. Perhaps the renewal of the idea of the *khilāfah* (caliphate), and along with that the resumption of the subjects of 'Islamic legal politics', there was *in toto*, at the very heart of the matter, that new thing that was ushered in by this period. That new thing would come to cause a sharp break with the Islamic Reformist legacy in the field, and it would enter the political question into conceptual mazes wherein a view of the horizon would be obscured.

There is not, in this assertion, excess or exaggeration. That is, the transition from the subject of the nation state to the subject of the *khilāfah* is not an ordinary detail in the autobiography of modern Islamic political thought, and not only an experimental, functional and conceptual substitution: it is, more precisely, a *revolution* in theory and problematic which reformulates the political question in this concept on an entirely different basis from that upon which it had come to rest in the nineteenth century. The provocative departure that leads to astonishment and impelled this revolution against the thought of Reformism and against the thought of the nation state is none other than one of the personas of that latter-day Reformism! We mean by this, Rashīd Riḍā – the student of sheikh Muḥammad 'Abdūh and his nearest associate in the battle of Reform and Renewal!

This conceptual revolution presented itself in a retrograde fashion as reverting from the problematic of Reformism in the matter of the nation state towards constructing the problematic of the *khilāfah*, and Rashīd Riḍā's book *Al-Khilāfah aw al-Imāmah al-'Uẓmā* (*The Khilāfah or the Grand Imāmah)* is the founding and authoritatively referential text that provided its context and theories. It was published in straitened political circumstances but would have the greatest of effects on the renewal of its nature and in stamping it in a way that is entirely unique in the field of the subject. However, this revolution encompassed, in regard to the concept, the sources of thinking as well! Thus, the texts of Rashīd Riḍā came after Reformism to score a transformation in regard to its authoritativeness in drawing from principles and foundations that Reformist thought – and that of Rashīd Riḍā formerly while he was still within the scope of it – had transcended.[1]

Rashīd Riḍā is counted among the Reformists and proponents of the *Nahḍah* (Arab 'Renaissance') and among their later generation: the generation of al-Kawākabī and Qāsim Amīn. He was among the students closest to Muḥammad 'Abdūh when he established his journal *al-Manār* (*The Lighthouse*) in 1899. He remained loyal to the Reformist idea until after the death of sheikh Muḥammad 'Abdūh in 1905. He defended constitutional life and democracy in the Ottoman state, after the deposing of 'Abd al-Ḥamīd II and the ascension of the Unionists ('al-Ittiḥād wa al-Taraqqī') to power;[2] and he supported the Unionists before subsequently attacking them, just as he supported that decentralization movement against the separatists.[3] He even stood by Mustafa Kemal (Atatürk) in his political initiative before reversing his position entirely, reverting to the idea of the *khilāfah,* and retrieving its traditional, theoretical subject matter along the same lines in which it had been expressed in literature of 'Islamic legal politics'.

On the Causes of the Return to the Idea of the *Khilāfah*

Before us are the causes that explain the regress to the idea of the *khilāfah* in the thought of Rashīd Riḍā; some of them are Islamic legal causes (*shar'ī*) and some are political, even if it is among the laws of impossibility to distinguish between or separate the two. There is a consummate need of the political for the Islamic legitimacy of the religion and a consummate need of the Islamic legal for the justification of politics.

On the Islamic Legal Causes

Rashīd Riḍā, defends, like any *faqīh*, the system of the *khilāfah* – or the *imamate* (*al-imāmah*) – on the account of its being a religious obligation: 'The pious ancestors (*salaf*) of the *ummah* were in consensus, and the Sunnis, as well as the masses of the other sects that the position of the imam – that is, the appointing him as trustee over the *ummah*, is obligatory for Muslims according to the *sharī'ah*.'[4] He, in this, is reiterating what the *fuqahā'* of Islamic legal politics (*al-sīyāsah al-sharī'yah*) asserted, such as Abū al-Ḥasan al-Mawardī and Ibn Taymīyah in their view of the *khilāfah*. Al-Mawardī, for example, when he writes: 'that Allah granted this *ummah* a leader, who is a *khalīfah* (caliph) of the Prophet, gave him powers in politics and about whom the people gathered around',[5] and that 'the *imāmah* is in the station of the Prophetic *khilāfah* in protecting the religion and the politics of the world', concluding with the assertion that 'the contracting of it to whoever will engage in it in the *ummah* is obligatory (*wājib*) by means of consensus (*ijmā'*)...'.[6] This is exactly what Ibn Taymīyah specified when he wrote 'the trusteeship of the matter of the people (*wilāyat amr al-nās*) is among the most tremendous obligations of the religion; rather, there is no persistence for religion or for the world except through it.'[7]

Rashīd Riḍā does not contribute anything new as regards a definition in specifying the necessity of the *imāmah* for the religion and the world and the compulsory nature of appointing the imam over the Muslims. Perhaps, the difference between him and between his predecessors among the *fuqahā'* of the *khilāfah*, such as al-Mawardī, al-Ghazālī, Ibn Taymīyah or Ibn al-Qayyim al-Jawzī is that these discussed an extant *imāmah*: an *imāmah* of reality – whether this was in the form of a unified group *khilāfah*, as in the case of al-Mawardī; or whether this was in the form of a *khilāfah* divided among different centers and countries in isolation from one another, as in the case of al-Ghazālī and Ibn Taymīyah and his students. Rashīd Riḍā, however, directed his discussion towards an *imāmah* and a *khilāfah* and towards preaching about a position that had no existence in reality – given that he did not consider it permissible to account the Ottoman *khilāfah* as being among that which deserved the term or was representative of it! Thus, the discourse of al-Mawardī – and whoever took the same position among the *fuqahā'* – was 'positivist' and based on an extant reality, whereas the discourse of Rashīd Riḍā remained somehow normative and propagandist. True, Rashīd Riḍā lived under the aegis of the Ottoman *khilāfah*, as we shall see; however his conceptual relation to that *khilāfah* was incompatible and not identifiable with the relation of the *fuqahā'* of Islamic legal politics of the Islamic Middle Ages to the *khilāfah* of that period.

Comprehending Riḍā's discourse in regard to the *khilāfah* is not possible without paying attention to the sense of pressure he felt due to the prevailing Islamic legal political vacuum as a result of the absence of the position of the *khilāfah* in modern Islamic countries outside of its nominal or *pro forma* existence. If this explains his lack of sorrow over Sultan 'Abd al-Ḥamīd's dethronement – due to his rule being nothing more than a *pro forma khilāfah* – and his support of the constitution and the rule of the Unionists ('al-Ittiḥād wa al-Taraqqī') in the Ottoman State, then it also explains his reversal with regard to these in what came afterwards and his accusing them of incompetence in policies and of tearing apart the unity of the sultanate. That is, 'Islamic unity' was of no less importance for him than the existence of the system of the *khilāfah* itself; rather, this system does not acquire its value except through its being the political vessel that preserves the *ummah*, the group (*al-jamā'ah*) and its unity.[8] The fierceness of that pressure increased upon him for the reason that Muslims were in dire need of a unified, authoritative referent (*marja'īyah*) for themselves: even in its conceptual and religious form along the lines of what the Reformist movement attempted to express in failed fashion, where its failure was attributable to resistance to reform and not to reform itself.

Here, we will indulge in exhibiting the remainder of these reasons through a lengthy comprehensive text wherein Rashīd Riḍā gathers together the different sources and causative justifications for the existence of what he terms 'revival of the position of the *khilāfah* (*iḥyā' manṣib al-khilāfah*)' saying:[9]

> The Islamic world is in a state of anguish over the matter of its religion and the rulings of its *sharī'ah*; subject to the whims of its rulers of different religions and confessions, the opinions of its *'ulamā'*, the guides of different

> *madhāhib* and schools of thought, and the control of its enemies in religion and the world; and it does not have a source of agreed-upon general guidance to which to resort in that of which it is ignorant. Whenever there appears within it a reformer who castigates the people of whim, the corruptors rush to confront him and cast aspersions upon his religion and his knowledge;[10] there is no cure for these corrupting factors and deviations except the revival of the position of the *imāmah*, and the establishing the rightful imam who brings together the Islamic legal qualifications (in his person)...it is he who will make every Muslim willingly submit to the obligation to follow him in what issues from him of matters of general reform to the extent of (their) ability...and if the *imāmah* is not like that, then the ruling of the *shar*ʿ on it is that it is an authority that dominates by force and obedience to the one who dominates by force (*al-mutaghallib*) which is not mandated in Islamic law and not even in regard to what is in agreement with the *sharīʿah*, except for he who is victorious over them. Sultan ʿAbd al-Ḥamīd might have been called the caliph, except he did not possess the legal qualifications and was not acting according to their strictures. The Muslims of Afghanistan, and Yemen and the Najd and the far reaches of the Maghreb did not believe in the veracity of his *khilāfah* and they were not convinced of the obligation to obey him...rather, the people of Egypt who were under his political sovereignty did not acknowledge his *khilāfah*...their recognition was *pro forma* and a spiritual support of him in resistance to British control over them...

There are in this text, then, two sources that catalyze the 'revival' of the position of the *khilāfah* in the view of Rashīd Riḍā, and they are: the absence of an authoritative religious reference (*marja*ʿ *dīnī*) to which (or to whom) the Muslims may resort in matters of their religion and their worldly life; and the *pro forma* nature of the extant Ottoman *khilāfah* and the absence of its responding to this need – aside from compulsory support for its formal role in checking the aggression of foreign domination. The like of these justifications seem to be closer to political reasons than Islamic legal ones except that the religious basis is confirmed and there is no ambiguity about it: the obligation to establish the system of the *imāmah* is according to the dictates of the rulings (*aḥkām*) of the *sharīʿah*. If the function of the political factor here is confirmatory and induces the elevation of the level of observance to the Islamic legal dimension in the subject, then its presence is enmeshed with the Islamic factor, except it is not other than an expression of that confluence of identity between the political and the religious which we indicated previously.

However, this observation is not a justification for the conviction that the political reasons for the revival of the idea of the *khilāfah*, and the renewal of work in the subjects of Islamic legal politics, were welded to Islamic legal reasons as an effect follows its cause; rather they were almost the very fulcrum upon which the Islamic religious reasons rested!

On the Political Causes

The idea of the *khilāfah* did not emerge, in modern Islamic political thought, from a void, nor did it come spontaneously, but rather it had 'occasions of descent' (*asbāb al-nuzūl*), and these causes were political, in the first instance, produced by developments and new phenomena suddenly overtaking the political scene and authority in Islamic countries and within the realm of the Ottoman State in particular. When Rashīd Riḍā wrote that 'the matter of the *khilāfah* was one of silence, before the new Turkish revolution made it among the most important issues that is a subject of research',[11] he was acknowledging objectively the fact that the pressure of the political factor was what awakened the religious preoccupation with the matter of the *khilāfah* – transferring it from the realm of silence to the realm of inquiry and debate. He says in a demonstration of his explication of the causes of its liberation in his book *al-Khilāfah aw al-Imāmah al-'Uẓmā*:[12]

> The *khilāfah* and the sultanate were a *fitnah* (trial) for people and Muslims[13] as the government of kings was a *fitnah* for them in the remainder of other communities and denominations. This matter was dormant and the sudden events of these days awakened them when the Turks brought down the Ottoman House and established on its debris a republican state in a new form, where among its fundamental principles (*uṣūl*) is that they will not accept that there should be in their new government authority for any individual – neither by the name of 'caliph' nor by the name of 'sultan', and that they have separated religion from politics completely; however, they have named one of the members of the family of the previous sultans as a 'spiritual caliph' for all Muslims, and they have restricted this *khilāfah* to this family...thus, many newspapers have plunged into the matter of the *khilāfah* and its rulings, and there has been much confusion and stampeding in the matter,[14] and the truth has been enshrouded in falsehood; so, we saw it as incumbent upon ourselves to clarify the rulings of our *sharī'ah* in regard to it in detail that which is dictated by the station in order that truth be known from the false.

The text indicates the political context in three subjects that point to the major events that catalyzed the writing of the book.[15] The first of these 'sudden unexpected events' was the abolition of the Ottoman sultanate and the separation of it from the *khilāfah*; and this was an abolition promulgated by a decision taken by the Nationalist Assembly in Turkey – on 4 November 1922, building upon a recommendation by Mustafa Kemal (Atatürk) who ordered the abolition of the central position of the Sultan while retaining the position of the *khilāfah* but constraining it to the scope of religious questions.[16] The second of these events was the setting up of the Ottoman Republican system that separated religion from politics entirely, along the lines that the Muslims had no guarantee in it. As for the third of these events, it was the transformation of the position of the *khilāfah* into a symbolic, pro forma one, and appointing one of the members of the family of the Ottoman house – disgraced in their *khilāfah* – to it!

The three events are not ordinary details of the Ottoman political scene at the time. They constitute, more precisely, a tremendous revolution in the course of development of the Ottoman State and the remainder of the Islamic countries that fell under its control. It is not without significance – in relation to the *fiqh* of Rashīd Riḍā for example – that the abolition of the sultanate, the establishment of a secular Republican system and the transformation of the position of the *khilāfah* into a pro forma one were all transpiring at the time. While it is true that there is no doubt that separating the *khilāfah* from the sultanate 'does not mean in relation to Rashīd Riḍā calling for the position to persist on the basis of defense of the incapable Sultan who did not correlate with the rulings of the *imāmah* for him';[17] there is also no doubt that Rashīd Riḍā remained counting on Mustafa Kemal (naturally only in the period before he took the final step of abolishing the *khilāfah* itself in 1924) and that he remained hopeful of his return to Islam which seemed to him as though it were still connected, if but weakly, to him.[18] This is to say nothing of the fact that Riḍā was able to comprehend the causes that invoked the support of many of the Muslim *'ulamā'* for this pro forma *khilāfah*,[19] or 'the *khilāfah* of necessity' as he termed it. Despite all of that, it was not easy for him to swallow the decision to separate religion from politics and the state; rather he was not able to see in it anything other than the victory of 'Westernized (lit., Francofied) apostates' over the Muslims[20] in the battle which began before the abolition of the sultanate, and from the period of the rule of Unionists of 'al-Ittiḥād wa al-Taraqqī'.

Rashīd Riḍā did not grieve over the separation of the *khilāfah* from the sultanate because he did not consider the Sultan to be the caliph. However, the separation obliged him to re-posit the question of the *khilāfah* in the Islamic legal order fearing that it would transform, after the separation, into a symbolic vessel empty of content. With the fact that it is not certain for us that Rashīd Riḍā was apprehensive about and in fear of the machinations of Mustafa Kemal, when he was writing his book, it is possible that he undertook it upon the abolition of the position of the *khilāfah* itself, except that what he wrote in *al-Khilāfah aw al-Imāmah al-ʿUẓmā* about the impediments to making the Ḥijāz the center of the *khilāfah,*[21] or impediments to or motives for his citizenship in Turkey,[22] or his call for establishment of 'Ḥizb al-Iṣlāḥ' (The Reform Party) and his presenting suggestions for making it work as a system of *khilāfah*[23] all would seem to indicate the extent of his wariness in his view of these ongoing political developments, and a measure of what he was ready to accept of possibilities.

These were the sum total of Islamic legal and political reasons that compelled Rashīd Riḍā to write *al-Khilāfah aw al-Imāmah al-ʿUẓmā*, and to set up the problematic of the *khalīfah* in contemporary Islamic thought on the debris of problematic of the nation state upon which Islamic Reformism of the nineteenth century had been anchored. However, constructing the political question on the subject of the *khilāfah* is not merely an analogous, formal, conceptual substitution, it is also a transference from one theoretical order to another: from the order of Modern liberal political conceptions to the appropriate problematic of the nation state, along the lines of what it represented to the Reformers who expressed it in their writings, to the Islamic legal political order appropriate to the idea of the *khilāfah*, along the lines of what Muḥammad Rashīd Riḍā expressed.

On the Renewal of 'Islamic Legal Politics'

The subjects of 'Islamic legal politics' reappeared with Rashīd Riḍā in well-known political conditions that re-opened the case of the *khilāfah* in the Islamic *fiqh* perspective. That does not mean that a cessation obtained in traditional political Islamic thought, taking the position of the Islamic legal political order during the Islamic Reformist epoch in the nineteenth century, this thought continued to connect the links anew for the *fuqahā'* and in the traditional religious centers such as al-Azhar and Qayrawān and al-Zaytūnah. However, this thought was not concerned to any great extent with the political question, and the state was not among its preoccupations. If there is value to Rashīd Riḍā in this context, it is that he reconnected the relation between this thought and the question of the state, and that he did that emerging from the womb of a conceptual heritage piled high with accumulations of givens in the field of political question.

We intend by 'Islamic legal politics' the sum total of traditional political conceptions by which means the *fuqahā'* thought about the political question and the field of rule in Islam, and the sum total of concepts that they produced about the nature of rule (the *khilāfah* or the *imāmah*) as well as the means of filling the position of the imam, who might aspire to it and what characteristics were required of him that would verify the conditions of eligibility for the *wilāyah* and so on.[24] The Medieval classical Islamic *fiqh* culture was replete with a tremendous legacy of conceptual production in this regard, and perhaps the most important of it was that bequeathed by Abū al-Ḥasan al-Mawardī in his writings, especially his authoritative reference book: *al-Aḥkām al-Sulṭānīyah* (Sultanate Rules) which was the first Islamic conceptual expose to take the matter of the state from the realm of the *kalām* (theology) to that of *fiqh*,[25] subjecting it to a theoretical complexity that would remain an authoritative referential *marja'īyah* for the remainder of subsequent writings on the subject. And it is a *marja'īyah* for which little has changed as many of the givens of *fiqh* of the *khilāfah* for al-Mawardī are not predicated on the dictates of the texts of the *sharī'ah* but inhere on the basis of the facts of political reality[26] as well.

Perhaps, what will attract the attention of the reader of the texts of Rashīd Riḍā who took positions on the subjects of Islamic legal politics – especially his book *al-Khilāfah aw al-Imāmah al-'Uẓmā* – is the great deal that was drawn from the ideas of al-Mawardī, there is little referral to them. Rather, the texts of this latter are almost not worthy of mention in comparison to the texts of later thinkers such as Ibn al-Qayyim al-Jawzī! This comparison is hardly less evident than with his intense focus upon Ibn Taymīyah and his book *al-Sīyāsah al-Shar'īyyah fī Iṣlāḥ al-Rā'ī wa al-Ra'īyah* despite that this work is unconcerned with the question of the *khilāfah*![27] In every case, the texts of the *fuqahā'* (al-Mawardī, al-Ghazālī, Ibn Taymīyah, Ibn al-Qayyim al-Jawzī, al-Qarāfī, al-Taftazānī) return to life with Rashīd Riḍā in order to exercise their knowledge and authority anew in a matter which had, after the Reformist epoch, almost become lost to memory.

Rashīd Riḍā, in regard to the *khilāfah* or the grand *imāmah*, did nothing other than to retrieve subjects from those who preceded him in regard to the significance of the *khilāfah*, its conditions, and the means to convene it. He did not have it, in any case, in his capacity other than to restore this due to the nature of the question that he chose and for which only one type of knowledge was appropriate – the *fuqahā'* had reached the furthest limit of *ifāḍāt* (redundancies) and *nawāfil* (supererogatory practices)! In the thesis of 'Islamic legal politics', as in the political *fiqh* discourse of Rashīd Riḍā, there are key concepts, the consciousness of this thesis, (however) unawares, does not comprehend its theoretical status in traditional political theory that the student of Muḥammad 'Abdūh would bring back to life: the theory of the *khilāfah*. Perhaps in the forefront of these key concepts is the *khilāfah* (or the *imāmah*) and the conditions of the *wilāyah* (trusteeship) and then the *ahl al-ḥal wa al-'aqd*.

On the Meaning of the Khilāfah

Al-Mawardī preceded others in his definition of the *imāmah* (or the *khilāfah*) as 'the Prophetic *khilāfah* was put in place for safeguarding the religion and the politics of the world.'[28] It was upon this same loom that those who came after him would weave in subsequent ages of Islamic political *fiqh*, and among them, the renewal of the matter of 'Islamic legal politics', Rashīd Riḍā who would define its significances with the assertion: 'the *khilāfah*, the grand *imāmah* and the emirate of the believers (*imārat al-mu'minīn*) are three expressions of one meaning and that is the leadership of Islamic government combining the interests of the religion and the world.'[29] If the concept of the *khilāfah* was not distinct from the conception of prophethood on the account of its being a '*khilāfah* for the prophethood (*khilāfah li-l-nubūwwah*)', then this *khilāfah* is possessed of a dual political – religious stamp arising from the reality of the temporal and religious duality inherent in prophethood itself. Thus, the caliph or the imam, or the 'commander of the faithful' (*amīr al-mu'minīn*) is the deputy representative (*nā'ib*) of the prophet who was the proxy of Allah.[30] This is what explains the occurrence of intervention in the Medieval Islamic interchange between the terms 'the caliph of Allah (*khalīfat Allāh*)' and the 'caliph of the Messenger of Allah (*khalīfat rasūl Allāh*)'[31]. This does not mean that the *imāmah*, for Rashid Riḍā and its Sunni *fiqh* referential authoritative points of reference was that which was signified by Shī'ite *fiqh* where the imam, in its conception, is *not* infallible (*ma'ṣūm*),[32] and nothing other than the caliph in the meaning commended by Sunni political *fiqh*. The original meaning here, of the '*khilāfah*', is in the connotation of *al-istikhlāf* ('to succeed' or 'successorship'),[33] as for the term '*imāmah*', it is an appendage to it.[34] The import of that is that the system of the *khilāfah* – if it is derivative from the constraints of the *sharī'ah*[35] – is a civil political system,[36] or say: Muslims endorse it by way of the '*ahl al-ḥal wa al-'aqd*' by means of the pledge of the *bay'ah* (oath of allegiance).

Rashīd Riḍā repeats what the *fuqahā'* stipulated in regard to the position of the imam or the caliph when he proceeds upon that which the Sunnis have concurred through *ijmā'* (consensus): 'the position of the caliph is a *farḍ kifāyah* (an obligation contingent upon sufficiency) and that those who are obliged to fill it are the *ahl al-ḥal wa al-'aqd* in the *ummah*',[37] and he specifies that this position is obligatory according to the dictates of the rulings of the *shar'*[38] without providing, in regard to its (ancient) precursors, supporting evidence to justify the assertion of its obligation.[39] He also retrieves the traditional subjects in 'Islamic legal politics' about the means of installation of the imam; that is, the *bay'ah*, and about whom the *ahl al-ḥal wa al-'aqd* – or the '*ahl al-ikhtīyār*' – the 'people of choice' (in the parlance of al-Mawardī) are permitted to choose as *khalīfah*, along lines that would seem to suggest he is a late, direct descendent of the ancients in what they conferred upon him. We will examine this further when the subject of the characteristics of the caliph arises as well as what Riḍā posits as conditions for the verification of the qualifications for the position of the *khilāfah*, and finally in regard to the subject of the *bay'ah* and how it is contracted.

Rashīd Riḍā delimits the conditions considered in regard to who the people of the *khilāfah* are when he asserts:[40] 'the legalists among the *'ulamā'* agreed that it is not permissible to swear the *bay'ah* to the caliph except in the case that he combines in his person what they mentioned of qualifications – especially justice and competence and his being Qurayshī'. This is an expanded version of the position taken by al-Mawardī[41] and Ibn Khaldūn according to a different order (interpolating sources in another).[42] However, the *fuqahā'* considered the condition of the caliph being a member of Quraysh (tribe) as a matter of contention; whereas Rashīd Riḍā considered it as being among the conditions that, if unfulfilled, would de-legitimate the *khilāfah* or would enter its matter into 'the rule of necessities' that are taken to account in circumstances where special rulings apply.

Exactly the same thing is said about the *bay'ah* or the one to whom it is sworn,[43] in its being the contract or the form whereby the entrusting of affairs proceeds: the entrusting (*tawlīyah*) of the imam or the caliph. Riḍā's definition of it is not extracted from the definition[44] of the *fuqahā'*; rather, it seems to almost not differ from that of al-Mawardī in the possibility that one for whom the *khilāfah* is contracted might be sworn the *bay'ah* *without* the choice of the *ahl al-ḥal wa al-'aqd* so long as he comprises comprehensively in this contract and succession all the requisite conditions for the *khilāfah*,[45] indicating in this the succession of ʿUmar bin al-Khaṭṭāb to Abū Bakr al-Ṣiddīq! In any case, there is a theoretical and political point of articulation in the 'Islamic legal politics' in the theory of the *khilāfah*: for Rashīd Riḍā and those who preceded him among the *fuqahā'*; and this point of articulation is the *ahl al-ḥal wa al-ʿaqd*. Who are these in the order of the *khilāfah*?

On the Concept of Ahl al-Ḥal wa al-ʿAqd

In all of the texts affiliated with the thesis of 'Islamic legal politics', there is a marked attention to the '*ahl al-ḥal wa al-ʿaqd*' as a special expression ascribable to political and religious function; imbued with the strategic importance that they accord it in the field of formation of state and with significant political importance in Islam. If Abū al-Ḥasan al-Mawardī was the most capable at translating their role and tracing the scope and modality of it, then those who succeed him among the *fuqahā'* did not do more than throw some light on the measure of his excellence in the explication of that role without engaging in any further significant struggle to develop its meaning.[46]

Rashīd Riḍā, sated by the perspectives of the traditional *fuqahā'*, attempts to discuss some of the expansion in the meaning of the '*ahl al-ḥal wa al-ʿaqd*' through subjecting it to functional politicization, when he defines those who are 'the central elite (*surāt*) of the *ummah*, its leaders and its heads', and when he considers that the welfare of the *ummah* and the welfare of its leaders is on the basis of the welfare of this group.[47] However, when he considers them the group to be addressed in the Qur'ān in regard to the rulings (*al-aḥkām*), and that their command to obey is dual: to obey 'those given command/charge of the matter' (*ulīy al-amr*) and to obey the masses; and they are charged according to Islamic law with 'executing the command and supervising its execution,[48] the nonfeasance of the *'ulamā'* of the Muslims to rise to this role can be noticed with regret, and to this culpability, without forgetting the comparison of the delinquent Sunni *'ulamā'* and the level of negligence which the *mujtahidūn* of the Shīʿite *'ulamā'* have reached, especially in the capacity of the political leadership of the people of the *madhab*.[49]

Perhaps, the problem of Rashīd Riḍā in this regard is binary: he, from one angle, conceives of a model for the *ahl al-ḥal wa al-ʿaqd* that has yet to come into existence. That is, a model of the *'ulamā'* of the religion who are capable of exercising accountability over the sultan and putting him into position or removing him according to the dictates of the rulings of the *sharī'ah*. However, he conceives, from another angle, of a political and social role for this group which was never comprehensive due to the rise of a new political class that monopolized that role! Rashīd Riḍā is torn between the polar examples of al-Ghazālī and Ibn *Taymīyah* on the one hand and the model of Sa'd Zaghlūl and Mustafa Kemal on the other. The problem is that the correlation between religious charisma and political charisma has not yet been possible: al-Ghazālī could not have been Sa'd Zaghlūl, nor could Mustafa Kemal have possibly been Ibn Taymīyah. The isolation between the two archetypes is a stubborn reality: it might have been in the capacity of Jamāl al-Dīn al-Afghānī, in principle, or Muḥammad 'Abdūh as well[50] to bridge the chasm between the archetypes; rather it might have been in the capacity of the personality of Rashīd Riḍā himself to have afforded the possibility of forging a link and a mutual interest between the two along the lines of the alliance and rapprochement he was attempting to effect – this *faqīh* who was struggling to establish a new meaning for the '*ahl al-ḥal wa al-'aqd*'. However, that would remain, in the end, to be enumerated among the exceptions that failed to refute the principle: the principle here being the deep fissure in the corpus of the '*ahl al-ḥal wa al-'aqd*' – between *knowledge* and *practice*!

Rashīd Riḍā, to a certain degree, realizes what confronts the idea of the *khilāfah* among difficulties in reception and realization. With that, he evinces an intense persistence in the defense of it against its circumstances of deterioration. True, his defense, in the first instance, is a defense of a principle which he considers to be an Islamic legal obligation: the establishing of the *khilāfah* and the installation of the imam through the *bay'ah* of the *ahl al-ḥal wa al-'aqd* to him. However the political facet in that defense is not difficult to clarify: the need of the Muslims, in the end of the first quarter of the twentieth century of the *khilāfah* for a sphere reflective of their identity as a group and their belief in *al-tawḥīd* (the unicity of Allah); and this was especially so after colonialism had marched into their homes and taken them one after the other and after the vow to terminate the position of the *khilāfah* itself appeared on the horizon as among the derivative results of the separation of the sultanate from the *khilāfah*.

The problem of that political defense of the *khilāfah* and its Islamic legal necessity is that it can be a successful religious defense, as it was with Rashīd Riḍā. However, in the end, it was unable to become – due to ambiguities of reality – nothing more than a defense of the *existing* system of the *khilāfah* which did not possess the requisite religious conditions that would enable it to transcend its pro forma nature and rise to the legitimate level of the religious *sharī'ah*. Thus, the function of the religion and religious support could do nothing more than confer the patina of the *sharī'ah* upon a *khilāfah* that was not legitimate!

Is this a dead end or impasse in the theory of the *khilāfah* for Rashīd Riḍā? Decisively, not: it is the segue into its theoretical establishment according to the dictates of the necessary equilibrium between the (religiously) obligatory and the (politically) possible, and the segue into the return of consciousness of it, not as a *fiqh* thesis on the *khilāfah*, but as its being a (realistic) political approach to that *khilāfah*. The truth is that understanding this matter is not clear except when we ascend to the idea of the '*khilāfah* of necessity' in the hypothesis of Rashīd Riḍā, because it is the focal point wherein all the sources of the realistic political objective are drawn together – not to say the *pragmatic* – in his political thinking.

The *Khilāfah* of Necessity, the Necessity of the *Khilāfah*

When the Islamic legal prerequisite conditions for the *khilāfah* are not provided, this does *not* bring down the *khilāfah* but rather it persists according to the dictates of what is obligatory and necessary, and then an attempt is made to gather together that which was missing among its conditions. We read in *al-Khilāfah aw al-Imāmah al-'Uẓmā*:

> the legalists of the *'ulamā'* agreed that it is not permissible to swear the *bay'ah* for the *khilāfah* to any except one who combines (in his person) what they mentioned of requisite qualifications, especially justice, and competence, and his being Qurayshī; but, if some of the requisite conditions are not present, then the matter enters into the rule of necessities, and the necessities dictate according to their measure that it is obligatory in that instance to swear the *bay'ah* to him who gathers together (in his person) *most* of the requisite qualifications from among its people (i.e., the people of the *khilāfah*) with *ijtihād* and hastening to accumulate all of these.[51]

Rashīd Riḍā points to the situation of the caliphs of the Umayyads and the Abbasids, indicating that they achieved the obedience of the *'ulamā'* and the masses despite the absence of their possessing the two qualities of knowledge (*'ilm*) and justice (*'adālah*), and pointing out that that upon which the Ḥanafīs relied in 'their imamate was absolutely correct because knowledge and justice for them are not among the requisite conditions for the swearing of the pledge.'[52] He takes the position of two types of 'compulsory *khilāfah*' (*khilāfat al-iḍṭirār*): between that which is obtained according to the dictates of the pledge of the *bay'ah* by the *ahl al-ḥal wa al-'aqd* to the 'caliph of necessity' and between that which comes into existence through 'domination' (*al-taghallub*) saying:

> the difference between this *khilāfah* – the familiar *khilāfah* of 'domination' and what came before it when both of them being permissible due to necessity is that the first issues from the *ahl al-ḥal wa al-'aqd* by their choice of one who represents those who have lost some of the requisite conditions... whereas the second is an assailant of the *khilāfah* by force of tribalism, not by the choice of the *ahl al-ḥal wa al-'aqd* ...[53]

Both of them are subsumed under the rule of compulsion due to the loss of some of the requisite conditions, except that that which radiates from their power is different: obedience to the first is obtained by choice whereas in the second it is imposed.

There is not in this distinction, within the *khilāfah* of compulsion, what implies that Rashīd Riḍā was casting aspersions on the legitimacy of the *khilāfah* that obtained through tribalism and domination – the intended referent being the *khilāfah* of the Ottoman House – as he does not divest it of legitimacy despite that in which it is deviant, but rather solicits rulings for it saying: 'the authority of domination is like the one who eats something dead or the flesh of a pig in a time of necessity; it is executed by force and is less [detrimental] than chaos'.[54] Here Riḍā reworks the principle long employed by the *fuqahā'* – all during the age of the state in Islam – and that is to solicit legitimacy for political power (the sultan) as some entity that was fraudulently attributing religious legitimacy to itself, in the fear that the political void that would obtain in the absence of the state would lead to *fitnah* (strife):[55] and this is worse than killing in the Islamic conception.

Is there not in this assertion of the permissibility of the authority of necessity the most telling expression of the realistic political objective?

We are not in doubt of that. However the *faqīh* – that which remained secluded in the conscience and the reason of Rashīd Riḍā – did not desire that reality should distract from Islamic legal obligation, and thus, saw it fit to rebut those who saw the permissibility of multiplicity of imams according to the law of necessity, deriving in that what al-Mawardī commended in this regard,[56] considering that the unity of the imamate was fixed in terms of Islam on the consideration that:

> the original principle of the *shar'* is that the head of the government be one imam, and that is because the 'matter of government is primary among all

> general matters which have many people, because it is necessary that it have a single orientation and that he regiment the system in order to stave off chaos...[57]

Nothing will change the fact that Rashīd Riḍā was serious when he said: 'the unity of the *imāmah* follows on the unity of the *ummah*', and that this is exposed to the tearing asunder wrought by the 'chauvinism of the *madhāhib*' and 'racism',[58] and that the occupation of countries of the Muslims did not aid in the unity of the *ummah* 'upon which the *imāmah* rests.'[59] That is, the Ottoman *khilāfah* of necessity – persisting through domination – was not a true, unified *khilāfah* for all the Muslims, and accordingly, there was no justification for the demand to bring it back. Similarly, the *khilāfah* that the 'Government of Ankara' created after the abolition of the sultanate is not of a clear nature, even in the writings of his book.[60]

We, thus, infer from this context that the chief derivative in the exhibition of the analysis of the logic of the *fiqh*-political discourse of Rashīd Riḍā is the call for the *khilāfah* as being an Islamic legal obligation, expanded to admit the possibility of awareness and observation and laws of compulsion, and from this, that it does not find possibility of being acknowledged as one of the types of the *khilāfah* that satisfies the Islamic legal perquisite conditions for the type that might be termed 'the *khilāfah* of necessity' or the '*khilāfah* of compulsion'. However this realistic possibility is not transmitted from Rashīd Riḍā and its rules are not permanent but only temporary. It rests on the positions of the *shar'*; and without that, nothing is permissible and no formulations can be made for its matter. In other words, what *appears* as political realism in the thinking of Rashīd Riḍā, is *not* anything more than the *fiqh* permissibility (*ibāḥah*) for what is subsumed by the *'ulamā'* under the category of 'mercy' (*al-raḥmah*) and 'forbearance/dispensation' (*al-'afwu*) as in the case of necessity, and accordingly, it is not possible to approach it with the terminology of politics or political thought.

Muḥammad Rashīd Riḍā is subject to a great deal of criticism from his opponents for taking Islamic political thought back to the fetters of 'Islamic legal politics', while he also enjoys the praise of those who surpassed him in the voice of public Islam in the age of the regress of the discourse of *al-shar'*. Yūsuf al-Qaraḍāwī, for example, described him as being nearer to the strictures of the *sharī'ah* than 'Abduh or al-Afghānī;[61] and this is the position taken, in another form, by Bertrand Badie,[62] just as the writings of the contemporary Islamic 'Revival' (*al-Ṣaḥwah*) refer to him as one of the most important authoritative Modern, conceptual referents for it. If the conceptual contribution of Rashīd Riḍā has a particular significance in the field of approaching the political question in Islam, then it is as its being indicative of the force of resistance manifested by the traditional political order in confronting the modern concept of the state and authority in the field of politics! And, this is a fact which is self-evident – and of the widest scope – in the last part of the 1920s.

Three features mark the discourse of Rashīd Riḍā in the political question and in the subject of a state of the *khilāfah* in particular:

The first hallmark is that the discourse is repetitious and retrograde. It does not add anything new to conceptions of the theses of Islamic legal politics, but rather it is a retrieval of its givens – a verbatim reiteration almost to the letter. It might be said here that the Islamic legal character of this thesis prohibited him from *ijtihād* and adding to it from within; however, this is an inadmissible assertion, that is, this thesis is not a text from the Qur'ān or the *ḥadīth* but rather a supposition set down by *fuqahā'* such as al-Mawardī, Ibn Taymīyah and Ibn al-Qayyim al-Jawzī, and moreover, the door to modification of it is open until opinion engaged in its concepts of *ijtihād* and in issues of development, renewal and adaptation are settled. What bespeaks this is that since the beginning of the 1930s, thinkers of the 'Revival' (*al-Ṣaḥwah*) have *ignored* al-Mawardī and the concept of the *khilāfah* as well as the concepts particular to it, without that having cast aspersions on the 'Islamic' character of their discourse.

The second hallmark is that it is a discourse that breaks from the Islamic Reformist readings of the concepts of 'Islamic legal politics' (*al-bay'ah*, *ahl al-ḥal wa al-'aqd*, and *al-shūrā*), and it is a reading through which the partisans of the 'Renaissance' (*al-Nahḍawīyīn*) attempted to accord to those concepts that were compatible with the nature of modern politics and the modern political system and then to transform them from closed concepts into open ones that might be enriched with new meanings. Riḍā's break was not with that Reformist interpretation except as a return of those concepts to traditional significations that the *fuqahā'* had defined – rather to view these significations from a *creedal* perspective and *not* a *functional* one that was susceptible to modification or updating.

As for the third hallmark, it is that it was instrumental as a founding discourse upon which his successors would build. The return of the state and the political field to the theory of the *khilāfah* is the cradle for the gestation of a new political idea in contemporary Islamic consciousness, and it is the idea of the Islamic state that would witness its theoretical formulation in the texts of Ḥasan al-Bannā and the thinkers of the Muslim

Brotherhood (al-Ikhwān al-Muslimīn) movement in Egypt, initially, then subsequently in the remainder of the Arab countries. If it had not been for the conceptual moment that Rashīd Riḍā represented and the idea of the *khilāfah* – it would have not have been possible for the idea of the Islamic state to have witnessed such an easy birth; Rashīd Riḍā was the rendezvous point for the major academic argument that would be used to argue for the transition to the defense of the new idea.[63]

Perhaps the basic distinction in the political thought of Rashīd Riḍā, and his defiant *fiqh* and ideological defense of the *khilāfah* is that his conceptual effort was not in the interest of the idea of the *khilāfah*, as this remained suspended in the unknown and a transitional idea without a contemporary point of reference or a clearly-defined goal. Rather, no one after him followed the subject with the same religious perseverance or the same academic acumen – except in the case of texts which register defenses of it, or rather, texts that attack detractors of it (the foremost among them being 'Alī 'Abd al-Rāziq). Thus, the function of Rashīd Riḍā's contribution – in view of reality and the results – was nothing more than license to break with Islamic Reformist thought and to open the widest of gates for the inception of Islamic 'Revivalist' thought: the thought of the Muslim Brotherhood and all those who belong to their lineage.

Notes

1. Raḍwān al-Sayyid comments over this intellectual transformation, saying: 'Muḥammad Rashīd Riḍā was one of the reformists who veered towards Salafism by the second half of the second decade of this century. At that time, he had access to works of Ibn Taymīyah, and later on sheikh Muḥammad bin 'Abd al-Wahhāb, and devoted himself to study *sunnah* adhering to it in his jurisprudential interpretations. He never, though, regarded his own approach as fundamentalism, and it was even not clear to him. However, there is a reference that he was concerned during that period with a book entitled *al-I'tiṣām* by the prominent Mālikī jurist: al-Shāṭibī, meanwhile his teacher – sheikh Muḥammad 'Abdūh – focused on another book by al-Shāṭibī entitled *al-Muwwāfaqāt*. In this book, al-Shāṭibī concentrates on the subject of *maqāṣid al-sharī'ah*, whereas in *al-I'tiṣām* he delves into themes of self and private identification of the faithful ones, and the necessity for distinction from among idolaters and People of the Book equally. These themes are also found in Ibn Taymīyah's book *Iqtiḍā' al-Sirāṭ al-Mustaqīm* which had also been scrutinized by Muḥammad Rashīd Riḍā'. Available at: Al-Sayyid, Raḍwān, *Sīyāsāt al-Islām al-Mu'āṣir: Murāja'āt wa Mutāba'āt* (Beirut: Dār al-Kitāb al-'Arabī, 1997), p. 42.

2. Rashīd Riḍā defended 'al-Itiḥād wa al-Tarraqī' in one of his articles in *al-Manār* journal, in which he stated: 'the foundation upon which we should build our present time and future is allegiance to our state and union with Turks and all other Ottoman subjects as far as these subjects are united with the state and loyal to it, we should be

strong supporters for "al-Itiḥād wa al-Tarraqī" in order to propagate the essence of constitution among all classes, we ought to be observers for the functioning of this government so that democracy grow consolidated in it'. Available at: Riḍā, Muḥammad Rashīd, *Mukhtārāt Sīyāsīyah min Majalat al-Manār*, Silsilat al-Turāth al-'Arabī al-Mu'āṣir (Beirut: Dār al-Ṭalī'ah, 1980), p. 172.

3. In spite of the fact that Rashīd Riḍā believed in the idea that (to have an independent state pours in the Arabs' political interest) by considering Arabs (one of the oldest independent nations in the world), and in spite of his keen belief that (the language of Qur'ān shall survive with an Arab state, and Islamic sharī'ah shall live as far as this state lives....), however, if this goal is (difficult or impossible), then one has to defend the unity of the Ottoman state (which is the only state Muslims are left with), holding 'al-Itiḥād wa al-Tarraqī Group' (the unsophisticated elitists) responsible for demolishing this state. Available at: Riḍā, *Mukhtārāt Sīyāsīyah*, pp. 195–6.

4. Riḍā, 'al-Khilāfah aw al-Imāmah al-'Uzmā' in: *al-Dawlah wa al-Khilāfah fī al-Khiṭāb al-'Arabī ibbān al-Thawrah al-Kamālīyah fī Turkīyah, Rashīd Riḍā- 'Alī 'Abd al-Rāziq- 'Abd al-Raḥmān al-Shāhbandar: Dirāsah wa nuṣūṣ*. Preface by Wajīh Kawtharānī, Silsilat al-Turāth al-'Arabī (Beirut: Dār al-Ṭalī'ah, 1996), p. 54.

5. Al-Mawardī, Abū al-Ḥasan 'Alī bin Muḥammad, *al-Aḥkām al-Sulṭānīyah wa al-Wilāyāt al-Dīnīyah* (Beirut: Dār al-Kutub al-'Ilmīyah, [199?]), p. 3.

6. Al-Mawardī, *al-Aḥkām al-Sulṭānīyah*, p. 5.

7. Ibn Taymīyah, Taqqī al-Dīn, *al-Sīyāsah al-Shar'īyah fī Iṣlāḥ al-Rā'ī wa al-Ra'īyah* (Beirut: Dār al-Kutub al-'Ilmīyah, 1988), p. 137.

8. Rashīd Riḍā represents here the intersection between reformists: between the discourses of Islamic unity according to al-Afghānī and that of constitution and civil order according to 'Abdūh and al-Kawākibī.

9. Riḍā, '*al-Khilāfah aw al-Imāmah*', p. 121.

10. Implicitly pointing out to his teacher Muḥammad 'Abdūh.

11. Riḍā, '*al-Khilāfah aw al-Imāmah*', p. 92.

12. Riḍā, '*al-Khilāfah aw al-Imāmah*', p. 53.

13. His statement here is similar to that of Abī al-Ḥasan Al-Ash'arī (the first dispute among Muslims...was the question of Imamate). Available at: Al-Ash'arī, Abū al-Ḥasan 'Alī bin Ismā'īl, *Maqālāt al-Islāmīyīn wa Ikhtilāf al-Muṣalīn,* Muḥammad Muḥyī al-Dīn 'Abd al-Ḥamīd, 2nd edn (Cairo: Maktabat al-Nahḍah al-Miṣrīyah, 1969), p. 39.

14. Again, this was interpreted by another contemporary researcher who took notice that 'as the Islamic lore embarks on establishing a theory for authority and caliphate, the political muddle gets even more aggravated to the degree of destroying the unity of faithfuls eventually...' Available at: Corm, Georges, *Ta'addud al-Adyān wa Anẓimat al-Ḥukm: Dirāsah Susīyulujīyah wa Qānūnīyah Muqāranah*, 2nd edn (Beirut: Dār al-Nahār li-al-Nashr, 1992), p. 217.

15. It is noteworthy that Muḥammad Rashīd Riḍā had started writing his book *al-Khilāfah aw al-Imāmah al-'Uzmah* in 1922 in the form of a series of studies published in his own journal *al-Manār*; two years before Mustafa Kemal terminated *al-Khilāfah*.

16. It was a ploy by Mustafa Kemal Atatürk to win the approval of Muslim grassroots, as well as Muslim clerics, in his battle against the termination of the effects of the Treaty of Sèvres which was imposed on Sultan Mehmet VI in 1920, in which Izmir (then Smyrna) and Dardanelles would become part of Greece, he accepted it in terms of establishing an Armenian state in eastern Anatolia, granting autonomy to Kurdistan, and rendering Bosphorus demilitarized. Moreover, Mustafa Kemal was in need of Muslims' support to win the political battle at the Lausanne conference in 1923.

Available at: Lewis, Bernard, *The Emergence of Modern Turkey*, Oxford Paperbacks; no. 135, 2nd edn (London: Oxford University Press, 1968), pp. 249–50.

17. Riḍā, *al-Dawlah aw al-Khilāfah*, p. 18.

18. Muḥammad Rashīd Riḍā says: 'Mustafa Kemal Pasha is a smart and eloquent man, still though not fundamentalist nor a jurist, he gives his opinion in religious issues [issues pertinent to the nexus of religion and politics] with the military audacity that he possesses, and humiliates with his political leadership. So that common people consent and jurists dare not object...'.

19. 'I debated many Egyptian elites – clerics and non-clerics – in this issue, and I discovered that they all agree that the intent of supporting the new caliphate innovated by the republican government of Ankara in Istanbul is to disrupt the British machinations that intend to render this eminent Islamic position a handy tool at a time when Britain instated King Hussayn in Mecca and Sultan Waḥīd al-Dīn in Astāna (Istanbul now) and what resulted from these British endeavors in gathering the two after secretly transferring the latter to Malta. None of the Egyptians meant to hail the new caliphate with felicitations or homage is to regard him as the great Imam of Muslims for this *ummah*, whose government are subject to his authority in which he is capable of instating princes and rulers, deposing them, controlling the collection of taxes, sending troops to *jihad*, and other caliphate functions cited by Islamic clerics...as we may see, this is a political purpose with negative benefit and it is due to the general Islamic sensation that was provoked by the foreign pressure...it doesn't stop at the existence of a right caliphate, nor a just Imam or group, nay it is a form of political demonstration for the political leader (Sa'd Pāshā Zaghlūl) and even fainter an example. For the sake of this, they care not about the conditions and functions of this caliphate, resembling in this case the rest of Muslims in Africa and elsewhere...'. Riḍā, *al-Dawlah wa al-Khilāfah*, pp. 65–96.

20. 'Westernized heretics deem religion non-compatible with politics, science and civilization in this age, and that the state that adheres to religion strictly would never be able to grow stronger and richer, nor would it outrace strong states....and the opinion of many is that the government should be non-religious...' Riḍā, *al-Dawlah wa al-Khilāfah*, p. 92.

21. Riḍā, *al-Dawlah aw al-Khilāfah*, pp. 100–1.

22. Riḍā, *al-Dawlah aw al-Khilāfah*, pp. 102–3.

23. Riḍā, *al-Dawlah aw al-Khilāfah*, pp. 103–5.

24. We presented a descriptive definition for the legitimate policy. However, jurists are not satisfied with this specification; *de facto* they behold it from an evaluative angle that assesses the nexus between this system and *sharī'ah*. A contemporary Islamic apologist states his opinion in this issue: 'the legitimate policy as an idiom according to our imams is to conduct public interests, governorship affairs, and judiciary in a way that do not collide with *sharī'ah*'. Yāsīn, 'Abd al-Salām, *al-Minhāj al-Nabawī: Tarbīyatan wa Tanẓīman wa Zaḥfan* ([n.pb.]; [n.d]), p. 23.

25. In this regard he states: 'al-Mawardī represents a distinguished phase in the history of political thinking in Islam...in the entire history of Islam, one relatively constant question poses, that which is connected to the political organization in Islam, the nature of appropriate governorship for this organization, i.e. the Islamic state *in toto*, al-Mawardī's phase is important compared to the previous ones as the political research was known with the Ash'arī thought...as a transformation that shifted...from argument to legislation, i.e. from scholastic theology to *fiqh*.' Al-'Alawī, Sa'īd bin-Sa'īd, *Dawlat al-Khilāfah: Dirāsah fī al-Tafkīr al-Siyāsī 'inda al-Mawardī*, Silsilat al-Uṭrūḥāt

wa al-Rasā'il; 6 (Rabat: Kullīyat al-Ādāb wa al-'Ulūm al-Insānīyah, [n.d]), p. 157.

26. 'The main dilemma in Islamic state is legislation, he didn't take the theoretical requirements for *sharī'ah* as launching points to start with, he constantly tried – instead – to achieve some sort of compatibility between these requirements – especially when they are not clear enough – and the political reality…'. Al-'Alawī, *Dawlat al-Khilāfah*, p. 23.

27. Verily he notices that when he writes: 'let's open Ibn Taymīyah's book *al-Sīyāsah al-Shar'īyah,* the first thing that drags our attention is that the author does not speak about caliphate as much as he is expounding in one thing, i.e. the implementation of *sharī'ah*, he means by the Islamic state as the state of *shar'* and nothing else. The jurist, in definition, is the one who craves for implementing *shar'* in reality, who does not return to his aspirations in his judgments but rather to the surrounding circumstances. Thus he speaks much of *sharī'ah* and little of *khilāfah.*' Al-'Arawī, 'Abdullah, *Mafhūm al-Dawlah*, 2nd edn (Casablanca: al-Markaz al-Thaqāfī al-'Arabī,1983), p. 101.

28. Al-Mawardī, *al-Aḥkām al-Sulṭānīyah*, p. 5.

29. Riḍā, '*al-Khilāfah aw al-Imāmah*', p. 53.

30. He maintains here that 'human beings are slaves of God; rulers are His deputies over them'. Ibn Taymīyah, *al-Sīyāsah al-Shar'īyah*, p. 19

31. Gardet, Louis, *La Cité Musulmane: Vie Sociale et Politique* (Paris: Vrin, 1961), p. 181; Al-Sayyid, *al-Jamā'ah wa al-Mujtama'*, pp. 25–6; and Al-Mawardī, *al-Aḥkām al-Sulṭānīyah*, p. 17.

32. 'For Muslims, the caliph is not infallible, nor is he a source of revelation, nor does he have the right to monopolize the Qur'ān and *sunnah* …he is to be obeyed, as far as he is to be argued and follows the Qur'ān and *sunnah*…'. Riḍā, '*al-Khilāfah aw al-Imāmah*', p. 138.

33. Al-Sayyid says about the definition of *al-khilāfah* : 'first Muslims perceive their authority, conquests and their subsequent legitimacy as being the *ummah* of the Prophet, whose prophethood was transferred to him after being taken away from *Bani Israel*, and who is *mustakhlaf* (given the authority) in the lands seized from Persia and Roman Empire…since God is the Owner of authority, and He may give authority to whoever He likes, and may take it away from whoever He likes…apparently, this may have denoted the first authority to Muslims after the death of the Prophet.' Al-Sayyid, *al-Jamā'ah wa al-Mujtama'*, p. 25.

34. Ibn Khaldūn says 'in the question of why we call him as Imam, since he resembles the Imam in praying who should be followed and taken as model, for this reason the term *al-Imāmatu al-Kubrā* is used. Whereas in the question of why he is called as Caliph, since he succeeds the Prophet in *ummah*, so he is the successor of *rasūl Allāh* (the Prophet).' Available at: Ibn Khaldūn, *al-Muqadimah,* p. 185.

Also another contemporary Islamic apologist delves into this term when he writes: 'Imam in the Islamic tradition is the successor who rules *ummah* on the behalf of the Prophet to consolidate religion and to run life in lights of it'. Available at: Al-Qaraḍāwī, Yūsuf, *al-Sīyāsah al-Shar'īyah fī Ḍaw' Nuṣūṣ al-Sharī'ah al-Islāmīyah wa Maqaṣiduhā* (Cairo: Maktabat Wahbah, 1998), p. 48.

35. We never mentioned it is derived from the texts, because texts refer to nothing in this regard. The most pertinent of all is implicit, and which has been adopted by many – especially al-Mawardī and Ibn Taymīyah – to observe the question of *al-khilāfah* (First) or to observe the question of laws in *Sharī'ah's* texts that address *wilāyat al-amr*. The most important among these texts, are the verses 58 and 59 in *sūrat al-nisā'*. Qur'ān, *sūrat al-nisā'* (4: 58–9).

36. Riḍā, '*al-Khilāfah aw al-Imāmah*', p. 124.
37. Riḍā, '*al-Khilāfah aw al-Imāmah*', p. 54.
38. Riḍā, '*al-Khilāfah aw al-Imāmah*', p. 54
39. Ibn Khaldūn does not find such an excuse, for instance, except in the deeds of *al-ṣaḥābah* when he writes: 'instating Imam is unanimously recognized duty in *al-shar'* by *al-ṣaḥābah* and *al-tabi'īn,* as upon the Prophet's death *al-ṣaḥābah* swore the oath of allegiance to Abī Bakr to be their new leader. The same mechanism is true to all subsequent ages in choosing the Caliph, no chaos had been stirred up in any period, and this became unanimously agreed upon in the necessity to instate an Imam'. Ibn Khaldūn, *al-Muqadimah*, p. 186.
40. Riḍā, '*al-Khilāfah aw al-Imāmah*', p. 72.
41. Compare with: Al-Mawardī, *al-Aḥkām al-Sulṭānīyah*, pp. 6 and 18.
42. Ibn Khaldūn, *al-Muqadimah*, p. 187.
43. See in this regard: Laroui, *Les Origines Sociales et Culturelles du Nationalisme Marocain, 1830–1912,* textes à l'appui, (Paris: Maspéro, 1980), p. 73, and Gardet, *La Cité Musulmane,* p. 181.
44. Riḍā, '*al-Khilāfah aw al-Imāmah*', pp. 64–5.
45. Compare with: Riḍā, '*al-Khilāfah aw al-Imāmah*', p. 71, and Al-Mawardī, *al-Aḥkām al-Sulṭānīyah*, p. 11.
46. We make an exception here, for sure, the attempt of reformists in the nineteenth century to develop the concept by fusing the concept of '*ahl al-ḥal wa al-'aqd*' with that of '*nuwwāb al-ummah*'. However, it is an attempt that was originated, as we know, from outside the legitimate political system and that holds against taking it into account in the context of self-development of a given concept from within its own theoretical-referential framework.
47. Riḍā, '*al-Khilāfah aw al-Imāmah*', p. 89.
48. Riḍā, '*al-Khilāfah aw al-Imāmah*', pp. 56–7.
49. Riḍā, '*al-Khilāfah aw al-Imāmah*', p. 90
50. Riḍā admits this fact when he writes 'our teacher – 'Abdū – may he rest in peace – achieved a leadership position in this *ummah* and the rank of *ahl al-ḥal wa al-'aqd* in religious and mundane issues from politics and so forth, he would have almost been the leader of the entire Islamic *ummah,* however, with force and not deed…'. Available at: Riḍā, '*al-Khilāfah aw al-Imāmah*', p. 90.
51. Riḍā, '*al-Khilāfah aw al-Imāmah*', p. 72.
52. Riḍā, '*al-Khilāfah aw al-Imāmah*', p. 73.
53. Riḍā, '*al-Khilāfah aw al-Imāmah*', p. 74.
54. Riḍā, '*al-Khilāfah aw al-Imāmah*', p. 74.
55. Djaît, Hichem, *La Grande Discorde: Religion et Politique dans L'Islam des Origines,* Bibliothèque des Histoires (Paris: Gallimard, 1989), p. 151.
56. 'if the *imāmah* was appointed to two imams in two countries, their *imāmah* shall never meet, for the *ummah* is never meant to be ruled by two Imams simultaneously, otherwise, if people go astray then authorize it.' Available at: Al-Mawardī, *al-Aḥkām al-Sulṭānīyah*, p. 7.
57. Riḍā, '*al-Khilāfah aw al-Imāmah*', p. 81.
58. Riḍā, '*al-Khilāfah aw al-Imāmah*', p. 84.
59. Riḍā, '*al-Khilāfah aw al-Imāmah*', p. 88.
60. He definitively says about this *khilāfah* '…if it is a spiritual *khilāfah* that has no influence over the policy of *ummah* and its government, then it is different from *the imamah* which we have expounded its rules'. Available at: Riḍā, '*al-Khilāfah aw al-Imāmah*', p. 87.

61. 'Muḥammad 'Abdūh was nearer to discipline in rules of *Shar'* than were his teacher al-Afghānī due to his profound Azhar education...al-sayyid Riḍā was nearer to discipline in rules of *shar'* than his teacher al-Imam due to his profuse knowledge in books of *sunnah* and *āthār*, and the establishment of the *salafist* school which is represented by Ibn Taymīyah and his pupil Ibn al-Qayyim...'. Al-Qaraḍāwī, *min Ajl Ṣaḥwah Islāmīyah Rāshidah* (Casablanca: Dār al-Ma'rifah, [n.d]), p. 41.

62. 'Riḍā's discourse – in a sense – is the least confused...as it does not involve – as the case with the rest of revivalists – references to western paradigms'. Available at: Badie, Bertrand, *Les Deux Etats: Pouvoir et Société en Occident et en Terre d'Islam, l'Espace du Politique* (Paris: Fayard, 1986), p. 99.

63. Ḥasan al-Bannā never denied how he received intellectual tutoring from thoughts of Rashīd Riḍā. This is the strongest clue of the intellectual nexus between the two in spite of their difference among issues of *al-khilāfah* and the Islamic State.

Chapter 5

On the Theoretical Criticism of the *Khilāfah*

> The truth is that the Islamic religion is absolved of this *khilāfah* that Muslims acknowledge, and absolved of all that they attribute to it of desire and fear and of pride and might.
>
> – ʿAlī ʿAbd al-Rāziq, *al-Islām wa Uṣūl al-Ḥukm* (*Islam and the Origin of Rule*)

The Blessed *Khilāfah*: Theoretical Tragedy and Political Impediment

ʿAbd al-Raḥmān bin Khaldūn distinguishes between three modes of rule[1] which are: natural rule (*al-mulk al-ṭabīʿī*), political rule (*al-mulk al-sīyāsī*) and the *khilāfah*; and he defines the *khilāfah* as: 'the inducement of people [to conform] to the dictates of the Islamically-legal view of their interests in the life of the afterlife and the world and referring to them.'[2] If the differences between them are in regard to the foundation or the principle upon which each of these two rest, according to Ibn Khaldūn, then the differences are between appetitive desire (*al-shahwah*) – the basis of natural rule; reason (*al-ʿaql*) – the basis of political rule; and Islamic law (*al-sharʿ*), the basis of the *khilāfah*. The difference between the *khilāfah* and the other two types – in terms of the end goal – is that it strives to realize the interests of both the afterlife and the life of the world whereas natural and political rule strive to effect worldly interests only.

This definition of Ibn Khaldūn is extremely perspicacious; it is a key to understanding the matter of the *khilāfah* and the foundations upon which its system rests. We will leave the matter for a moment and inquire with ʿAbdullah Laroui about the extent of correspondence between this order of evaluation (or idealized measure) of the systems of rule (natural rule, rational rule, and the *khilāfah*), and between the chronological sequence of them. Laroui replies with the assertion that:

> at the level of universal history, there is a correspondence that cannot be denied: the *khilāfah* came after rational politics (*al-sīyāsah al-ʿaqlīyah*), and this was preceded by natural rule. However, in the realities of Islam, there is a difference and a disjuncture because the Arabs did not know rational politics as they did not know urban civilization before Islam. Islam is what civilized them; thus, the stage of the *khilāfah* came immediately after the stage of natural rule...soon enough, it would collide with rational politics – Persian, in particular – and it would disappear under its blows for reasons well-known...[3]

The *khilāfah*, then, did not triumph over rational politics in Islam; but rather, it was defeated by it. With that, we mean that with this transformation that occurred from the *khilāfah* to the 'mordacious monarchy' (*al-mulk al-ʿaḍūḍ*), in the widely-transmitted Islamic expression, and then the 'Islamic state' that rose upon the debris of the *khilāfah* did not break completely with the dictates of the *khilāfah* (that is, Islamic law – *al-sharʿ*), and neither were its caliphs – outside the scope of the (Shīʿite) Imāmī *madhab* – viewed as being heretics or *kuffār* (unbelievers)[4] – except in contemporary Islamist writings;[5] but rather, it remained capable, by virtue of the nature of its formation,[6] of acquiring for itself a religious legitimacy – not simply by force of claim, but by implementation of Islamic law (*al-sharʿ*) as well, even if only in a limited sphere. That is that 'all agree,' says ʿAbdullah Laroui, 'that the hallmarks of Islamic law (*al-sharʿ*) were extant under the rule of Muʿāwīyah',[7] and accordingly, that differentiation between the Islamic state in existence in the Umayyad and Abbasid periods and between the *khilāfah* did *not* persist on the basis of the implementation of Islamic law.

This observation brings us back to our point of departure, and we are inquiring in regard to the definition of Ibn Khaldūn, and it is the relation of the *khilāfah* – without or after worldly interests, and moreover, its separation from natural rule and rational politics according to the terminology of Ibn Khaldūn's lexicon, and at precisely this level. We reiterate here the question posited about the *khilāfah* in another way: is the *khilāfah* the political system that correlates to Islamic law (*al-sharʿ*) so long as it persists 'according to the dictates of the Islamic-legal perspective' as Ibn

Khaldūn says? However, we have seen the assertion that none would argue in regard to the implementation of Islamic law during the rule of Mu'āwīyah. And yet, despite that, none has termed his rule a *khilāfah*. It would be said that the state: the state of the Umayyads, and after them the state of the Abbasids *usurped* the *khilāfah*; and, moreover, it is not permissible in regard to their kings to assert that they were caliphs. However, what of 'Umar bin 'Abd al-'Azīz, was he not considered a caliph as Laroui has noted in his regard – to the exclusion of the rest of the Umayyads? Rather, was not he described as being the 'fifth caliph' who continued the series of the *Rāshidūn* caliphs?

Laroui aids us again in the answer to the meaning of the *khilāfah* far from the supposition of the correlation between it and the implementation of Islamic law by asserting: 'What separates monarchy from the *khilāfah* is not the implementation of Islamic law, but the *intended goal* of that implementation.' As for the goal which Laroui intends – rather, say: that which is intended by those asserting the *khilāfah* – is *the realization of the intents* of the *sharī'ah,* that is the pinnacle of morality; and it is connected to what falls outside the locus of immediate worldly demands to which monarchy responds.[8]

The *khilāfah* was not realized in this meaning that was delimited by the *fuqahā'*,[9] except in the era of the rule of the four Companions – the *Rāshidūn* Caliphs. Moreover, the Islamic affection for this ideal and authoritatively referential epoch is nothing except yearning for the *khilāfah* and a willingness to return to restore it or to set it up anew. Given that the *fuqahā'* of the Sultans (the Umayyads and the Abbasids) realized the impossibility of that, they constructed a political order that was in agreement with the obligation of Islamic law and what was *feasible* politically – between the *ideal* (that is, the *khilāfah*) and the *real* (that is, the state of the sultanate) and that is the order of 'legitimate' or 'Islamic legal politics' (*al-sīyāsah al-shar'īyah*) except that the blessedness of the *khilāfah* would remain perpetually renewed and casting a rosy glow on the imagination of *fiqh* and Islamic politics. If the *faqīh* is 'still tenaciously clinging to the blessedness of the *khilāfah*,'[10] as 'Abdullah Laroui says, 'then, it increases the imamate (*al-a'immah*) in legitimacy'. And what most calls for bewilderment is that it did that – along the lines of what we have seen with Rashīd Riḍā – when the distance – the distance of politics and the possible increased further and rendered the *khilāfah* a goal that was far from being reached.

The discourse of Rashīd Riḍā, in this sense, is a *utopian* discourse: precluded from realization for reason of the tremendous chasm separating the logic of the state from the logic of the *khilāfah*. Perhaps it seemed to him that the problem of the *khilāfah* was latent in the existence of a pro forma sultanate calling for that *khilāfah*, and that the solution of this problem rested on the removal of this sultanate, and with it, the removal of that claim. However, his enthusiasm for that would soon wane when he ascertained that the results of the abolition of the sultanate would entail the abolition of the *khilāfah* itself;[11] and that the establishment of the *khilāfah* did not hinge upon desire or decision, as indicated by the failure of the Islamic Religion Conference (convened in May of 1926 to look into the matter of the *khilāfah* after its abolition and the communiqué of senior *'ulamā'* in Cairo decreeing the nullification of the Islamic-legal *bay'ah* [pledge of allegiance] to the emir 'Abd al-Majīd) to reach a decision on the subject of the *khilāfah* and delaying inquiry into the matter.[12] However, the most important source of political impediment, which rendered whoever called for the *khilāfah* purely utopian, was the disintegration of the Islamic world in the aftermath of the First World War and the Sykes Picot Agreement that mandated the atomization of the East into mini-states, just as in the aftermath of the fall of Libya and Morocco – after Egypt and Tunisia – into the grip of colonialism, and the setting up of a separate Arab state in the Ḥijāz, as well as the breakup of geographic and political connections in the remainder of Muslim countries. This was the matter that had become for him the point of refuge in the 'Islamic legal solution': the *khilāfah*, in something which was actually nearer to the politics of escaping into the future than anything else!

There existed, along with that, those who were ready to respond to this theory and blessedness conceptually – in a rebuttal from within the conceptual Islamic order itself. Despite that this response was not intended directly, and necessarily, at the hypoth'esis of Rashīd Riḍā, but rather it dealt with the matter in general terms; even if it was clear who was actually being accused in the history of thought – namely, that it was the subjects of Rashīd Riḍā about the *khilāfah* that were the basis of what catalyzed the like of this critical response. Our indication for this is not only the *timing* of the response which followed directly on the publication of *Al-Khilāfah aw al-Imāmah al-'Uẓmā*, but also the types of cases and thoughts that this critical response took as a subject for rebuttal: these are precisely those Rashīd Riḍā exhibited in his book. Perhaps, the most important critical text to confront – at that moment – to thoroughly exhaust and pulverize the theory of the *khilāfah* was the book *al-Islām wa Uṣūl al-Ḥukm* (*Islam and the Origin of Rule*)[13] by the renegade al-Azhar scholar 'Alī 'Abd al-Rāziq on the 'legitimate political order'.

A *Khilāfah* Without an Islamic Legal Origin: The Thesis of 'Abd al-Rāziq

Four theoretical subjects regulate the discourse of 'Alī 'Abd al-Rāziq in the matter of the *khilāfah*, and form the major critical assertions of *Al-Islām wa Uṣūl al-Ḥukm* and these pertain to the nature of absolute authority upon which the system of the *khilāfah* is established; the impermissibility and illegitimacy of this system from the viewpoint of Islam; the foundations upon which it is established (material force and not willful obedience); then, to the *political* nature of government in Islam. These are the critical subjects that, today, have not ceased, even after the passing of thirteen centuries since their formulation, to represent a critical ceiling for the remainder of attempts at theoretical rebuttal of the idea of the connection between politics and religion, in contemporary Islamic thought that different pens of various currents and inclinations have confronted in contemporary Arab thought.

The Absolute Sultanate or 'Sublimity in Politics' (al-Ta'ālī bi-l-Sīyāsah)[14]

'Alī 'Abd al-Rāziq notices in the preface of his book that the significance of the *khalīfah* (caliph) for the Muslims engenders an absolute blurring between him and the Messenger (*al-rasūl*)[15] when it is the case that 'he stands according to his affiliation in the station of the Messenger, the peace and blessings of Allah be upon him'; and he 'occupies the station of the Messenger for the believers; he has a general trusteeship (*wilāyah 'āmah*) over them, [their] complete obedience, and total power, and he has the right to implement their religion, to execute the *ḥudūd* (penalties) and implement its *sharī'ah* and he also has the primary right in the matter of their worldly affairs as well.'[16] When the *khalīfah* has these attributes, he is above any accountability or censure, and the position to which he accedes – which is an analog of prophethood in its jurisdiction – transcends the stations of those who might imagine they have an Islamic-legal duty to question him – and among these are, naturally, the '*ahl al-ḥal wa al-'aqd*'.

Originating from this Islamic conception of the *khalīfah* – in the view of 'Abd al-Rāziq are three distinctions:

First: the position of the caliph becomes – in the eyes of Muslims and their *fuqahā'* – a *religious* center and not only a political one. If the incentive for that does not proceed according to a parallel between the political *wilāyah* and the religious, in the texts of the *fuqahā'* and the historical political experience, then among its reasons also is the attribution of the agnomen of '*khalīfah* of the Messenger of Allah', that has caused ambiguity among Muslims, 'so it seems to them that the *khilāfah* is a religious center, and that he who has come to be entrusted with the matter of the Muslims (*wālī amr al-Muslimīn*) has come to hold the position that the Messenger of Allah had held.'[17]

Second: The *khalīfah* became a sultan with absolute powers, where no form of discipline constrained him and none could stop him as 'he alone has [the power of] command and prohibition, and in is hand are the reigns of the *ummah* and the disposal of its affairs whether they be mighty or trivial. Any trusteeship (*wilāyah*) other than him derives from him, every function under him is subsumed under his power, and every religious or temporal plan branches from his position.'[18]

Third: This absolute authority that he holds is not amenable to any type of division or redistribution, but rather the utmost that is possible is that he may bestow it on the people of politics and this is a conferral or dispensation from him, that is from his position, with significances distinct to it, specified by the one and only God.[19] This, in fact, is the point where 'deification' may be noticed in the model of *khilāfah* asserted by the sultan's *fuqahā'*.

'Abd al-Rāziq ridicules such a *fiqh* perception of the *khalīfah*, and he also expresses his astonishment over attitudes of the *fuqahā'* as they avoid explicating their evidences for such glorified positions towards the *khilāfah* and the *khalīfah*, maintaining that 'it is their duty – since they handed all the keys of power over to the *khalīfah* and enabled him to attain to this rank, especially with all this authority – to explain to us the source of all these powers which they claimed for the *khalīfah*. Where did he get these? Who permitted him and helped him to acquire these?'[20] Since he knows from the outset, that there is no answer for such questions due to their negligence in studying such a problem, he justifies this by the fact that they dare not question the eminent position of *khilāfah*:[21] which is a position too great to be questioned.

'Abd al-Rāziq is not looking for an answer; he, in fact, initiates an approach to this issue from its main entrance: seeking the legal attitude towards *khilāfah*, and then looking for effectiveness of the theory of *khilāfah* according to the views of the *fuqahā'*.

The Khilāfah *in the Measure of Islamic Law*

'Abd al-Rāziq proceeds from the *ijmā'* (consensus) of the Muslims, or – more precisely – the *ijmā'* of their *fuqahā'* that the position of the caliph is *obligatory* and that abandoning it is a 'sin', in order to demonstrate a glaring gap in their texts, and that is the absence of an Islamic legal proof for the position which they have taken, and furthermore, their being obliged as a result of that textual vacuum to find a substitute for this among principles that fail to carry sufficient argumentative weight in terms of the *sharīʿah* such as that which the text confers through their resorting to *al-ijmāʿ* at times and their resorting to the 'dictates of logic and the laws of reason'[22] at others.

Our rebellious Azhar sheikh raises the challenge in the face of those calling for the *khilāfah* and who protect it and defend its legitimacy, when he demands a legal 'document' (*wathīqah*) of them for the textual evidence of the trustworthiness of their assertion, writing in firm, confident terms: 'We have not found in what has come to us of the researches of the *ʿulamāʾ* who presumed that the setting up of the imam is an obligation (*farḍ*) anyone who has attempted to proffer an indication of its obligation in a verse from the noble Book of Allah [the Qurʾān]. And, verily, if there were indeed a single indication of that in the Book, the *ʿulamāʾ* would not have hesitated to extol and laud it…'.[23] Is there an argument in the *ḥawzah* of our sheikh greater than this: the absence in the Qurʾānic text of any verse indicating a matter and yet not only conferring upon it religious legitimacy but actually raising its station to rival that of prophethood?

This argument does not suffice ʿAbd al-Rāziq, and he adds to it, and to the balance of the challenge, another argument which is the absence of that proof in the *sunnah* as well. He writes decisively:

> It is not the Qurʾān alone which omits mention of this *khilāfah* and does not confront it; rather the *sunnah*, like the Qurʾān, also leaves it and does not exhibit it. This indicates to you that the *ʿulamāʾ* were not able to indicate in regard to this topic anything from the *ḥadīth*, as if they had found any indication in the *ḥadīth*, they would have provided it as a proof instead of [resorting to] *al-ijmāʿ*.[24]

There is no relation for the *khilāfah* in anything – in what ʿAbd al-Rāziq sees – in Islam and the obligation of Islamic law. All that which was produced of theory and formulation for it is *invalid* from the perspective of the religion; and, moreover, what is said about it and other functions does not belong to the realm of *al-daʿwah*, but rather is more appropriately connected to the sphere of interest and benefit: *the interest of those arguing for the system* of the *khilāfah* in order to benefit from the restorations of *their* position in it.[25] Muslims are not in need of this *khilāfah*, and those among them who call for its religious necessity and assert that upon it rests 'establishment of the religious maxims and the welfare of the flock', are disavowed by Islamic law (*al-shar'*) as well as historical reality where:

> tangible reality that is supported by reason and witnessed by history – both ancient and modern, confirm that the ordinations of Allah the Most Exalted and the manifestations of his noble religion do not rest upon that type of government which the *fuqahā'* term '*khilāfah*' nor upon those to whom people have conferred the agnomen *khulafā'* (caliphs). Reality is also that the public good of the Muslims in their world does not rest upon anything of that.[26]

The logic of the criticism according to 'Abd al-Rāziq not only dictates that this *khilāfah* does not persist on the basis of a relation to Islamic law, but rather he takes the position, proceeding from this segue, of deducing that it is *illegitimate* and that it is among that which has besmirched Islam in the name of Islam as 'the religion of Islam is absolved of this *khilāfah* which is recognized by the Muslims and absolved of all that which they attribute to it of desire and awe and pride and might.'[27] There is no need for us, then, of the *khilāfah* – says 'Abd al-Rāziq – to regulate the affairs of the world and the religion. Still, this does not suffice him, and he goes further than that to decree the harshest verdict possible in regard to it saying: 'the *khilāfah* was and has not ceased to be a *catastrophe* for Islam and the Muslims, and it has given rise to evil and corruption...'[28]

The removal of Islamic legitimacy from the *khilāfah* does not imply anything more than the knowledge of its intrinsic nature and its alienation from the values of Islam and its principles. And that, in particular, is what confirms its matter for 'Abd al-Rāziq: he does not stop at the limit of decoupling the connection between it and between Islam only, but rather he goes on to uncover the true nature of the glaring contradiction between the principles upon which its edifice rests and between the values of Islam in the sphere of the political order, at least *vis-à-vis* the Prophetic experience – if the Qur'ānic text has not been explicit about this.

Brute Force is the Basis of the Khilāfah

In order for the *khilāfah* to be legitimate, and trustworthy in the expression of the system of Islamic values, there ought to be a just person to renounce wrongdoing, oppression and injustice, who operates according to the constraints of the good pleasure and acceptance of the 'group' (*al-jamā'ah*): being an expression of them in the choice of *ahl al-ḥal wa al-'aqd* (the people of authority) and respect of the principle of '*al-shūrā*' in the practice of the functions of the *wilāyah* (trusteeship) over Muslims. That is what those calling for the *khilāfah* and its partisans suppose, and that also is precisely what sheikh 'Alī 'Abd al-Rāziq disavows of them in the most stringent repudiation. He mentions the connotation of the *khilāfah* for the Muslims and their assertion that it 'goes back to the choice of the *ahl al-ḥal wa al-'aqd*, resting for support in that on the definition of Ibn Khaldūn of the imamate as 'a contract' (*'aqd*) obtained by pledge of the *bay'ah* of the *ahl al-ḥal wa al-'aqd* to whom they have chosen as an imam for the *ummah* after their mutual consultation.'[29] Then, he analyzes that critically by asserting:

> the meaning of this might be that the *khilāfah* persists for the Muslims on the basis of the voluntary *bay'ah* and that it centers on the desire of the *ahl al-ḥal wa al-'aqd* of the Muslims and with their good pleasure. Or, it might be reasonable to assume that in the world there is a *khilāfah* along the lines of what they have mentioned, except that if we return to reality...we find that the *khilāfah* in Islam was *never* centered upon anything except on the basis of *terrifying force* and that this force, except rarely, was *armed material force*. Nothing surrounded the position of the *khalīfah* except spears and swords, armies armed to the teeth and severe torment [if challenged]. This, at the exclusion of all else assured the security of its center and perfected its command.[30]

There is no basis, in what 'Abd al-Rāziq sees, for the supposition of the *khilāfah* ever having had its basis in any foundation or any legitimate principle attaching to the good pleasure of the group and the *ummah* for the institution of the *khilāfah*, and that what buttressed it was force and domination, and these are, moreover, its *only* sources of 'legitimacy'. Rather, without force there would be no formula for it to rule and no surety of its existence. It is here as Ibn Khaldūn described 'natural kingship', but rather it intersects, generally, with his concept of the state that is not realized *except through domination.*

'Abd al-Rāziq knows that there are those who may be able to follow him in his general supposition, but who may demand clarification of his sequence and ask whether or not this connotation of the *khilāfah* corresponded to the *khilāfah* of the *Rāshidūn* as well; and, he hastens to assert uncertainty or hesitation in describing the *khilāfah* of 'the first three' – implying that some uncertainty is possible, then digresses and responds with a rhetorical question: 'However, is it not of little doubt that 'Alī and Mu'āwīyah...did not vie for accession to the throne of the *khilāfah* except in shadow of swords and on the tips of spears; and likewise also the caliphs after them up to our present day?'.[31] While it is difficult to determine if 'Abd al-Rāziq distinguished between the *khilāfah* of the *Rāshidūn* and the *khilāfah* in general, it is *not* difficult to demonstrate the degree of his readiness to posit the *khilāfah* of the *Rāshidūn* itself as a subject for question! However, this readiness reaches its peak when he decrees that the goal of research into the *khilāfah* is the demonstration of its nature and its points of articulation, and the true form of its existence in reality, *not* the sources that draw from it its personalities or the extent that they enjoyed rational or religious legitimacy.[32]

Is the entire history of the *khilāfah* a history of the sword, brute force and hegemony?

The like of this question may be leveled at 'Abd al-Rāziq, and any choosing to level it may resort to the indication that the factor of material force was omnipresent in the experience of the *khilāfah*; and when our sheikh acknowledges that this force was armed and that it was in support of the *khilāfah*, the phenomenon of its existence was not always generally perceptible in all of history and that 'there were periods wherein this force was not employed due to the absence of a need to use it',[33] except that he does not consider that sufficient to invalidate the principle which he has enunciated that 'force is present *incontrovertibly*',[34] because it is *indispensible* within the *nature* of kingship and the *nature* of the *khilāfah*, this is to say that 'if there is anything in this world that drives man to despotism and wrongdoing,' says 'Abd al-Rāziq, 'and facilitates for him hostility and overweening excess, it is the position of the *khalīfah*.'[35]

Moving from there to thinking about the phenomenon of the *khilāfah* as it presents itself in reality – remote from the texts, 'Abd al-Rāziq attempts to push the analysis much further – to the point where the basic sanction latent in this goal for draconian power lies in the *khilāfah*, and he stumbles upon it in (the concept of) interest (*maṣlaḥah*): the interest that leads, in its turn, to jealous concern about what is possessed. Thus, 'jealous concern over dominion prompts the king to safeguard his throne against every thing that might shake its pillars, or that might detract from its sanctity or lessen its holiness; thus it was natural that the king might be transformed into a wild, Satanic, gargantuan butcher when his hands were apt to clutch any who attempted to escape from obedience to him or to undermine his throne…'.[36]

The *khilāfah* is *not* a religious institution in the view of 'Abd al-Rāziq, and it does not persist according to the dictates of *al-bay'ah* or choice of the *ahl al-ḥal wa al-'aqd*, but rather, it is a *political* institution persisting on the principles of force and domination. The fact is that this hypothesis of 'Abd al-Rāziq does not pertain to the *khilāfah* known to many as the 'mordacious rule' (unjust rule) (*al-mulk al-'aḍūḍ*); that is, political and civil character is inseparable from all types of governments known to Islam, and moreover, its rule over the *khilāfah* encompasses all of these.

Government in Islam is Political

'Abd al-Rāziq does not take a negative position towards government or the political system: his negative position was in regard to the *khilāfah* exclusively when it was asserted that it was successive to prophethood and reviving of its religious message role. As for government, or say, the principle of establishing a government, he was among those who did not oppose it; rather he was among those who designated its obligation and the need for it. That, for example, is what we gain from this text wherein he says:

> It is known that the political scientists have been satisfied with the fact that there was no doubt that its matter be established in a religious-civil community – whether it was possessed of a religion or not, and whether it was Muslim, Christian or Jewish or of mixed religions, there was no doubt that an organized community whatever its creed was or whatever its race, color or language, that a government be established to administer its affairs and to implement matters in it. The forms and characteristics of the government might differ – from constitutional to autocratic, from republican to Bolshevik or other than that. The political scientists competed to praise the merits of one form of government over another. However, we do not know of any among them or other than they who suggested otherwise for any community among communities – that some type of rule was necessary for them.[37]

The first question which is posited by this text and in light of it is: does it not imply the possibility that the same thing might be said about the *khilāfah*? And, thus, why should these aspersions be cast upon it?

'Abd al-Rāziq does not have a problem with the idea that there should be a *khilāfah* in this connotation – as posited by political scientists. With it, the Muslims should have the right to enjoy a system of political rule that is particular to them. The problem begins only when the *fuqahā'* desire by the *khilāfah* the connotation which they have formulated for it which is not supported by anything in Islamic law or reality.[38]

'Abd al-Rāziq's view was that government in Islam has a civil and political character. And, this not only correlates with the sultanate states which designated the term *khilāfah* for their systems, but it *also* encompassed the order of the *Rāshidūn* caliphs as well: the state which they set up or which they were preparing to establish 'was an Arab state persisting on the basis of a religious call. Its raison-d'être was the protection of this call and the engaging in it',[39] and the condition with Islam is that it is not only an Arab religion but it is a religion for all mankind. And this also is the condition of a logic practiced by this state which was political when 'many of those which were termed wars of "apostasy" in the first days of the *khilāfah* of Abū Bakr were not, in fact, *religious* wars but were unadulterated *political* ones, and not all of them were for the sake of the religion'.[40]

The highest form of evidence and proof of all, for our sheikh, is that which pertained to the nature of what he termed the 'Prophetic kingdom' (*al-mamlakah al-nabawīyah*).[41] This, according to his position, represented political government as well, where its matter was the like of other political governments. It ought not be conceived except from within the supposition that it 'operates in isolation from the *da'wah* (call) of Islam and outside the limits of the Message'.[42] Perhaps, the indications of that are numerous, but among them are two primary ones: the first is that the Prophetic *da'wah* had recourse occasionally 'to force and fear (*al-rahbah*)'. This is what is not moot for a religious call because the components of this are preaching and conviction, 'whereas force and coercion are not appropriate to a call where the goal of it is the guidance of hearts and the purification of creeds'.[43] Thus, whatever transpired from it in the way of force or fear, 'was not in the way of the *da'wah* (call) to the religion and the conveying of its message to the worlds, and it is not possible for us to understand except that it was in the way of dominion (*al-mulk*) and formation of the Islamic government'.[44] The second primary indication is with regard to what obtained in the administrative systemization in Medina in regard to collection of wealth (*al-māl*) and the disposal of it. This also represents, in his view, a phenomenon among the phenomena of kingship that is 'outside the function of the Message as it is'.[45]

If the distinction between these Prophetic actions with a political character and the Message is possible, then this will inform the consciousness of politics in a way that is far removed from the imperativeness of the religion, and if so, then the Prophet is simply the bearer of a religious call and nothing more. This is the content of the approach of 'Alī 'Abd al-Rāziq to the Prophetic experience and the relation between the religious and the political in it.

The critic of the *khilāfah* and the theory of the *khilāfah* concludes his criticism in a focused and dense text, clarifying in it the invalidity of calls to support the institution of the *khilāfah* while resting on religious supports and covering up its essential political nature by writing:

> The *khilāfah* is not in aught of religious planning and not of the judiciary (*al-qaḍā'*) or other than these among the functions of rule and the centers of state. Rather this is, entirely, unadulterated political planning with no relation to the religion in it, it is neither acknowledged nor denied by it [i.e., the religion], and it neither commands it nor prohibits it, but rather it leaves that to us, to have recourse in regard to it to the dictates of our reason and the experiences of communities and the bases of politics.[46]

It is decisive and abundantly clear that 'Abd al-Rāziq separates between the political and the religious through his separation of the *khilāfah* from its presumed authoritative religious referent. He does not say something new, and certainly in this regard many preceded him in that: Adīb Isḥāq, Faraḥ Anthon, as well as Khayr al-Dīn al-Tūnsī, Muḥammad 'Abdūh, and 'Abd al-Raḥmān al-Kawākibī and so on. However, he differs from all of these: he differs from the liberals in the Levant, because he said what he said in regard to the *khilāfah*, and he is a Muslim and from al-Azhar, *not* being 'excused' on the basis of his membership in Christianity as was the case with others among the liberals, or his being 'excused' on account of estrangement from al-Azhar: the homeland of religious creed and the hitching post for researches into the 'decisive assertion' in the matters of world and religion. Then, he also differs from the Islamic Reformers – in Tunisia, Egypt and Syria – in his writing what he did in a stage of religious expansionism that was inaugurated by the subject of the *khilāfah* of Rashīd Riḍā, and drove him to collapse the epoch of that Reformism! This is among that which the Reformers of the nineteenth century did not undertake with the same degree of strength. Al-Ṭahṭāwī built on Ḥasan al-'Aṭṭār, and al-Tūnsī built on al-Ṭahṭāwī, and Muḥammad 'Abdūh built on al-Afghānī, and al-Kawākibī and Qāsim Amīn built on 'Abdūh and so on. As for 'Abd al-Rāziq, Rashīd Riḍā did not leave anything for him on which to build after his bringing down of the whole structure on everyone in it!

The discourse of 'Alī 'Abd al-Rāziq on the criticism of the *khilāfah* and its theory of the remnants of the Islamic Reformist discourse is not stifled by the pressure of the rising tide of the conceptual authoritative referent. Rather, it remains an indication that the theoretical and political subjects that the Reformers attempted to cultivate remained able to grow despite all the destructive elements that threatened its tree.

Was he alone in his conception? No, there were others whose existence indicated that 'Alī 'Abd al-Rāziq was not only a witness standing on the tomb of Reformism, but rather he was a sign of a new establishment for the renewal of its message. And, among these was a sheikh among the *'ulamā'* of Algeria: 'Abd al-Ḥamīd bin Bādīs.

Criticism of the *Khilāfah*...from Afar

'Abd al-Ḥamīd bin Bādīs did not carve out a particular conceptual endeavor in the criticism of the *khalīfah*, and that was not among the premonitions of the theory. However, he examined the subject in other contexts that were governed by preoccupation with the relation between politics and religion in Algeria in the third decade of the twentieth century. Even though he scarcely dealt with the subject outside a limited number of paragraphs, his texts about the Islamic system – and from them a conception for it in the subject of the origin of the *wilāyah* (trusteeship) – expose the threads connecting his view of politics in the Islamic sphere and his position with regard to the issue of the *khilāfah*.

Like the rest of Islamic thinkers and believers in the idea of the *khilāfah* and its authoritatively referential model in the first period of Islam, 'Abd al-Ḥamīd bin Bādīs expresses his positive position towards it describing it as 'the supreme Islamic position which engages in executing Islamic law (*al-shar'*) and that which surrounds it through the means of *al-shūrā* of the *ahl al-ḥal wa al-'aqd* of those possessed of knowledge and experience and insight, and through the force of soldiers and cadres and the remainder of means of defense';[47] however this position, as viewed by Ibn Bādīs – does not remain thus throughout the history of Islam, because of the collapse of its central political position, as 'it was possible that this position could be occupied by one person at the dawn of Islam or a time thereafter – on the basis of schism and disorder – then necessity would dictate the multiplicity of it in the East and the West'.[48] This collapse was not, due to the multiplicity, without result on the image of the *khilāfah* and its original significance; but rather it visited destruction upon them as well.

This was the point of departure in his view of the matter of the *khilāfah* in the contemporary period, when voices of Azhar sheikhs were raised demanding the attribution of the *khilāfah* to the King of Egypt – a matter to which 'Alī 'Abd al-Rāziq responded and one which Ibn Bādīs disavowed. The *khilāfah*, in his opinion, was not only impossible today, but it had entered a scope of intractability ever since its central position had collapsed and split apart. As for what came to persist on the debris of that collapse, it was a rule that was entirely different even if it applied the name of *khalīfah* to itself. Thus, 'on the day when the Turks abolished the *khilāfah*, and we do not justify all their actions, they did not abolish the Islamic *khilāfah* in the Islamic sense, but rather they abolished a governing system that was particular to them, and they brought down an imaginary symbol with which Muslims were uselessly infatuated'.[49]

The *khilāfah*, then, is nothing more than an imaginary symbol. And, those who attempt, today, to revive it (and the intended meaning here refers to some of the sheikhs of al-Azhar) engage people uselessly and degrade them in what is not possible to realize. Thus, he says at times in remonstrative language: 'Enough of this arrogance and deception the Islamic nations today – even those that are oppressed among them have come to not be deceived by this intimidation – even if comes from under the *jubbahs* and turbans!' So that for which there is no duplicity is that 'imagination of the *khalīfah* will not be realized and that Muslims will one day, God willing, agree to this opinion.'[50]

It is clear then, that 'Abd al-Ḥamīd bin Bādīs shared 'Alī 'Abd al-Rāziq's critical opinion of the *khilāfah*, and specifically in regard to the impossibility of setting it up and in the obligation to not attempt to revive the idea of it in the minds of people. However, the correspondence between the two of them stops here as Ibn Bādīs did not take the position of disavowing the principle of the *khilāfah* itself, as 'Abd al-Rāziq had done, but rather he gauges the distance between the authoritatively referential realization of it at the dawn of it and between what it eventually became in terms of division and atomization and collapse. However, with this, he does not wager on its revival, and this is the salient point: it is not important here that Ibn Bādīs read the history of the *khilāfah* in a way that was different from the reading of 'Abd al-Rāziq, but what is important is that they both read its present and future along shared lines.

There is an Algerian nationalist dimension in the position of Ibn Bādīs towards the *khilāfah*, or say from the relation of the religious to the political. If his criticism of the *khilāfah* meant – scientifically – its separation of the field of politics from religion, or from the religious claim that the *khilāfah* represented, then his goal was Algerian in that as he was pushing the French occupation towards the conviction that the *'ulamā'* were not desirous of intervening in political affairs, and that served to abate their aspirations to control the religious and cultural institutions. And, in this matter, we share the views of Fahmī Jad'ān in his explication of the position of Ibn Bādīs with regard to the *khilāfah*.[51]

We have a strong argument from the texts of Ibn Bādīs that indicates his positive position towards the principle of the *khilāfah*, not withdrawn from a future conception of it, and not an incentive to wager on its renewal. The argument which we mean is the text that was distributed in the journal *al-Shahāb* (*The Spark*) in 1938, where he framed his concept of the Islamic system,[52] delimiting in it the *uṣūl* (origins) of the *wilāyah* as thirteen. This text and article clarifies beyond all doubt that the man was not thinking about the model of the *khilāfah* from any standpoint, but rather that he was emphasizing an entirely different concept of the state and the system of rule, even if he indicates that this conception was inspired by the *khuṭbah* (sermon) of Abū Bakr al-Ṣiddīq after he was sworn the *bay'ah*.

The constraints of space do not permit the examination of the text of Ibn Bādīs' conception of the system of rule in Islam in complete form, so we will consider it sufficient to present representative excerpts from it; and by this, we mean the thirteen *uṣūl* which are as follows:

i 'No one has the right of *wilāyah* (trusteeship) of any matter among the matters of the *ummah* except by the conferral of trusteeship by the *ummah*. The *ummah* has the right and the authority to confer trusteeship and remove it...' (the first of the *uṣūl*).

ii And that 'the one who is entrusted with a matter (*amr*) from among the matters of the *ummah* is the most competent in regard to it and not the best of it in terms of his behavior'[53] (the second of the *uṣūl*).

iii And that 'None is by virtue of his being entrusted with any matter among the matters of the *ummah* better than *ummah*...' (the third of the *uṣūl*).

iv And that 'the *ummah* has the right to censure those charged with the matter (*ulīy al-amr*) because it is the source of their authority and has supervision in their trusteeship and their removal' (the fourth of the *uṣūl*).

v And that there is a duty for the *wālī* (trustee) over the *ummah* 'in what it provides to him of help if it sees its rectitude...and it is a partner with him in responsibility...' (the fifth of the *uṣūl*).

vi Along with 'the right of the *wālī* over the *ummah* in his advice and guidance' (the sixth of the *uṣūl*).

vii And 'the right of the *ummah* to discuss with those charged with the matter and to take them to account for their actions and to oblige them to act as it [i.e., the *ummah*] sees fit and not as they see fit...' (the seventh of the *uṣūl*).

viii And that 'whoever is charged with a matter among the matters of the *ummah* it is incumbent for him to clarify the line upon which he is proceeding in order that they be eminently aware and that he proceeds along that line with the approval of the *ummah* …' (the eighth of the *uṣūl*).

ix And that 'he not rule the *ummah* except by laws that it has approved for itself…and the *wilāyah* is nothing other than an executor of its will, as it obeys the law because it is its law not because another authority – whether individual or group – imposed it upon it…so that it feels that is free in its conduct, and that it is directing itself by itself, and that it not the property of other than itself among people…' (the ninth of the *uṣūl*).

x And that 'All people are equal before the law…' (the tenth of the *uṣūl*).

xi And that it is mandatory 'to safeguard rights…and not to squander the right of the weak…' (the eleventh of the *uṣūl*).

xii And that it is mandatory 'to preserve balance between the classes of the *ummah* in the safeguarding of rights…' (the twelfth of the *uṣūl*).

xiii And finally that it is mandatory 'for the guardian (*al-rāʿī*) and those with whom he is charged (*al-raʿīyah*) to share in mutual responsibility between them in the welfare of the society'[54] (the thirteenth of the *uṣūl*).

It is entirely clear that this conception of the political order in Islam has no thread of affinity with the theory of the *khilāfah* but rather is established on a contemporary conception of politics and the state and very strongly connected to the concept of Islamic Reformism that we presented in the first three chapters of this study. Its center and what is present in its design is the *ummah* and not the caliph – rather, the latter is not even mentioned at all in the initiative. Fahmī Jadʿān may have been very correct when he noticed that:

> the purport of the thirteen *uṣūl* which he posits for the political order in Islam…engenders the distinct impression that Ibn Bādīs saw that the *ummah* was the source of all authority and that he did not consider it permissible that the *ummah* should be governed except by law that it approved for itself and charged its *wilāyah* with executing, and that responsibility was mutual between the state and the citizens within the limits of the law.[55]

In sum, the system that Ibn Bādīs exhibited in his conception of this is not the system of the *khilāfah*, despite his inspiration from the *khuṭbah* of the First Caliph, but rather it was *the system of the nation state*.

The two theses of 'Abd al-Rāziq and Ibn Bādīs on the criticism of the *khilāfah* represent a difficult, though bold, attempt to effect a return to the political question to the territory of the Reformist concept that was overturned by Rashīd Riḍā. Its difficulty was latent in the conditions in the second quarter of the twentieth century – which were not the same circumstances of the Reformist thesis of three decades before. True, the order of the Ottoman *khilāfah* had collapsed and its official abolition transpired in Turkey, and most of the countries of the Islamic world fell under the grip of colonial occupation wherein its untenable and pro forma unity was rent asunder. Along with that, the idea of the *khilāfah* coexisted as a response to two events: to its abolition (in Turkey) and to Colonial occupation. It was not in the capacity of its criticism to slash open a path from within the Islamic conceptual order, even if it was able to do that more easily in the locus of liberal or nationalist thought. Even those who attempted to redraw the map anew and to subject the *khilāfah* to criticism were soon compelled by the opposition to recant and announce repentance and to assume the lead in the movement of culturally authentic thought. This is, for example, what happened to Khālid Muḥammad Khālid[56] in regard to this subject, or what happened to the symbol of modernity in Arab thought – Ṭāhā Ḥussayn – who returned to the ranks of culturally authentic thought in the 1930s[57] after his sojourn and tour of conceptual rebellion against traditional reason.

Just as the movement of the criticism of the *khilāfah* lost its battle with its opponents, so did the movement for the *khilāfah* lose its wager with those who would spring from its loins. However, Rashīd Riḍā's loss of this wager is not comparable to the huge loss that was inflicted upon the thesis of 'Abd al-Rāziq. That is, that Rashīd Riḍā, at least, won over a new generation of Islamic intellectuals who studied under the tutelage of his subjects in the political question and would take it far in adaptation and modification so that it might take on the form of a new problematic – the problematic of the Islamic state. On the other hand, the other would not remain to transform into a wellspring for exaggerated conceptions of state and authority vying for precedence with the concept of theocracy.

Notes

1. We explained this distinction previously in Chapter 1 of this book.
2. Ibn Khaldūn, *al-Muqadimah*, p. 185.
3. Al-'Arawī, *Mafhūm al-Dawlah*, p. 95.
4. Ibn Khaldūn says: 'when the dispute between 'Alī and Mu'āwīyah occurred... the twain sought for the right and returned to *ijtihād,* both never sought in their

confrontation for mundane cause or preference for wrong or ran after personal feuds as may wrongly be perceived by others or may be inclined to be believed by infidels, they disputed in right and each one argued the other according to his own *ijtihād* and so they battled for the sake of right nevertheless 'Alī was rightful. Mu'āwīyah intended the right and erred but never sought the wrong'. Ibn Khaldūn, *al-Muqadimah*, p. 198.

5. Writings of sheikh 'Abd al-Salām Yāsīn are the best representation for them in the last three decades.

6. Al-'Arawī specifies this composition by saying: 'We perceive how obvious are the components that form what we call the Islamic state: Arab *al-Dahrīyah* (Natural Law), Islamic morality, and the Asian hierarchical system...apparently ancient and modern historians felt the same way when they addressed the Islamic state of *al-khulafā' al-Rāshidūn,* the Arab Umayyad state and the Persian Abbasid state...when we speak of the Islamic state today we mean necessarily the composition of all three elements: the Arab element, the Islamic element and the Asian element.' Available in: Al-'Arawī, *Mafhūm al-Dawlah*, pp. 92–3.

7. Al-'Arawī, *Mafhūm al-Dawlah*, p. 102.

8. 'It is not enough to state that the main purpose of *al-shar'* is interest, even if we include the public interest, i.e. prosperity, scientific progress, and establishment of peace and security...as for *al-khilāfah*, it is the governorship that aims through achieved mundane interest to the purpose of *sharī'ah*, to what Muslim jurists would call *makārim al-akhlāq,* as expressed by the Prophet's own words. Governorship is not a caliphate only in the sense of regarding itself as an instrument that serves a superior goal, a state will never be a caliphate only if it transcends its own self-motives.' Available in: Al-'Arawī, *Mafhūm al-Dawlah*, p. 103.

9. Ibn Taymīyah has two statements in this context in his book *al-Sīyāsah al-Shar'īyah*, when he says, 'It is a duty to take the *imārah* as a faith and a way to come closer to God', and when he says 'if power and wealth were meant to bring someone closer to God, that would have been the uprightness of religion and life. However, if power is separated from religion, or vice versa, people's affairs are blighted.' Available in: Ibn Taymīyah, *al-Sīyāsah al-Shar'īyah*, pp. 139 and 141 respectively.

10. Al-'Arawī, *Mafhūm al-Dawlah*, p. 137.

11. In response to the resolution of Mustafa Kemal and the People's Party to abolish the *khilāfah* on 13 March 1924, many Turkish procedures of extirpation had been launched against Islam and the Muslim grass-roots in the country, among which were: cancellation of religious teaching and the Qur'ānic teaching book, disbandment of Sufi lodges and dervish rituals, cancellation of the *Hijri* calendar, revocation of Islamic *awqāf* (endowments) and annexing them to the state properties, dropping the Arabic script in the writing of Turkish language and utilization of the Latin one instead, and adoption of modern European laws instead of those derived from the *sharī'ah*...etc. For details, see: Stewart, Desmond, *The Middle East: Temple of Janus*, Translated into Arabic by Zuhdī Jār-Allah (Beirut: Dār al-Nahār li-l-Nashr, 1974), pp. 238–9.

12. For details see: Kawtharānī, Wajīh, ed., *al-Dawlah wa al-Khilāfah fī al-Khiṭāb al-'Arabī ibbān al-Thawrah al-Kamālīyah fī Turkīyah, Rashīd Riḍā- 'Alī 'Abd al-Rāziq- 'Abd al-Raḥmān al-Shāhbandar: Dirāsah wa nuṣūṣ,* Silsilat al-Turāth al-'Arabī (Beirut: Dār al-Ṭalī'ah, 1996), pp. 21–4.

13. The book was released in Egypt in 1925.

14. Statement can be found in: Al-Jabri, *al-'Aql al-Sīyāsī al-'Arabī,* p. 321.

15. Al-Jabri expounds further in his analysis of the sultanate's ideology and the *fiqh* of politics, to the degree of maintaining that the rank of the caliph belongs – in the discourse of *al-ta'ālī bi-l-sīyāsah* – to that of God. Al-Jabri, *al-'Aql al-Sīyāsī al-'Arabī,* pp. 360–4.

16. 'Abd al-Rāziq, 'Alī, *al-Islām wa Uṣūl al-Ḥukm* (Beirut: Dār Maktabat al-Ḥayyāh, 1978), pp. 13–14.

17. 'Abd al-Rāziq, *al-Islām wa Uṣūl al-Ḥukm,* p. 199.

18. 'Abd al-Rāziq, *al-Islām wa Uṣūl al-Ḥukm,* p. 15.

19. 'The caliph shares no one his tenure, nor does anyone have *wilāyah* (trusteeship) over Muslims, only for a *wilāyah* that is derived from the caliphal position'. Available in: 'Abd al-Rāziq, *al-Islām wa Uṣūl al-Ḥukm,* p. 15.

20. 'Abd al-Rāziq, *al-Islām wa Uṣūl al-Ḥukm,* p. 18.

21. 'Abd al-Rāziq, *al-Islām wa Uṣūl al-Ḥukm,* p. 19.

22. 'Abd al-Rāziq, *al-Islām wa Uṣūl al-Ḥukm,* p. 39.

23. 'Abd al-Rāziq, *al-Islām wa Uṣūl al-Ḥukm,* p. 39.

24. 'Abd al-Rāziq, *al-Islām wa Uṣūl al-Ḥukm,* p. 42.

25. Al-Jabri clearly stated this when he presented the attitude of proponents of the *khilāfah* among modern intellectuals, he writes: 'When the *salafist* demands the revivalism of the "real" Islamic caliphate, he didn't in fact think of – and never favored the establishment of a rule pattern similar to the one Europe had experienced in the Medieval Ages...but rather he called for retrieving that optimal model of governorship in its referential framework, which was epitomized by the caliphate of 'Umar bin al-Khaṭṭāb, i.e. the governor who adopts the concept of "*al-shūrā and al-'adl*". Consequently, what the *salafist* really demands is that kind of governorship in which he has – since he represents the majority – a position and a rank, and that is achieved through *shūrā* which he considers himself, as a result, one of its components, i.e. "*ahl al-ḥal wa al-'aqd*"'. Available in: Al-Jabri, *al-Khiṭāb al-'Arabī al-Mu'āṣir: Dirāsah Taḥlīlīyah Naqdīyah* (Beirut: al-Markaz al-Thaqāfī al-'Arabī; Dār al-Ṭalī'ah, 1982), pp. 93–4.

26. 'Abd al-Rāziq, *al-Islām wa Uṣūl al-Ḥukm,* pp. 80–3.

27. 'Abd al-Rāziq, *al-Islām wa Uṣūl al-Ḥukm,* p. 201.

28. 'Abd al-Rāziq, *al-Islām wa Uṣūl al-Ḥukm,* p. 83.

29. 'Abd al-Rāziq, *al-Islām wa Uṣūl al-Ḥukm,* p. 69.

30. 'Abd al-Rāziq, *al-Islām wa Uṣūl al-Ḥukm,* p. 70.

31. 'Abd al-Rāziq, *al-Islām wa Uṣūl al-Ḥukm,* p. 71.

32. 'What concerns us here is to maintain that the reliance of the *khilāfah* upon power is undoubtedly an inevitable truth. In both ways it is the same, whether this tangible reality coped with reason or not, and whether it was concordant with laws of religion or not.' 'Abd al-Rāziq, *al-Islām wa Uṣūl al-Ḥukm,* pp. 73–4.

33. This point of view was also expressed by Ibn Khaldūn in a rare textual synthesis which is unique in its theoretical approach in categorizing history of the state, especially the history of using sword (physical force) and pen (scientific force). In spite of its relative extension, we put it here for its significance and relation to the idea expressed by 'Abd al-Rāziq, Ibn Khaldūn: 'I know that both sword and pen are two instruments for the ruler, however the need for sword is superior to the use of pen in the beginning of the establishment of state as far as its citizens are still in the beginning of arranging their own lives, as the pen in this case is a minion for the sultan's rule. The sword is an associate in this concern. This is true even in the decline of the state as it grows weaker and its citizens become older, so the state needs to be backed up by swordbearers and the need for them to defend the state is as it was the case during its birth. So the sword has a merit in two regards over the pen, so the swordbearers are thus the wealthier and more influential. Whereas in the middle period, the ruler lays down the sword somehow and concentrates upon the establishment of the state – on levying taxes, imposing order, implementing rules and, in this case, the pen is the supporter of him. So swords become neglected unless needed in a conflict or dire

conditions, otherwise they are useless. Thus the pen-holders become the highest in rank and the wealthier...and even closer to the sultan...as the pen – here – is the instrument by which he reaps the fruits of his state...'. Available in: Ibn Khaldūn, *al-Muqadimah*, pp. 242–3. Compare this to the categorization set by Althusser as he explains the use of sword and pen in the tyrant regimes and the ideological systems of the state and how they are implemented within the social framework of the state. Available at: Althusser, Louis, 'idéologie et appareils idéologiques d'état, in: *positions, 1964–1975* (Paris: Editions socials, 1976).

34. 'Abd al-Rāziq, *al-Islām wa Uṣūl al-Ḥukm,* p. 71.
35. 'Abd al-Rāziq, *al-Islām wa Uṣūl al-Ḥukm,* p. 75.
36. 'Abd al-Rāziq, *al-Islām wa Uṣūl al-Ḥukm,* p. 76.
37. 'Abd al-Rāziq, *al-Islām wa Uṣūl al-Ḥukm,* pp. 80–1.
38. 'Abd al-Rāziq, *al-Islām wa Uṣūl al-Ḥukm,* p. 83.
39. 'Abd al-Rāziq, *al-Islām wa Uṣūl al-Ḥukm,* p. 184.
40. 'Abd al-Rāziq, *al-Islām wa Uṣūl al-Ḥukm,* p. 196.
41. The appellation was not used arbitrarily or inadvertently, in fact it meant that the Prophet was like a king for the state of Medina.
42. 'Abd al-Rāziq, *al-Islām wa Uṣūl al-Ḥukm,* pp. 119–20.
43. 'Abd al-Rāziq, *al-Islām wa Uṣūl al-Ḥukm,* p. 117.
44. 'Abd al-Rāziq, *al-Islām wa Uṣūl al-Ḥukm,* p. 118.
45. 'Abd al-Rāziq, *al-Islām wa Uṣūl al-Ḥukm,* p. 118.
46. 'Abd al-Rāziq, *al-Islām wa Uṣūl al-Ḥukm,* p. 201.
47. Ibn Bādīs, 'Abd al-Ḥamīd, *Āthār Ibn Bādīs*, edited and compiled by 'Amār al-Ṭālibī (Algiers: Dār wa Maktabat al-Sharikah al-Jazā'irīyah, 1986), vol. 1, p. 410.
48. Ibn Bādīs, *Āthār Ibn Bādīs*, p. 411.
49. Ibn Bādīs, *Āthār Ibn Bādīs*, p. 412.
50. Ibn Bādīs, *Āthār Ibn Bādīs*, p. 412.
51. '...what Ibn Bādīs meant by this is to hint that even though 'Jam'īyat 'Ulamā' al-Muslimīn' operated during the French occupation period and that it had to keep the occupier's hands off it, still, that was not an excuse for it to meddle in politics. So during that time, when he called for instating "Jamā'at al-Muslimīn" – who are supposed to be the *ahl al-'ilm wa al-khibrah* (people who possess knowledge and expertise) and are capable of running Muslim interests from a literary religious view that is remote from politics or intervention from any government whether Islamic or non-Islamic in the position of the *khilāfah*'s authority, he meant that primarily to prevent the occupier from managing religious affairs in Algeria to preserve, ultimately, their Arab-Islamic Algerian identity, and to have Algerians' affairs being run by themselves and not the French...' Available in: Jad'ān, Fahmī, *al-Māḍī fī al-Ḥāḍir: Dirāsah fī Tashakkulat wa Masālik al-Tajrubah al-Fikrīyah al-'Arabīyah* (Beirut: al-Mu'asasah al-'Arabīyah li-al-Dirāsāt wa al-Nashr, 1997), p. 135.
52. The text is available in: Ibn Bādīs, *Āthār Ibn Bādīs*, pp. 401–5.
53. This is a reference to his famous statement upon the speech of instating Abū Bakr.
54. Ibn Bādīs, *Āthār Ibn Bādīs*, pp. 401–5.
55. Jad'ān, *al-Māḍī fī al-Ḥāḍir*, p. 136.
56. Khālid, Khālid Muḥammad, *min Hunā Nabda',* 4th edn (Cairo: Dār al-Nīl, 1950).
57. See analysis of the reasons behind this transformation and its context in the thought of Ṭāhā Ḥussayn. Available in: Omlīl, *Al-Iṣlāḥīyah al-'Arabīyah.*

Part Two

From the Islamic State to the Religious State

Chapter 6

On the 'Islamic State' – Religious and Political Aspects

> Rule (*al-ḥukm*) is counted as among our books of *fiqh*, creed and *uṣul*, and not among the derivative branches (*furuʿ*) and jurisprudential interpretations (*fiqhīyāt*)
>
> Ḥasan al-Bannā

> The system of Islamic rule is not separated in principle or practice from the remainder of the obligations (*furūḍ*) of the religion.
>
> ʿAbd al-Salām Yāsīn

Despite the call of ʿAlī ʿAbd al-Rāziq, and what spawned from it of analogous calls – spreading in its wake – among modern conceptual currents, there did not occur a major change in the relation of the connection between religion and state, from the standpoint of some form of division between them, as the aforementioned theses endeavored to effect. 'Rather there was a strong trend against this separation calling for binding between the two, advocating rooting and demanding a reconstruction of "the Islamic state" or "the Islamic society" shaded by the Islamic *sharīʿah*.'[1] This trend, upon which we previously touched, was not an extension of the thesis of Rashīd Riḍā in the political question – of the *khilāfah* specifically – even if it might not have appealed to the thesis of the *khilāfah* in its problematic or counted it among the true Islamic problematics (*ishkālīyāt*) in the field of politics. Ḥasan al-Bannā, the leader of the Muslim Brotherhood (*al-Ikhwān al-Muslimīn*) in Egypt, was the founder of that trend and an early theorist and proponent of its theses; contentions that would come to fruition and spread – in place – to cross the borders of Egypt and reach most of the countries of the Arab and

Islamic worlds, and subsequently spread – in time – to span an era of seven decades between the birth of the discourse and movement of the Muslim Brotherhood until the end of the twentieth century.[2]

The Birth of the Problematic of the 'Islamic State'

Ḥasan al-Bannā was a student, in an indirect way, of *sayyid* Muḥammad Rashīd Riḍā, and counted him among his contemporary points of reference; however, he did not pay heed – either closely or remotely – to the matter which had engaged his teacher: the *khilāfah* (caliphate). The reader of the texts of the founder of the Muslim Brotherhood movement and its guide is not about to find anything more than a few sparse indications of the subject of the *khilāfah*, designating it with the frank analysis that it is a matter to be delayed, if it *is* in fact an Islamic legal matter for which there is no way to drop religious culpability (*al-taklīf*).[3] Perhaps the reason for his refraining from delving into it was a political one – in the first instance – and not a religious one (nothing absolved him in any case as an Islamic preacher graduating from the school of Rashīd Riḍā); and, 'what was occupying his mind with regard to this matter,' according to Fahmī Jad'ān was 'the establishment of true "Islamic government".'[4] That is, the realization of a *realistic* political initiative if the sanctified content of the idea of the *khilāfah* could not be taken into consideration. As for that initiative, it was the building of an Islamic state in a region and nation within the reaches of the Islamic world – in Egypt, which, in turn, might become a nucleus for this *khilāfah*, or a precursor on the road to its realization.

It is not possible to read the absence of the subject of the *khilāfah* in the thought of Ḥasan al-Bannā or the inheritance bequeathed by the Muslim Brotherhood, except as its being the main objective indicator of the weighty presence in his thought of the realistic objective. In this sense, if the subject of the 'Islamic state' displaced the subject of the *khilāfah* in Islamic political thought, and it inherited it on the basis of its being the sole inheritance, then that displacement is not – in aught – a contradiction of its logic or a departure from its rhetorical limits, but rather it is a modification of its sacrosanct content and an attempt to slash open a possible path leading to it. Rather, we would speculate here that the thesis of the 'Islamic state', along the lines of the features and divisions which Ḥasan al-Bannā drew for it, is nothing, in its nature, other than a miniature, idealized incarnation of the *khilāfah*. And, if we are aware – methodologically – then we might assert that while it is not like that in the sense of its details, we would add that it does not diverge from that in its *essence* or content, as we shall discuss shortly.

Should we understand from this that the problematic of the 'Islamic state' represents a continuation of the problematic of the *khilāfah* in contemporary Islamic political thought?

This is in exact conformity at the level of the system of understanding employed in the two 'theories' of the *khilāfah* and the Islamic state: which appears to be one despite numerous differences in the two forms. As for the matter from the standpoint of the limits of the *wilāyah* (trusteeship), and the sphere of the sultan, that is in terms of what we might express in contemporary parlance by the term the 'political geography of the state', there is a real and decisive distinction which the researcher cannot deny, especially in the supposition that the factor of political geography is not an ordinary detail of the matter, but rather that it *is* the matter, itself. In it, at least, is that to which this conceptual and political reality bears witness – that the subject of the 'Islamic state' is subsumed, in apposition to the *khilāfah* and its sanctity. In any case, we have a number of indications of the relation of the tension between the subject of the *khilāfah* and the subject of the Islamic state as well as its fluctuation between the limit of (the relation of) intertwinement and self-identification and between the limit of estrangement and separation. Possibly what best represents this relation between them are the following two matters: the first being the necessity of the state for the Islamic group, and the second being the content – or significance – of the 'Islamic' character of this state.

On the Need for a State

Along the lines of those who advocate the *khilāfah* and take the position that setting up an imam is obligatory for Muslims and sinful if they abandon the matter, Ḥasan al-Bannā asserted, along with the rest of those who called for the 'Islamic state' after him, that establishing the state was an obligatory act (*fi'l wājib*) in Islam; that it was among the matters specified by the requirements of Islamic commandment; and that separation between religion and politics was among that which had no basis in principle. Al-Bannā wrote about this import:

> Orthodox Islam imposes government as a basis among the foundations of the social system that it brought to people – it does not sanction chaos nor does it leave the Muslim group without an imam...whoever speculates that religion or, more precisely, Islam, is not concerned with politics or that politics

> is not within its realm of inquiry has wronged himself and has wronged his knowledge by this [sort of] Islam.[5]

The principle of the state, and what carries it forward then, is the need to prevent chaos and ensure the stability of the system: a need expressed by the ancients as the necessity of guarding against *fitnah* (strife) and a precautionary measure to ensure the unity of the group and the means of its protection and safeguarding. Modernists later continued to reiterate these formulae in terms different in form but similar in meaning. However, what does 'stability of the system' signify in this assertion about the necessity of the state in Islam and its necessity for Islam?

It means, in the first instance, that Islam is not only a religious creed (*'aqīdah*), but rather that it is also a social and political system which cannot exist or persist without a state to express it and to impose its rulings; and this is what the Prophetic experience connoted in the construction of a state in Medina after the immigration (*hijrah*) to it. In this sense Muḥammad al-Mubārak says:

> The state is necessary in Islam because it is not possible to execute the rulings of the Qur'ān without a state (in what there are among the rulings of *al-zakāt* and the *ḥudūd* penalties and the like of these) because in the Qur'ānic understanding of existence, there is no doubt that there must be a social sphere in order for it to be realized and that is the Islamic state; and secondly, because the Prophet himself set up a state.[6]

The remainder of contemporary thinkers of Islam, or rather the Islamist activists, repeat the essential viewpoint of this assertion almost verbatim; does that mean that establishing a state is among the *uṣūl* (root sources) of Islam?[7]

Among the contemporary thinkers of Islam there was contention between those taking the position of the idea of the 'Islamic state'. Many of them among the Shī'ite *madhab* took the position that the state and the imams (*al-a'immah*) were a source among the *uṣūl* of the religion. Others rejected that in accounting it as being of among the *furū'* (derivative branches) which did not reflect either negatively or positively on the Islamic character of the person asserting either of the two opinions in the matter. Ḥasan al-Bannā wrote frankly about the first connotation that:

> Rule (*al-hukm*) is enumerated in our books of *fiqh* among the creed (*al-'aqīdah*) and the *uṣūl*, it is not of the derivative jurisprudential interpretations (*al-fiqhīyāt*) or the *furū'* (branches). Islam is rule and implementation just as

it is legislation and education just as it is law and judiciary – one part is not disconnected from the other.[8]

This assertion, without doubt, is a very interesting turn in Sunni thinking about the political issue and political authority.

If Ḥasan al-Bannā, as far as we know, was the first contemporary Sunni Muslim thinker of those who took the position that the matter of political authority in Islam was a matter of creed and not *fiqh* and that it was among the original *uṣūl* and not the branches of *furū'*, then he was certainly not the last. Many followed him, became students of him and partook of his political theses; or rather, his assertion opened up a wide path before them to establish an '*uṣūlī* theory' (*naẓarīyah uṣūlīyah*) on politics and the state which had never been undertaken previously – whether it bridged the gap between it and the Shī'ite theory of the imamate or not, to invest its product with new political terminology. This is what would ultimately have the greatest applicability to what he unleashed in this realm with Taqqī al-Dīn al-Nabahānī, Sayyid Quṭb, Muḥammad Quṭb and others of the same ilk such as will be examined in another chapter of this study.

The contemporary Islamist writer Muḥammad Ibrāhīm Mabrūk took the position of the *madhab* of Ḥasan al-Bannā in assertion of the creedal and *uṣūlī* nature of the matter of political authority and the state in Islam. He intones: 'The establishment of the state (*al-imāmah*) for Muslims is a religious obligation (*wājib dīnī*) incumbent upon the Islamic *ummah* and the affairs of their religion and their life cannot be conducted except by it.' He pronounces 'a refutation of any thesis put forth by any person who aims to avert the mandatory responsibility of the Muslims to establish this rule (*al-ḥukm*)'.[9] This was in response to Muḥammad 'Amārah who asserted that establishing a state is not among the pillars (*arkān*) of the religion which are five when he said: 'Talk about these five pillars pertains to the Islam of the individual not to the group because it is not reasonable that it should be said to the individual Muslim that it is among the pillars of your Islam that you as – an individual – establish a state; discussion of this matter is not directed towards any except the *group*.'[10]

Along these lines, an Islamic thinker and *mujtahid*, or one who is supposedly so, such as sheikh Muḥammad Yūsuf al-Qaraḍāwī acknowledges the matter of the imamate or the *khilāfah* as being among the *uṣūl* of the religion and among the legitimate inquiries of creed and *al-tawḥīd* (the Islamic unicity of Allah) among the Shī'ah, whereas among the Sunnis it is 'among the inquires of the *furū'* (branches) because it attaches to *practice* (*'amal*) not to belief as a basis'. He asserts that he submits to this 'without a doubt' except that he fritters away his definition entirely and plants doubt in the very fabric of his supposition when he acknowledges:

> but this does not imply disdain for this matter because Islam is not only the tenets of creed, but rather it is creed and work (*'amal*); and faith is what is revered in the heart and confirmed by deed. And, if we look at the basic obligations (*farā'iḍ asāsīyah*) like *al-ṣalāt* (prayer) and *al-zakāt* (alms), we see that they are among the branches (*al-furū'*) and not among the *uṣūl* because they are deeds and not among the tenets of the creed, but this does not take them out of their consideration as being pillars (*arkān*) of Islam...on the basis of the conviction (*i'tiqād*) of their necessity, as faith (*al-īmān*) in its status as a pillar in the religion is among the *uṣūl* and not among the branches.[11] For this reason whoever denies their obligatory status (*farḍīyatihā*) or who doesn't take them seriously is considered a *kāfir* (unbeliever) and an apostate from the religion – outside of the faith...and thus it is said that the imamate or rule by what Allah has sent down is among the branches, but conviction in its necessity and imperativeness...is certainly among the *uṣūl*...and in this sense, rule by what Allah has sent down enters into the locus of faith, and it is enumerated among the *uṣūl* without any dispute.[12]

The first result of the assertion of the necessity of the Islamic state in Islam and the consideration of the espousal of the 'Islamic state' to be a necessity is a transfer of the political question from the scope of general *fiqh* and political *fiqh* to the world of *al-kalām* (Islamic theology) where it becomes a *creedal* matter from among those of the *uṣūl* of the religion. The significance of this is that contemporary Islamic political discourse, the discourse of al-Bannā and whoever takes him as a model, is not sufficed with merely defending the relation between the religious–political connection in Islam against whoever attempts to sever the tie between them, but rather it goes to the extreme of according this relation a sacrosanct character and cutting off any questioning of it in a way parallel to the position of Shī'ite *fiqh* in regard to the matter of the imamate and its religious *uṣūlī* character in Islam.

Does this imply that the state in Islam is a *religious* state?

The Islamic State and the Religious State

Contemporary Islamists, especially those relying on the thought of Ḥasan al-Bannā and the inheritance of the Muslim Brotherhood strive to emphasize the separation and distinctions between the concept of the Islamic state and the concept of the *religious* state, according to their regard of the second as alien to the teachings of Islam and its political experience. That endeavor is essentially nothing more than a reaffirmation of the maxim that 'there is no monasticism in Islam' (*lā rahbanah fi-l-Islām*), and an insistence that men of the Islamic religion are *not* the like the clergymen (*al-Iklīyurus*) of Europe but rather that 'the authority of Muslim men of religion is circumscribed and limited,' according to the assertion of al-Bannā, 'it is not able to change the status quo or the heart of the system'[13]

A source of comparison between the Islamic experience and the European experience is present in the density of texts of Islamists pertaining to this matter; we direct the comparison to the group of men of religion, both here and there, and set forth a general principle: every religion has a need for 'men' whose mission is to teach people the matters of their religion – many of which might be obscure for them. At this point, however, differences begin: if

> when religion is a creed and a motto and a *sharīʿah* (i.e., a total system of law), and a knowledge about the life of the world and the afterlife, then these 'men' are *ʿulamāʾ* and *fuqahāʾ* and preachers and instructors (*murabbīn*)...as for the case when religion is only a creed, without a *sharīʿah*...then the mission of these 'men' is circumscribed and limited to an attempt to connect people with their Lord only along the spiritual path in that religion...and these 'men' of religion as dictated by that state – turn into soothsayers (*kahanah*) who preserve the 'secrets'...the mysteries that evade the understanding of people, and they become...'intermediaries between the slave and the Lord...'. That has nothing to do with the religion – it is the situation of the Church and the state – on of whether or not the Church itself is an innovation (*bidʿah*) innovated without any authority having been sent down from God.

The sole ruling power imposed itself by force and not by right, and that was an encroachment of rights; 'when the Church came to be a political power along with its being a spiritual one, there began the idolatrous excess – *al-ṭughyān*.' That was the result of the religion 'transforming...at the hands of the Church into a restraining force on life...oblivious to the life of the world due to the whim of working exclusively for the spirit.'[14]

There is no sphere – in the discourse of those asserting the idea of the Islamic state – for the establishing of a correspondence between the functions of men of religion in the Christian Church and their functions in Islam. The first present themselves as intermediaries between the human being and the Lord, and this is what the latter reject as Islam dispenses with the system of monasticism just as it imposes the creed of *al-tawḥīd* (divine unicity). The first turn away from the societal dimension and do not operate outside the spiritual; this being the matter which exposes the social life of those believers in the Christian message to a separation of *sharīʿah* from creed and one of life from religion,[15] establishing by that a new 'deviant' creed that has no connections to the teachings of the Messiah and so on.[16] Whereas, these others believe that a separation between creed and *al-sharīʿah* is alien to the teachings of their religion, and that those asserting this are carrying out a theft of sorts in the domain of politics which, *in toto*, is the proper domain of the creed. Rather, the contemporary Islamist preacher goes to the extent of denying the existence of 'men of religion' in Islam, considering the assertion of that to be irrelevant to its nature and the interconnectedness and connection between creed and *al-sharīʿah* in it.[17]

If Ḥasan al-Bannā was the originator of the idea of the 'Islamic state', he was among those who called attention to the distinguishing differences between this state and the religious state. Theorizing about the distinction between the two, however, was not something to which he devoted a place in his texts, but rather the matter sees light in the works of other preachers among his students – the most important contemporary of these who is still living being Yūsuf al-Qaraḍāwī. The latter has expended considerable effort to clarify that distinction and the difference between the two conceptions in a number of his texts. With his fidelity to the teachings of his sheikh al-Bannā – and he had been a contemporary of him in his youth, before his assassination at the end of the 1940s – sheikh al-Qaraḍāwī has attempted to prosper from al-Bannā's thesis about the Islamic state and the inherent differences between it and the religious state with new ideas culled from the concept of the modern state. Thus, the reader of these texts feels as though al-Qaraḍāwī is leaving behind the conceptual realm of understandings upon which al-Bannā had relied in his construction of a political thesis in the matter of the Islamic state in order to vie for precedence with new (modern) theses, erected upon modifications of these assumptions. Nevertheless, on the other hand…these feelings are not, in the truth of the matter, more than a formal retreat, perfected in the political writings of sheikh al-Qaraḍāwī – indebted to a degree to the Islamic political thesis of the Muslim Brotherhood, to the fortress of its (purportedly) obligatory nature and its objectivity. That is, sheikh al-Qaraḍāwī himself was soon afflicted by feelings of boredom with the monotony of a bare *ijtihād* role and reverted to his original temperament in desiring to be loyal to the teachings of his sheikh.[18]

We read al-Qaraḍāwī defining the Islamic state in contradistinction to the religious state where he says:

> The Islamic state which Islam brought, and as is known in the history of the Muslims, is a *civil* state (*dawlah madanīyah*); political power is set up in it on the basis of the pledge of allegiance (*al-bay'ah*) and choice (*al-ikhtiyār*) and *al-shūrā* (consultation), and the ruler in it is the agent (*wakīl*) of the *ummah* or its employee (*ajīr*). It is the right of the *ummah* – represented in the people of authority (*ahl al-ḥal wa al-'aqd*) among them – to take him to account; to supervise or censure him; to command him and prohibit him; and to rectify his course if he deviates, and if not – to remove him. It is among the rights of every Muslim, rather of every national citizen (*muwāṭin*), to disavow him if he sees him sinning and engaging in reprehensible actions, or failing to enjoin what is just. Rather, it is incumbent on the people to declare revolution (*al-thawrah*) against him if they see that he is a *kāfir* according to the criteria of Allah. As for the religious 'theocratic' state which the West knew in the Middle Ages, and which was ruled by the men of religion who retained their rule by the necks – and conscience – of people in the name of the 'divine right'...it is rejected by Islam.[19]

Al-Qaraḍāwī leads from this distinction to an overt and explicit utterance: '...We declare frankly: Yes...to the Islamic state, and no, and again no...to the religious "theocratic" state.'[20]

It might appear to the reader of this text that al-Qaraḍāwī's distinction between the Islamic state and the religious state goes to the limits of the assertion that the state in Islam is, in fact, *civil* (*madanīyah*) as he says, and this is not true, that the meaning of civil (*al-madanīyah*) for him is constrained only to the absence of the 'men of religion'; as for the presence of the *'ulamā'* of the religion, that does not represent, in his opinion, a detraction from its civil character, even if they are the people of authority (*ahl al-ḥal wa al-'aqd*) in it! If we have only presented what is a small measure towards understanding the significance of 'civil' (*al-madanī*) and constitutional (*al-dustūrī*) for this Islamic state – in the discourse of al-Qaraḍāwī – we find that this significance does not go beyond what al-Bannā asserted in that the system of the Islamic state is nothing other than the system of *al-sharī'ah*.[21] 'The Islamic state,' says al-Qaraḍāwī, 'is a "constitutional state" (*dawlah dustūrīyah*) or "Islamically-legal" (*sharī'īyah*), which has a constitution governing in it and law referring to it, and its constitution is represented in the principles and rulings of *al-sharī'ah*...'.[22]

The constitution of this state, then, is the *sharī'ah*, or it might be said that the *sharī'ah* is what is given the patina of 'constitutionality'. However, this constitution has no analog among modern constitutions, as it does not permit any modification – whether by elimination [of articles] or addition [to them] to respond to the requirements of development in the realm of political society. Thus, in regard to this state: 'It is not an option to respect its constitution or law, as this is required by the dictates of Islam and a proof of faith in it'.[23] It is not Islamic except *through* it. So, its legitimacy is neither social nor civil (*madanīyah*), rather it is *religious*, and that is 'the observance by the state of the law (*qānūn*) of *al-sharī'ah* is what gives it its legitimacy...as for the case if it diverges from this method (*manhaj*)...then the right of legitimacy is forfeited and people are no longer obligated to follow it...'. And, this constitution 'is not one which was put in place by it (i.e., the state) but by an authority higher than it (i.e., God).'[24]

We will attempt to effect an exit from these overgeneralizations, the precursor being the definition of the 'Islamic state', in order to approach the geography of this state as its topography was charted in the theoretical discourse of its founder Ḥasan al-Bannā in his political theses, not in his theoretical definitions.

The Islamic State in the Discourse of Ḥasan al-Bannā: Divergences in Understanding

The transference or oscillation between the religious concept of the state and the modern civil conception of it, especially as exemplified by the discourse of al-Qaraḍāwī is not to the exclusion of the remainder of contemporary Islamist intellectuals, rather it is the legacy of Ḥasan al-Bannā who was one of the most proficient practitioners of it – to the extent that none equaled him in it. The truth is that the reader of the texts of the founder of the Muslim Brotherhood movement does not experience any difficulty in locating a fascinating divergence originating in his discourse about the state: one of extreme open-mindedness and extreme close-mindedness! This is the divergence that takes his discourse to the furthest limits of tension as a result of the force of attraction between the two opposing poles of openness and closedness. We recognize this – in an extremely clear fashion – in his defense of the constitution and parliamentary representational choice and in his withering attack on multiple political parties!

The State and the Constitution

The vast majority of readers of his conceptual texts, or those who have looked over his political positions, know that Ḥasan al-Bannā was positively disposed towards the question of the constitution and political, parliamentary choice, and that he pushed his Muslim Brotherhood movement to participate politically in public life – far from thoughts of violent options, especially before the establishment of the 'Special Apparatus' (*Tanẓīm al-Khāṣ*)[25] which became a shock troop in armed confrontation with the huge and expansive Republican organization of the Egyptian state.[26] Despite the fact that his position is positive towards this, it was, in all that he thought, of pure Islam; that is, the constitution and parliamentary representation were *not* among ideas extraneous to the creed of Islam or its *sharīʿah*; rather, they were *of* its teachings even if it might appear that Muslims were borrowing them from the West. That is, the systems of Islam, as far as he could see, were 'more perfect and more beneficial than what is known to people of either modern or ancient systems.'[27] Even when he was defending the principle of citizenship (*al-muwāṭanah*) – which is a modern concept in political thought – he was doing that from within his religious authoritative point of reference arguing: 'It is thought...that holding fast to Islam and making it a basis for the system of life is a negation of the existence of non-Muslim minorities in the Muslim *ummah* and a negation of the unity between different races of the *ummah*,' clarifying, 'the truth is entirely contrary to that.'[28] It is very interesting, here, that al-Bannā does not use expressions like the 'protected peoples' (*ahl al-dhimmah*), in this context, and he doesn't deal with the experience of the Ottoman '*millet* system' in treating the question of non-Muslim minorities, rather he goes directly to constructing his position for the welfare of the unity of the nation and society through the consideration of a number of Qur'ānic verses that encourage the fraternity of believers and their unity, ending with the conclusion that '[in] this Islam, which is built upon this just sentiment and this far-reaching equity it is not possible for its follower to be a cause of rupture of its interconnected unity, rather the opposite: this unity has a connotation of religious holiness rather than that which might derive from only a civil text.'[29]

In al-Bannā's discussion of the constitution, distinction is necessary between two positions both in it and from it: between the positive, open position towards the constitution in general as a political document and relation, and between his position with regard to the Egyptian Constitution, which was a critical one and about which it appears he had considerable reservation, even if this reservation didn't take him to the limit of rejecting it outright. Al-Bannā says, addressing the Brotherhood:

> The researcher, when he looks at the principles of constitutional government which are dedicated to preservation of personal freedom, in all its types; and *al-shūrā* and the derivation of authority (*al-sulṭah*) from the *ummah*; and the responsibility of the rulers before the people and their taking them to account for what they do; and the explication of the limits of all the power of the authorities – these are the sources (*uṣūl*) – all of them – that commend to the researcher that they are absolutely compatible with the teachings of Islam and its systems and its foundations in every form of rule. And for this, the Muslim Brotherhood are convinced that the constitutional system of rule is the nearest existing system of rule, in all the world, to Islam, and they do not place it on a par with any other system.[30]

Al-Bannā, here blurs between the modern liberal system and the systems of rule in Islam apparently without the slightest hesitation. With his assertion that 'the constitutional system of rule is the nearest system of rule...to the Islamic system', it might be inferred that this system is external and being compared from within (the Islamic system) except that his previous expression that the principles of constitutional rule 'are absolutely compatible with the teachings of Islam' breaks down the barriers between these two systems and renders them a single system. Thus, we end with Ḥasan al-Bannā asserting that the political system in Islam – the system of the 'Islamic state' is a *constitutional* system.

This positive openness in principle and theory turns to guarded reservation when the matter attaches to the particular text of the Egyptian Constitution. Despite the fact that al-Bannā greatly welcomes the implementation of a constitution for the country, he does not hesitate to direct criticisms towards it, and especially when it involves – in his opinion – ambiguity and the means of putting it in motion. We read from him in this regard:

> Among the texts of the Egyptian Constitution are what the Muslim Brotherhood see to be ambiguous and obscure, leaving a vast scope of interpretation and explication, filled with conjecture and whims; and it is in need of clarification, delimitation and explanation. This is one thing, and another is that way of executing that which is in conformity with the Constitution...is one which has been fraught with the confirmed failures of experience whereby the *ummah* has been subjected to harms and not benefit; and it is in dire need of editing and modification to realize its intent[s] and facilitate its

goal[s]...and it suffices us here to indicate the law of elections [by way of example]'.[31]

It is without doubt that the nebulous obscurities of the Egyptian Constitution would have to be cleared up before it could be considered compatible with the idealized conception of the constitution that al-Bannā had drawn for it in his imagination; rather, there was no doubt about rectifying its administration in order to bring the administration of it into accordance with its essence. And, it is precisely this matter that constitutes the essence of al-Bannā's reservation: diverting the law – or the laws – from the *spirit* of the constitution as in the case of the law of elections. The reality was that al-Bannā realized very well the difference between the constitution and the law: the constitution is tantamount to the general principles whereas the law is the systemization of operational procedures.[32] On this basis, the constitution and principles of Islam might be compatible, and he wrote in his preamble that Islam is the religion of the state, just as is the case in most Arab Islamic countries[33] in the event that these laws might not express this spirit and come to be dissociated from it. Al-Bannā is not restricted to attempting to cover this style of analysis of the constitution: declaring its theoretical principles, then their incompatibility with dissociated operational laws; rather, he goes further than bringing the laws into orbit and adjusting them to the authoritative reference point (*marja'īyah*) of the constitutional principles. He goes to the assertion – frankly – that in the Qur'ān there are sufficient laws to be put in place and promulgated, and its single law is that which springs from its rulings (*min aḥkāmihī*) and the Prophetic *sunnah*.[34]

Is there a contradiction in this?

Decisively not; in it there is a logical steadfastness and harmony with the initial presumptions put forth about it as, when we consider the constitutional system and the Islamic system to be one and the same, the assertion follows that positive laws are promulgated as an expression of the principles of the constitution and it is not possible except if they are Islamic, and if not, then they do not express anything of the spirit of the law or its founding principles.

***

Tethered to the defense of the constitution and the constitutional system in the texts of Ḥasan al-Bannā is the defense of the parliamentary representational system as a branch is connected to a root and an effect to its cause. However, the connection is nourished – also – by the drastic political need of al-Bannā and the Muslim Brotherhood for a sphere of political participation from a higher position: from a position of approbate stability. It was a need called for by the masses of the Muslim Brotherhood during the 1930s and in the beginning of the 1940s, to not follow the path of revolution and violence, and to respect the line of peaceful political work, just as it called for considering the proportion of benefits – or political benefit – that would accrue from proceeding to power via the path of elections and representation. This is a fact which is impossible to overlook in realizing the measure of realistic political perception with which Ḥasan al-Bannā was inculcated despite the stamp of an idealist or sacrosanct preacher which many thereafter him would confer upon him!

In marked contrast to his position with regard to the origins of the constitutional concept – which he reckoned as being Islamic and not alien – he acknowledged that the *origin* of the parliamentary system was foreign. If he asserted that 'It is among the rights of the Islamic *ummah* to supervise the ruler with the utmost censure, and to indicate to him what they perceive to be good, then it is incumbent upon him to consult them and to honor their desires…', then this does not suffice – other Islamist thinkers – on the account of this being a matter which is considered a principle of (Islamic) evaluation of the ruler. Rather, he goes to the assertion – in a candid indication of the foreign source of this principle: 'The "Islamic system" in this context – does not signify either forms or names when these basic founding principles are realized whereby rule is not sound without them,' ending in the extremely unambiguous acknowledgement that 'in [the period of] our modern life, we transferred from Europe this parliamentary system which now persists under the auspices of our governments.'[35] It is – for the record or to be honest – an audacious, decisive acknowledgement, the like of which is not found in many of those who attribute either themselves or their thought to Ḥasan al-Bannā among contemporary Islamist intellectuals.

If al-Bannā affirms that 'there is nothing in the foundations of this parliamentary system that contradicts the foundations which Islam put in place for the system of rule,'[36] he inclines to proving that through mention of 'techniques' of enlisting (*ishrāk*) the *ummah* in rule, and he emphasizes that Islam 'was not conditioned on the solicitation of the opinion of all its members in every instance (lit., 'descent')'. It is a general expression of what in modern terminology is a public referendum. However, in normal circumstances, the 'people of authority' (*ahl al-ḥal wa al-ʿaqd*) are sufficient.[37] If this indication from him does not diminish the matter of the referendum, to some degree it confirms the principle of representation, but if so, it brings into question the matter of the connection of representation to the 'people of authority' and the significance of this group as to who they are and how this particular group is composed.

Al-Bannā does not hide the fact that Islam did not put forth an authoritatively referential definition for these people (i.e., the *ahl al-ḥal wa al-ʿaqd*), 'and it did not appoint them by name or by their persons', but he covers this gap by drawing upon the assertions of the *fuqahāʾ* and enlisting them in the '*ijtihād*' that describes them as: 'being composed of three groups: 1) the *mujtahidūn* of the *fuqahāʾ* whose assertions can be depended upon in *fatwas* and matters of implementation of the rulings (*al-aḥkām*); 2) the people of experience (*ahl al-khibrah*) in general matters; 3) whoever has a position as a leader or chief among people...all of these may be correctly subsumed under the rubric of 'the people of authority' (*ahl al-ḥal wa al-ʿaqd*).'

Along the lines of the Islamic Reformers in the nineteenth century, he concludes a marriage between the 'people of the authority' (*ahl al-ḥal wa al-ʿaqd*) and the representatives of the *ummah* in the parliament when he writes: 'The modern parliamentary system establishes the protocol for arriving at the people of authority (*ahl al-ḥal wa al-ʿaqd*) through what the constitutional *fuqahāʾ* put in place of systems of elections and their various means,' with the result that, 'this system ought not be declined so long as it leads to the choice of the people of authority (*ahl al-ḥal wa al-ʿaqd*).'[38]

However, the problem of Ḥasan al-Bannā stems from the basis that he does not defend the parliamentary system as he does the constitution and does not take his defense of it to a logical end as it may readily be discovered that his acknowledgement of this parliamentary system is a *conditional acknowledgement*; that is, it hinges on the basis of providing the necessary condition which is the absence of partisanship (*al-ḥizbīyah*) or, in contemporary parlance, the multiplicity of political parties.[39] So how, then, are we able to conceive of a parliamentary political system – structured on electoral partisan competition – without political parties?

This, in fact, is the primary problem among all problems in the thought of Ḥasan al-Bannā and in his political conception of the system of the 'Islamic state'.

The Multiplicity of Political Parties or the Specter of Civil Strife (al-Fitnah)

Al-Bannā's position rested on a convulsive rejection of partisanship (*al-ḥizbīyah*) in general and of it in Egypt in particular. He does that in spite of his candid admission that the *Ikhwān al-Muslimīn* is a particular political group – alongside its concern for the religion and creed – in the state and the political system.[40] And, in that, he exceeds others in what will permit it for himself, obliged, against his will, to present a negative picture of it and of its political program due to his conflict, rather his endeavor to pulverize the very political measure of that which he attempts to defend in his defense of constitutional rule and the system of parliamentary representation!

In concert with the logic of his call, from the standpoint of peaceful, political gradualism,[41] al-Bannā defends reform and Reformist methodology in political, conceptual and educational work and in building society and the state; and in all of what he defends of 'reform', 'the overcoming of (political) partisanship and the orienting of the political forces of the *ummah* towards a united front and single line…'[42] He does not hesitate in calling upon the (Egyptian) political parties to join the ranks of the Muslim Brotherhood in order 'to unite under the banner of the mighty Qur'ān'; enjoining them to respond and thus be 'the best of them and the most pleased in the life of the world and the afterlife', and admonishing that 'appealing to them would shorten the time and the [required] efforts'; and threatening them that if they refused, they would be 'compelled to act for the call (*al-da'wah*) as minions while they could act for it as leaders!'[43] Is this 'Reformist' in any respect; or is it moderate? What is it that drove al-Bannā to this nihilistic position, this hostile stance towards political partisanship and parties?

There are, in reality, numerous reasons wherein political obstruction is mixed with creedal, and both intervene in what precludes for him the making of a distinction or separation. We distill from among these two reasons: the first pertains to the conviction of al-Bannā of the effects and results of political partisanship in national society; and the second to what he believes is in conflict between partisanship and the idea of unity of the *ummah* in Islam and a threat of *fitnah* (strife) to its system.

We read from al-Bannā, in regard to the first aspect:

> The Muslim Brotherhood believes that all Egyptian political parties came into existence under special conditions, and most of these were personal…and the Brotherhood, similarly, believes that this partisanship has corrupted for the people all aspects of their lives and hindered their interests, twisted their morals and torn asunder their connections, and that it has had in their general and private lives, the worst possible effect.[44]

Thus, political partisanship, in what he sees, has been nothing more than political investment in building personal success, and that it has yet to have any effect other than hindering production, distracting people, corrupting values and tearing the social fabric that is unified about the concept of the *ummah* and the group; and, thus, it has not been of any benefit worth noting. In regard to the second aspect, we read in al-Bannā:

> The [Muslim] Brotherhood believes that there is a difference between freedom of opinion and thought, clarification and elucidation, and *al-shūrā* and advice – and that is what Islam obligates – and between fanaticism of opinion (*al-taʿaṣṣub li-l-raʾīy*) and departing from the group, and concerted effort to widen the chasm of schism in the *ummah* and exacerbate the tempest about the power of the rulers; and this is all brought on by political partisanship. Islam refuses this and forbids it in the sternest of terms.[45]

Political partisanship – in this conception – is not the sum of political rights for individuals and groups, and it is not a manifestation among manifestations of the right of free expression or freedom of opinion; rather, it is an analog of fanaticism, rebelliousness and insurrection against the opinion of the group, and it is a tempest in terms of political stability. It is, for these reasons, religiously forbidden, or one might say that the standpoint of rejection of it is not only a political position, but rather an *Islamic legal* position as well.

Despite the fact that Ḥasan al-Bannā attempts to dodge the liability of apparent hostility towards political partisanship because of political competition – especially that which was ongoing with the Ḥizb al-Wafd – his call for the obligation to dissolve these political parties was not ever for the sake of the interest of Egypt, as might be inferred, but rather it was for the sake of clearing the field for *one* party and that was the Muslim Brotherhood movement, or to form a political group sphere wherein the Movement would occupy the central position of leadership.[46] Thus, the similarity of Ḥasan al-Bannā to those groups calling for a single party – Egyptian Communists being among these – has the effect of putting question marks about all the support and loyalty that he intimates in his texts for the modern political system: this is what cannot be reconciled – either selectively or comparatively – between its principles and what al-Bannā and others did.

If some of the symbolic representatives of the second, moderate generation of thinkers of the Muslim Brotherhood attempted to rectify this conception from the legacy of the Brotherhood in reviewing the position of al-Bannā and defending multiplicity of political parties, or rather attempting to re-root these from within the authoritative referent of the *sharīʿah*,[47] then it is within our capacity to understand the reason for that glaring contradiction upon which the discourse of al-Bannā about the state rested and which pushed him to vacillation between a strident defense of the constitution and the representative system and between an even stronger attack on political partisanship and political pluralism. We posit that the reason for this is his conception of 'the group' (*al-jamāʿah*)[48] and the *ummah*: this group – unified in the creed of Islam – deserves a constitution to ensconce the principles of its religion in rule and laws that correlate to its *sharīʿah*, as well as a representative system that sets apart the *ahl al-ḥal wa al-ʿaqd* (people of authority). These are all acceptable means to enable the group and the *ummah* to attain to a system of rule which is expressive of its identity as a group – rather, which is demanded and desired. However, that does not correlate to multiplicity of political parties in any way, shape or form. If we leave aside the matter of political sanction, where there was no benefit for al-Bannā in the existence of political parties competing with the Brotherhood in their turn and their social representation, then the main reason which drove him to the position that he took with regard to political partisanship was a *religious* reason: the fear of breaking apart the unity of the group, dividing it, and drowning it in *fitnah* (strife).

Without tarnishing the image of Ḥasan al-Bannā or casting doubt on his political calculations in distinguishing between the constitutional question and representation and between the question of political pluralism, it is possible to assert decisively that what he did in his division between them was reflective, in its essence, of what would occur after him in the experience of the exercise of power – from the standpoint of the Arab and Islamic ruling elites, and especially since the beginning of the second half of the twentieth century. The reality of the matter would confirm that these elites would be able to accept the setting up of a constitution for these countries (an idealized constitution in some cases), that they would institute a parliamentary system and promulgate laws of election, and that voting for 'representatives' of the people or the *ummah* could take place and so on, and at the same time that they could prohibit political parties from existing![49]

Ḥasan al-Bannā was not only a sheikh practicing *fiqh* in the matters of creed and the *sharīʿah* who possessed boldness in the expression of what he saw as being a position in conformity with the *sharīʿah* in the matters of politics and leadership, he was, in addition to that, a political preacher with an ample measure of sophistication and cunning, realistic political ability, and even possessed of *pragmatic* inclinations. All of that helped him to produce political theses that would have the greatest effect on the masses during the twentieth century and which would establish one of the most vast mass political movements in the contemporary Islamic world with the inception of the Muslim Brotherhood. Just as his ideas would achieve success and overspill the borders of Egypt – reaching most of the Arab-Islamic countries, so would the political movement that emerged from the Egyptian national context become a popular, worldwide organization. Few things would bear greater witness to his ability to forge a rare marriage between the temporal and the holy the like of which neither ancients nor moderns had been previously able to effect.

The subject of the Islamic state in the thought of al-Bannā is itself alone an indication of what has been emphasized: that he took it from Rashīd Riḍā after modification (transforming it from a *khilāfah* which was sacrosanct but obstructed into an Islamic state that was practical and realistic);[50] however, he saw in this that the call for Islamic law and obligation did not correspond to politics and the possible, and immediately commenced researching this 'state' the matter of which had come to prominence in a society invaded and attacked by Modernity – political and cultural, after the invasion of colonialism. Thus, he did not find the object of his search among the subjects of the Islamic Reformers who had preceded him by a quarter of a century, and while he did not stray far from the course they charted, he made a decisive break while still drawing from it fruits that would be employed in his writings on the constitutional idea and representational democracy.

Does this mean that the 'Islamic state' according to al-Bannā – is analogous to the significance of the 'nation state' in the thinking of the Reformers?

No. It is a constitutional state, taken from the (parliamentary) representative system, except that the source of authority in it is the Islamic *sharī'ah*. It is a state of the *sharī'ah*, and the *sharī'ah* has not ceased to be the 'constitution' of Muslims in regulating their civil and political societies in his opinion.

Notes

1. Jad'ān, *al-Māḍī fī al-Ḥāḍir*, p. 137.
2. Mitchell, Richard P., *The Society of Muslim Brothers,* translated by 'Abd al-Salām Raḍwān & Munā Anīs (Cairo: Maktabat Madbūlī, 1977), vol. 2.
3. Al-Bannā says: 'The Muslim Brotherhood believes that the *khilāfah* is the symbol of Islamic unity, and a feature for the connection of Islamic states, it is an Islamic

ritual that Muslims contemplate and in which they should take an interest. The caliph has many rules in the religion of Allah...*ḥadīth* that were cited in the context of instating the imam, explicating the rules of the *imāmah* and expounding what is relevant to it – leaving no doubt that it is the Muslims' duty to think of the issue of their *khilāfah* from the times when it was distorted, passing through the times when it was revoked, and up to now. For this reason, the Muslim Brotherhood makes the idea of *khilāfah* and the endeavors to restore it the main point in their approach; they believe that it requires some preliminary steps to achieve it and the direct step for re-establishing it requires some preceding ones beforehand: furthermore, there has to be a social and economic cooperation between all Islamic peoples, then the forging of alliances and treaties, holding symposia and conferences between them...and the establishment of a league of Islamic nations, until then Muslims can choose an imam who is the medium of this contract....and *ẓil Allāh fī al-'arḍ* (the shadow of Allah on earth)'. Available in: Al-Bannā, Ḥasan, *Majmū'at Rasā'il al-Imām al-Shahīd Ḥasan al-Bannā* (Beirut: al-Mu'asasah al-Islāmīyah, [n.d]), pp. 178–9.

4. Jad'ān, *al-Māḍī fī al-Ḥāḍir*, p. 137.

5. Al-Bannā, Ḥasan, *Majmū'at Rasā'il*, p. 211.

6. Al-Mubārak, Muḥammad, *Niẓām al-Islām: al-Ḥukm wa al-Dawlah*, 4th edn (Beirut: Dār al-Fikr, 1981), pp. 12–18.

7. In the history of the debate about numerous issues in Islam including that of authority, questions arose concerning categorization among the *fuqahā'*, *'ulamā'* and others as to where to assign particular matters – and at the most basic level as to whether they pertained to the *uṣūl* – the original sources and literally 'roots' – of the religion (*al-dīn*) or creed (*al-'aqīdah*) or whether they were 'derivative' and, thus, pertained to the *furū'* or 'branches' of the religion or creed. Within a given *madhab* (Islamic school of law), matters judged to be among the *uṣūl* were not open to debate as they were understood to be matters of consensus (*al-ijmā'*) as opposed to matters of the *furū'* which could ultimately be the product of human interpretation in *ijtihād*, and thus, at least in theory, subject to reinterpretation or discussion. As discussed by the author throughout the book, assigning a matter such as the obligation to establish a political authority or 'state' to the *uṣūl* has definite implications for Muslims – especially in terms of their Islamic legal 'culpability' (*al-taklif*) and responsibility. Thus, for example, if a matter such as *jihad* or the imamate (*al-imāmah*) is subsumed under and considered to be among the *uṣūl* – as is the case with the Shī'ah, in general, then the assertion of the necessity of these becomes identical or tantamount to *belief* in the religion or creed itself. –Translator.

8. Al-Bannā, Ḥasan, *Majmū'at Rasā'il*, p. 170.

9. Two recurrent issues in *fiqh* and pertinent to this debate are whether or not a matter is obligatory and thus expressed in technical terms as *farḍ* or *wājib* (as in this case); and also whether or not it pertains to the *individual* Muslim or to the Muslim *group* (*al-jamā'ah*). The individual Muslim is obliged to discharge certain duties such as prayer (*al-ṣalāt*) and alms (*al-zakāt*); however, there may be other potential duties which cannot be performed by a Muslim individually. – Translator.

10. Mabrūk, Muḥammad Ibrāhīm, *Mūwājahat al-Mūwājahah* (Cairo: Dār Thābit, 1994), p. 51.

11. Here, the crux of the matter with which the author takes issue – as well as his legitimate basis for hesitation – in his criticism is apparent. That is, close reading suggests that al-Qaraḍāwī in this has, at one and the same, time 'reversed' his previous position, albeit through a sort of categorical subterfuge. That is, an individual Muslim's 'conviction' and 'faith' in the necessity of establishing a system of Islamic rule (which is

among the *furū'*) effectively subsumes this system under the *uṣūl* (and the creed) by extension – due to the fact that Al-Qaraḍāwī considers this to be, in fact, a matter of faith where any who denies the 'obligatory status' of it is a *kāfir*. – Translator.

12. Al-Qaraḍāwī, *al-Sīyāsah al-Shar'īyah*, pp. 16–17.

13. Al-Bannā, Ḥasan, *Majmū'at Rasā'il*, p. 72.

14. Quṭb, Muḥammad, *al-'Ilmānyūn wa al-Islām* (Cairo; Beirut: Dār al-Shurūq, 1994), pp. 11–17.

15. 'Distortion was not limited in the scope of creed alone – which is, itself, very dangerous – but, it beset another issue which is the separation of creed from *sharī'ah* and presenting religion to people as a creed with no legislation! This in fact had serious impact on life in Europe...socially, politically, economically, and intellectually...'. Available in: Quṭb, Muḥammad, *al-'Ilmānyūn wa al-Islām*, p. 10.

16. Muḥammad Quṭb states: 'Europe never knew the real religion of God that was revealed to Jesus son of Mary, but rather knew a distorted image, which was propagated by the apostle Paul who spread it in the earth, especially Europe'. Also he says: 'We Muslims are not the ones who said that the religion that Europe espoused is not the one already revealed to Jesus by God, this is acknowledged by their own historians and writers...'. Available in: Quṭb, Muḥammad, *al-'Ilmānyūn wa al-Islām*, pp. 7 and 10 respectively.

17. 'As a result of this schizophrenia, some people posit the term "men of religion" as a counterpart to that other term – "men of state" or "politics" or "knowledge"; however, Islamic reason did not know the idea of "men of religion" as the Christian West did, but rather it knows "the scholars of religion" who are specialized in studying and understanding it. After all, every Muslim is a man of his own religion.' Available in: Al-Qaraḍāwī, *al-Ḥilūl al-Mustawradah wa kayfa janat 'alā Ummatinā*, Silsilat Ḥatmīyat al-Ḥal al-Islāmī; (Beirut: Mu'asasah al-Risālah, 1971), p. 48.

18. This may be clearly noticed in: Al-Qaraḍāwī, *al-Sīyāsah al-Shar'īyah*.

19. Al-Qaraḍāwī, *al-Ṣaḥwah al-Islāmīyah* (Cairo: Dār al-Ṣaḥwah, 1988), p. 188.

20. Al-Qaraḍāwī, *al-Ṣaḥwah*, p. 189.

21. Al-Bannā, Ḥasan, *Majmū'at Rasā'il*, p. 172.

22. Al-Qaraḍāwī, *min Fiqh al-Dawlah fī al-Islām* (Cairo; Beirut: Dār al-Shurūq, 1997), p. 32.

23. Al-Qaraḍāwī, *min Fiqh al-Dawlah*, p. 33.

24. Al-Qaraḍāwī, *min Fiqh al-Dawlah*, p. 33.

25. Mitchell, *The Society of Muslim Brothers*.

26. The grassroots shifted from half a million in 1945 to one million in 1946, to two million in 1948 and 1949 in favor of the Muslim Brotherhood. Available in: Carré, Olivier, *Mystique et Politique: Lecture Révolutionnairre du Coran par Sayyid Qutub, Frère Musulman radical, Patrimoines Islam* (Paris: Cerf; Presses de la Fondation Nationale des Sciences Politique, 1984), p. 8.

27. Al-Bannā, Ḥasan, *Majmū'at Rasā'il*, p. 69.

28. Al-Bannā, Ḥasan, *Majmū'at Rasā'il*, p. 69.

29. Al-Bannā, Ḥasan, *Majmū'at Rasā'il*, p. 70.

30. Al-Bannā, Ḥasan, *Majmū'at Rasā'il*, p. 172.

31. Al-Bannā, Ḥasan, *Majmū'at Rasā'il*, p. 172.

32. Al-Bannā stresses this distinction to the supporters of the Muslim Brotherhood in his last message in the Fifth Conference of the movement. Available in: Al-Bannā, Ḥasan, *Majmū'at Rasā'il*, p. 172.

33. Jad'ān writes of the reasons for the rise of the Islamist current: 'One of the impacts of this current that the modern Islamic states urged to integrate is the clause

of "the religion of the state is Islam" in their charters and constitutions, or to consider *sharīʿah* as one of the sources for legislation, even if it is not the "main source" for that given state.' Available in: Jadʿān, *al-Māḍī fī al-Ḥāḍir*, pp. 137–8.

34. 'Islam did not come without regulations or rules, and much legislation was addressed, whether financial or criminal, mercantile or international. The Qur'ān and *ḥadīth* are replete with what indicate these; books of jurists also address these various aspects; foreigners and non-Muslims themselves admitted this fact and acknowledged it at the Hague Convention before representatives in the field of law from around the world. Thus, it would be illogical for an Islamic state to have a law that is contradictory to the rules of its religion and text of the Qur'ān and *sunnah*.' Available in: Al-Bannā, Ḥasan, *Majmūʿat Rasāʾil*, p. 173.

35. Al-Bannā, Ḥasan, *Majmūʿat Rasāʾil*, p. 213.

36. Al-Bannā, Ḥasan, *Majmūʿat Rasāʾil*, p. 216.

37. Al-Bannā, Ḥasan, *Majmūʿat Rasāʾil*, p. 222.

38. Al-Bannā, Ḥasan, *Majmūʿat Rasāʾil*, p. 222.

39. 'Scholars in constitutional *fiqh* maintain that the parliamentary system depends on the responsibility of the ruler, the authority of *ummah,* and the respect of its free will, and nothing deters it from having the *ummah* unified...even if some might claim that one of the pillars of the parliamentary system is partisanship, this is a *tradition* and *not* a fundamental issue in the establishment of such a system since it can be implemented without all of this partisanship and alteration of its fundamental bases.' Available in: Al-Bannā, Ḥasan, *Majmūʿat Rasāʾil*, pp. 215–16.

40. Al-Bannā says: 'He is terribly wrong whoever thinks that the Muslim Brotherhood is a group of dervishes, who confine themselves to a constricted locus of Islamic rituals, where all their concern is simply for prayer, fasting, and supplication. The first Muslims did not understand Islam this way...they conceived of it as a practical and spiritual system at one and the same time, so they had a state and a religion, a *muṣḥaf* (of the Qur'ān) and a sword.' Available in: Al-Bannā, Ḥasan, *Majmūʿat Rasāʾil*, p. 78.

41. Al-Bannā, Ḥasan, *Majmūʿat Rasāʾil*, pp. 155–61.

42. Al-Bannā, Ḥasan, *Majmūʿat Rasāʾil*, p. 74.

43. Al-Bannā, Ḥasan, *Majmūʿat Rasāʾil*, p. 159.

44. Al-Bannā, Ḥasan, *Majmūʿat Rasāʾil*, p. 180.

45. Al-Bannā, Ḥasan, *Majmūʿat Rasāʾil*, pp. 180–1.

46. 'The Muslim Brotherhood does not perpetuate a feud with any party for its own, they believe that the best option for Egypt is to have all of these parties dissolved, and to form an effective national assembly that leads the *ummah* in light of instructions in the Qur'ān.' Available in: Al-Bannā, Ḥasan, *Majmūʿat Rasāʾil*, p. 181.

47. Al-Qaraḍāwī writes: 'The multi-party system in politics resembles multi-sectarianism in *fiqh*'. He also writes: 'Parties are sects in politics, as sects are parties in *fiqh*.' Al-Qaraḍāwī disagrees with al-Bannā when he states: 'I know for certain that the martyr Imam al-Bannā denied partisanship and the multi-party system in Islam due to the partisanship he witnessed that had ripped *ummah* into pieces before its enemy. It is an *ijtihād* on his part – may he rest in peace; our *ijtihād* may disagree with his as he did not impose upon those who came after him to make *ijtihād* such as his, especially due to changing and developing circumstances and thoughts. Maybe, he would alter his *fatwas* if he lived in our times, as *fatwas* change with changes in time and place and manner, especially in the ever-changing matters of politics.' Available in: Al-Qaraḍāwī, *min Fiqh al-Dawlah*, pp. 151, 153 and 157 respectively.

48. Regarding the concept of the *jamā'ah* – 'the group' in Islam, see: Al-Sayyid, *al-Ummah wa al-Jamā'ah*, pp. 125–45, and Al-Sayyid, *al-Jamā'ah wa al-Mujtama'*, pp. 39–48.

49. This is in addition to some of those who unabashedly implement and assert the concept of 'whoever rallies, soon betrays'.

50. Those who are skeptical about the possibility of establishing an Islamic state – indeed – are ignoring substantially the example of Iran since the rise of its Revolution over twenty years ago, and partially the two examples of Afghanistan and the Sudan.

Chapter 7

The State and *al-Sharīʿah* in the Criticism of the Secular Idea

> The sultan has contended with the Qurʾān and forsaken it in our history since the earliest times; and the matter of the *ummah* will not be rectified nor brought together except through the mending the rift between the *sharīʿah* of the Qurʾān and the restraint of the sultan.
>
> ʿAbd al-Salām Yāsīn

The *Sharīʿah* of the State

We have analyzed the discourse of Ḥasan al-Bannā and some of his pupils in regard to two central subjects in the construction of the understanding of the 'Islamic state' in that discourse.[1] The first of them is the subject of the thesis of the necessity of the state in Islam. The second of them is the subject of the thesis of the belonging of the matter of the state and rule to creed (*ʿaqīdah*) and the *uṣūl* as opposed to the interpretive judgments of *fiqh* (*al-fiqhīyāt*) and the derivative branches (*al-furūʿ*). Between the two subjects is a connection, rather they are almost expressive of the same thing: that the state is a *necessity* in Islam; meaning that it is *not* among the optional acts of worship (*al-nawāfil*) but rather is among the *mandatory* and *obligatory* acts (*al-furūḍ wa al-wājibāt*). That the matter should be among the *uṣūl* of Islam means that its necessity and obligatory nature are among the fundamental axioms of the religion. This connection between the two subjects was made clear in the consciousness of those advocating them when we presented the clarification of the relation between the state and the *sharīʿah* in Islam along the lines of what it signifies for those calling for the idea of the 'Islamic state' among contemporary Islamists.

Yūsuf al-Qaraḍāwī transmits proofs of the comprehensiveness of Islam and its teachings in the political arena, and the system of rule and the state in his book *Min Fiqh al-Dawlah fī-l-Islām* (*On the Fiqh of the State in Islam*).[2] Among the proofs are four primary ones and these are: first 'the proof from the texts (*nuṣūṣ*) of Islam';[3] second, 'the proof from the history of Islam'[4] where he turns to the experience of the Prophetic state in Medina;[5] third, 'the proof from the nature of Islam', where he emphasizes the need of Islam in order for it to express its attendant teachings in organization and responsibility; and fourth, 'the need for the state to embrace Islam', and that is need which is elucidated in another text on another occasion: 'Islam, even if its texts did not directly express the obligation of establishing a state for it, it is in need of a state – there is no doubt about it.'[6]

What concerns us among these 'proofs' for our subject are the third and the fourth: the need of Islam for a state to 'express its teachings' and its need for a state 'to embrace it', that is to defend it and to spread its message. Islamic *sharī'ah* has a relation to both needs: in the first, it is upon the basis of the state needing to engage in the obligation of implementing its rulings in the land(s) of Islam,[7] and upon those belonging to its creed, on the account of its rulings, needing a political authority to engage in the obligation to spread the message of Islam in 'the worlds' (*al-'ālamīn*), and the transformation of the rulings (*aḥkām*) of *al-sharī'ah* into universal law (*qānūn kawnī*) instead of the protection of Islam itself from within by surrounding itself within the law of *al-sharī'ah* inside its *ḥawzah*. Both cases purport to the same fact – in the opinion of al-Qaraḍāwī – and the call for the 'Islamic state' – and that is the conclusion that Islam endorses the rulings (*aḥkām*) of its *sharī'ah* and enjoins all Muslims to operate according to its dictates; it imposes the state *as an instrument* to implement these rulings. Thus, the *sharī'ah* is the basis of the Islamic state and the source of the legitimacy of the political system in it.

This conclusion does not leave any scope for – or significance to – questioning the extent of the compulsory nature (*ilzāmīyah*) of the rulings of Islamic *sharī'ah*; that is, 'The original state in the life of this *ummah*,' says Muḥammad Quṭb, 'is that the divine *sharī'ah* is the *ḥākimīyah* (ruling authority)[8] in it, without there being any need to demand that of either an individual or a group because it is a divine obligation (*ilzām rabbānī*).' And along these lines, 'the arbitration (*taḥkīm*) of *al-sharī'ah* is not a matter of choice for people and they are consulted for their opinion.'[9] Thus, the Islamic state is a demand for 'rule (*al-ḥukm*) by what Allah sent down', and it is, in this, unique among all other types of states according to Mūnīr Shafīq.[10] This is that its role exceeds the bounds of what are known of human attempts to make it an instrument for social systemization only, if 'what the state legislates,' says 'Allāl al-Fāsī, 'is nothing except for the good (*maṣlaḥah*) of the religion, and what it has made as the *khilāfah* is only for the execution of the rulings of the *sharīʿah*'[11].

The Islamic state is not a state for the *sharīʿah*, and the *sharīʿah* of this state is not Islamic *sharīʿah* except for a consciousness that constructs bonds and bridges between religion and the world – between creed (*ʿaqīdah*) and *sharīʿah*. The connection between them is incomprehensible except from the standpoint that it is a relation of communication and connection not a relation of segregation and separation along the lines of the position taken in the theses of a large segment among secularist intellectuals. This is because defending the idea of the connection between religion and politics (and society), between creed and *sharīʿah*, and the defense of the obligation to 'implement Islamic *sharīʿah*' was – in one of its aspects – an attack on those asserting the separation between religion and politics (the state). It might, due to its nature, take the form of a contest or debate between the advocates for the implementation of the *sharīʿah* – from among the contemporary Islamist thinkers – and the advocates for the separation between the state and politics from religion among those termed 'secularists'[12] or 'Laicists' as the Islamist preacher sheikh 'Abd al-Salām Yāsīn prefers to call them.

A Debate Against the Secular Idea

The first recorded Islamic writings against the idea of secularism go back to Jamāl al-Dīn al-Afghānī in his rebuttal of the 'Naturalists' (*al-Dahrīyīn*) in India and to the debate of Muḥammad 'Abdūh with Faraḥ Anthon. That debate, in its early stages, is considerably less fanatical for two reasons. The first is that those who openly entertained the idea of a separation between religion and the state were in a minority which did not merit much consideration, and its subject matter did not constitute a danger to the prevailing Islamic system of thought – in the nineteenth century. The second reason was that Islamic Reformism was not entirely removed from the assertion, in one way or another, of the separation between the religious sphere and the political sphere in what was advanced about the relation between the two,[13] especially in its understanding of the nation state. However, this debate would witness an increasing sharpness from the 1930s onwards and would reach the threshold of ripping apart the Arab-Islamic consciousness and precipitating a conceptual civil war, among the ranks of the elites, from which it has yet to emerge, even to this day.[14]

Advocates of the connection between the state and religion emerge from a conceptual creed which dictates the concomitance of their essences – self-identifying the two, and the impossibility of considering creed as something outside the sphere of Islamic society and outside the obligations of its systemization according to creedal requirements and the necessity of submitting to them. They, for that reason, see that whoever calls for separation between the two wants, in the expression of Yūsuf al-Qaraḍāwī:[15] 'spiritual Islam (*al-islām al-rūhī*)' or 'priestly Islam (*al-islām al-kahanūtī*) which is epitomized in the recitation of the Qur'ān for the dead, not for the living, and which seeks blessing in decorating the walls with its verses, or opening concerts and gatherings with reading what is easy from it, and then leaving Caesar to rule according to whatever he wants and do whatever he desires.'[16] This is what is not permissible, in his view, because Islam is 'a method and worship and morals and practices, and law and orientation, and brotherhood and organization' because it 'is one in its connections which do not permit division'.[17] The challenge takes sheikh al-Qaraḍāwī to the position where he asserts that Islam, from the standpoint of its comprehensiveness and completeness, 'is directed towards...the individual Muslim in his personal, family, social and political life from the etiquette of high morals to the primacy of rule, and the relations of peace and war.'[18]

This defense belongs to the concept of the *comprehensiveness* of Islam in *both* religious and temporal spheres, and of the concept of the necessity of the submission of the temporal sphere to the rulings (*aḥkām*) of the *sharī'ah*, in the perpetual ideational struggle between the concept of secularism and its representatives among contemporary Arab and Muslim intellectuals. It is not possible to comprehend the tremendous shock which was precipitated by Ṭāhā Ḥussayn's book *al-Shi'r al-Jāhilī* (*Poetry of the Jāhilīyah*) or *al-Islām wa Uṣūl al-Ḥukm* (*Islam and the Origins of Rule*) of 'Alī 'Abd al-Rāziq on the *'ulamā'* of al-Azhar, except by describing it as a seminal moment in the long struggle between the advocates of the 'Islamic state' and the advocates of the 'secular state', or so the first would assume, at least, even if the latter did not agree with them necessarily in this assessment of theirs.[19] The struggle took this as a known point of departure: the accusation of the intellectuals calling for the separation between the state and religion of putting into circulation an intruding Western concept in the thought of Islam and its historical experience in which Islamic *sharī'ah* was the authoritative referent for politics and rule and the basis for the judiciary (*al-qaḍā'*) and *fatwas;*[20] where this idea reflects the non-religious character of the state, and that is basis for the consideration of the state as 'natural/atheistic' (*dahrīyah*) – to use the expression of the nineteenth century – or temporal/historical (*zamanīyyah*) and secular in contemporary parlance.

There is no doubt that three factors had the most decisive of roles in the magnitude of the apprehension (obsession) about the defense of the *sharī'ah* and the obligation to implement it among the elites of contemporary thinkers, and especially since the founding of the movement of the Muslim Brotherhood (*Ikhwān al-Muslimīn*) at the end of the 1920s. The first of these factors was the fall of the Arab and Islamic countries into the grip of colonial occupation, and what radiated from that in the reinforcing of its political authority throughout its entities, and its submission of its political and administrative systems to positive law derived from an authoritative referent of Western, political and secular stamp, alienated from the logic of Islamic *sharī'ah*. Further, colonialism imposed this secular system 'from above', and 'the people, in that, had no choice...';[21] if it had not been for colonialism, this secular positivism would not have been able to compete with the *sharī'ah*, or to remove it from its place at the center of power and referential authority (*al-marja'īyah*)[22] which had persisted for thirteen centuries.

The problem was not restricted to the colonial interregnum only, but rather it persisted after it; that is, after the evacuation of direct foreign colonization. The Arab and Islamic, which had surrendered the political authority of the state, did nothing other than devise a method based on the same (colonial) method in the domain of positive laws and legislation: politics and civil society (*al-madanīyah*), and reproduced – through that – in the view of the Islamists – the secular system itself from the standpoint that it resulted in 'constraining religion to the mosques and some insignificant side-aspects of life'. In addition it imposed:

> the understanding of the Christian West on religion where it is only a relationship between the human being and his Lord, and it disseminated among people obscure and deviant slogans such as 'religion is for God and the nation is for all'...and in that it affirmed the despicable interfering colonial conception that religion has no concern in politics and that the state has no relation to religion.[23]

This was the first epoch for the countries of Islam of this tremendous upset which had taken them out of the realm of the authority of the *sharīʿah* and into the realm of secular authority and positive law.

The second of these factors was the splitting off of Turkey from the Islamic world and its choice of secularism as a political system for its state, as well as its success in acquiring legitimacy for itself 'by the edge of the sword'.[24] Among the results of that was that building would begin along the lines of the Turkish precedent in some of the Islamic countries – even if some of the elites did not possess the public audacity of Mustafa Kemal Atatürk – when their countries endorsed positive laws that replaced the rulings (*aḥkām*) of the *sharīʿah*, which was pigeonholed into the narrow corner of personal status law.[25]

As for the third of these factors, it was the ascendancy of an explicit secular discourse incapable of defending its positivist issues on behalf of a large segment among Arab intellectuals in the second quarter of the twentieth century. This factor might be the most important of the three, especially because of its role in mobilizing its Islamic adversary, or due to the fierce reaction it (i.e., the secular discourse) instigated, and which constituted a genuine factor in provoking the appeal to the socio-cultural authenticity (*al-aṣālah*) of the religion and the *sharīʿah*. This provocation did not attach to the defense of the separation between the religion and the state alone, as other Islamist intellectuals had done that, but rather it attached also to the defense of the Western civilization and culture and the attack on the civilization of Islam. So, when Salāmah Mūsā, for example, asserts that the exegesis of contemporary Arab man whose '...history does not go back more than five hundred years, when the Europeans legislated, depending upon scientific knowledge instead of inherited creeds';[26] or when he says 'the worst of what I fear is that we will be victorious over the colonizers and expel them, and that we will be victorious over the exploiters and restrain them, but that we will be unable to rout the Middle Ages from our lives and we will revert to the call: "Return to the ancients."';[27] or when Zakī Najīb Maḥmūd says that 'There is no hope in our contemporary conceptual life unless we decisively sever the heritage (*al-turāth*) and live alongside with those who are living in our age...'.[28] In this is what is really a genuine provocation[29] of the contrary sentiments of the Islamists and their religious zeal.

Perhaps, this liberal secular trend was unambiguous about its Western cultural allegiance, and moreover, it is accounted – in the view of the Islamists – according to the scope of its elite who are withdrawn from the masses of the surrounding cultural environment, and its effects, and who, for that reason, will not be – in the end – significantly detrimental to the society, the culture and the creed. The most major problem lies in Arab intellectuals, from a background of Islamic knowledge, and from among graduates of the great religious institutions who were affected by secular thoughts which drove them to treat as they did what they penned of texts about the political question in Islam. These[30] constitute a proof of the success of the operation of the Western cultural 'invasion' (*ghazw*) in arriving at its desired goal: pushing the Muslims to doubt their cultural religious identity, and positing the solution of their problems in the Western order of thought and politics!

Islamist discourse asserts that these do not resemble, in their danger, anything but those who take a position of hostility towards the West and colonialism emphatically asserting that they take the side of the ranks of the people and their culture; while what they are doing is to effect disintegration in the cultural and religious order for un-Islamic goals which they dare not declare openly for their fear of losing the trust of the people! That, for example, is what we read in sheikh 'Abd al-Salām Yāsīn in this context where he says:

> The secular danger which the people of faith must watch closely and guard against most vigilantly is not the secularism which is uncovered and baring its fangs...but it is the secularism of mirage phantom spots presented to Muslims which wears the garb of falsehood. It is the secularism of the 'geography of *al-kalām*' of the new cultural futurism; that which glorifies Islam and denounces Marxism and imperialism and ingratiates for itself a place among the masses![31]

It should be clarified that this critical remark goes on to blame a particular conceptual current, and that is the trend of contemporary cultural studies and the symbols of its founding icons including the likes of Mohammed Abed al-Jabri, Muḥammad Arkoun, and Ḥasan Ḥanafī;[32] and that is the same accusation which sheikh Yāsīn directs towards other Muslim politicians for whom he is in doubt in regard to their positions and the goals of their radical Islamic claims.[33]

The colonial invasion and its distorting effects on the political fabric of the state in Muslim countries; the secular precedent in Turkey as well as its political and psychological effects among the ruling elites in independent Islamic countries; and subsequently the ascendancy of the secular call in the midst of the liberal, left-wing and Islamic elites are the primary factors in the crystallization of the Islamist formulation of a defense of the *sharīʿah*, and a rebuttal of those advocating the separation between state and religion.

However, this debate is not possible except on two conditions: the condition of establishing a proof of a lack of potential benefit from the secular idea for society and state in Islamic lands; and the establishing of a proof that the execution of the rulings of the *sharī'ah* is, in fact, the execution of the *actual* rulings of the *sharī'ah* and not human, *fiqh* interpretations of *ijtihād* as asserted by those opposing the call for them. This is what we will address briefly in the following section.

***

Islamist discourse emerges, in its debating the call of its secular opponents demanding the separation of state and religion, as a result of its consideration that secularism is a philosophy unique to the West, expressive of the particulars of its historical and religious experience, and that the system existing on its basis is not compatible with the reality of political society in Islamic lands. Al-Qaraḍāwī is representative of the distinction, current among Islamist thinkers, that is posed between the science of the West and its technical capabilities and the philosophy of its political system. This distinction emphasizes the Islamic need for that science and those techniques as being what is indispensable in accounting science and technical capability as two formative bases for renaissance and that this is among that which bears no correlation to its culture and its values or to the mode of rule in them because this is not only lacking in an objective connection to the renaissance of the Muslims, but it actually may be an impediment to that renaissance! 'The philosophy of the West', says al-Qaraḍāwī:

> its system for life, its view of religion and the state...and its organizations, traditions and institutions – which are established on the basis of this philosophy and that 'ideological' view... are not among that which our Muslim East needs nor among that which will benefit it, but rather – decisively – among that which will harm and injure it.

That is not, in his opinion, for any reason other than that this Muslim East 'is not "an empty vessel" which accepts whatever is poured into it of the pure and impure, but rather it is a "full vessel" which has no space or capacity for anything new.'[34]

The Muslim East does not know any interstice in meaning, view and understanding – according to this view – in its conception of society and the state, to the extent that it is self-sufficient and can dispense with any example other than that of itself. Or, in more precise terms, in the context which concerns us here, it has a particular system of rule and that is the 'Islamic state' which derives its legitimacy from Islamic legislation (*al-*

tashrīʿ) – textually, and in *fiqh*, which has its particular laws that are compatible with it: the rulings (*aḥkām*) of the *sharīʿah*. And, moreover, it is not in need of borrowing from the secular political system which separates between the state and its religious support, and this is among that which is not commensurate with the teachings of Islam in the political sphere.

Islamist thinkers are not ignorant of the secular theoretical heritage and its modern political history in Europe, as might be incorrectly assumed. Rather, they have profound knowledge and extensive awareness in this regard,[35] and they understand very well why secularism developed a political philosophy in the West, or one may say, they understand why it was incumbent for it to develop in such a way in the prevailing Medieval European conditions. This is not to say that they have an understanding of its origin, but this does not broker justification or legitimacy for it.[36] Nevertheless, they concur that, whether it was beneficial or not for the West, it represents – in Islamic societies – a complete reversal of the teachings of Islam in the matter of politics and rule and their connection to creed. Thus, there is nothing which justifies the appeal of Arab or Muslim intellectuals to this idea, diametrically opposed to the logic of the creed, and that connotes nothing more than their Westernization and their fidelity to a foreign culture.

The debate does not stop at this point – at the point of a clarification of the alienation of secularism from the system of rule in Islam – on account of its being an idea cultivated in the soil of a civilization, culture and religion that is the West; but rather, it takes another step towards attempting to stultify secular propagandists through rebuttal of the arguments of their opposition to Islamic *sharīʿah* and a clarification of the decisiveness of this assertion with regard to the authoritative referent of this *sharīʿah* in systemizing the Islamic political sphere.

The Islamist advocate Muḥammad Quṭb knows well the opposition of secularists to the implementation of Islamic *sharīʿah* and the bases upon which they construct these objections as he writes:

> Among these is the thesis that there is nothing in reality which may be termed 'implementation of the *sharīʿah*' (*taṭbīq al-sharīʿah*) as what is implemented, in fact, is *not* the divine *sharīʿah*, but rather it is the human understanding of the text transmitted in the *sharīʿah*, and from this standpoint it is *human* legislation in reality! But, despite its human characteristic – it assumes for itself a sanctity deriving from divine inspiration (*al-waḥīy al-rabbānī*). And, it threatens by way of this sanctity, any who opposes it with accusations that they have gone out of the religion! Whereas exclusively human legislation,

> which human beings make by themselves – who are not affiliated by it to the religion – does not have any sanctity for those who promulgate it or those who oppose it. Therefore, it may be discussed freely and modified or cancelled if necessity dictates that without any fear or trepidation! On the basis of that, there follow two consequences: first, the impossibility of implementation of authority, and second, leaving human beings to legislate as they see fit, modifying and replacing, without any fear in what they propound or in allegations of apostasy from the religion.[37]

Despite the fact that Muḥammad Quṭb transmits the opinion of these opponents with a measure of objectivity, he does not find that which will permit him to respond to their position other than the assertion that differences in understanding and *ijtihād* are, in fact, what is not refuted in the matter of the text, and that these differences are intended (*maqṣūd*).[38] He finds it sufficient to indicate that these differences are not a vindication for mixing between *ijtihād* that constrained to Islamic legal constraints and another system entirely devoid of any restraints, in the name of public good (*al-maṣlaḥah*). Even if he confesses that the matter in regard to implementation of *al-sharīʿah* attaches in practice to *ijtihād* and not to a text in all cases, he asserts the unique place of *ijtihād* in the Islamic legal justification for it from the standpoint that it is *ijtihād* constrained by the strictures of Islam and concluding with the assertion of the legitimacy of the state in deciding between multiple interpretations of *ijtihād* and depending upon one of them – after ascertaining the opinion of the *fuqahāʾ* in that – according to his expression 'the law respected in its statutes and administrative and legal organizations.'[39]

If we leave the matter of *ijtihād* in promulgation of Islamic legal rulings on the side – as it is a matter of contention between the two groups over the understanding of *ijtihād* and the limits of its authority as well as one which pertains to the issue of who has the right to engage in it, we might ask Quṭb about the rulings (*aḥkām*) which are *not* disputed among the *fuqahāʾ*, or what are a point of consensus (*ijmāʿ*) among them. If we were to do so, we would find that he has no answer other than that they are the rulings of the *ḥudūd* penalties (*aḥkām al-ḥudūd*)![40] It goes without saying that they represent the most essential basis of all bases in the problem among those who are termed secularists with the assertion of the 'Islamic state' and 'the implementation of Islamic *sharīʿah*'.

The previous context puts us in the heart of the political problem as evinced by the call for the 'Islamic state' among the advocates of it as among its opponents; we mean the question of the '*implementation* of *al-*

sharī'ah'. What does this mean in the discourse of those who defend it, and what are its chances in terms of real political possibility? Rather, what is chance of the 'state of *al-sharī'ah*' (*dawlat al-sharī'ah*) coming into material existence?

On the Subject of 'Implementation of the *Sharī'ah*'

In a text not devoid of an air of dramaticism, 'Abd al-Salām Yāsīn writes regretfully:

> Since the time when rule between the Muslims became a possession and a growling [and gnashing of teeth] and a morsel [to be fought over], carving out the *da'wah* (Islamic call) and its men, the state has not been the supervisor of the *da'wah* as was the case before. The sword no longer is in the service of the *muṣḥaf* (of the Qur'ān), and the sultan and the Qur'ān have been rent asunder.[41]

The like of this opinion is not that taken by al-Qaraḍāwī, as the latter emerges – as we explored in this chapter – from the standpoint of a different supposition and that is that *al-sharī'ah* remained the source of recourse for rule and the state in the history of Islam for thirteen centuries before the entrance of colonialism. The fact is that Yāsīn is more practical than al-Qaraḍāwī in his concept of the divergence of politics and the state – in Islam – from the path of *al-shar'* since the caliphate turned into [the] 'mordacious rule' [of Ibn Khaldūn] and this is the idea to which the Islamic *salafīyah* have remained intensely loyal. The import of the assertion is that the difference between the two opinions is not an ordinary distinction in a *fiqh* context of *ijtihād*, but rather the assertion of it follows from obvious results in the differing natures of significance among which two are primary. The first of them is that the endeavor to implement *al-sharī'ah* – as al-Qaraḍāwī posits it – is an endeavor to confront the positivist secular idea that was accorded a place by colonialism and which was re-instated by its deputies among the local elites who were tied to it culturally;[42] whereas as represented in the opinion Yāsīn, it is an endeavor to confront this secular idea, on the one hand, and on the other, to effect the rapprochement of the relation between the Qur'ān and the sultan – between the religion and the state as the point of departure for the political experience of Muḥammad in Medina and what followed it in the period of the *Rāshidūn* Caliphs, where there is a necessary correlation between religion and state and a unity between the Qur'ān and the sultan.[43] The second of these is that the obstacle to implementation of the *sharīʿah* in the view of al-Qaraḍāwī is a foreign impediment in the first instance: colonialism and its systems imposed by violence; whereas Yāsīn goes to the conviction that this obstacle is also – on the side of colonialism – *internal*, represented in the Islamic societies deprived of their *sharīʿah* by force of the politics of the rulers, the cowardice of the *fuqahāʾ*, and the timidity of those he terms 'book worms'. For this reason, the battle is an internal battle as well as one for the sake of returning Islam to its original wellsprings.[44]

The return of the *sharīʿah* as the definitive authoritative point of reference in the administration of the affairs of rule or the state is among that which cannot be a subject of debate or point of view. Islam does not accept, in the view of ʿAllāl al-Fāsī, for example,[45] that the constitution and the law should be outside the *uṣūl* of the *sharīʿah* – as defined in the sources of the *sharīʿah* – the Qurʾān and the *sunnah* – because that is among which is incompatible with its conception of politics and the *wilāyah* (trusteeship). Additionally, it is also what pertains to the Islamic character (*islāmīyah*) of the Muslim as we 'are not Muslims,' says ʿAbd al-Salām Yāsīn, 'if we imagine that we worship Him [i.e., God] in prayers and alms (*al-zakāt*) while we rule by other than His *sharīʿah* in public matters.'[46] However, is emphasizing the obligation of this need legally sufficient to bring about its realization? Is that possible by the force of the laws of reality? And if it is not possible, does that suggest that it is incumbent upon Muslims to rebel against the rule of law which is not Islamically legal as currently imposed upon them?

ʿAbd al-Salām Yāsīn answers that by endorsing a *sharʿī* principle for which there is no margin for dispute and that is that 'there is no obedience in rebelling against God' (*maʿṣīyat* Allah); the political translation of which is that it is not possible to impose among laws on the Muslims that which is incompatible with the rulings of their *sharīʿah* where 'there is no recourse to its spirit or its legal intents'. This is what is among that which is not possible to accept from the standpoint of the matter of Islamic legitimacy: 'to simply shrug and kowtow so long as a Muslim remains under the domination of excessive idolatrous rules (*al-ḥukm al-ṭāghūtī*)'.[47,48]

We, in this observation, are in the crux of the question about the feasibility or infeasibility of implementing the *sharīʿah*, or one may say, in regard to the feasibility of the various measures conceived by Islamist intellectuals for that implementation. However, we are in need, before approaching this question, of assessing an elementary conceptual matter which is the *meaning* of *al-sharīʿah*. What is the understanding of *sharīʿah* in the discourse of the Islamic 're-rooting' (*al-taʾṣīl*) – and what are its connections to what preceded it or to what coexists along with customs and laws, and finally, how is the view of it from within the duality of the text and *ijtihād*?

Sharīʿah and Ijtihād

Modern thinkers of Islam are in consensus that Islamic *sharīʿah* has two sources: the Qurʾān and the *sunnah*. Thus it is a divine *sharīʿah* (*sharīʿah ilāhīyah*)[49] or a Providential *sharīʿah* (*sharīʿah rabbānīyah*)[50] in the expression of some of them. The understanding of *al-sharīʿah* here is constrained to the scope of religious teachings: revelation (*al-waḥīy*) and Prophetic practice. This is regardless of the fact that the Sunni *fuqahāʾ* expand this when they add to these two sources consensus (*al-ijmāʿ*) and analogical reasoning (*al-qiyās*); and in what others augment of *al-istiḥsān* ([public] good) and *al-maṣāliḥ al-mursalah* (allowable interests); as well as *istiṣḥāb* [*al-ḥāl*] (transference of the legal import of previous law), and the authority of custom (*al-ʿurf*) and instrumentalism (*al-dharāʾiʿ*) and so on.[51] The significance of this is that we have moved – through this *fiqh* derivation of the *sharīʿah* – from its original signification as passed down Islamic legal rulings (*aḥkām*), and what distinguishes them in terms of religious obedience to them, to a new signification. In this new signification the *sharīʿah* is an amalgam of both text and derivation together, along with what is among that of *fiqh* derivation – comprising variations and clarifications in accordance with the particular explication of the various *madhāhib* (schools of Islamic law) and interpretations of *ijtihād*, which conflict with this obligation to obey it except in cases when it is viewed as being a political or legal obligation.

Islamist thinkers have not given pause before this contradiction: between the assertion that Islamic *sharīʿah* is of divine origin and the assertion that among its sources are the interpretations of *ijtihād* of the *fuqahāʾ* (the matter that cannot be reconciled with the first premise), and between the assertion that it is a 'divine ordination' (*ilzām rabbānī*)[52] as well as deafening silence on the fact that this obeisance is *political* in the first instance, engaged in by the 'commander of the faithful' (*amīr al-muʾminīn*) (who today is the president of the republic or the king in Islamic countries) after he consults one *fiqh* opinion instead of another – giving preponderance to it over others as it best conforms to the requirements of his view! ʿAllāl al-Fāsī was clear in his expression of this opinion when he said that Islam 'gave to the commander of the faithful the power of granting preponderance (*al-tarjīḥ*) in matters about which Muslims among rulers differ in the locus of legitimacy'. And, even if we suspend the ambiguity inherent in the signification of the phrase 'commander of the faithful', it cannot be understood from this whether it is intended to indicate exclusively the *Rāshidūn* Caliphs. He adds for clarification: 'the authoritative rulings of the sultan (*al-aḥkām al-sulṭānīyah*) from the standpoint of the sources of internal legislation in the scope of Islamic-legal politics (*al-sīyāsah al-shar'īyah*) necessitate obedience to them if they do not contravene an *aṣl* among the *uṣūl* of the religion; that is, if they are within its Islamic-legal scope', adding to that his absolute conviction that:

> the *ummah* has attained consensus in the consideration of the interpretations of *ijtihād* of the emirs of the Muslims, as long as they are within their Islamic-legal scope[53]; and similarly it is just as though the *ummah* were to accept it and the communities of the *mujtahidūn* were to reach consensus on it, as it becomes counted among the *sharī'ah* which is obligatory to follow.'[54]

The suppositions of 'Allāl al-Fāsī, Yūsuf al-Qaraḍāwī, and Muḥammad Quṭb impel us in the matter – despite what differences may persist in their assertions – to pose the question of the connection between the *sharī'ah* and between the text (*al-naṣṣ*) and *ijtihād*: the text in its unadulterated form and its primacy, and *ijtihād* in the absence of a text from the Qur'ān or the *sunnah*, and the subsequent occurrence of a 'legislative void' (*farāgh tashrī'ī*) – or even with the existence of a text. That is that these suppositions – especially in the cases of al-Fāsī and al-Qaraḍāwī – give precedence to the idea of *ijtihād* and consider it to be an '*aṣl* (among the *uṣūl*) and a source in constructing an Islamically-legal civil society (*al-mudawwanah al-shar'īyah*).

In an elementary sense, it is a certainty that this opinion is *not* general among Islamists; and in particular for those who take the position that *ijtihād* and *al-tajdīd* (renewal) are among the matters of religion, it is a very sensitive matter – where it is feared that it might lead to a collision with the fixed principles (*thawābit*) of Islam.[55] For this, 'Abd al-Qādir 'Awdah[56] (for example) writes about the subject:

> The *sharī'ah* was not a set of a few foundational principles (*qawā'id*) which then multiplied, nor diverse principles which were then collected together, nor initial theories which were then refined. The *sharī'ah* was not born as a infant along with the Islamic group which then went on to develop and grow as it grew, but rather it was born at birth in its complete maturity and sent

> down from Allah as a perfect, comprehensive and impenetrable *sharīʿah* – you will not see in it any divergence (*ʿawaj*) nor witness in it any deficiency.[57]

This opinion, despite its resonance today among a number of the 'Revivalists', was not an original basis for the construction of the understanding of the 'Islamic state' for Ḥasan al-Bannā or those of his generation and was not a method depended upon among those whom al-Qaraḍāwī calls the moderate people of the 'middle trend' among the Islamists who are in the vast majority today. Discussion of this will be delayed until the following chapter to cover the moment of the huge ideological–creedal expansion in contemporary Islamic discourse.

Islamist intellectuals do not differ that Islamic *sharīʿah* is 'suitable for every time and place', and that 'none in the world is exempt, in any age, from obeying the divine command'.[58] However, this obliges them to acknowledge the obligation of putting the rulings of the *sharīʿah* into effect at the levels of transformations and changes of place and time in light of the fact of the existence of a 'region of void' (*manṭiqat farāgh*) or a 'area of toleration' (*manṭiqat ʿafwu*), or 'mercy' (*raḥmah*) as al-Qaraḍāwī terms it – in the text of the *sharīʿah* that is not completed – in what they themselves confirm – other than through *ijtihād*. So, what then does *ijtihād* signify – in the contemporary discourse of Islam – and what is the realm of its operation and what are its limits?

Al-Qaraḍāwī has written on this topic, defining *ijtihād*:

> exertion of the utmost effort (*ghāyat al-juhd*), and exhausting the full extent in the derivation of the rulings of the *sharīʿah* from their indications (*adillah*) by way of consideration (*al-naẓar*) and using thought; and it is a *farḍ kifāyah* for the *ummah in toto*, wherein it is in a state of sin if it fails to provide for this task a number of its sons to meet its need for it. And it is *farḍ ʿayn* for whoever finds within himself sufficient qualifications to engage in it, and ability for it, when or if he does not find from among fellow Muslims one who will meet the need...[59]

Ijtihād is obligatory (*farḍīyah*), then, in the estimation of al-Qaraḍāwī, but it occurs in the first station as *kifāyah*, that is, as it confronts the *fuqahāʾ*. As for its being *farḍ ʿayn*, the meaning of that is not that *ijtihād* is the duty of the general population, but rather it is restricted to whomever senses that he has the ability to engage in it, and in the conditional state where the *ʿulamāʾ* fall short in awareness of the matter.[60] Most important for what concerns us is that *ijtihād* is necessary for the religion in order to *meet a need*; this need is either intrinsic – pertaining to the rulings of the *sharīʿah*: what is ambiguous of them and what is absent; or this need is objective – pertaining to change and interactive exchange in the flow of reality and what it imposes of rulings which are compatible with it or which respond to its questions.

That puts us before the question of the scope in which *ijtihād* operates: is it only the scope wherein no (explicit) text of *sharīʿah* is supplied, or is it *also* in the scope of the text itself? And in this case, is *ijtihād* possible along with the existence of the text, and what are the limits of its possibility if it is, indeed, possible?

We detect in previous citation of al-Qaraḍāwī answers to these questions. He states:

> *ijtihād* is done in two areas: one of them is the area wherein there is no text, which the legislator (*al-shāriʿ*, i.e., Allah) has intentionally left up to us, as a mercy unto us and not due to forgetfulness...for the *mujtahidūn* to fill in this empty space with what will realize the legal intent of the legislator, in agreement with the ways of *ijtihād* that the *mujtahidūn* follow...and the second of two areas is the area of texts wherein speculation inheres (*al-nuṣūṣ al-ẓannīyah*), whether with regard to speculation about its soundness (*ẓannīyāt al-thubūt*), and most of the Prophetic *ḥadīth* are like that, or whether there is speculation as to what it indicates (*ẓannīyāt al-dalālah*), and most of the texts of the Qurʾān and *sunnah* are thus...so the existence of the text does not prohibit *ijtihād* as some people whimsically imagine, rather nine out of ten texts or more are amenable to *ijtihād* and to multiplicity of points of view, even the noble Qurʾān itself allows for multiplicity of understandings in derivation from it.[61]

Two primary ideas formulate the assertion in this citation: the first of them is there are intentional legislative empty spaces (*farāgh*) in the Qurʾān and the *sunnah* to the end that they impel the Muslims to engage theoretical reasoning (*al-naẓar al-ʿaqlī*) and *ijtihād* with the intention of deriving the rulings (*instinbāṭ al-aḥkām*), and moreover, engaging in *ijtihād* is an act among the *uṣūl* where there is no exemption from it. The second of these is that the texts of the Qurʾān and the *sunnah* involve a measure of speculation (*al-ẓann*): whether in regard to the issue of legitimacy or soundness – in the case of the Prophetic *aḥādīth* – or in the indications which appear to be indecisive; and thus *ijtihād* is necessary to confirm what is doubtful in regard to the law (*al-sharʿ*) or to lift obscurity or ambiguity from signification of the particular proclamation within. In both cases, the locus of *ijtihād* has expanded – according to our sheikh – to encompass what is absent (*al-ghāʾib*) among rulings and the textually specified among these as well. If the first matter (*ijtihād* in instances where there is no text transmitted) is a matter of consensus among many throughout the history of Islamic *fiqh*, the 'new' concept of al-Qaraḍāwī with regard to the subject of *ijtihād* is the assertion of an Islamic legal duty/right of *ijtihād with the existence of the text.*

However, the object of scrutiny in his assertion rests at the limits of this last type of *ijtihād*: in the area of that which is textually specified (*al-manṣūṣ 'alayhī*). That is, al-Qaraḍāwī constrains this *ijtihād* exclusively to two domains: the domains of confirmation (*al-ta'akkud*) and verification (*al-ibānah*), while he does not assert this right/duty by extension to the case of the existence of an explicit text which tenders no speculation in regard to its signification (*al-manṣūṣ 'alayhī ghayr al-maẓnūn fī dalālatihī*). This is among that which indicates, for him, that *ijtihād* with the existence of a text is conditional *ijtihād* (*mashrūṭ*), and moreover, the limits of its permissibility are those that are steeped in doubt or obscurity: doubt in the soundness of the attribution of a text, or obscurity in its signification.

With 'Allāl al-Fāsī, the matter differs to a small extent where we find that the locus of *ijtihād* with the existence of a text appears to be wider than that of what has been previously noted for al-Qaraḍāwī despite the fact that the Moroccan *faqīh* and *mujtahid* wrote what he did more than a third of a century ago! If 'Allāl al-Fāsī proceeds from the standpoint of the concept of the Islamic legal intents of the *sharī'ah* (*maqāṣid al-sharī'ah*),[62] which the great Mālikī *faqīh* al-Shāṭibī asserted, he takes the position that the Islamic legal intents transform in their role into the measure which delimits the means of implementation of the explicit texts of the *sharī'ah*. We read in this sense:

> ...the Islamic legal intents of the *sharī'ah* affect even what is textually specified in the case of need, and 'Umar bin al-Khaṭṭāb's suspension of the penalty for theft in the year of the famine, despite its textual specification in the Qur'ān, is for no other reason than the intent of the lawgiver (i.e., Allah) is the punishment of the thief not those who are compelled by need to appear as thieves; this is because if people go hungry, and other than they have an excess of what they need [of food], it becomes their right to take it and to fight them for it.[63]

Is this audacity?

No doubt, except that firstly it is completely understandable from within the order of the Islamic legal intents which proffered the richest Islamic *fiqh* contribution in approaching the rulings of the religious texts on the basis that they are *objective* rulings to the utmost extent: they exceed the literal expression of them and verification of them is incumbent through reason. Then, secondly, this is an understanding from 'Allāl al-Fāsī who was, by right, the last of the Muslim Reformers of the *Nahḍah* after the collapse of the edifice of their ideas under the conceptual blows of the concept of the new 'Reawakening' (*Ṣaḥwah*); and he was the last one to remain, among their line, respecting the procedural approach of the legal intents. The boldness of 'Allāl al-Fāsī cannot be apprehended except in apposition to the boldness of Muṣṭafā al-Sibāʿī who was the general guide of the *Ikhwān al-Muslimīn* movement in Syria.[64] Al-Sibāʿī – the staunch defender of the 'socialism of Islam' – did not waste any effort or opportunity to attack the *fuqahā'* who had clung tenaciously to the texts or to *fiqh* opinions 'propounded in recent ages' that were not commensurate with the problems of our age, and not compatible with the spirit (*rūḥ*) of the *sharīʿah;*[65] calling for treating these problems in light of the principles of the *sharīʿah not* in the light of these texts.

Like 'Allāl al-Fāsī, Muṣṭafā al-Sibāʿī proceeds from the idea that public good (*al-maṣlaḥah*) is that which establishes the principles of the *sharīʿah* and delimits its legal intents; and, secondly, that any *ijtihād* in *fiqh* which contravenes or appears in conflict with this principle is 'contradicting the *spirit* of the *sharīʿah* and its social message in life'.[66] It is not possible, in the estimation of al-Sibāʿī, to understand this fact except when the *sharīʿah* is expressed as *universal* and indivisible, and viewed in the context of development (*al-taṭawwur*). Thus, he attacks *fuqahā'* who 'understand the *sharīʿah* in an atomized and disconnected way, not oriented towards a general goal or as a comprehensive message for life'[67] finding it sufficient to view the texts on the basis of their literal verbatim rulings, and in consideration of those rulings as being from the intent of the *sharīʿah* in them. Al-Sibāʿī propounds an example in the position of the *fuqahā'* with regard to the nationalization of land ownership when they refused this nationalization on the basis of the assertion that it stripped ownership from those who had a right to it legally saying that they:

> did not ever consider the afflictions of the peasant farmers who were living in the exploitative system in a state of abject poverty, disease, ignorance, pain and dispossession; they only thought about protecting the 'right' of the owner of vast lands and that his state of ownership should persist in order that he not be 'wronged'. They became enraged at the wronging of 'a single individual' but were not angered by the wronging of 'thousands and tens of thousands' on the basis of arguing that the *sharīʿah* gave the land owner the right in this ownership from which originated this despicable injustice.[68]

If we leave aside the excessive social dimension of this citation, which characterizes most of the writings of al-Sibā'ī and pushes them to borrow from understandings of class analysis, we find that the axis of his thought is the defense of an *ijtihād* unfettered by the rulings of the explicit text, rather a re-reading of these rulings in light of their original legal intents as well as in light of the facts of historical and social development. And, in this, he succeeds, along with 'Allāl al-Fāsī in the concept of the duty/right of *ijtihād* with the existence of an explicit text in regard to the signification, on the basis that its actual operative signification is attained through the *intents* of its rulings rather than through its direct verbatim (literal) utterance.

Ijtihād is necessary for the *sharī'ah* and not a conceptual extravagance for the *fuqahā'*. It is an *ijtihād* which goes to limits of the earth: filling up the empty spaces of legislation to the farthest boundaries – adjusting the rulings in accordance with requirements of the legal intents of the *sharī'ah* and the demands of development, and even with customary laws (*al-a'rāf*).[69] If the need of the *sharī'ah* for *ijtihād* is from its need to be 'beneficial for every time and place', then it is expressive – in parallel – of the need of 'the Islamic state' for legitimacy in order to be a system and source for legislation rather a theme for its Islamic identity. However, it is not sufficient to say that any state is an Islamic state because it is *textually specified* that the *sharī'ah* is the source of legislation and laws in it, rather it is necessary for it to be as such – in the consciousness of those calling for it – to implement the rulings of the *sharī'ah*. So how, then, is that feasible and how does Islamist discourse deal with this question?

The Rulings of the Sharī'ah: *Descent and Gradual Implementation*

Regardless of whether Islamic *sharī'ah* descended complete as 'Abd al-Qādir 'Awdah asserts, or whether its rulings are enriched by the *fiqh* of the *sharī'ah* and the derivations of the *fuqahā'* as most Islamists assert, the matter of implementing its rulings today puts forward – for those calling for it – the question about the required means for that implementation. They do not differ about the implementation of the *sharī'ah*, but rather their opinions are distinguished on the basis of the type of preparations that must be undertaken in the endeavor to reach that goal. And, in our opinion, this clarification hinges first upon the meaning of the phrase 'implementation of the *sharī'ah*': by that, is the refining of laws and filling them with rulings of the *sharī'ah* intended, or is changing the system of rule – republic or kingdom – to establish an Islamic political system that which is demanded?

In regard to the appeal for the Islamic state, for those partaking of the conceptual and political subjects of Ḥasan al-Bannā and the movement of the *Ikhwān al-Muslimīn* during his tenure – there is no sphere for connecting between implementation of the *sharīʿah* and an overthrow of the extant system of government. They say that disparately, there being nothing to gather the variations of the assertion together other than their rejection of violence as a means of arriving in power.[70] Yet despite that, not one of them admits frankly the possibility of implementing Islamic *sharīʿah* without establishing an Islamic state! This among that which opens the door to the belief that demand for the realization of the *sharīʿah* is bifurcated in terms of goals: entailing a first-stage goal of Islamizing what can be Islamized among laws in the scope of the extant (positivist) states where this is a transitional goal – its accumulations and gains opening the way before the end-goal: the establishment of the Islamic state, after the system of social and political relations has matured. That is not, however, a reason which justifies any slackening in the call for total implementation of the rulings of Islam – even under the auspices of the existing state and not only in the sphere of law[71] just as al-Qaraḍāwī asserts.

If we leave aside the writings of some extremist Islamists – those who came out of the womb of the *Ikhwān al-Muslimīn* and renounced the moderate ideas of al-Bannā – such as Sayyid Quṭb, Muḥammad Quṭb and even ʿAbd al-Qādir ʿAwdah himself, we find that most contemporary Islamist thinkers assert the obligation to pave the way for gradual and staged implementation of the rulings of the *sharīʿah* – operating according to that for which the Prophet had called and that for which al-Bannā had been calling since the second quarter of the twentieth century. While it is true that they do not back down from the matter of the obligation of its complete implementation without any selectivity,[72] they do not find any deficiencies in that occurring easily and in stages if 'gradualism is a *sunnah* among the *sunnan* (a norm among the norms) of Allah in his creation,' as al-Qaraḍāwī says, 'and the *sharīʿah* was perfected without doubt,' except that its implementation 'requires encouragement and preparation in order to transform society into one of genuine Islamic obedience.'[73]

According to this sense, ʿAllāl al-Fāsī took the justification further and more explicitly when he wrote:

> Our return to the *sharīʿah* does not need to be in one stroke, rather we are in a situation which resembles the situation when revelation (*al-waḥīy*) was descending upon the Messenger of Allah...as he charged a course of gradu-

> alism in the declaration of rulings and their implementation, preferring that this be a result of the conviction of the people and their acceptance...and it suffices us to accept a characteristic which is not indicative of indulgence or doubt concerning the principle of the return to the *sharī'ah*. And if, after that, there persists a necessity of delaying work according to the requirements of a rule among the rules of Allah, then we will take it as an example from our highest values for which we work and exert effort to realize its implementation. The meaning of this is not that we permit the obstruction of any ruling among the rulings of Allah – woe to me if I should intend or accept that – but, I know that Muslims today, if the *sharī'ah* were implemented upon them in one stroke, would not be able to bear it; and for that reason, there is not doubt in attracting them by good preaching and to create a favorable atmosphere...

He concludes with an assertion that has more than a little 'jurisprudential pragmatism' saying: 'It is better that working according to a rule or the rules of Allah of the *sharī'ah* be delayed than to scuttle the *sharī'ah* entirely because what is not fully apprehended is also not entirely abandoned.'[74]

It is not possible to implement the *sharī'ah* altogether – in the view of al-Fāsī – for a number of reasons and among these are the absence of a general readiness to facilitate that, and the need to avoid alienating Muslims from the rulings of their religion as a result of hastiness. Thus, it is incumbent to choose the realistic way to thread this path towards the goal without major costs to the *sharī'ah*. This way is not an innovation (*bid'ah*), and it is not the way of concessions, it is the *Prophetic* way itself of settling in the rulings.

'Allāl al-Fāsī was not the like of al-Bannā or al-Qaraḍāwī, among the leading personae of the *Ikhwān al-Muslimīn*. He was a leader of a national party – Ḥizb al-Istiqlāl (the Independence Party) and was not among those who called for 'the Islamic state'. He was among those who called for the 'nation–state', and it was the last cry of Reformism after the Second World War. Along with that, his background was Islamic and it impelled him to intersect with the thought of the Islamists just as the latter would push the reformist tendency of al-Qaraḍāwī – coming from the womb of the Muslim Brotherhood – to intersect from time to time with Arab Renaissance Reformist thought in some of his books.

How can the 'Islamic state' be a state for the *sharī'ah* in what is conceived of by its proponents as a 'civil' state (*dawlah madanīyah*) not religious and 'constitutional' not tyrannical, where the *ummah* should be the source of political authority in it?

This brings us face-to-face with the matter of the political system in this state, its nature, and the bases upon which its formation turns, and – in a word – before the matter of *al-shūrā*. What does this connote and what is the connection of its significance – in the consciousness of the contemporary Islamist – to the understanding of democracy?

Notes

1. See Chapter 6 of this book.
2. Al-Qaraḍāwī, *Min Fiqh al-Dawlah*.
3. He quotes here the verse (*āyah*) number (59) from The Women (*sūrat al-nisā'*): 'O you who believe obey Allah, and obey the Messenger, and those given authority (*al-amr*) among you. If you differ in anything among yourselves, refer it to Allah and his Prophet' [Qur'ān, *sūrat al-nisā'*, (4:59)]. Also quoting the *ḥādīth* 'He who passed away without swearing a pledge of allegiance (*bay'ah*), died a death of paganism (i.e., as in the Jahiliyyah period).' (Cited by Muslim: *ḥādīth* no. 1851). Al-Qaraḍāwī, *min Fiqh al-Dawlah*, p. 15.
4. Al-Qaraḍāwī, *min Fiqh al-Dawlah*, pp. 15–21.
5. Al-Qaraḍāwī, *al-Ḥal al-Islāmī: Farīḍah wa Ḍarūrah*, p. 71.
6. There is a problem in the definitions given by both al-Bannā and al-Qaraḍāwī for the 'lands of Islam' and the 'lands of Muslims', in that they both expanded these definitions to include every spot in which Muslims had once settled. Al-Bannā states: 'The Muslim Brotherhood made every Muslim think that every bit of this earth, whereon a brother who follows the religion of the Qur'ān may exist, is a part of the general Islamic domain which Islam demands its believers to persevere to protect and delight in. As a result of that, the horizon of the Islamic homeland has expanded and even transcended its national geographic and national consanguineous boundaries to adopt a nationality of sublime principles, sheer righteous doctrines and the rights God bestowed for the world as the right path and a guiding light. And when Islam permits its sons to feel that meaning and ensconce it within their insides, it obliges them by religious duty to protect the land of Islam from aggressors' hostility, deliver it from invaders' captivity, and fortify it against intruders' interests.' Available in: Al-Bannā, *Majmū'at Rasā'il*, p. 50.

Al-Qaraḍāwī says: 'Every land once inhabited by Muslims that had Islamic rituals held upon and had minarets constructed for exclaiming 'God is Great!' (*Allahu akbar!*) or was claimed as such is a land of Islam and must be protected and defended.' Available in: Al-Qaraḍāwī, *al-Ḥal al-Islāmī*, p. 65.

The previous two texts refer to the concept of '*dār al-Islām*' (lit., 'house of Islam') which was coined by *fuqahā'*, and in opposition to it they posited the concept of '*dār al-ḥarb*' (lit., 'house of war') which also connotes '*dār al-kufr*' (lit., 'house of unbelief'), regarding the history of concept *dār al-Islām*. Available at: Al-Sayyid, *Sīyāsāt al-Islām al-Mu'āṣir*, pp. 77–95.

7. Quṭb, Muḥammad, *al-'Ilmānyūn wa al-Islām*, pp. 61–2.
8. Islam has been described at times as a 'nomocracy' (deriving from the Greek *νέμω*) which might be misleading if outside the strict connotation of a 'government ruled by or dispensing (the law of) justice' – in this case, the Islamic *sharī'ah*. There is no single correlate or precise analog in English for the term *ḥākimīyah*, but the essence of the concept is that the active and operative 'ruler' is the law – *al-sharī'ah* – itself. Specific individuals and groups are somewhat 'incidental' or 'tangential' to this rule,

their function being to simply 'implement' or 'execute' the ordinances of the law. What the author of this book aptly notes is the tendency among advocates of this theory to 'overlook' or 'minimize' the necessary interpretive role played by the human being in this process – that is the 'middle link' of the human endeavor known as *ijtihād* (which relies on analogy, reason, interpretation and extrapolation) between the *sharī'ah* (considered to be verbatim and divine) and actual implementation in the world (*al-taṭbīq*). – Translator.

9. Perhaps, the most precise definition for 'Islamic government' is 'to rule with what God has revealed to the Prophet' or to rule according to *al-sharī'ah* '...the ruler here, and then the government, nay the state as a whole, are assigned the task of ruling according to what God has revealed of laws, and to conduct and work according to these laws...so we are not, here, encountering a ruler governing by his own command, nor a faction or a group or a political party that brings in a ruler and a government and establishes a state concerned with achieving their personal interests and oppressing the other classes in society....as is the case with the models obtained from capitalist modes. And we are also not before a party that sets up a government and a state to render it *above* the society...and issue whatever it favors of laws as is the case with the Soviet model and those similar to it...indeed, we are before a unique condition, not similar to any other among the social models or modes of state, except for the models in which prophets heralded the Law of God...'. Shafīq, Munīr, *al-Islām wa Mūwājahat al-Dawlah al-Ḥadīthah*, 3rd edn (Tunis: al-Nāshir; Dār al-Bayraq, 1992).

10. Al-Fāsī, *Difā' 'an al-Sharī'ah* (Rabat: [n.pb.], 1966, p. 53.

11. About the idioms *al-'almānīyah* or *al-'ilmānīyah...'ālam* or *ālim*) see Chapter 1 in: Al-'Azmah, 'Azīz, *al-'Ilmānīyah min Manẓūr Mukhtalif* (Beirut: Center of Arab Unity Studies, 1992).

12. In respect to that 'Abd al-Salām Yāsīn took notice and wrote, commenting on Muḥammad 'Abdūh and al-Kawākibī: 'Reformers of the *Nahḍah* were criticizing the state of mental rigidity and imitation, while praising the privileged free mentality, however, they never felt, and are excused for that, that their fascination with Western civilization and their overwhelming national enthusiasm pushed them too far to the very opposite of what they used to criticize – even plunged them into rationalistic superficiality, where they were trapped in a web of secular thought; even their masters went on stating openly and frankly in their writings that religion is merely for the afterlife.' Yāsīn, 'Abd al-Salām, *al-Islām wa al-Qawmīyah al-'Ilmānīyah*, 2nd edn (Ṭanṭā: Dār al-Bashīr li-al-Thaqāfah wa al-'Ilūm al-Islāmīyah, 1985), pp. 115–16.

13. Ghalyūn, Burhān, *Ightīyāl al-'Aql: Miḥnat al-Thaqāfah al-'Arabīyah bayn al-Salafīyah wa al-Taba'īyah* (Beirut: Dār al-Tanwīr, 1985).

14. Al-Qaraḍāwī, *min Fiqh al-Dawlah*, p. 24.

15. Other Islamic intellects addressed this meaning before, so that we read for sheikh 'Abd al-Salām Yāsīn a rejoinder against 'Westernized Laity': 'To them, religion is extremism and terrorism, only to be divinely ascetic resting in a mosque's corner to laud and glorify what its resolution wills before the hands of eminent democrats who are experts in life's issues, capable of overcoming them, affiliates of Left, Right and Middle of life's geography. As for the mosque and those who belong to it, they have the duty of shrouding the dead.' Yāsīn, *Ḥiwār ma'a al-Fuḍalā' al-Dīmuqrāṭīyīn* (Casablanca: al-Mu'alif, 1994), p. 4.

Even before him, was 'Allāl al-Fāsī who wrote: 'Islam is a belief and a law, so it is not acceptable for us to stop at just believing in God, praying, almsgiving, going for pilgrimage, fasting and doing righteous deeds; in addition to these pillars, it orders us to apply *sharīʿah* in our daily transactions and issues and get it involved in our administration and government.' Al-Fāsī, *Difāʿ ʿan al-Sharīʿah*, p. 52.

16. Al-Qaraḍāwī, *al-Ṣaḥwah al-Islāmīyah* (Cairo: Dār al al-Ṣaḥwah, 1988), pp. 68–70.

17. Al-Qaraḍāwī, *min Fiqh al-Dawlah*.

18. If it was plausible to label Faraḥ Anthon as a 'secularist', and if the same appellation was applicable to Salāmah Mūsā, it would be difficult to accuse Sheikh ʿAlī ʿAbd al-Rāziq of that as done by sheikh Bikhīt and his Azhar colleagues, or even to accuse sheikh Khālid Muḥammad Khālid with secularism as done by sheik al-Ghazālī and others because the epistemological distance between them was not so great in order as to justify such an epithet.

19. Al-Qaraḍāwī, *al-Ṣaḥwah al-Islāmīyah*, p. 84.

20. Al-Qaraḍāwī, *al-Ḥilūl al-Mustawradah*, p. 42.

21. Al-Qaraḍāwī, *al-Ṣaḥwah al-Islāmīyah*, p. 84. Keppel also notices how religion shrank after the Second World War to become confined to personal and family dimensions. Available in: Keppel, Gilles, *La Revanche de Dieu: Chrétiens, Juifs et Musulmans à la reconquête du monde* (Paris: Seuil, 1991), p. 13.

22. Al-Qaraḍāwī, *al-Ḥilūl al-Mustawradah*, p. 47.

23. Al-Qaraḍāwī, *al-Ḥilūl al-Mustawradah*, p. 46.

24. Mūsā, Salāmah, *al-Tathqīf al-Dhātī aw kayfa Narā Anfusinā* (Cairo: Maṭbaʿat al-Taqaddum, [n.d]), p. 80.

25. In countries such as Egypt this has resulted in multiple court systems including civil/criminal, military and family courts – where the latter is the only one which maintains a relation to Islamic *sharīʿah* in matters of 'personal status' such as marriage and divorce. In the case of the other courts, positive laws are modeled on various European civil codes. – Translator.

26. Mūsā, *Ma Hiya al-Nahḍah* (Cairo: Dār al-Jīl, [n.d]), p. 10.

27. Maḥmūd, Zakī Najīb, *Tajdīd al-Fikr al-ʿArabī* (Beirut: Dār al-Shurūq, 1971), p. 13.

28. Al-Qaraḍāwī paraphrased some other provocative texts of this type belonging to Mūsā and Jamīl Maʿlūf, disavowing them harshly. Al-Qaraḍāwī, *al-Ḥilūl al-Mustawradah*, pp. 37–9.

29. 'The most serious incident in the "house of Islam" was that Western secular ideology did not stop at the generations educated by a secular culture, nay it invaded some minds of the Islamic culture, which graduated from religious institutes like al-Azhar.' Among those meant by al-Qaraḍāwī in this statement are ʿAlī ʿAbd al-Rāziq and Khālid Muḥammad Khālid.

Al-Qaraḍāwī, *al-Ḥilūl al-Mustawradah*, p. 48.

30. Yāsīn, *al-Islām wa al-Qawmīyah*, p. 128.

31. ʿAbd al-Salām Yāsīn did not hold back any criticism in his book: *al-Islām wa al-Qawmīyah* against the Egyptian researcher in the field of cultural heritage Dr. Ḥasan Ḥanafī.

32. Among these, for instance, is the Iranian apologist and researcher ʿAlī Sharīʿatī – whom Ayatollah al-Khomeini treated fairly after the Revolution and whom ʿAbd al-SalāmYāsīn labeled as 'the hypocrite writer'! Yāsīn, *al-Islām wa al-Qawmīyah*, p. 36.

33. Al-Qaraḍāwī, *al-Ḥilūl al-Mustawradah*, p. 108.

34. Sheikh ʿAbd al-Salām Yāsīn sets examples for those, as he presents abundant and detailed givens – in their material – about the historical context for the development of secularization in the recent and contemporary West, and about the various political forms that it acquired in countries of dissimilar political experiences such as

France, the UK, and the USA. Available in: Yassine, Abdessalam, *Islamiser la Modernité* (Rabat: Al-Ofok impressions, 1998), pp. 65–7.

35. Among these, for instance, is al-Qaraḍāwī who wrote: 'Secularism may be accepted in a Christian society...Christianity is not comprised of laws or a system for living that orders the believer in it to be especially committed to this system of these laws. In fact, The Gospel itself accepted dividing life into two halves: one for God or faith, the other for Caesar or the state, so it commands "Render unto Caesar what is Caesar's and what is God's to God". In this way, a Christian can live under secular rule with a relieved conscience and unscathed faith.' Al-Qaraḍāwī, *al-Ḥilūl al-Mustawradah*, pp. 111–112.

36. Quṭb, Muḥammad, *al-ʿIlmānyūn wa al-Islām*, p. 56.

37. Difference of the *fuqahāʾ* is among the advantages of this religion...since God left many issues free for interpretation, as a mercy from Him and never due to obliviousness...and God knows – and allowed interpretation in whichever issue not revealed in a sacred text human's perceptions differ....as if God allowed such a distinction in implementation of *sharīʿah*.' Available in: Quṭb, Muḥammad, *al-ʿIlmānyūn wa al-Islām*, p. 59.

38. Quṭb, Muḥammad, *al-ʿIlmānyūn wa al-Islām*, p. 60.

39. Quṭb, Muḥammad, *al-ʿIlmānyūn wa al-Islām*, p. 57.

40. Yāsīn, *al-Islām wa al-Qawmīyah*, p. 91.

41. In this context ʿAllāl al-Fāsī states: 'Some Muslims – a majority of whom are officials in Islamic governments – started to act as the colonialists themselves in spreading foreign thought which is represented by modern laws. And, they stood consistently against Islamic *fiqh, fuqahāʾ* and apologists. Meanwhile, proponents and the *ulamāʾ* of the *sharīʿah* helplessly stood agape before the colonialist onslaught in the guise of Westernized Muslims that achieved rule in the name of their own Muslim peoples and their struggle for the sake of freedom.' Available in: Al-Fāsī, *Difāʿ ʿan al-Sharīʿah*, pp. 4–5.

42. 'The sultan has forsaken the Qur'ān since the dawn of our history; the state of our *ummah* shall not be rectified or regained provided that the rift between the *sharīʿah* of the Qur'ān and the restraint of the sultan not repaired.' Available in: Yāsīn, *al-Shūrā wa al-Dīmuqrāṭīyah* (Casablanca: Maṭbūʿāt al-Ufuq, 1996), p. 270.

43. According to al-Qaraḍāwī, Westernized secularists represent nothing but an internal faint repercussion of that external imperial secular propaganda; as a result, extirpation of these depends on cutting off imperial ideological influx towards our Islamic communities.

44. Maybe this difference between the two sheikhs – al-Qaraḍāwī and Yāsīn – in handling and evaluating the matter explains the openness of the former to current official politics in a moderate critical fashion and the campaign of the latter against them in an unprecedented way!

45. Al-Fāsī, *Difāʿ ʿan al-Sharīʿah*, p. 52.

46. Yāsīn, *al-Islām wa al-Qawmīyah*, p. 67.

47. A pivotal term in considerable Islamic discourse is *al-ṭāghūt* and its derivatives as found in the Qur'ān. There is no direct cognate, but the underlying connotation of the Arabic root is to 'overspill' or 'exceed boundaries' – to be 'excessive'. In the Qur'ān, wood and stone idols are referred to as *ṭāghūt* as are appeals made to soothsayers. Pharaoh is also referred to as *ṭāghūt*. For this reason, the term has been rendered to connote 'idolatrous excess' – in order to indicate the implied implication between 'overstepping bounds' and 'taking idols in worship' in the Islamic source texts. – Translator.

48. Yāsīn, *al-Islām wa al-Qawmīyah*, p. 68.

49. Al-Fāsī, *Maqāṣid al-sharī'ah al-Islāmīyah wa Makārimuhā* (Casablanca: Maktabat al-Wiḥdah al-'Arabīyah, 1963), p. 54.

50. Al-Qaraḍāwī, *al-Ṣaḥwah al-Islāmīyah*, p. 82.

51. Al-Fāsī, *Maqāṣid al-sharī'ah*, p. 80.

52. Quṭb, Muḥammad, *al-'Ilmānyūn wa al-Islām*, p. 61.

53. In Sunni Islam the sources or *uṣūl* of law are three: the Qur'ān, the *sunnah* of the Prophet (i.e., the transmitted accounts of the injunctions and normative sayings and practices of Muḥammad), and *ijmā'* – consensus (of the scholars). The attainment of the last or ascertaining the comprehensiveness of it – outside certain widely-accepted principles – is difficult to measure, and therefore the category is not as 'flexible' or 'accommodating' as it might appear. – Translator.

54. Al-Fāsī, *Maqāṣid al-sharī'ah*, pp. 54–5.

55. When Yāsīn says – for instance – that renewal 'is not...transformation of what is constant in the *shar'* of Allah bearing in mind that the *aḥkām* of the Qur'ān and *sunnah* continue to operate until the Day of Judgment', he reaffirms the rule of 'what all of those who called for *ijtihād* have followed and the stipulated conditions for it, and all of those who have objected to it and warned of its consequences.' Available in: Yāsīn, *al-Minhāj al-Nabawī*, p. 31.

56. He was one of the significant leaders and teachers for the Muslim Brotherhood after Ḥasan al-Bannā's death. His thoughts profoundly affected most of the second generation of the Muslim Brotherhood: the generation of Sayyid Quṭb and Muḥammad Quṭb, especially in making these thoughts root deeper and prompting a sense of restrictive absolutism among them.

57. 'Awdah, 'Abd al-Qādir, *al-Tashrī' al-Jinā'ī al-Islāmī Muqāranan bil-Qānūn al-Waḍ'ī*, Silsilat al-Thaqāfah al-'Āmmah, vol. 2 (Cairo: Maktabat Dār al-'Urūbah, 1960), pp. 15–16.

58. Al-Fāsī, *Difā' 'an al-Sharī'ah*, p. 140.

59. Al-Qaraḍāwī, *min Ajl Ṣaḥwah Islāmīyah*, p. 42.

60. Among the categories of *fiqh* in Islamic law is that of *farḍ* which describes actions and duties that are obligatory and which must be observed as failure or neglect to do so (in the absence of mitigating circumstances or a legally acceptable excuse – such as incapacity or illness) will incur sin (*ithm*). This category breaks down into two major subcategories: *farḍ 'ayn* and *farḍ kifāyah*, where the first connotes what is binding and obligatory upon the legally-culpable Muslim individual and where the second is contingent upon sufficiency which may be distributed over the Muslim group and where a given task or duty may not be the responsibility of an individual Muslim if there are other Muslims 'sufficient' to the task carrying it out. – Translator.

61. Al-Qaraḍāwī, *min Ajl Ṣaḥwah Islāmīyah*, pp. 42–3.

62. This idea is the essence of his valuable book: *Maqāṣid al-sharī'ah al-Islāmīyah wa Makārimuhā*.

63. Al-Fāsī, *Difā' 'an al-Sharī'ah*, p. 140.

64. See a profound analysis of Muṣṭafā al-Sibā'ī's thought in: Bārūt, Muḥammad Jamāl, *Yathrib al-Jadīdah: al-Ḥarakāt al-Islāmīyah al-Rāhinah* (London: Rīyaḍ al-Rayyis, 1994), pp. 95–127.

65. Al-Sibā'ī, Muṣṭafā, *Ishtirākīyat al-Islām*, 2nd edn (Damascus: Mu'asasat al-Maṭbū'āt al-'Arabīyah, 1960), p. 380.

66. Al-Sibā'ī, *Ishtirākīyat al-Islām*, p. 384.

67. Al-Sibā'ī, *Ishtirākīyat al-Islām*, p. 384.

68. Al-Sibā'ī, *Ishtirākīyat al-Islām*, pp. 386–7.

69. In this context, al-Bishrī writes: 'In the past, constant issues in *sharī'ah* expanded traditions and habitudes already extant in the lands conquered by Islam, *fiqh* was able to contain all traditions and habitudes that were compatible with it and capable of being integrated within the whole body of Islamic *sharī'ah* so it is feasible to enrich *fiqh* with many models of the present times as well' Available in: Al-Bishrī, Ṭāriq, *Al-Malāmiḥ al-'Āmah*, p. 51.

70. Al-Bannā, *Majmū'at Rasā'il*, pp. 85 and 168–70; Al-Qaraḍāwī, *al-Ḥal al-Islāmī*, pp. 155–173 and 182–3; and Yassine, *Islamiser la Modernité*, p. 291.

71. '...Islamic Revivalism demands more than mere substitution of positive laws with Islamic ones...that is why Islamists deny restricting *al-da'wah* (the "call") to Islam to the legal corner...and that is why "moderate Islam" calls for *al-da'wah* to Islam for all Muslims, not only in implementing *sharī'ah* in a narrow sense as understood by many.' Available in: Al-Qaraḍāwī, *al-Ṣaḥwah al-Islāmīyah*, p. 86.

72. 'It is not applicable to implement one part of *sharī'ah* while not implementing others.' Available at: Yāsīn, *al-Shūrā wa al-Dīmuqrāṭīyah*, p. 70.

73. Al-Qaraḍāwī, *al-Ṣaḥwah al-Islāmīyah*, pp. 87–8.

74. Al-Fāsī, *Difā' 'an al-Sharī'ah*, pp. 231–2.

Chapter 8

Al-Shūrā and Democracy – Connection and Disjuncture

> Democracy presents the best tool or device for rule – enabling the citizens through its use – to practice the basic freedoms and, among them, the political liberties.
>
> Rāshid al-Ghanūshī

> Many researchers...rather, many Modernists among them...detract from the understanding of *al-shūrā* and give *al-shūrā* a connotation akin to their understanding of democracy, and this is what is a denigration of Islamic thought and a deviation from the true meaning of *al-shūrā*.
>
> Fatḥī Yakan

Contemporary Islamists almost do not differ in the central issue of the principle of *al-shūrā* (consultation) in Islam and, particularly, in the systemization of the political sphere in it. Perhaps, there are points of clarification among them in regard to opinions about the connotation of the expression or in the extent of its applicability or its correlation with that particular connotation. That is, perhaps it might be subjected to the endeavor of some to expand the locus of the application of its signification to understanding it from the standpoint of blurring between or reconciling with the locus of signification of modern political understandings, or an endeavor by others to restrict the total components of its comprehension as a signification to the narrow Islamic scope and to not extend it outside this and so on. Most of the modalities of explication of this type apply to the derivative and detailed ruling respectively where there is no great impact on Islamic *uṣūlī* group-consciousness in regard to the principle of *shūrā* as a founding principle in the view of Islam of politics.

With that having been said, the researcher into the history of the understanding of *shūrā* – and into the forms of its varied presence in contemporary political writings – notices two phenomena worthy of attention which cast light on the context of the cognitive, political and Islamic conception of the matter of *shūrā*, and the limited character of the conceptual accumulations which occurred or accrued through its use (that is, the understanding of it). The first of these is that we do not find in the ancient texts concern for the subject of *shūrā* in Islam, rather it is almost not even indicated in the authoritative referential political Islamic legal corpus! Ḥasan al-Turābī may well have been correct and accurate when he noticed that:

> Modern Islamic literature is that which circulated the word and attributed to it its value and its salient content after the ancient books of *fiqh* had not meant much by it and had not conferred upon it this magnificent value because consultative political practice [based on *shūrā*] was not widespread and not possessed of much significance in Islamic history.[1]

The second of these is that we are almost unable to detect – in what Islamist intellectuals have published on the subject – anything at the conceptual level in contemplating the matter of *al-shūrā*, or in producing an epistemology of its order that goes beyond repeated generalizations: as witnessed in glosses on the two verses on *al-shūrā* (in the Qurʾān) or minor attempts to transfer its experience in the political Prophetic context and what was subsequent to it in the era of the Rāshidūn caliphs (even if the aspect of backward-projection in this reference is overlooked).

The two previous observations benefit us in recognizing two facts which impose themselves on the researchers into the question: the first is that the ideology of *al-shūrā* is a *contemporary* ideology, even if the idea of *shūrā* itself is ancient and presented among the teachings of politics in Islam. Radiating from this is that a contemporary exploitation of the idea of *al-shūrā* has occurred with Islamist discourse under pressure of new political questions imposed upon it and challenging the establishment of a modern political system and a political ideology to express it[2] (that is, liberal democratic ideology), and that it was not possible for the idea of *shūrā* to fully cover this extent, and garner all this significance in the contemporary Islamic conscience. If it had not been for the existence of an objective sanction to promulgate the code of Islam before the questions of the age, and at the heart of them the question of the extent of capability of that code to extend to Muslims a political answer to the question of rule and the state and the rights of the group and the *ummah* in power.

The second of these facets is the absence of academic classical *fiqh* accumulation on the matter of *al-shūrā* which had the most far reaching impact in the branding of contemporary Islamist thought about it. This marked theoretical poverty pushed a large segment of contemporary thinkers to borrow some of the modern theoretical subjects of democracy and to attribute them to *shūrā*, endeavoring to cover the need of according the understanding with an adequate measure of signification in order to be able to employ it in the discourse. Similarly many did not succeed, as we shall see, in achieving a victory for the authenticity of the understanding of *shūrā* with the assertion that the understanding of modern Western democracy is nothing more than an inspiration drawn from it. Correspondingly, many also did not succeed in achieving the like of that victory from the standpoint of their emphasis of the distinction and differences between the understanding of *shūrā* and the understanding of democracy and the original authenticity of the first in comparison to the spuriousness of the second.

Thinking about *shūrā* – in contemporary Islamist thought – poses three primary questions: What is the meaning of *shūrā*? What is its position in the Islamist conception of politics?; and finally, what is the nature of the relation between *al-shūrā* and democracy?

On the Meaning of *al-Shūrā*

Islamists talk much about *al-shūrā*, but they seldom give pause for theoretical considerations about the understanding of its definition. This creates a type of impression that the meaning of *al-shūrā* was abundantly clear in a spontaneous, intuitive way to the minds (of the ancients) – to the effect that it was utterly without need for clarification: that is for theoretical specification. The case, however, is not like that at all; rather the reluctance to define it is an indication of the measure of the theoretical poverty exhibited in contemporary Islamist 'thought' which hinders the practice of an operation of theoretical analysis of the subjects which it comprises just as it is also an indication of the extent of the obscurity of the understanding among its users! Among the factors of this obscurity are, in our estimation, vigilance by most of them to not enter its meaning into connotations and modern understandings similar to it in signification such as the concept of democracy. However, also among the causes of this obscurity is an ignorance of the need to consider the understanding academically and, instead, finding it sufficient, to reference the two Qur'ānic verses and the landmark engaging in it in the Prophetic experience and that of the *Rāshidūn* Caliphs, as well as the consideration that mere reference to this word is decisive in the subject.

Perhaps, we may find exception in what a few among contemporary Islamist thinkers have written – a trace of concern for that need (to define the term) that drives towards theoretical consideration of an understanding that goes beyond the utility of the mere mention of it (that is, the referencing of the term) which most Islamist 'researchers' circulate in regard to the matter. Ḥasan al-Turābī and Rāshid al-Ghanūshī are two among these few who are worthy of note.[3] They do not leave the concept of thinking about *al-shūrā* in apposition to or as a relative correlate of democracy but strive to delimit it in its theoretical and semantic placement within the order of Islam.

We read on the definition of *shūrā* according to sheikh Rāshid al-Ghanūshī:

> *Al-shūrā* in Islam is not a derivative ruling of the branches (*ḥukm farʿī*) among the rulings of the religion indicated by a [Qur'ānic] verse or two and some *aḥādīth* and (historical) events. Rather it is a source (*aṣl*) among the *uṣūl* of the religion and dictated by the requirements of human vice-regency (*al-istikhlāf*), that is, conferral of the divine authority on the slaves (i.e., upon humans)...and from there, *al-shūrā* was the backbone of the political power of the *ummah* and their means of rising to rule...[4]

Al-shūrā is not, according to the citation, a detail among the details of politics in Islam where the sultan might be inclined to ignore it – so long as it did not fall into a category that necessitated its respect.[5] Rather, it is a binding contractual source (*aṣl ʿaqdī*) which is not subject to disabling. It is the expression of the idea of human vice-regency on the Earth and in authority; that is, the vice-regency of the *ummah* in ruling its affairs according to the dictates of consensus (*al-ijmāʿ*)[6] contracted in it for the affairs of its *wilāyah* (trusteeship) over itself. This, for the same reason, is the essence of the concept of authority in Islam and the expression of the *wilāyah* of the *ummah* over itself.

Ḥasan al-Turābī goes to the same meaning when he writes:

> *al-shūrā* in Islam is a rule issuing from the *uṣūl* of the religion and its universal foundations before derivative branching specifications for it were asserted in the texts of law (*al-sharʿ*). Among the tenets of the creed is that the Islam of divine ordination and that rule and political authority belong to Allah as well as the belief that human beings are equal in the worship of

> Allah. Thus, political liberation which the system of *al-shūrā* requires is...if people become, without exception, those who are vice-regents of political authority on the earth where every one of them has a rightful share of power...the principle of the absolute divine sovereignty (*al-ḥākimīyah*) of Allah and the vice-regency of the human being on the earth are what gave them this freedom and power to practice political authority in things and among people, and all of this renders the slaves free, equal partners who do not engage in anything except through *al-shūrā* (consultation). It is cooperation by attaining to consensus of opinion in a particular matter rather than the decision resting with the one to whom it pertains, and such is the case of responsibility and any public matter from the standpoint that no individual behaves autocratically but rather all are consulted about it.[7]

Al-shūrā, then is a matter of the *uṣūl* in Islam. It is among that granted its status among the *uṣūl* as a result of the primary principle that, in Islam, worship and servitude (*al-'ubūdīyah*) are for Allah alone without any partner. This is a principle of equality between human beings in their rights; and it is among that which Allah has charged to individuals in worship, and they are free in what is between them, and equal before the law (*al-shar'*) in duties and rights. This equality of theirs is what impose *shūrā* as a system of politics for them from the standpoint that no one of their members can act individually in political power, thereby setting up [a system of] worship or impinging upon the principle of equality which Islam has specified. On the basis of this, political freedom does not belong to the people – it is a sub-condition for engaging *shūrā* as a system for them – if not being of the fruits of the worship of Allah. Thus, *shūrā* – in the view of al-Turābī – is a political matter in its direct definition, a product of a creedal principle of the *uṣūl*: the worship of and servitude to Allah that is also a matter of the *uṣūl*.

The first of the results of this definition of *shūrā* is the assertion that the system of rule in Islam is a *shūrā* system.

The System of *al-Shūrā*

Islamists concur that 'the system of Islamic, Qur'ānic Prophetic rule is the system of *al-shūrā*', and that 'Muslims are obligated to not entrust their affairs to anyone except through [an occasion of] *shūrā*'.[8] That assertion presupposes that establishment of a system of rule – in Islam – occurs in the milieu of the Muslims and with agreement among them, or between those who have been elevated among them to the task of representation; that is, it does not submit to an administration *above* the group, and it does not proceed according to dictates of confiscation or usurpation – and among these are usurpation of succession as well as inheritance of rule in it.[9] However, the assertion of this poses questions about the system of *al-shūrā*: its essence, its means of realization, and what might possibly serve as an authoritative referent upon which to build, or even upon which to rely? It is the question of the initiative which, in the first instance, entails an absence of Islamic legislation on the subject, and difficulty in ascertaining the Prophetic system of *shūrā* or that of the *Rāshidūn* caliphs – in Medina – as represented by attempts to graft it onto new experiences characterized by markedly different conditions and variables.

We read in sheikh Muḥammad al-Ghazālī of an attempt to approach the question:

> *Al-shūrā* is a great Islamic principle! But, the means of realizing *shūrā* and setting up its apparatus has not been specified for us. It would appear that this is intended for differences in environment and level of civilization; rather we notice that one *ummah* of a high civilization changed the means of *shūrā* in it a number of times depending upon its experiences and the relative benefits. What occurred in France during a period of less than half a century is a model for that change. *Al-shūrā* in the caliphal state came into prominence in manifold forms, and it is not important which type we embrace, rather what is important is that we provide the guarantees and the modes that will make *shūrā* an observable reality so that the exploited individual will disappear and political idolatry will die out, and the correct opinion will return triumphant without fetters, and the capable man will be without resentment...[10]

There is not, in the opinion of al-Ghazālī, an authoritatively referential text, or a model experience, specifying the system of *shūrā* in either one or the other; rather, that is not even necessary in his opinion when we consider that the absence of legislation is 'intended' (*maqṣūd*) in order to observe clarifications and differences in circumstance and historical period and when we consider that the lesson is in *principle* and not by way of a model. The 'intended' thing is that what al-Ghazālī mentions as the 'main point' in the subject from the perspective of the defenders of the idea of the *shūrā* of the political system in Islam. It is a legal encouragement of the obligation of *ijtihād* in establishing that system in accordance with the constraints of particular needs and conditions. The most important thing in all of this is that he specifies a tenet assumed by the contemporary *mujtahidūn* of Islam, or more precisely, one which they deduce in their interpretation of the silence on the matter in the texts of the *sharīʿah*. The upshot of this tenet is that refraining from legislation in the political question, generally, and for *shūrā* specifically, is an endorsement (contextually or specifically, depending upon the degree of interpretation) of the *wilāyah* (trusteeship) of the *ummah* over itself, and its right in choosing the system of rule that it desires.[11] That is not, as ʿAllāl al-Fāsī asserts for any other reason than the idea that 'political authority is latent in the *ummah*, and from it, it ascends to the hands of the leaders (*al-ruʾasāʾ*) and those who have been given command (*ulīy al-amr*).'[12]

When Muḥammad al-Ghazālī or ʿAbd al-Salām Yāsīn says that *al-shūrā* is not a ready-made description in the texts of Islam but rather a *principle* left to *ijtihād*,[13] and when al-Qaraḍāwī interprets the like of that assertion as a byproduct of the Islamic state being a 'constitutional' state,[14] or that it is 'the state of rights and freedoms',[15] it ought not be believed that *al-shūrā* connotes establishment of a civil rule agreed upon by people (that is, the group or the *ummah*) on agreed upon (or positive) bases and laws with their consent, and in isolation from an authoritative referent of their *sharīʿah*. That is what conflicts with the existing logic of the Islamic state that rests upon the authoritative referent of the *sharīʿah* in its social and political system. The truth of the matter in the Islamic state is that the state of *al-sharīʿah* and *al-shūrā* is *not* a civil right, but rather it is the right of Allah; and on the basis of this: 'it is the right of any Muslim – male or female,' says al-Qaraḍāwī, 'if the rule commands him or her in what clearly contradicts the *sharīʿah* of Allah, to refuse, rather it is his or her obligation to refuse; because if he or she is confronted with the right of rule and the right of Allah, then the right of Allah takes precedence without doubt.'[16]

It is not possible to comprehend this theoretical chemistry which precipitates concepts of the Islamic state, *al-sharīʿah*, and *al-shūrā* along with concepts of the trusteeship (*wilāyah*) of the *ummah* over itself, and the *ummah* as the source of political power except through understanding of the meaning of the term '*ummah*' in Islamist discourse. The *ummah* (community) which this discourse intends, in its widely-disseminated discussion of it, is not the national/popular *ummah* or the social or civil one as defined in modern political thought, but rather it is the *ummah* of the denomination: the *religious ummah* which can be summarized by the concept of 'the group' – the group of Muslims (*jamāʿat al-muslimīn*). It is, in the definition of one of the Islamist writers[17] 'a human society established on a shared creedal basis'. Thus, it is not free to choose a political system other than one resting for support on its *sharīʿah*; that is, 'it is not free to choose whether or not to respect this constitution' (*al-sharī'ah*), as al-Qaraḍāwī says,[18] because 'ruling by *al-sharī'ah* is a command wherein the people have no choice nor are they consulted for their opinion' as Muḥammad Quṭb says.[19]

If we temporarily overlook these necessary, precise challenges, and find it sufficient to work with the concept of *al-shūrā* in its general Islamic form – from the standpoint that it is synonymous with signifying the specification of the right of the *ummah* to choose its leaders and to take them to account – then that which imposes itself in this connection is the question of the supposed status of *al-shūrā* in Islam: is it to be respected with a respect that is tantamount to that for the *sharī'ah* itself, or is it only a principle where operating by it does not fall within the locus of obligation?

Perhaps sheikh al-Qaraḍāwī is the most important among Islamist thinkers to have struggled to deal with this matter from the standpoint of the potential connection between adopting the principle of operating according to the opinion of the imam – and Ḥasan al-Bannā asserted and espoused this while al-Qaraḍāwī resurrected it – and adopting the principle of *al-shūrā* or *al-mashūrāh* within the Muslim group or from the group of *ahl al-ḥal wa al-'aqd* (people of authority) among them. If al-Qaraḍāwī confirms the necessity of operating according to the opinion of the imam, he delineates that obligation in three spheres:

a. In the sphere of 'that for which there is not text (*naṣṣ*)', and he means by that: 'that for which there is no Islamic legal signification (*dalīl shar'ī*) transmitted in the Qur'ān or the true *sunnah*', considering that this sphere represents a 'free region (*minṭaqah ḥurrah*)' or an 'empty region (*minṭaqah fārighah*)' in the particular Islamic-legal (*shar'ī*) texts'. And, these are what al-Qaraḍāwī terms a 'region of dispensation (*minṭaqah al-'afwu*)' in other instances.
b. In the sphere of 'what allows for multiple facets (*wujūh 'iddah*)'; and this has two meanings: 'that from which the imam may choose' and 'what exhibits multiplicity of opinions and endeavors in *ijtihād*'.
c. In the sphere of 'consigned (public) good (*al-maṣāliḥ al-mursalah*)'; that is, the absolute and unlimited, and 'we mean by that the (public) good (*al-maṣlaḥah*) which is not indicated by a particular signification among the texts of *al-shar'* according to their consideration and not according to their cancellation'.[20]

Al-Qaraḍāwī does not stop at these limits, repeating the theses of the *fuqahā'* of Islamic legal politics concerning the obligation to operate according to the opinion of the imam, but rather he goes beyond, or specifies conditions for it from the standpoint that he asserts 'what is obligatory is that this be completed after consulting the people of opinion and specialization (*ahl al-ra'īy wa al-ikhtiṣāṣ*)';[21] and it is not for the imam, moreover, to consider himself above the need for that, or exempt from its command, because 'if even the Prophet – supported by revelation (*al-waḥīy*) – was commanded to engage in consultation, then other than he must certainly do so.'[22] In an extension of the givens of this context, the question which arises is whether or not *al-shūrā* is, then, *mandatory.*

Al-Qaraḍāwī takes this position when he writes: 'We assert the obligation of *al-shūrā* because its results are mandatory so long as they issue from its people in its place.'[23] But, who are these 'people of it' for which it is not mandatory except in the case of their existence? They are the *ahl al-ḥal wa al-'aqd* (the people of authority); and the opinion of these 'is mandatory for the imam'.[24]

Thinking about *al-shūrā* in its contemporary political contexts is best done by raising the level of attention to this principle in Islam; and the context of that is Western civil society and the modern liberal political system: the system of the nation state. Undoubtedly the contemplative pause given by the Reformers of the nineteenth century to meditation on the relation of *al-shūrā* to democracy and to researching that relationship, which gives rise to the thesis that it is a relation of intersection, was renewed by Islamic Reformers since the 1930s and took on two orientations: the orientation of researching the similar aspects or the reconciliation of the two concepts; and the orientation of researching the divergences and distinctions between them.

Al-shūrā and Democracy: On Relations of Proximity

Sheikh Muḥammad al-Ghazālī notices, with pain, how Muslims have failed to realize the system of *al-shūrā*, while they are its exponents, where others have succeeded in that, saying: 'It distresses us that *al-shūrā* reached its fruition in a wide region outside the domains of Islam,'[25] and the 'outside the domains of Islam' which he intends, refers to nothing more than the countries of the West: Europe and USA. The fact is that many among Islamist intellectuals do not hesitate over an acknowledgement of the sort of sheikh al-Ghazālī, in the success of the West in systematizing its social, civil and political fairs according to the requirements of '*al-shūrā*' (i.e., democracy), along the lines of succeeding in its goal of social guidance and expression of the demands of society.[26] That acknowledgement was implicit on the sidelines of what is indicated by a scientific impartiality – a chapter among chapters in contemporary Islamic intellectual openness to the experiences of other peoples and communities in administrating political affairs and the state. Perhaps we may find the best example of that openness in what sheikh Rāshid al-Ghanūshī wrote in defining the modern democratic system and delimiting its distinguishing particulars.

Al-Ghanūshī embarks on his discussion of democracy from the conceptual basis ingrained in his consciousness and its outcome is that, 'Democracy offers the best instrument or device for rule, enabling the citizens, through its use, to practice basic freedoms, and among these are the political liberties.'[27] He does not assert that incidentally, and does not reiterate generalizations on the subject that many have contributed to the thesis unthinkingly, but rather he does that decisively in sober knowledge of the history of democracy in the modern West.[28] The democratic system – as far as our *mujtahid* sheikh sees – is form and content. From the standpoint of *form*: it is an assertion of the principle of the sovereignty of the people and it is the source of political authority; it is sovereignty exercised in elections and what is enjoyed among rights in equality, a separation of power, political and union organization, and the right of rule of the majority; as well as the right of the minority to mount opposition in order that political authority may attain to legitimacy. As for the matter from the standpoint of *content*, it is an acknowledgement of the essence of human beings and their dignity, and a textual specification of their right to political participation in the administration of general affairs given the consideration that '*participation* in the social and political dimension is the essence of the ideal towards which the democratic model fixes its gaze and not representation' and, subsequently, the consideration that 'the highest ideal of democracy is that the governed should become rulers in order to realize for themselves and by themselves what they aspire towards among goals and ends.'[29]

Al-Ghanūshī, however, like most Islamist *mujtahidūn*, gives pause in the acknowledgement, at the point of critical realization that demands recourse to his position as a Muslim extolling a different order of values, and evaluating through it the necessary distance with a subject he fears will overwhelm him and which threatens to strip him of his identity. At the point of this realization, he registers, like the others,[30] his *philosophical* reservation, not his *political*, about Western democracy and writes:

> the point of concern (lit., disease) is not in the apparatus of democracy – elections, parliament, majority, multiplicity of political parties or freedom of the

press – not to the extent that it is latent in the political philosophies of the West...which separate between the spirit (*al-rūḥ*) and the body (*al-jasad*) – the philosophy of Descartes – and then ignore the spirit, burying it alive; and [these philosophies] make war on Allah and struggle to the utmost to displace the human being from his [rightful] place so that there does not remain anything in the universe or within the human being other than material substrate, motion, appetite and control and struggle and the legitimacy of raw force. The afflictions of humanity are not latent in the democratic system or its familiar techniques, which permit it to function successfully and to constitute a sound device for the systemization of the relation between the rulers and the ruled and to transfer legitimacy from the person of the ruler...to the institution of rule derived from the will of the people.[31]

Al-Ghanūshī's critical realization, however, does not compel him – like others – to decree the necessity of the democratic system and the relativity of its model, and its rejection is not justifiable for him under any circumstances; rather, he is unequivocal in that 'it is the best system for the extension of the development of human thought,' warning with the assertion that one ought not 'dwell on the faults of this system in order to refute it, as to do so is to the benefit of dictatorship and even deficient or libertine freedom is preferable to tyranny. A society governed by deficient law is better than a society whose law is the will of idolatrously excessive rulers and their whims.'[32] What is not in need of clarification is that the like of this defense of the democratic system is far removed from the supposition of the incompatibility between it and between the Islamist view of the world and society and politics which engenders in the consciousness the binding together of democracy and *shūrā*, not from the standpoint that they are linked in support to two different philosophical backgrounds, but rather from the standpoint that they share in the same *political* principle, and that they are delimited by the same theoretical points of departure in the sphere of political consciousness.

The most prominent manifestation of constructing a connection of nearness and proximity between democracy and *shūrā* – in the contemporary Islamist consciousness – is the attribution of the first to the second on the consideration that *shūrā* is the *origin* of democracy.[33] It is not important that this consciousness constrained to a referential authority that evaluates it, but rather what is important is that it accompanies the idea of the juncture between the Islamic political legislative order and the legislative order of positive law.[34] That is what justifies the assertion of one making the assertion that *shūrā* is democracy or vice versa.[35]

This relation of proximity between democracy and *shūrā* posits a question: is it possible to realize *shūrā* – as an Islamic principle – in the scope of the existing democratic system, or must democracy be returned to 'its origin' of *al-shūrā*? If we open the door to the first possibility, there are greater opportunities for reconciliation between the two principles. If, however, we incline towards the second supposition, then we deny the existence of the possibility of Islam and Muslims engaging in contemporary democracy! Probably al-Ghanūshī was the boldest among the rest of contemporary Islamists when he emphasized that, in the scope of the Islamic system:

> it is possible to put into effect the political values that Islam brought such as *al-shūrā* and the pledge of allegiance (*al-bay'ah*) and consensus (*al-ijmā'*) and commanding what is just and forbidding what is unjust (*al-amr bi-l-ma'rūf wa al-nahīy 'an al-munkar*); that is, the teachings that came to establish justice and to effectuate human happiness. If so, it is possible for democratic implements, just as it is possible for manufactured implements – in the consideration that they are a human inheritance – to be employed in different cultural environs and different conceptual terrain.[36]

This means that there is no way to think about the supposition that *shūrā* is *outside* the reality of existing democracy.

If we want to enumerate the shared and similar sources of the system of *al-shūrā* and the system of democracy in the Islamist consciousness, we might give pause before three primary ones: representation (*al-tamthīl*); 'culpability' (*al-taklīf*); and the right of opposition.

'Allāl al-Fāsī effects a proximity between Islam and Western thought in their conceptions of the matter of political representation, and he notes[37] that Islam emerges from the principle of an absence of infallibility (*'iṣmah*) for any individual other than the Messenger, leading to the assertion of the absence of infallibility for the group, to the assertion of the impossibility of the group or the *ummah* expressing its opinion, and moreover, its need for deputizing representatives for these whom they choose. Then, he notices that this same gradation or progression is that tread by defenders of democracy in the West: the assertion that the original basis is one where individuals should govern themselves, and as that is not possible, each one is obliged to choose another who will represent them and who will assume the trusteeship of rule in their name.

The solid relation between Islam and Western thought – in the assessment of al-Fāsī – is on the side of the consideration of the value of political representation in establishing the system of rule – *al-shūrā*, democracy.

However, the question that this opinion poses is: if the modern democratic system reckons the idea of representation as the foundation of the principle of citizenship, on what principle would the system of *al-shūrā* consider this idea? Or, in other words, if citizenship which is a legal and material expression of the allegiance (*walā'*) of the nation, constitutes that in Western societies, then what does it constitute in Islamic societies where there is no allegiance in them except to the religion and the group of believers in the creed of Islam? Is it the right of non-Muslims to represent Muslims or to get votes of Muslims or to enter into coalitions with them in parliaments?

Al-Qaraḍāwī answers that – in an exhibition of his disapproval of the opinion of other deniers – saying:

> We should not be surprised to find those who prohibit the candidacy of non-Muslims to enter the house of representatives or the popular parliament or the *majlis* of *al-shūrā*...and who prohibit giving them the votes of Muslims as we might find those who prohibit Muslims themselves from presenting themselves for candidacy to these legislative bodies (*al-majālis*)! Their argument in that is that whoever presents himself as a candidate for this representative office might demand the trusteeship (*al-wilāyah*) for himself, and whoever demands the *wilāyah* is not entrusted with it, as has been reported in a sound *ḥadīth* of the Prophet when he said: 'Verily we do not accord trusteeship in this matter to any who asks for it or covets it'...and whoever sees that this representation of a segment of the people of a particular circle...does not consider it to fall under the rubric of emirates (*al-imāmah*) or trusteeship (*al-wilāyah*)...[38]

Given the fact that al-Qaraḍāwī acknowledges the right of non-Muslims to serve as representatives in a conditional form, that is, 'so long as the parliament in its overwhelming majority is of Muslims', he also acknowledges at the same time the right of these non-Muslims to be 'citizens' in the Islamic state.[39]

This preceding remark drives us to a question from which derives a maxim: if citizenship is what permits representation in both cases – in the case of Islamic *shūrā* and in the case of Western democracy – then are we led to perceive the concept of citizenship in Islam or is it in our capacity to build on this concept from within Islam,[40] or is it possible for us to find for it an Islamic correlate or what approximates that?

'Allāl al-Fāsī delves to dig up this correlate for the modern concept of citizenship in the Islamic lexicon, and he finds it in the concept of culpability (*al-taklīf*). Islam considers every individual to be culpable (*mukallaf*), that is, called upon to engage in his obligations towards Allah and towards society and towards himself as well as towards all humanity. The rights which obtain are those which obtain through the awareness of these obligations; and thus, 'culpability (*al-taklīf*) in Islamic customary law (*al-'urf*) occupies the place of citizenship in the modern democratic customary law.'[41] It is on the same loom that al-Qaraḍāwī weaves his attempt to construct the connection between the voter (*al-nākhib*) in the modern democratic political lexicon and the witness (*al-shāhid*) in the Islamic lexicon.[42]

Citizenship, then, is culpability (*taklīf*). However, it is known to us that this culpability is mandatory for Muslims; so, what about non-Muslims among those who live in the '*dār al-Islām*' (domains of Islam)? The citizenship of these is determined – in the view of most Islamist *mujtahidūn* – by their membership in the Islamic state[43] and by their possession of the right to equality with the Muslims, that is:

> the principle of the equality of citizenship in the Islamic state is fixed and the rights and obligations of Muslims do not differ from non-Muslims except in what is dictated by differences in creeds because equality among equals is just and equality in circumstances that are not equivalent is wrongdoing, and in that is confirmation of the principle of equality for which there is no exception.[44]

Equality in rights, for those asserting the imprint of *al-shūrā* on the political system in Islam, moves from equality in rights, equality possessed of a religious stamp (between Muslims and non-Muslims) to equality possessed of a political stamp – between the majority and the minority. Here, also, Islamists tend towards the assertion of resemblance of the givens of political rights in the system of *al-shūrā* with this determination in the modern democratic system, and on the basis of these rights is the right of opposition in its consideration as a right retained by the minority and a guarantee of the sponsorship of its interest in the face of the ruling majority. We read Muḥammad al-Ghazālī in this sense:

> Among the particulars of modern 'democracy' is that it considers opposition a part of the general system of the state! And, the opposition has a leader who is acknowledged and comes to an understanding with him without any duress! That is, that the possessor of political authority is a human being who has those who support him and those who criticize him, and neither of the two has more right to respect than the other...and the reality is that this theory approaches very closely the teachings of the *Rāshidūn* Caliphs. 'Alī bin Abī Ṭālib did not attempt to quash those who opposed him or to gather

> them together to strike them, rather he said to them: 'Keep your opinions as you will, on the condition that you do not ferment chaos or shed blood.' That is, the great man desired a *constructive* opposition not a destructive one, and he did not perceive opposition to his person as a wrong (*munkar*).[45]

What is clear is that sheikh al-Ghazālī does *not* find an Islamic legal text to convey for him a way of proving the similarity between the position of Islam in regard to the matter with the position of modern political democratic thought; however, realities aid him in some of their precedents of demonstration for the position that was taken. And these, generally, serve as the operational basis for the remainder of contemporary thinkers of Islam who have attempted to clarify the points of similarity or disjuncture between the political system in Islam and the modern political system!

Against this approach of reconciliation between *shūrā* and democracy among one strand of Islamist thinkers asserting *al-shūrā*, there is another approach with a different trend tending towards an adamant emphasis of the divergences and inherent distinctions between the two. Rather it vilifies with all alacrity any attempt to construct any kind of correlative comparison between the two!

Al-Shūrā is Religious and Democracy is Secular

> Among Muslims there are those who say: Democracy is a boon and profitable to the human being, and it is the way out – there is no other, and it is the sister of Islamic *shūrā* and its correlate and of the same type...and among Islamists are those who say frankly that democracy is unbelief (*kufr*)...and they might concede to accept that democracy, if it is not unbelief, is the sister of unbelief...Democracy is not the opposite of unbelief, it is the opposite of autocracy (*al-istibdād*). The opposite of unbelief is faith. If our world takes the position that the equation is democracy equals unbelief, then alongside it is the equation that faith equals autocracy. And if so, then we are, of a necessity, with every despot who says 'I am a Muslim against freedom' and says 'I am not democratic'.
>
> 'The term democracy means the rule of the people and the choice of the people and governance to the people. This is an issue for which we call, and we are not pleased with other than it. We are certain that Muslim people...will not choose rule other than that which Allah sent down, and it is Islamic rule, and it is our general program and the horizon of our initiative for change and transformation...If it happens that people choose, in this

> country or that or in this stage or that, to go along with the democrats we will take it upon ourselves to accuse them of paucity in the knowledge of what Islamic rule is and we will take measures granted by pure democracy and not granted by autocracy to lay out for people and explain to people and to associate with people until they know us according to our reality and they know the democrats according to their reality.'

The two citations are those of sheikh 'Abd al-Salām Yāsīn.[46] The reader of these excerpts will not doubt that their writer is extremely circumspect as to what democracy connotes as a value for consideration; rather extreme in his reliance on 'its clean means' as a means for change, instead of violence. The truth is that Yāsīn – influenced by the Moroccan political environment and the political conceptual legacy of the National Movement – wrote on different occasions what would imply that he exempts himself and his movement – Jamā'at al-'Adl wa al-Iḥsān (the Group of Justice and Benevolence) – from democratic choice, and he does not wager on any other way to approach the matter of political authority other than it.[47] However, the point of divergence in the thought of sheikh Yāsīn – and perhaps it is the reigning point of divergence in the consciousness of most contemporary thinkers of Islam – is that what he accords to democracy with the right hand of *politics*, he takes away with the left hand of *concept* and creed! He draws from it, *politically*, a realistic, open borrowing, pronouncing upon it, on the other hand, a death sentence when he approaches it from a *conceptual* angle from within the order of the *sharī'ah*. Thus, he arrives at an amalgam of two conflicting discourses about it: an open civil discourse and a closed religious one.

This schizophrenia in his consciousness – in the consciousness of many other than he – constitutes a dependence and an emendation: dependence on a matter or concept, then assailing it with a critical or attacking emendation! We read that for example – and in what pertains to our subject about the relation between *al-shūrā* and democracy – in the following citation:

> The people in the popular democratic state – in addition to race, language, shared interest and history – are bound together by a social contract...this social contract is represented in customary laws, precedents, and reserved implied rights which are unwritten...or in a written rational constitution...this is one aspect where the demand of democracy converges with the demand of *al-shūrā*: that people are bound together by contract (*'aqd*) and pledged agreement (*'ahd*) so that all people may behave according to the knowledge of what each possesses and what is incumbent upon each per-

> son...while on the other hand, the second proposition of the equation conflicts with a basis among the essential bases of the Islamic state. That is, that this society is predicated on the basis that it is nothing more than a civil society, bound together only on the basis of consensual goals. Believers are connected in the Islamic state from the standpoint of every interest of the *wilāyah* (trusteeship) between the believing men and women; and it is a religion. This is a condition in the context of *al-shūrā*; it is its spirit.[48]

This mode of dependence and emendation is repeated in much of what he has written about the subject of the relation between *shūrā* and democracy,[49] except that Yāsīn does not stop to liberate himself from this schizophrenia in the service of his conceptual and contractual definition of democracy according to his political definition of it, resulting in the assertion – as is the case with many other than he[50] – that *shūrā* is *other* than democracy in nature and essence when 'the difference between *al-shūrā* on the basis of the Qur'ān and democracy on the basis of a social contract is an essential difference', as the believer desires by *al-shūrā* 'his triumph in the abode of the afterlife, and his active participation in commanding what is just and forbidding what is unjust (*al-amr bi-l-ma'rūf wa al-nahīy 'an al-munkar*)'. As for the democrat, he desires by democracy 'citizenship of which he can be proud' and civil rights and a freedom guaranteed by law.[51] The tremendous difference between the two is tantamount to the difference between Muslim society and civil society.[52] While it might be true to suggest, analogously, that '*al-shūrā* is the term for "our democracy"' – according to the expression of Yāsīn[53] – the difference between them is impossible to deny, and it extends from the etymological difference (the source of the utterance)[54] to a difference in nature where it is not possible for democracy and the *sharī'ah* to coexist.[55] So long as both *al-shūrā* and democracy spring from a 'referential authority (*marja'īyah*) different at the root-level',[56] that is, so long as both the society of *al-shūrā* and the society of democracy have a particular and distinct criterion by which to measure the issue![57]

If 'Abd al-Salām Yāsīn establishes his theory of the relation between *al-shūrā* and democracy on a philosophical basis or a contractual one (*'aqdī*) – rather than a political one – he concludes by positing the divergences and differences between them on the basis of an indeterminate sharpness, where democracy becomes 'a natural law "*sharī'ah*" (*sharī'ah ṭabī'īyah*) and *al-shūrā* becomes a "divine *sharī'ah*";[58] rather, democracy is the sister of secularism just as *al-shūrā* is the sister of prayer (*al-ṣalāt*) and alms (*al-zakāt*)'.[59] In that, our Moroccan exponent is the greatest example of the assertion of the dissociation – in contemporary Islamic thought – and the rift between *al-shūrā* and democracy and its belonging to a 'philosophical' signification which he extracts from its political definition.[60] The significance of that is nothing but a correlate of its concept for the concept of secularism or *al-lā'ikīyah* (Laicism) in the expression of Yāsīn.

If we transfer the matter of the relation between *al-shūrā* and democracy from its comparative conceptual framework, along the lines of some of the givens entertained by 'Abd al-Salām Yāsīn, to the comparative political sphere, we find some of the manifestations of that divergence and separation abundantly clear without the slightest ambiguity. Thus, Fatḥī Yakan, for example, engages in the political opposition between the two on the presumption that democracy connotes 'the governance of the people and their ascendancy in the state', and this being that which implies the people 'rule themselves by a system which they themselves have created', and that *al-shūrā* 'does not solicit the consideration of the opinion of an individual or a group of people in the exegesis of Islamically legal rule or its comprehension or *ijtihād* in any matter among its affairs in light of the Islamic legislation.'[61] Whoever stands on the grounds of this opposition, endeavors to derive a result that rule in Islam is *individual* and that operation according to *al-shūrā* is specified under the rubric of *al-isti'nās* (amicable consultation/counsel) not that of obligation and mandatory observance (*al-wujūb wa-l-iltizām*)![62]

What is clear here is that establishing the disjuncture between *al-shūrā* and democracy is not to be found by tracing the prominence of the value of *al-shūrā* – religious or supra-political – but rather what is intended by it is to tarnish the image of *al-shūrā* and to usurp the right of the masses (the people, the group, the *ummah*) in political authority, in contradistinction to the ruler who enjoys absolute political authority to the point where they transfer to him the right to bring down the principle of *shūrā* itself! It is legislation for tyranny in the cloak of *al-shūrā* divested from all democratic content.

Approaching this meaning – without being identical to it – is what another Islamist pen wrote in distinguishing between legislative political authority in the democratic state and between the Islamic state when it wrote: 'Legislative political authority in present-day constitutional governments is entrusted to members of the representational parliaments, and they are those who engage in authoring the laws...whereas in the Islamic state the ones to whom legislative political authority is entrusted are the *mujtahidūn* and the legalists who issue *fatwās* (*ahl al-futayā*)'.[63] The people of democracy are elected and they represent and they legislate; as for the people of '*al-shūrā*, it is not moot for them to elect or to choose, and they have no right in legislation; the full extent of what they possess is to engage in 'making the text comprehendable and clarifying the rule which it specifies' or in formulating their analogy for that for which there is no text on the basis of that for which there is one in order to derive its ruling.[64]

The difference is categorical, then, between the two systems, and every attempt to reconcile between them – as the Reformers of the nineteenth century or the students of Ḥasan al-Bannā and 'Allāl al-Fāsī attempted – is attempting the impossible in what is essentially an attempt to square the circle. If so, then the relation between *al-shūrā* and democracy is a contradictory and mutually exclusive one; rather it is, in its essence, tantamount to the relation between Islam and the West, between Muslim society and civil society, between the *sharī'ah* and secularism and so on. It is, in sum, a relation the like of a chasm that cannot be bridged.

If we depend upon building on the givens of the preceding analysis, the meaning of *al-shūrā* in contemporary Islamist discourse is constrained, and it is not possible for us to define it as 'the implementation of democracy on the basis of the *sharī'ah*', or that it is 'the reciprocal right of political power in the scope of the *sharī'ah*'. When it is the case that the *sharī'ah* is sent down and there is no role for '*ijtihād*' other than commuting its rulings to new realities, then the marginalization of *shūrā* in the practice of political authority is a narrow marginal rule...rather it is only pro forma.

On this basis, if that justifies the legitimacy of establishing a distinction and disjuncture between *al-shūrā* and democracy, from one angle, then it explains the reasons that impelled many Islamists to take that separation and distinction to its furthest limits with the utmost passion: to the limit of identity transformation. That is, that this intrinsic, sharp distinction was not capable of bearing a connotation or a function other than that of bringing down the principle of *shūrā* itself from among the primary fundamentals of politics and authority through the detachment of its connection to the meaning of democracy with the goal of legislating for a religious state that has no constraints upon it whatsoever.

Notes

1. Al-Turābī, Ḥasan 'Abdullah, *Naẓarāt fi al-Fiqh al-Sīyāsī* (Khartoum: al-Sharikah al-'Ālamīyah li-Khadamāt al-I'lām, 1988), p. 72.

2. In this context, al-Sayyid states: '*Shūrā* is a deeply ingrained Islamic characteristic; it is a Qur'ānic text. Nevertheless, the political dimension it possessed during the first and second centuries of the *Hijrah* waned at the beginning of the third for the sake of

demarcating its moral and social dimensions up until the time when al-Ṭahṭāwī, al-Tūnsī and al-Afghānī rediscovered it, or rather rediscovered its political dimension due to their knowledge of Western charters – especially the French one – in the second third of the nineteenth century. Consequently *shūrā* grew in al-Ṭahṭāwī's view – and in that of the Reformers who came after him – to become synonymous with constitutional provision.' Al-Sayyid, *Sīyāsāt al-Islām al-Mu'āṣir,* pp. 157–8.

3. Undoubtedly, al-Turābī and al-Ghanūshī represent the most prominent Islamic apologists among contemporary thinkers in the last quarter of the twentieth century, their importance lies in their combining an encyclopedic and theoretical knowledge of Islamic tradition with a prudent political leadership; adding open conscience to modern human thought; and a high jurisprudential aptitude for interpretation. And, if the former was drawn away from openness, criticism, interpretation and remaining rooted to origins, al-Ghanūshī remained, however, adhering to the path of *ijtihād* and cognitive intrusion setting himself free from coercions of an authority with which he refused to affiliate himself – just as his contemporary al-Turābī did through soldiers!

4. Al-Ghanūshī, Rāshid, *al-Ḥurīyāt al-'Āmmah fī al-Dawlah al-Islāmīyah* (Beirut: Centre for Arab Unity Studies, 1992), p. 109.

5. It is fair enough for any individual to read the text by Islamist apologist Fatḥī Yakan to give pause at the value of al-Ghanūshī's opinion in the question of the compulsoriness of *shūrā*. Fatḥī Yakan writes: 'Leadership in Islam is individualistic...the inescapable truth about the leader in the Islamic system is that he has the authorization to manage the state affairs, however, he is not obliged to abide by the majority in running the various issues of *ummah,* the exegesis of the verse on *al-shūrā* is very plain in maintaining that the final say goes to the holder of authority and not the majority after conducting the consultation.' Available in: Yakan, Fatḥī, *Mushkilāt al-Da'wah wa al-Dā'īyah*, 3rd edn (Beirut: Mu'asasat al-Risālah, 1974), p. 173.

6. 'Consensus (*ijmā'*) which is deemed a source of the *sharī'ah* alongside the Qur'ān and the *sunnah,* is a sheer call for taking into account public opinion, with all its diverse, genuine and constant orientations and tendencies.' Available in: Al-Ghanūshī, *al-Ḥurīyāt al-'Āmmah*, pp. 119–20.

7. Al-Turābī, *Naẓarāt fī al-Fiqh,* pp. 73–4.

8. Yāsīn, *al-Shūrā wa al-Dīmuqrāṭīyah*, p. 239.

9. 'The Islamic state is not a replica of that of Khosrow or Caesar; it is not a state of succession privileged for a certain dynasty, or a branch of a family where descendants inherit it from their forefathers as if they inherit properties or a fortune.' Available in: Al-Qaraḍāwī, *min Fiqh al-Dawlah*, p. 35.

10. Al-Ghazālī, Muḥammad, *al-Sunnah al-Nabawīyah bayn Ahl al-Fiqh wa Ahl al-Ḥadīth* (Beirut: Dār al-Shurūq, 1989), p. 135.

11. In light of this, al-Qaraḍāwī goes on stating: 'Islam gave the *ummah* the authority to rule itself, so that it chooses its own Imam or ruler with conviction and gives allegiance to him with satisfaction, whenever it sees that he meets the necessary qualifications...thus, if the *ummah* chooses its ruler and gives its allegiance to him in satisfaction and submission, then it should have the right – and rather the duty – to monitor him with fidelity and to question his rule fastidiously...'. Available in: Al-Qaraḍāwī, *al-Ṣaḥwah al-Islāmīyah*, p. 80.

12. Al-Fāsī, *al-Naqd al-Dhātī,* 2nd edn (Tiṭwān, Morocco: Dār al-Fikr al-Maghribī, [undated]), p. 110.

13. 'The principle of *shūrā* in the Qur'ānic verse: "And those who have responded to their Lord and established the prayer; and their matter is one of a *shūrā* between them, and who spend of what We have given them in sustenance." [Qur'ān, *sūrat al-*

shūrā, (42:38)] fully cleared the way for *shūrā* to materialize and become convened for what is best for certain times and places, so that it acquired a certain form – or even forms – during the Prophetic and *Rāshidīn* periods, a form that was consistent with the simplicity of living and the closeness of Muslims then...and in order to meet the needs of our recent times, space, life conditions, and complex problems, we can not merely follow that simple form anymore. We have to take the essence though and pursue the perfection of faith as much as possible. And we should be diligent in convening this *shūrā*.' Available in: Yāsīn, *Ḥiwār ma'a al-Fuḍalā'*, p. 64.

14. Al-Qaraḍāwī, *min Fiqh al-Dawlah*, p. 33.
15. Al-Qaraḍāwī, *min Fiqh al-Dawlah*, p. 48.
16. Al-Qaraḍāwī, *min Fiqh al-Dawlah*, p. 58.
17. Mubārak, *Niẓām al-Islām,* p. 100.
18. Al-Qaraḍāwī, *min Fiqh al-Dawlah*, p. 33.
19. Quṭb, Muḥammad, *al-'Ilmānyūn wa al-Islām*, p. 62.
20. Al-Qaraḍāwī, *al-Sīyāsah al-Shar'īyah*, pp. 70–82.
21. Al-Qaraḍāwī, *al-Sīyāsah al-Shar'īyah*, p. 111.
22. Al-Qaraḍāwī, *al-Ṣaḥwah al-Islāmīyah*, p. 78.
23. Al-Qaraḍāwī, *al-Ṣaḥwah al-Islāmīyah*, p. 79.
24. Al-Qaraḍāwī, *al-Sīyāsah al-Shar'īyah*, p. 114.
25. Al-Ghazālī, *al-Sunnah al-Nabawī,* p. 136.
26. 'The victory of democracy in the prevailing regimes during the present era of citizenship has imposed the organization of the *ummah* in institutions that are capable of facilitating the orientation of people and manufacturing their real needs which might fade among the masses.' Available in: Al-Fāsī, *al-Naqd al-Dhātī,* p. 117.
27. Al-Ghanūshī, *al-Ḥurīyāt al-'Āmmah*, p. 75.
28. The following text is an example of this. Al-Ghanūshī states in his chronology of democracy in the West: 'Liberalism, equity, representation, pluralism, and competition remained as the primary subjects in the Western democracy until World War II, in which a number of economic, political, technological and social development factors played a role in prompting some sort of revolution against this regime, so that the role of the state is no more unbiased in the perpetual social struggle, confined in this way to preserving domestic and external security only, in fact under the new growing pressures of associations, public opinion and parties for the sake of founding a new equilibrium it had to actively get involved in social and political lives, this in turn led to having the democratic system in the West surpass the stage of formal freedoms represented by human rights advertisements; sovereignty of people, parliaments and elections; the majority's right to rule and the minority's right to oppose...to end up with an essence represented mainly in a system of communication between people and the governing institutions, a system that allows people to call, and the state to respond back. A system that enables people to take effective action and to participate in running general affairs and to contribute in forging decisions that control their own destiny, and not only to elect representatives for them...'. Available in: Al-Ghanūshī, *al-Ḥurīyāt al-'Āmmah*, p. 76.
29. Al-Ghanūshī, *al-Ḥurīyāt al-'Āmmah*, p. 77.
30. Al-Qaraḍāwī admits that 'the best aspect of Liberalism...is its political one, which is represented by the establishment of a parliamentary life in which the people are capable of choosing their own representatives...', he concludes by saying, 'the major fault of secular democratic Liberalism is its lacking a spiritual element, rather, its *deliberate* neglect of it.' Available in: Al-Qaraḍāwī, *al-Ḥilūl al-Mustawradah*, pp. 68 and 102 respectively.
31. Al-Ghanūshī, *al-Ḥurīyāt al-'Āmmah*, pp. 86–7.

32. Al-Ghanūshī, *al-Ḥurīyāt al-'Āmmah*, p. 87.

33. '...as for political democracy, its origins in our faith lie in *al-bay'ah* and *al-shūrā*.' Available in: Al-Qaraḍāwī, *al-Ṣaḥwah al-Islāmīyah*, p. 108.

34. Compare this with: al-Fāsī, *Maqāṣid al-sharī'ah*, p. 58.

35. 'For me, the modern concept of *shūrā* that Islam always recommended is parliamentary democracy...to have people elect deputies on their behalf who are capable of addressing the people's own free will and demands, and who act as guardians of the rights of this *ummah* in the state'. Available in: Khālid, Khālid Muḥammad, *al-Dawlah fī al-Islām* (Cairo: Dār Thābit, 1981), pp. 58–9.

36. Al-Ghanūshī, *al-Ḥurīyāt al-'Āmmah*, p. 88.

37. Al-Fāsī, *Maqāṣid al-sharī'ah*, p. 216.

38. Al-Qaraḍāwī, *min Fiqh al-Dawlah*, p. 194.

39. Al-Qaraḍāwī, *min Fiqh al-Dawlah*, pp. 194–15.

40. Al-Bishrī and al-Qaraḍāwī in: 'Mabda' al-mūwāṭanah', papers presented at: *al-ḥiwār al-qawmī-al-dīnī*: papers of the conference held by Centre for Arab Unity Studies (Beirut: Centre for Arab Unity Studies, 1989), pp. 139–40 and 156 respectively.

41. Al-Fāsī, *Maqāṣid al-sharī'ah*, p. 221.

42. Al-Qaraḍāwī, *min Fiqh al-Dawlah*, p. 37.

43. Al-Bannā, *Majmū'at Rasā'il*, p. 69.

44. Al-Ghanūshī, *Ḥuqūq al-Mūwāṭanah: Ḥuqūq Ghayr al-Muslim fī al-Mujtama' al-Islāmī* (Tunis: [n.pb.], 1989), p. 40.

45. Al-Ghazālī, *al-Sunnah al-Nabawī*, p. 136.

46. Yāsīn, *Ḥiwār ma'a al-Fuḍalā'*, pp. 57–9.

47. 'Since democracy is dialogue versus dialogue, and a solution for political disputes via civilized political means, rather than tanks mustered to liquidate the political rival that once prevailed over you, then we may say that hope is peering from the horizon, that we can protect ourselves and our people from massive turmoil.' Available in: Yāsīn, *Ḥiwār ma'a al-Fuḍalā'*, p. 62.

48. Yāsīn, *al-Shūrā wa al-Dīmuqrāṭīyah*, pp. 46–7.

49. For example, he writes: 'Democracy is rationalization of rule, human wisdom, the essence of an experience, and whatever you may cite of real or illusory virtues...our primary objection to democracy is not that it is the idea, purpose and rationalization that belongs to its own goal in which man may enjoy a decent prosperous life, but rather because it does not suggest for man any exit from *kufr* (unbelief), and this is a major injustice as it allows its own faith to let man die ill-advised of what might be awaiting him beyond death.' Available in: Yāsīn, *al-Shūrā wa al-Dīmuqrāṭīyah*, pp. 23–4.

50. 'Many authors and researchers in present and ancient times had misinterpreted *shūrā* directly or indirectly, when they took it out of its context which is concordant with the essence of religion and rules of legislation...even some modern writers accorded *shūrā* a concept similar to that of democracy and that is deemed a decline in Islamic thought and a detour from the real connotation of *shūrā* in the Islamic system.' Available in: Yakan, *Mushkilāt al-Da'wah*, p. 170.

51. Yāsīn, *al-Shūrā wa al-Dīmuqrāṭīyah*, p. 35.

52. Yāsīn, *al-Shūrā wa al-Dīmuqrāṭīyah*, pp. 154–6, and Yāsīn, *Ḥiwār ma'a al-Fuḍalā'*, pp. 82–5.

53. Yassine, *Islamiser la Modernité,* p. 309.

54. Yassine, *Islamiser la Modernité,* p. 309.

55. Yāsīn, *al-Shūrā wa al-Dīmuqrāṭīyah*, p. 291.

56. Yassine, *Islamiser la Modernité,* p. 310.

57. Yāsīn, *al-Shūrā wa al-Dīmuqrāṭīyah*, p. 291.
58. Yāsīn, *al-Shūrā wa al-Dīmuqrāṭīyah*, p. 297.
59. Yāsīn, *al-Shūrā wa al-Dīmuqrāṭīyah*, p. 349.
60. Al-Turābī enumerates the differences between democracy and *shūrā* by saying: 'The first difference between Western democracy and *shūrā* democracy in the Islamic context is that democracy according to the Western concept is implemented mostly via a non-religious rule...definitely, there is no space for any kind of popular rule that is detached from any sense of faith in Islam...so stripping democracy from a religious framework and making it a purely political one is considered heresy as it makes the free will of people equivalent to the will of God...the second difference is that *shūrā* in Islam is not an isolated political practice but rather *a system of living*...this means a great deal, as when democracy is abstracted and rendered a political expression, it is nothing but a superficial democracy...the third difference is that sovereignty in Western democracy is accorded in constitutional theory to the people...whereas in Islam people take charge of it on earth as a covenant of succession from God and under the condition of submission to God...moreover, democracy in Islam does not imply the absolute authority of people, but the authority of people in light of commitment to *sharī'ah*.' Available in: al-Turābī, *Naẓarāt fī al-Fiqh,* pp. 82–6.
61. Yakan, *Mushkilāt al-Da'wah*, p. 171.
62. Yakan, *Mushkilāt al-Da'wah*, p. 173.
63. Khallāf, 'Abd al-Wahhāb, *al-Sīyāsah al-Shar'īyah aw Niẓām al-Dawlah al-Islāmīyah fī al-Shu'ūn al-Dustūrīyah wa al-Khārijīyah wa al-Mālīyah* (Cairo: al-Maṭba'ah al-Salafīyah, 1931), p. 44.
64. Khallāf, *al-Sīyāsah al-Shar'īyah,* p. 45.

Chapter 9

Pseudo-Theocracy in the Rule of Allah – '*al-Ḥākimīyah*'

> They are only two matters, and there is not a third. Either to answer Allah and his Messenger, or to follow whim (*al-hawā*). Either the rule (*ḥukm*) of Allah or the rule of *al-Jāhilīyah*. Either government by all of what Allah sent down or strife (*al-fitnah*) against what Allah sent down.
>
> Sayyid Quṭb

> In the divine scales, there are only two types of rule: either the rule (*ḥukm*) of Allah or the rule of *al-Jāhilīyah*...democracy, in so far as it is not the rule of Allah in the measure of Allah, is that of *Jāhilīyah*.
>
> Muḥammad Quṭb

On the Destinies of the Expression 'Islamic State'

The idea of the 'Islamic state' *(al-dawlah al-islāmīyah)* which began with Ḥasan al-Bannā in the 1930s underwent essential modification from the second half of the 1950s onwards with Sayyid Quṭb and Muḥammad Quṭb to experience critical convolutions in content and its theoretical premises and to ultimately end as a lexical borrowing from 'the religious state' or the 'theocratic state' which Europe knew in the Middle Ages and which al-Bannā and his students had gone to great lengths to distinguish from the 'Islamic state'. Regardless of whatever may be said today about the various wings of Quṭb's followers in abandoning the scope of theoretical subjects of Ḥasan al-Bannā or 'Abd al-Qādir 'Awdah in regard to 'the Islamic state', in order to establish a sphere for the new thesis in the matter, there is not the least doubt that the bequest of al-Bannā's concept, as developed and exemplified by Sayyid Quṭb yet exhibits some of the trace 'nuclei' and preconceptions of al-Bannā's thought that had conferred the conditions of existence.

This does not necessarily mean that the idea of the 'religious state' emerged from the womb of the concept of the Islamic state, or that it is an extension of it. Rather, what this indicates is that some of the basics of the idea of the Islamic state – according to al-Bannā and 'Awdah – were entirely suitable to build upon; the structuring of the new idea was – in the final analysis – the *worst* possible exegesis of the original idea! And, what is more important is that these theoretical bases upon which the subject of the 'Islamic state' rested for al-Bannā, were those upon which extremist revivalists continued to build their theocratic political systems; the idea expressed by the slogan: 'Islam is a religion (*dīn*) and a state (*dawlah*)'. This is a concept which ushered forth from al-Bannā's famous contention that rule (*al-ḥukm*) – that is, the state (*al-dawlah*) – is counted among the annals of the *uṣūl* and the creed (*al-'aqā'id*) and *not* in the annals of the derivative branches (*al-furū'*) and formulations of *fiqh*.

'Abdullah al-'Arawī has rightly noted that 'the reductive formulation of "Islam is a religion and a state" is not possessed of any great deal of meaning because the first term is not defined. If it connotes for us *culture* (*al-thaqāfah*), then we might be able to arrive at the conclusion that Christianity is also, by the same token, a religion and a state. Whereas, if it connotes, more explicitly, *conviction* (faith, creed), then the term "state" is redundant.'[1] Therefore, the like of such a slogan as this 'defies or escapes any historical criticism of reality'.[2]

It is certain that the maxim 'Islam is a religion and a state' connoted – for the establishments of the Muslim Brotherhood – a new idea that came as a response to the appeal for a separation between religion and state among the Arab and Muslim secularists influenced by the modern, liberal political systems who were defending the formula of the nation state (and among them were *fuqahā'* – the most prominent of whom was al-Azhar sheikh 'Alī 'Abd al-Rāziq). Similarly, it connoted a defense of the authoritative Islamic legal *marja'īyah* of the political–legal system of the state, and was posited against recourse to positive law derived from the constitution and European civil codes. Despite this, the fact is that Ḥasan al-Bannā and his students after him did not posit the maxim of 'Islam is a religion and a state' as an obstacle before them which prevented them from taking positive and realistic steps in political life or from positive give and take with the achievements of the modern state: they recognized the constitution, and they believed in the political reality and in gradualism in meeting demands, and they respected the principle of operating according to that in practice, just as they were vigilant about entering into the political parliamentary game. They viewed it and peaceful political competition positively and, all the while, did not hesitate in any of that to assert that they were endeavoring to establish an Islamic state.

As for the generation of the 'Revival' (*Ṣaḥwah*) of al-Quṭb, they did not find in the maxim 'Islam is a religion and a state' anything except what justified for them turning completely towards the assertion that politics and political authority cannot be rectified except through being cut off from the society of '*al-Jāhilīyah*': the '*Jāhilīyah*' of the twentieth century as Muḥammad Quṭb termed it,[3] and building a religious state wherein *al-ḥākimīyah*[4] was for Allah alone according to the dictates of the Qur'ānic text 'Verily rule (*al-ḥukm*) is but unto Allah'. In order for Islam to be a religion and a state, it is not possible that Muslims live their Islam in a system of rule constrained by other than their religion: thus, 'When the conscience of the human being and his self-identity are ruled by a *sharī'ah*, and subsequently his reality and activities are ruled by a [different] *sharī'ah*...then his persona is afflicted with a malady which resembles schizophrenia' says Sayyid Quṭb.[5] We have no doubt that all those afflicted with 'schizophrenia' – according to Quṭb – include everyone who calls for the Islamic state and the constitution and democracy – and among them his teacher Ḥasan al-Bannā – and if that were not the case, then what is it that compels him to diverge from the conclusions settled upon by the legacy of the Muslim Brotherhood among fixed principles in politics – to warn his throng 'against this deviation which talks about "the *ummah* being the source of political power" and the right to vote and the freedom to choose...'?[6] What is it, then, that impels him to call for violence as a way to practice politics and to obtain power? Would not Ḥasan al-Bannā and his associates have opposed these people?

The downfall of the idea of 'the Islamic state' in the second half of the 1950s and the first half of the 1960s (before its return, in a limited context, since the mid-1970s), and the ascendancy of the idea of the theocratic state: the state of '*al-ḥākimīyah*' for which Sayyid Quṭb theorized – and before him Abū al-A'lā al-Mawdūdī – was, in a sense, one of the results of the orientation of that 'theoretical' slogan 'Islam is a religion and a state': the orientation that was comprised in large measure of the ambiguity which ultimately backfired to hinder the asserters of it in constructing a genuine, integrated and comprehensive conception of the political system![7]

Sayyid Quṭb[8] represents the second wave in the experience of the Muslim Brotherhood,[9] and the second conceptual moment in the heritance of the Islamic '*Ṣaḥwah*'. Likewise, he diverged radically from the Islamic thought of the *Ṣaḥwah*, and termed it extremism, just as he diverged from the experience of the Brotherhood to separate out extreme political manifestations that had never before been countenanced. Ṭāriq al-Bishrī asserts that roots of the thought of Quṭb are to be found in the 'Special Apparatus' (*al-Tanẓīm al-Khāṣ*) which the Muslim Brotherhood established in the 1940s[10] for security purposes pertaining to the protection of the political organization against the repression of the (Egyptian) political authorities, which was ultimately transformed, with the passing of time, into what resembled a closed military organization. A large base among the young men of the Brotherhood were immersed in security activities, and they gradually, step-by-step, became more and more distanced from legal political work and the conceptual and political orientation of the Brotherhood. These young men had an appointment with destiny – after the death of al-Bannā and the inception of the revolution – with the new political life with which they were unfamiliar and with its realities with which they were unable to coexist. Despite that Quṭb, himself, was not among their number, he *did* find in them that believing 'nucleus' that might be able to bear the burden of the *da'wah* (call) for the 'state of the Qur'ān', just as they found in his pen, the most capable form for expression of their rejection and rejectionist contentions!

The distance between the thought of al-Bannā and the thought of Quṭb is huge – to the extent that it appears that the fissure between them cannot be bridged, even to the extent that leads to the assertion that the relation between the two is one of a severance and divergence. The thought of Ḥasan al-Bannā, says Ṭāriq al-Bishrī:

> was a thought widely disseminated and as common currency, connecting to people in general and it is the thought of naked trust. The thought of Ḥasan al-Bannā is a thought which cultivates land, and spreads seeds, and waters a tree that spreads with the sun and the wind. As for the thought of Sayyid Quṭb, it digs a trench and builds a fortification of high fences and lofty towers, an impregnable fortress. The difference between them is the difference between peace and war.[11]

Far from suggesting a resemblance, and in what is very telling, there is what distinguishes greatly between the two men, rather there is that which posits a decisive distinction between them. Al-Bannā had something in himself of the Reformist that justified for him his political realism and which permitted him to acknowledge the constitution and the path of electoral democracy that compelled him to plunge into its deluge without reservation or hesitation. As for Quṭb, he purged whatever remained of the Reformist bent of the Brotherhood from within himself and charged the prevailing political reality with apostasy, mocked those who were convinced of the constitutional and electoral idea;[12] and he cut off and discarded, *in toto*, all that which Ḥasan al-Bannā had built.

The political realism of al-Bannā impelled him to establish a cultural, educational, guiding movement, rather than simply a political movement, evolving from the creed and spreading its teachings among people, moving towards conviction and the heart of the balance of cultural forces in society for the benefit of Islam. Thus, it was positively predisposed towards styles of construction, inculcating consciousness and guidance. As for the extremism of Sayyid Quṭb and his fanaticism, it compelled him to constrain that movement to a *political* movement, to transform it into a 'shock brigade' representing the believing, struggling 'vanguard' in order to establish the Islamic society. For this reason, there is the inclination towards techniques of instigation and rallying the mob employed through enchanting expository writing which brokers some success and effect in the conscience of those who encounter it. The result is that al-Bannā produced political thought whereas Quṭb produced a combative political communiqué, the climax of its expression being reached in his book *Milestones* (*Ma'ālim fī al-Ṭarīq*).[13]

Religious intervention in political work[14] was not Quṭb's innovation, rather al-Bannā preceded him in that; however, Quṭb pushed it to its farthest limit, while benefiting from his predecessor. This is almost identical to the way that the remainder of the forces of religious contention 'absorb the gains of their predecessors' in order to deepen and generalize their capabilities for social mobilization.[15] It would be confirmed that what Sayyid Quṭb sowed in the 1950s and 1960s would come to fruition 'conceptually' in a way that was decidedly more extremist and fanatical[16] in the 1970s and 1980s with 'Abbūd al-Zamur, 'Abd al-Salām Faraj, 'Umar 'Abd al-Raḥmān, 'Alī Bilḥāj and the remainder of those who fell out of their same political-genealogical tree.

With the Quṭbian trend, then, the subject of the Islamic state would inevitably precipitate out. We will not read on the slate of this state any themes or declarations of the sort such as: calls for the constitution; the *ummah* as being the source of political power; or adapting the rulings of *sharī'ah* according to the requirements of the age; *shūrā* and democracy; representation or elected parliaments and so on. Rather, what will confront us are the terms '*al-Jāhilīyah*', unbelief – *kufr*, faith – *imān*, *al-ḥākimīyah*, revolution against society, and the immigration – *hijrah* – out from the society of the unbelievers or the hypocrites and so on. We are, then, before a new political–conceptual discourse, representing a complete severance with what came before it and establishing for itself precursors of a system which does not permit a reading except within the scope of these terms.

The *Jāhilī* Society and the Muslim Society

Quṭbian political discourse sets up a sharp dichotomy: the *Jāhilī* society and the Muslim society, and it deals with the political issue from within this understood duality on the basis of its 'theoretical' givens that distribute all things along this vast expanse of contention. Quṭb defines the '*Jāhilī* society' by asserting:[17]

> the *Jāhilī* society is every society other than the Muslim society! And, if we want to delimit it objectively, we might say: it is every society which is not entirely dedicated to the worship of Allah alone...where this slavery (*'ubūdīyah*)(i.e., worship of Allah) is represented in the belief conception, in the slogans of obeisance, and in the legal maxims...and according to this objective definition the '*Jāhilī* society' comprises, in fact, all those societies in existence today on earth![18]

Quṭb names among these societies, the Communist societies; the 'idolatrous societies' (*al-mujtama'āt al-wathanīyah*) in India, Japan, the Philippines and Africa; the 'Judeo-Christian societies'; also enumerating among them 'those societies that consider themselves "Muslim"'!

It is possible that the reader of this text might suspect that the writer has placed himself in a contradiction when he defined '*Jāhilī* society' as 'every society other than Muslim society' and that 'every society which is not entirely devoted to the worship of Allah alone', at the same time that he subsumes the Islamic societies under the rule of the *Jāhilī* society. The fact is that he does not fall into a contradiction for reason of his conviction that the Islamic character of society is not solely delimited by the individual worship of Allah alone, but rather it rests on regarding the meaning of this slavery (to Allah) as *complete*, even in its social system, to the end that there is nothing left in it of the *ḥākimīyah* of Allah for the human being. Thus, these societies:

> do not enter into this scope (i.e., the author intends the '*Jāhilīyah*' societies) because they are convinced of the divinity of one other than Allah, and not because they tout slogans of subservience to other than Allah, but they enter into this sphere because they *do not practice* the religion (*taddayun*) of Allah – they attribute the most significant of divine particulars to other than Allah, and they practice religion according to the rule (*ḥākimīyah*) of other than Allah; and from this *ḥākimīyah* stems their system, their laws, their values, their criteria, their customs and their traditions...and nearly all the stations of their life.[19]

It is not sufficient, in the view of Quṭb, that Islam should be the creed of these societies and that their people should respect the maxims of worship, in order to be worthy of being counted as a 'Muslim society' in the sense he defines it to be, borrowing outmoded alien thoughts about *kufr* and *imān*. If there is no basis for equivalency for an intermediate solution between the two extremes that are not equal in the scales of the creed, then 'there is no Islam in a land where Islam does not rule according to its method and its law. Nor is there anything behind faith (*al-imān*) except unbelief (*al-kufr*), and there is nothing without Islam except *al-Jāhilīyah*...and nothing after the truth except going astray.'[20]

This uncompromising and extremist opinion which Quṭb set forth would transform over time into a political ideology of which a large segment of the intellectual extremists of the Revivalist order were convinced, and they would revisit the production of it in their texts and in that which they distributed to the masses among the enraged who were growing in number and in readiness. Possibly, one of the most important of these intellectuals, outside of Egypt, was the Syrian preacher Saʿīd Ḥawwā, guide of the *jihadist* trend of the Muslim Brotherhood in Syria during the 1970s who overturned the thought of its general guide Muṣṭafā al-Sibāʿī and the 'socialism of Islam' and open-minded implementation of *al-sharīʿah* in favor of accusations of unbelief (*al-takfīr*), violence, killing and coup.[21]

Saʿīd Ḥawwā appears less fierce in charging Islamic societies with unbelief when he terms them 'corrupt societies (*mujtamaʿāt fāsiqah*) ruled, in the main, by apostates or hypocrites or unbelievers'.[22] That, however, would be a shallow impression given that Ḥawwā takes the idea of complete divorce from existing societies to the limits of bewilderment. He calls for the believer to engage in what he terms 'the struggle within' (*al-mujāhadah al-dākhilīyah*) against the *Jāhilī* life and he asserts that it is against 'listening to the radio or watching television or reading newspapers and magazines or attending theatres or places of entertainment...and reading what the pens of disbelievers have produced of philosophy and sociology and morals and behavior and literature'[23]...as this is, all of it, of the culture of the 'unbelievers', and 'those who resemble disbelievers are *of* them.'[24] As for the 'struggle within', its function is to prevent the Muslim from falling into (idolatrous) collusion with these people, and to raise the degree of his readiness to engage in confrontation in defending his creed and his *sharī'ah*. That is 'the Muslim is in a perpetual struggle (*ṣirā' dā'im*) with the others',[25] and it is not for him to choose to engage in this or not as this is among the category of obligations wherein one cannot be a Muslim without engaging in them.

In the fellowship of Sayyid Quṭb, Sa'īd Ḥawwā, Fatḥī Yakan, and 'Abd al-Salām Faraj, Islam has an appointment of conflict with the age, and the Muslims have an appointment to struggle with their societies: a struggle in which they enter against '*al-Jāhilīyah*' and disbelief, and the emigrate in order to set up the '*dār al-Islām*', the nucleus in the *hijrah,* in order to return to the conquest of the bastion of unbelief and to spread the creed of Islam in it, operating according to the Prophetic experience.[26] Among the fruits of this retrospective view towards the Prophetic experience is the movements of *al-takfīr wa al-hijrah* (unbelief and emigration) that began in Egypt and spread to various reaches of Islamic societies – the most recent of them being in Pakistan and Afghanistan.

If the *Jāhilīyah* – in the definition of Quṭb, is the 'enslavement of people to people (*'ubūdīyah al-nās bi-l-nās*): in the legislation of some people for people what Allah did not permit,'[27] then what of Muslim society or Islamic society?

It is, in the definition of the asserter of this dichotomy – Sayyid Quṭb – 'the society in which Islam is implemented...as creed and worship as a *sharī'ah* and as a system, as morals and behavior...'[28] or it is 'that which takes the Islamic method, all of it, as the method for its life entirely'.[29] Therefore, when other societies are either unbelieving (as in the case of the idolatrous societies – *al-mujtama'āt al-wathanīyah*), or without a *sharī'ah* (the Christians),[30] or their *sharī'ah* is deviant (the Jews), then the Islamic society remains the only human society able to offer a definitive answer to the material and spiritual questions of human society;[31] and in the opinion of Quṭb, 'all humankind is in need of us'[32] and it is not possible for us to ignore this need when we – insofar as Quṭb sees – are the companions of the greatest message to the worlds, rather 'the chosen people of Allah' in fact.[33]

Thus, Islamic society, then, is the most successful in the balance of preferences, and its success derives from its being the one society that provides within it the most important conditions for splitting off from the remainder of *Jāhilī* societies in its being, simply, the society of Islam; and, Islam is not just any religion, rather it is the only one with which Allah is pleased for his slaves. It differs from the remainder of religions on the basis of its being 'the slavery of people to Allah alone in their taking orders from him alone and their conceptions, their creeds, their laws (*sharā'i'ahum wa qawānīnahum*), their values, their criteria and the liberation from slavery to [other] slaves',[34]: that is from the slavery which is connoted by the '*Jāhilī* society.

This sharp duality of the '*Jāhilī* society' and the Muslim society does not belong to the political thought of the Muslim Brotherhood among the foundational subject matter of Ḥasan al-Bannā or as subsequently developed by 'Abd al-Qādir 'Awdah,[35] but rather it draws its precursors from another Islamic political thought originating and flourishing outside the Arab sphere from the 1930s to the 1970s – and especially with Abū al-Ḥasan al-Nadawī and Abū al-A'lā al-Mawdūdī. If the first outstripped Quṭb in pressing for the institution of that intrinsic distinction between the two societies – the *Jāhilī* and the Muslim – subsequently it was the second who outstripped him in concern for the idea of '*al-ḥākimīyah*' and its becoming the essence, for him, of the formulation for the matter of the state and the political system.

Abū al-Ḥasan 'Alī al-Ḥusanī al-Nadawī pushes the idea of distinguishing between the two societies far, writing:

> For rational historical reasons...Christian Europe transformed into a materialistic *Jāhilīyah*, it was stripped of all that prophethood had bequeathed to it of spiritual teachings and moral excellences and human principles, and it came to believe in nothing for personal life except pleasure and utility, and in political life in nothing but strength and conquest...and it revolted against human nature...and it took licentiousness to the extremes, and it forgot the purpose of life...and with the withdrawal of the Muslims from the field of life, and their coming down from the leadership of the world and the *imāmah* of the *ummah*, and their neglect of the religion and the world...Europe took the communities (of the world) by the forelock, and succeeded them in leadership of the world, and they directed the course of the ship of life and civil society from which its masters had withdrawn, and in that, the entire world – in its communities and peoples and civilizations – became a fast engine driven by a materialistic *Jāhilī* engineer towards its own ends, and the Muslims – like other communities – augmented this human train in hastening towards the *Jāhilīyah* end of fire and destruction, compulsion and combat, social chaos and backward decline and economic woe and spiritual poverty.'[36]

This text might leave the impression on the reader that Europe is responsible for steering the world towards '*al-Jāhilīyah*' due to the type of values upon which its social entity persists, and the type of (material) goals which chart for it the ends of its civilizational progression. The fact is that al-Nadawī puts European responsibility in second place after the responsibility of Muslims for what is occurring today in the world. True, he does not hide his worry over the vast extent of the '*Jāhilīyah*' which Europe opened up and in which the world is immersed due to its might and the triumph of its civilization in universal competition. However, he does not see that what it is doing as anything but the result of the retreat of Islamic society in its leading role in spreading the civilizational message; and it is a retreat the price of which is paid not only in the loss of its leadership position but also in its falling into idolatrous partnership with Europe in the '*Jāhilīyah*'.

Al-Nadawī, however, who knows both Medieval and modern European history precisely in what, no doubt, bespeaks a very wide breadth of familiarity,[37] in no time forgets all that he has said in regard to the decline of the Muslims in the age of the triumphant Europe, and he accords to them a major role of salvation: classifying the '*Jāhilīyah*' not in their domains, but rather in the entire world. Thus, he writes:

> The world – both East and West – has come into an essential spiritual, social and economic crisis which demands a rapid and expedited solution...the sole solution is the transformation of world leadership and the transfer of the rudder of life from the hand of deviant sin which has besmirched its use to another pure and innocent hand...the clear and effective transformation is the transfer of leadership from Europe...which is driven by materialism and *al-Jāhilīyah* to the Islamic world which is driven by Muḥammad in his eternal message and his wise religion. This is the transformation that will change the face of history.'[38] The like of this opinion is what Sayyid Quṭb intimated in his famous dictum: 'Verily, humankind, all of it, is in need of us.'[39]

We are not beset by any doubt that the concept of '*al-Jāhilīyah*' for Sayyid Quṭb finds its origin with al-Nadawī. Al-Nadawī preceded Quṭb in his use of this concept in his writings and clearly affected the latter, and his 'concealment' in the book of al-Nadawī is one of the strongest indications: that is, it should be indicated here that Quṭb wrote the preface for al-Nadawī's book. However, Quṭb, did not confine uses of the concept, like al-Nadawī, to the scope of instilling religion in the contemporary, European materialistic civilization and extolling a spiritual way out from its contradictions. Rather, he took this far – to the extent that it became a key for the 'understanding' of contemporary Islamic societies, and sending down religious rulings within them, to the extent of charging them with unbelief and declaring holy '*jihad*' against the prevailing '*Jāhilīyah*' in them.

The consciousness of the '*Jāhilīyah*' societies in the countries of Islam, according to Sayyid Quṭb as well as his disciples and students among extremist Revivalists is tied to consciousness of the causes and factors of this '*Jāhilīyah*': the establishing of the state and politics according to the dictates of the rule of people by people, not according to the dictates of the salvation of the rulings of Islamic *sharī'ah*, and this is what may be described as a 'theory' of politics for '*al-ḥākimīyah*'.

On the Concept of '*al-Ḥākimīyah*'

Sayyid Quṭb was not the first 'advocate' for the use of the term '*al-ḥākimīyah*' in approaching the matter of the state and the political system in Islam; he was preceded in that by the Pakistani preacher Abū al-A'lā al-Mawdūdī by nearly a decade and a half. However, Quṭb was the most capable of all Islamists in rendering the term one of general usage and transforming it into a 'theoretical' key for apprehending the political question in Islam and as a precursor to that the mater of the system of rule in it. It is certain that he took the conception of '*al-ḥākimīyah*' from al-Mawdūdī just as he took the conception of '*al-Jāhilīyah*' from al-Nadawī – except that he did, as he had done with the concept of '*al-Jāhilīyah*', and took '*al-ḥākimīyah*' to limits that quite possibly never crossed the mind of al-Mawdūdī. The end result of this is that he submitted it to intense scrutiny that transformed it into a key concept in contemporary Islamic political thought: the thought of the *Ṣaḥwah* in its new *Khārijī* incarnation.

Those who have considered the '*ḥākimīyah* ' of Sayyid Quṭb – among contemporary Arab researchers – to be an inversion in modern political Islamic thought and its theoretical precursors in regard to the matter of politics and the state[40] and as exceeding the basic principles upon which its order rested[41] are not excessive in what they have asserted. Rather, they are, to a high degree, accurate in according a point of *imbalance* in the procession of this thought in departing from its precursors and establishing other precursors for the new assertion. The truth is that is what Sayyid Quṭb did as did all those who would subsequently weave their concepts on his loom among his followers. They all inclined to the production of subjects and political ideas unprecedented in the modern history of Islamic political thought (in the Arab realm and that of the Muslim Brotherhood) for which is not possible to detect precursors or a source in it. The texts of Sayyid Quṭb in this regard suffice us to provide sufficient proof of what we have indicated. They are texts almost entirely bereft of any consideration of what preceded them in thought or production of the Muslim Brotherhood, if they were not without a very ancient source: the ideas of the *Khawārij* about rule.[42]

First, however, we shall read sources of the idea of '*al-ḥākimīyah*' according to Quṭb upon which he drew and from which he partook – namely, the texts and ideas of al-Mawdūdī.

Abū al-A'lā al-Mawdūdī defines the Islamic state by saying:

> The foundation upon which building it rests is the concept of the idea of the *ḥākimīyah* of Allah, the one and only, and its basic theory is that the earth – all of it – belongs to Allah, and He is its Lord intervening in its affairs. Command (*al-amr*) and rule (*al-ḥukm*) and legislation (*al-tashrī'*) are all the particular province of Allah alone; and it is not for any individual or any family or class or people nor for human kind to have any authority in command or in legislation. There is no scope in the confines of Islam or the locus of its implementation except for the state wherein man engages in the function of *khalīfat* Allah.[43]

Al-ḥākimīyah then, belongs to Allah and *not* to the human being. However, this idea is very nebulous in relation to the apparent clarity of its form. In its apparent import, it simply implies that Allah rules. However, the question which must be asked is *how*? Perhaps, the answer is direct in the conclusion of the text of al-Mawdūdī where the state is one in which 'man engages in the function of *khalīfat* Allah'. Should it be understood from that that the human being rules as a deputy representative (*bil-nīyābah*) of Allah? That is what the apparent meaning of the assertion would seem to imply. However, al-Mawdūdī obliterates this connotation quickly when he summarizes that:

> the basis upon which the support of the political theory in Islam is that all authority for command and legislation is removed from the hands of human beings – both individuals and groups – and it is not permitted for any of them to execute his command in regard to a human being the like of him or that he should be obeyed or that he should ordain a law for them that they should find fault with it or follow it. Verily, these are matters entirely reserved to Allah alone and He does not enlist the participation of any other than Himself in them.'[44]

This text belongs to decisive acts and forms in translating the meaning. It establishes the distinction between the *ḥākimīyah* of Allah and *ḥākimīyah* of the human being, considering the latter to be in hostile apposition to the divine right, with the result of instilling in the reader the idea that rule belongs to none, in so far as al-Mawdūdī knows, where everyone also knows, that 'rule according to what Allah has sent down' is engaged in by human beings who have no infallibility (*'iṣmah*);[45] and, moreover, that their implementation of the rulings (*aḥkām*) of the *sharī'ah* is not a spontaneous action but rather imposes a measure of *ijtihād* on them; and moreover, they rule, in the end, not by what Allah sent down, but by what they esteem to be the rule of Allah! In particular, the scope of operation for the ruler or the imam, when he is '*khalīfah* of the Highest Ruler'[46] is very wide: Islamic *sharī'ah*, in the view of al-Mawdūdī, is ultra-comprehensive – extending in its comprehensiveness even to 'food, and sitting, and the family and financial affairs and the rights of citizenship as well as relations between the communities',[47], and these are, *in toto*, spheres capable of considerable expansion due to the details of life which are not dealt with in a specific text. Furthermore, there is no realm for ruling in them except through recourse to the *ijtihād* of *fiqh*.[48]

The system of *al-ḥākimīyah* – along the lines of the bases demonstrated by al-Mawdūdī – inevitably produces a political–religious class (theocracy) that enjoys absolute power deriving from the 'divine deputization' of it! An authority which is completely above reproach or being taken into critical account (because it does not rule in the name of any civil idea, nor in the name of any social force), resembling the type of authority enjoyed by the clergy in Medieval Christian Europe before the Protestant Reformation and the revolution. Al-Mawdūdī was frank, himself, in defining the system of *al-ḥākimīyah* as a theocratic system when he wrote: 'It is not correct to assert the term democracy for the system of the Islamic state, rather what is a more accurate expression is the term the "divine government" (*al-ḥukūmah al-ilāhīyah*) or *theocracy*.'[49] And, in that Abū al-A'lā al-Mawdūdī is the first modern Islamist thinker to talk positively about the concept of politics and political authority in Islam, outside the circles of the Shī'ah, and to ultimately blur between the concept of *Imāmī Shī'ism* – the idea of the '*wilāyat al-faqīh*' – and the theory of the 'Divine Right' (Droit divin) which was the political ideology of the pre-Renaissance Christian state in Europe.

How did that occur, and what are the causes and factors that were at the basis of the production of this assertion that was outside normative political assertions in Islam – or the Sunni ones at least?

'Alī Omlīl, for example, in researching these causes and factors, finds them in the Indian Islamic political context, that is, in the call, itself, for the independence of Indian Muslims and a special state for them – namely, Pakistan. It is a call espoused by al-Mawdūdī in the face of the calls of others who entertained the possibility of coexistence with the Hindus, under the auspices of an un-Islamic state so long as that did not affect the creed of the Muslims of India.

Al-Mawdūdī – in the assessment of Omlīl – was not about to acknowledge the possibility of that 'according to the thesis that Islam was a religion and a political system, that is, that Islam itself is not possible *except* in an Islamic state.'[50] From here, comes the idea of '*al-ḥākimīyah*' that 'dictates that the state of the Muslims observe the *sharī'ah* alone, and that the state of Pakistan in particular must observe that, because Islam was the original justification for its establishment'; and similarly, in the call for '*al-ḥākimīyah*' 'respect for and obedience to this state, after its establishment, rests on this condition; that is, complete observance of the Islamic *Sharī'ah*, and if not, then justification for its establishment comes to an end'.[51]

It is from these subjects – not from the thought of the Muslim Brotherhood – that Sayyid Quṭb drew his ideas about the political question and especially in the matter of the 'Islamic state'. The profound effect of the thought of al-Mawdūdī on his consciousness is very clear, especially in his famous book *Ma'ālim fī al-Ṭarīq* (*Milestones*), which was distributed to the far horizons[52] and would ultimately come to resemble the 'ideological manifesto' of confrontational Islamist movements of the last three decades. The idea of '*al-ḥākimīyah*' was among the fruits of that effect, and at least three seminal presumptions would emerge from the concept of '*al-ḥākimīyah*' with Quṭb.

First, there is a strong connection between the nature of the social system and the nature of the 'creedal conception' from the standpoint that it is not possible to suppose an antithetical relation between the two as to do so would imply that the social system is an 'unnatural' system. Rather, the relation between them presupposes a tie between them of the firmest sort to the extent that the founding assumption is that the operative emanation of this social system is from the creedal conception.[53]

Second, there is no breach between religion and the world when 'It is not natural for 'religion' (*al-dīn*) to dedicate a limited, minor negative sphere of a human's life to Allah, while reserving the major positive realistic sphere for rival demigods who ordain laws and form sects, systems, groups and conditions according to their own whims without even returning to Allah.'[54] That is, the system of life and society emanate from belief and are not separate from it.

Thirdly, every system has its distinct general conception/outlook and philosophy, and problems particular to and originating from it. Moreover, solutions and answers are applicable and germane to the type of problems and the nature of that specific system where it is not possible to co-opt one system in order to find solutions for the problems of another. From the standpoint that Islam as a 'complete social system', and the interconnectedness of its sources, wherein it differs from all other systems in existence,[55] it is not possible to demand tangible solutions for problems alien to its system as produced by other systems[56].

On the basis of these presumptions, rests the concept of '*al-ḥākimīyah*' for Quṭb. Thus, for the Muslims who are convinced of the message of Islam, it is not possible that their social system should derive from anything except their creed (the first presumption); and Islam is not only a creed and a faith, but rather, it is a *sharī'ah* which puts rulings (*aḥkām*) in place for the complete system of life (the second presumption); and finally, Islam alone is a particular entity distinct from the remainder of other creedal systems and prevailing forms of rule (the third presumption). In sum, Islam is the creedal and Islamic legal system that is encapsulated by the principle of the *ḥākimīyah* of Allah as opposed to the *ḥākimīyah* of the human being – the status quo 'in the *Jāhilī* societies'.

The thesis of '*ḥākimīyah*' is synonymous with the assertion of the rule of Islamic *sharī'ah* as the system for Islamic societies on account of that being considered to be the sum total of rulings which Allah sent down: that takes the call for '*al-ḥākimīyah*' as a foundation for the assertion of it. However, Sayyid Quṭb goes further than this meaning in his definition of '*al-ḥākimīyah*' and the *sharī'ah* to encompass a locus that he extends to include implications where he writes:

> The implication (*madlūl*) of '*al-ḥākimīyah*' in the Islamic conception is not constrained to the collection of legal rulings (*al-sharā'i' al-qānūnīyah*) from Allah alone, or to seeking recourse to them alone, or to ruling according to them alone...the implication of '*al-sharī'ah*' in Islam is not constrained to legal legislation, and not even to the sources (*uṣūl*) of rule and its system or posited elements. This narrow implication does not represent the (true) implication of '*al-sharī'ah*' and the Islamic conception! The '*sharī'ah* of Allah' means that every thing which Allah has decreed for regulating the life of the human being...and this is represented in the *uṣūl* (sources) of belief, and the *uṣūl* of rule and the *uṣūl* of morals, and in the *uṣūl* of ethical behavior and in the *uṣūl* of knowledge (*ma'rifah*) as well.[57]

The *sharī'ah*, then, is *not* tantamount to laws (*qawānīn*), and not even to the principles of rule and the system of politics. It is, over and above that, a social, ethical and epistemological system: that is, a system for life in its totality – in all its various spheres; the Muslim is not able to glean any matter attached to his creed, his thought, his behavior, his values and his social and political system 'except from that divine source',[58] and if not, then he has exceeded the bounds of Islam and been satisfied with the worship of other than Allah. The state is that 'when the supreme "*ḥākimīyah*" in society is for Allah alone, represented in the prevailing divine *sharī'ah*, then this is the one conceivable vision wherein the human being is completely and actually liberated from the worship of another human being…'[59]

It is according to this understanding of '*al-ḥākimīyah*', that Sayyid Quṭb makes a complete break from the ideas of all who preceded him among Muslim thinkers about the political development of the constitution and parliamentary representation, about gradual implementation of the rulings of the *sharī'ah*, about the establishment of a political system according to the dictates of *al-shūrā*[60] in order to advance a new conception for politics and political authority[61] buttressed by a perfect identification between the religious and the political to the extent of asserting a religious state: a state which does not derive its legitimacy from society or from the *ummah*, but rather from the religion, and from religion *alone*. It is, as we have seen, a conception which originated in a non-Arab Islamic sphere – that of India and Pakistan – and Quṭb borrowed from it and introduced its product into contemporary Islamic thought without there being any source or precursors in the Arab-Sunni Islamic sphere. Even though many have attempted to present the matter of '*al-ḥākimīyah*' along different lines, and were attempting to attribute it to Islamic sources (*uṣūl*),[62] this was nothing more than an attempt to lessen the vehemence of criticism that was directed towards the thought of Sayyid Quṭb in the (erroneous) consideration of it being representative of a phase in the development of the Muslim Brotherhood movement!

These thoughts did not cease with the tragic end of the thinker. The execution of Sayyid Quṭb only served to add weight to his value as a symbol and to manifestly extend the dimensions of this symbolism among the new generation of confrontational Islamist forces,[63] to ultimately transform his ideas into the operational guide for the new violent revolution driven by radical Islamist forces – which have yet to cease – against prevailing political systems such as those known by the names of 'al-Takfīr wa al-Hijrah', 'Islamic Jihad', 'al-Jamā'ah al-Islāmīyah', 'Jund Allāh' and others.

Subsequently, the precursors of the new ideas would become more extreme than the ones which preceded them, as espoused by the guides and leaderships of the organizations of violence whose consciousness emerged from the 'womb' of *Ma'ālim fī al-Ṭarīq* (*Milestones*).[64] Possibly, the most prominent of these – in the last two decades – is Muḥammad 'Abd al-Salām Faraj, one of the leaders of the organization 'al-Jihād' who was executed on charges of planning the assassination of former Egyptian president Anwar al-Sadat. He authored a famous treatise by the name of 'Al-Farīḍah al-Ghā'ibah' ('The Absent Duty'), which transformed into an authoritative referential text for the '*jihadist*' Islamist movements over the next twenty years.

'Abd al-Salām Faraj says in this treatise:

> Verily, the rulings that Muslims promote today are the rulings of unbelief (*al-kufr*); they are laws posited by the unbelievers and according to which the Muslims have operated. Allah, the Most Glorified and Exalted, says: 'Whoever does not rule according to what Allah has sent down, then these are unbelievers'.[65] After the *khilāfah* was finally gone in 1924, and the extirpation of the rulings of Islam in entirety and the replacing of them with rulings enacted by the unbelievers...their condition became exactly like that of the Tartars as is confirmed in the *tafsīr* of Ibn Kathīr about the saying of Allah 'Do they desire the rule (*ḥukm*) of *al-Jāhilīyah*? But who is a better ruler than Allah for people who are god-fearing?'[66] ...And, as for the rulers of the age the number of gates of unbelief through which they have passed in going out of the Islamic community have multiplied to the extent that the matter is not in doubt for any who follow in their path.[67]

The like of this assertion establishes an idea of *al-takfīr* (accusation of apostasy) such as that asserted by the *Rawāfiḍ* (the 'Rejectors') in the age of the '*fitnah*'. However, it is an assertion which moves rapidly, seriously and persistently to renew that '*fitnah*' inside the *ummah*, and is among that which is indicated by the frequent use of the concept of '*jihad*' (precisely that which is indicated by the expression of the 'absent duty') which does not connote, in the assertion of Faraj, what it does in Islamic *fiqh*; but rather carries new import at the level of a *rejection* of what has traditionally been transmitted. Raḍwān al-Sayyid says:

> What is new in the treatise of Faraj is the consideration of *jihad* as an obligation (*farīḍah*); whereas it is well-known in traditional Sunni *fiqh* that it is a *farḍ kifāyah* and not a *farḍ 'ayn*. However, what is more important is the consideration of *jihad* as an obligation *inside* Islamic society, whereas it is

traditionally well-known that it does not persist except in the confrontation of what is external and not Islamic.[68]

Thus, it was not among the fruits of the sharp Quṭbian dichotomies – the *Jāhilī* society and the Muslim society; the party of Satan (*ḥizb al-shayṭān*) and the party of God (*ḥizb allāh*); and the *hākimīyah* of the human being and the *ḥākimīyah* of Allah – so much as it was a product of a new dichotomy of creed and politics – faith and unbelief – that signified an entry into a phase of conceptual debasement in Islamic reasoning (and that of political parties in particular) from which sprang nothing other than ideas of *al-takfīr* and accusation of sin (*al-ta'thīm*) and calls for '*al-hijrah*' (immigration) out of the *Jāhilī* society and *jihad* against it. We have even witnessed those who have attempted to defend illiteracy on the grounds that the Prophet was illiterate, and there are even graver secrets waiting to be unveiled.

These Quṭbian subjects – and what is generated from them – do not come into existence haphazardly, rather they have social and political '*asbāb al-nuzūl*' ('occasions of descent'), and among these are three primary ones:

The first occasion is the context of the Egyptian political experience lived by Quṭb and the second generation of his followers among the rejectionists. It is true that there is no doubt that the '*hākimīyah* of Quṭb' was a reaction to the experience of the nation state in Egypt, and the Nasserist state in particular'.[69] It was similarly a reaction against the fierce inquisition that was being faced by Islamists imprisoned in Egypt and elsewhere for more than four decades. There is no doubt that this inquisition kindled within them feelings of absolute divorce from state and society and notions of immigration, revenge and violence. This fact was confirmed in Algeria in the 1990s when the military coup over the democratic elections pushed Algerian Islamists to abandon the idea of peaceful democratic work in favor of adopting armed and violent means, or '*jihad*' in their discourse.

The second occasion is connoted by the repercussions of setting up an 'Islamic state' in Pakistan for the Muslims of India and what this suggested about the possibility of establishing Islamic rule. This was the basis for undertaking the reading of the works of Abū al-Aʿlā al-Mawdūdī and Abū al-Ḥasan al-Nadawī. And, the effects and repercussions would similarly be repeated in the wake of the success of the Iranian Revolution and the establishment of the 'Islamic Republic' just as with the success of the 'Afghan Mujāhidīn' in turning back the Soviets and bringing down a Communist regime and setting up an Islamic state in Afghanistan. It was not a coincidence the movement of confrontational and '*jihadist*' Islam would witness its second major impetus since the end of the 1970s with the Iranian Revolution and in the context of the Islamic Afghani resistance of the Soviet occupation where an atmosphere conducive to the acceptance of an Islamic state was created.

The third occasion was the increasing consciousness of the importance of religious work in social mobilization and political recruitment after scrutinizing the successes of organizations in utilizing the weapon of religion in effecting dominance.[70] Radiating from the gains of religion, politically, from the standpoint of groups of political Islam – was the transformation of religion into an ideology for the masses,[71] and secondarily, the increase in demand for it on behalf of these groups, and in particular the ideas which more greatly expressed fury and confrontationalism and which augmented politics for reasons of manufacturing sanctity – religious devotion as opposed to worldly weakness.

These were the 'milestones' in the ascendancy of '*al-ḥākimīyah*' in the Islamic political consciousness and the dominant conceptions of it on the path of its adherents towards wandering absentmindedly in the new conceptual wilderness of the subject of the 'Islamic state', even if they were not predisposed towards calling it a *theocratic* state. If the matter of this '*ḥākimīyah*' pertains directly to the Sunni Islamist Revival discourse, then it has analogs, resemblances and shared views in Shī'ite Islamic discourse, and among the most important analogs of all is that of the concept of the '*wilāyat al-faqīh*'.

Notes

1. Laroui, *Islamisme, Modernisme, Libéralisme: Esquisses Critiques* (Casablanca: Centre Culturel Arabe, 1997), p. 179.
2. Laroui, *Islamisme, Modernisme*, pp. 179–80.
3. Quṭb, Muḥammad, *Jāhilīyat al-Qarn al-'Ishrīn* (Cairo: Dār al-Shurūq, 1980).
4. Quṭb, Sayyid, *Ma'ālim fī al-Ṭarīq*, 10th edn (Cairo; Beirut: Dār al-Shurūq, 1983).
5. Quṭb, Sayyid, *al-Mustaqbal li-Hādhā al-Dīn*, 12th edn (Cairo; Beirut: Dār al-Shurūq, 1992), p. 16.
6. Quṭb, Sayyid, *Ma'rakat al-Islām wa al-Ra'smālīyah*, 13th edn (Cairo; Beirut: Dār al-Shurūq, 1993), p. 11.
7. Jad'ān says in this sense: 'The truth is that the elements of the Muslim Brotherhood's understanding for an Islamic political system have not crystallized definitely up to this very moment.' Available in: Jad'ān, *al-Māḍī fī al-Ḥāḍir*, p. 139.
8. Khālidī, Ṣalāḥ 'Abd al-Fattāḥ, *Sayyid Quṭb al-Shahīd al-Ḥay* (Amman: Maktabat al-Aqṣā, 1981).

9. According to the Testimony of Sheikh Muḥammad al-Ghazālī, Sayyid Quṭb did not join – up until 1950 – the 'Muslim Brotherhood'. Available in: Various, *al-ḥarakāt al-Islāmīyah al-mu'āṣirah fī al-waṭan al-'Arabī (Conference), Maktabat al-Mustaqbalāt al-'Arabīyah al-Badīlah,* 4th edn (Beirut: Centre for Arab Unity Studies, 1998), p. 99.

10. Al-Bishrī, Ṭāriq, *Al-Malāmiḥ al-'Āmah*, p. 33.

11. Al-Bishrī, Ṭāriq, *Al-Malāmiḥ al-'Āmah*, p. 33.

12. 'The talk about charters and parliaments is a rich humorous material enjoyed mostly by inane people.' Available in: Quṭb, Sayyid, *Ma'rakat al-Islām*, p. 12.

13. Al-Bishrī did not stray far from truth when he wrote: 'It is evident to me that Sayyid Quṭb's book [referring to *Ma'ālim fī al-Ṭarīq*] represents a theory for the movement in the context of Islamic political thought, and resembles Lenin's book *What is to be Done?* in the context of Marxism by the time of its release. The importance of Lenin's book during that time came from its rejection of the syndicate approach and its concentration on a political approach that is oriented towards the governing institution, also the book focused on the Party as an institution to the non-spontaneous movement in its political activity, and as a nexus between theory and Marxism, i.e. it established this nexus via organizing itself as a party and a state. *Ma'ālim fī al-Ṭarīq* prompts a similar question, as it states that reviving creed is a task of the "vanguard", which is considered as a shock battalion and represents some kind of isolation from the *Jāhilī* society.' Available in: Al-Bishrī, Ṭāriq, *Al-Malāmiḥ al-'Āmah*, p. 40.

14. Keppel also described the book as the *What is to be Done?* of the Islamists. Available in: Keppel, *La Revanche de Dieu*, p. 39.

15. Badie, *Les Deux Etats,* p. 100.

16. Badie, *Les Deux Etats,* p. 267.

17. 'The tragedy of execution of the man of discourse [referring to Quṭb] did not put an end to this approach and its political practice, as the case with its equivalents and counterparts, it acquired the capability for dissemination around the Islamic world, roaming from one place to another and lingering within the ideologies and practices of its various movements.' Available in: Dyāb, Muḥammad Ḥāfiẓ, *Sayyid Quṭb: al-Khiṭāb wa al-Īdyulujīyā,* 2nd edn (Beirut: Dār al-Ṭalī'ah, 1988), p. 113.

18. Quṭb, Sayyid *Ma'ālim*, p. 98.

19. Muḥammad Quṭb – who wrote the book *Jāhilīyat al-Qarn al-'Ishrīn* – does the same thing when he converts the equation Islam/*Jāhilīyah*, from the framework of sociology to that of state and authority, he writes: 'In the divine balance, there are two types of rule: the rule of God, and that of *Jāhilīyah*...consequently any rule that is not of God is a rule of *Jāhilīyah*. Thus democracy is not a rule of God, so it is in God's balance the rule of *Jāhilīyah*.' Available in: Quṭb, Muḥammad, *al-'Ilmānyūn wa al-Islām*, p. 64.

20. Quṭb, Sayyid, *Ma'ālim*, p. 101.

21. It might well be argued that Sayyid Quṭb's method – and that of his followers or those who can be traced to him directly or indirectly – is simple in essence; constituting a reduction of virtually every issue to a bare dichotomy – a bifurcation. In this world-view there are no gradations but only 'either/or' propositions. What is termed the *takfīrī* trend emphasizes or exemplifies this tendency where not only non-Muslims but also Muslims are subject to a rule of exclusion that is predicated upon total acceptance of the tenets of a particular creed and set of interpretations and where any deviation from this evinces the accusation that the person in question – especially a fellow Muslim – is an unbeliever or *kāfir*; and hence the term for this trend. – Translator.

22. Quṭb, Sayyid, *Ma'ālim*, p. 101.

23. Ḥawwā, Sa'īd, *Jund Allāh: Thaqāfatan wa Akhlāqan*, 2nd edn (Cairo: Dār al-Ṭibā'ah al-Ḥadīthah, 1977), p. 10.

24. Ḥawwā, *Jund Allāh,* p. 324.
25. Ḥawwā, *Jund Allāh,* p. 185.
26. Ḥawwā, *Jund Allāh,* p. 66.
27. Djaït was not far from truth when he noticed that the Prophetic persona and path salvaged all revolts, state founders, and leaders in the Islamic aspect 'however, here, they salvaged the extremist Islamists by establishing an unprecedented model of schism'. Available in: Djaït, *La Personnalité et le devenir Arabo-Islamique collection esprit* (Paris: Seuil, 1974), p. 179.
28. Quṭb, Sayyid, *Ma'ālim*, p. 163.
29. Quṭb, Sayyid, *Ma'ālim*, p. 116.
30. Quṭb, Sayyid, *al-Islām wa Mushkilāt al-Ḥaḍārah*, 11th edn (Cairo; Beirut: Dār al-Shurūq, 1992), p. 193.
31. 'Christianity is merely a call for spiritual purification, it never included a legislation for life...in fact it left this issue for Caesar,' accordingly, Europe 'did not find any legislation for life in Christianity, and found in it only a spiritual creed and praying.' Available in: Quṭb, Sayyid, *Ma'rakat al-Islām*, pp. 56–7.
32. The Islamic community is 'the only way out for a humanity threatened with destruction...'. Available in: Quṭb, Sayyid, *al-Islām wa Mushkilāt*, p. 186.
33. Quṭb, Sayyid, *Naḥwa Mujtama' Islāmī,* 10th edn (Cairo; Beirut: Dār al-Shurūq, 1993), p. 11.
34. 'The chosen people of God are really the Muslim *ummah* which will forever stay shaded by the banner of God however diverse it may be in its races, colors and nations.' Available in: Quṭb, Sayyid, *Ma'ālim*, p. 160.
35. Quṭb, Sayyid, *Ma'ālim*, p. 163.
36. In his book *al-Māḍī fī al-Ḥāḍr,* Jad'ān is inclined to believe that some subjects which were discussed by 'Awdeh had a great influence in the thought of Quṭb, much in the same way the influence of al-Nabahānī had affected him. Al-Nadawī, Abū al-Ḥasan 'Alī al-Ḥasanī, *Mādhā Khasira al-'Ālam bi-Inḥiṭāṭ al-Muslimīn* (Kuwait: al-Markaz al-'Ālamī lil-Kitāb al-Islāmī, [n.d]), pp. 258–9.
37. He presents very solid evidence concerning extensive knowledge of the history of Europe and this can be found in the index, item no. 35 of the same book.
38. Al-Nadawī, *Mādhā Khasira*, p. 262.
39. See index, no. 31.
40. '*Al-Ḥākimīyah* is another turning point in modern Islamic political thought that totally differed from the logic of Islamic constitutional Reformism in the last century...indeed, *al-ḥākimīyah* intersects with Islamic Reformism which was established on the basis of a constitutional discourse, and endeavored to create a nexus between philosophy and the system of a nation state and other specific Islamic concepts.' Available in: Omlīl, *Al-Iṣlāḥīyah al-'Arabīyah,* pp. 167–9.
41. 'Whatever "*amr al-jāhilīyah*" as explained by Sayyid Quṭb might be, and whatever "*amr al-ḥākimīyah*" might be, this derivation is bizarre and unfamiliar to the Arab ear. We may be able to gain a sense of it in a criticism of the principle that considers the *ummah* to be a source of sovereignty as assumed by modern political thought and contemporary constitutional *fiqh*. Perhaps, there must be some kind of opposition, in a mathematical sense, between the two concepts: that of "sovereignty" on the one hand and *al-ḥākimīyah* on the other.' Al-'Alawī, Sa'īd bin-Sa'īd, *al-Īdyulujīyā wa al-Ḥadāthah: Qirā'āt fī al-Fikr al-'Ārabī al-Mu'āṣir* (Beirut; Casablanca: al-Markaz al-Thaqāfī al-'Ārabī, 1987), p. 113.
42. 'It is noted that Quṭb was influenced in bringing this concept to light by the first rebellion of the *Khawārij* on the eve of establishment of the Umayyad state (no rule but

for God) in which they were confused between (*ḥukm Allah*) which connotes the religious ordination for which God was the only route, and "government" which connotes political rule, so they made the state and political rule pure religion, and then refused to let people have any involvement in politics and government.' Available in: Dyāb, *Sayyid Quṭb,* p. 92.

43. Al-Mawdūdī, Abū al-'Alā, *Naẓarīyat al-Islām wa Hadyih fī al-Sīyāsah wa al-Qānūn wa al-Dustūr* (Beirut: Mu'asasat al-Risālah, 1980), pp. 77–8.

44. Al-Mawdūdī, *Naẓarīyat,* p. 31.

45. Which is not present in Shī'ite *fiqh*.

46. Al-Mawdūdī, *Naẓarīyat,* p. 49.

47. Al-Mawdūdī, *Naẓarīyat,* p. 158.

48. Sayyid Quṭb does not approve of such a conclusion taking into account that 'Islamic *sharī'ah* is one thing, and Islamic *fiqh* is another, and they are not equal in terms of source, nor in resourcefulness'. Available in: Al-Mawdūdī, *Naẓarīyat,* p. 47.

49. Al-Mawdūdī, *Naẓarīyat,* p. 34.

50. Omlīl, *Al-Iṣlāḥīyah al-'Arabīyah,* p. 172.

51. Omlīl, *Al-Iṣlāḥīyah al-'Arabīyah,* pp. 172–3.

52. 'The book *Ma'ālim fī al-Ṭarīq* was distributed and reprinted five times between January and June of 1965, i.e., at a rate of one edition per month.' Available in: Carré, *Mystique et Politique,* p. 19.

53. Quṭb, Sayyid, *al-Mustaqbal,* p. 12.

54. Quṭb, Sayyid, *al-Mustaqbal,* p. 24.

55. 'The main problem in the privilege of the Islamic community of having a unique system is that it is a community made by a special *sharī'ah* that was revealed by our God, so that this *sharī'ah* which was born complete...is the one that founded this religion.' Available in: Quṭb, Sayyid, *Naḥwa Mujtama',* p. 63.

56. Sayyid Quṭb wonders 'how Islam is questioned oftentimes about such issues, and is demanded to have solutions for them, or how Islam's opinion is sought for issues it did not engender or participate in creating...', he even wonders further how 'clerics' responses and their involvement with those inquirers in arguments about Islam's position and attitude in such trivia in a state that does not rule by Islam and nor does it implement the system of Islam. He continues wondering 'What does the issue of having or not having women in the parliament have to do with Islam? What concerns Islam in having genders socialize or not? Or to have women work or not? Or any problem of the systems utilized in this community which are not Islamic and do not accept the rule of Islam?' Available in: Quṭb, Sayyid, *Dirāsāt Islāmīyah,* 9th edn (Cairo; Beirut: Dār al-Shurūq, 1993), pp. 87–8.

57. Quṭb, Sayyid, *Ma'ālim,* pp. 135–6.

58. Quṭb, Sayyid, *Ma'ālim,* p. 138.

59. Quṭb, Sayyid, *Ma'ālim,* pp. 118–119.

60. Olivier Carré was correct when he noticed that the *Manār* exegesis by Rashīd Riḍā (referring to the exegesis published in *al- Manār* magazine) concentrated on *al-shūrā,* whereas Sayyid Quṭb concentrated on the *bay'ah* in his *Ẓilāl al-Qur'ān* exegesis. Available in: Carré, *Mystique et Politique,* pp. 213–14.

61. Mawṣillī, Aḥmad, *al-Uṣūlīyah al-Islāmīyah: Dirāsah fī al-Khiṭāb al-Īdyulujī wa al-Sīyāsī 'ind Sayyid Quṭb: Baḥth Muqāran li-Mabādi' al-Uṣūlīyīn wa al-Iṣlāḥīyīn* (Beirut: al-Nāshir, 1993).

62. It is applicable, for instance, to al-Qaraḍāwī when he writes: '...some people think the issue of governorship as being divine and belonging to God was innovated by al-Mawdūdī, then Sayyid Quṭb, as they explained this issue and reiterated it over

and over in their books. However, if anyone reads books such as those of the *uṣūl al-fiqh*, he will find that among the chapters and introductions of these books is the chapter that addresses "the ruler/governor": Who is the ruler? Many have agreed that the ruler is *God*…'. Available in: Al-Qaraḍawī, *al-Sīyāsah al-Shar'īyah*, p. 18.

63. Aḥmad, Rif'at Sayyid, *al-Nabī al-Musallaḥ,* (Beirut: Rīyaḍ al-Rayyis, 1991), vol. 1: al-Rāfiḍūn; 'Abd al-Fattāḥ, Nabīl, *al-Muṣḥaf wa al-Sayf: Ṣirā' al-Dīn wa al-Dawlah fī Miṣr* (Cairo: Maktabat Madbūlī, 1984); Bārūt, *Yathrib al-Jadīdah*; and Haykal, Muḥammad Ḥasanayn, 'al-Islām al-Sīyāsī' in: *Kharīf al-Ghaḍab: Qiṣṣat Bidāyat wa Nihāyat 'Aṣr Anwar al-Sādāt*, 2nd edn (Beirut: Sharikat al-Maṭbū'āt, 1983).

64. Al-Sayyid was not mistaken when he considered this book 'the foundational text for resistance- and political-party Islam and from between its lines all Islamist groups that emerged, at least in the Arab world.' Available in: Al-Sayyid, *Sīyāsāt al-Islām,* p. 192.

65. Qur'ān, *surat al-mā'idah,* (5:44).

66. Qur'ān, *surat al-mā'idah,* (5:50).

67. Faraj, 'Abd al-Salām, 'al-farīḍah al-ghā'ibah' in: Aḥmad, Rif'at Sayyid, *al-Nabī al-Musallaḥ*, vol. 1: al-Rāfiḍūn, pp. 130–1.

68. Al-Sayyid, *Sīyāsāt al-Islām,* p. 185.

69. Omlīl, *Al-Iṣlāḥīyah al-'Arabīyah,* p. 179.

70. There is a difference in the implementation of religion by Iran and in Arab kingdoms. Available in: Badie, *Culture et Politique, collection politique compare* (Paris: Economica, 1983), p. 152.

71. Djaît, *L'Europe et l'Islam, collections esprit* (Paris: Seuil, 1978), p. 135.

Chapter 10

Pseudo-Theocracy: On the '*Wilāyat al-Faqīh*'

> The qualified *fuqahā'* are charged with and commanded to engage in all the matters that persisted in the era of the Prophets.
>
> Khomeini

> As the government of Islam is the government of law, it is incumbent upon the scholars of law – rather more importantly – on the *'ulamā'* of the religion – that is, the *fuqahā'* – and they are the ones engaging in it.
>
> Khomeini

From 'Conditional' to the 'Imamate': The Context of Retreat

The constitutional idea was witnessing an abatement in the (Sunni) Islamic consciousness from the middle of the 1950s onwards due to the effect of the waning of the liberal epoch in Egypt and the birth of the 'Islamic state' in Pakistan, as well as the absence of the leaders of the Muslim Brotherhood and then the ascendancy of the subject of *'al-ḥākimīyah'* to pride of place in the political thinking of the second generation of the 'Awakening' – *al-Ṣaḥwah*. During exactly the same time period, the same idea was suffering the same fate in the Shī'ite Islamic consciousness in Iran. Perhaps, the reasons were similar to a certain extent: Iran was experiencing its second constitutional movement – at the end of the 1940s and the beginning of the 1950s – after the debacle of the first constitutional movement in the second half of the first decade of the century, and shortly, it would experience a black political moment characterized by a sudden and ferocious dictatorial assault on the political gains it had obtained since the end of the First World War, and at its heart was democratic constitutional development.

The Iranian Nationalist Movement had secured a tremendous advance in establishing its force and its facility by benefiting from two factors: the weakness of the young Shah Muḥammad Rezza Pahlavi – who succeeded his father who abdicated in 1941 – and the unity of its political forces: the Communists (the Tudeh Party) and the Liberals. The upshot of that advance secured the ascendancy of the government of the 'National Front' under the leadership of Dr Muḥaammad Mosaddeq in its rise to power. However, the program for national government of Mosaddeq – directed towards restraining the absolute royal power of the Shah in an attempt to transform it into a constitutional monarchy, and subsequently, the nationalization of the oil were rapidly leading to his confrontation, due to their rejection of this, with the army and the foreign forces that were adversely affected by the nationalization, and the rescinding by the men of religion among the institutions of the *ḥawzah 'ilmīyah* of their support for the national initiative for government. The result of that is the American Central Intelligence Agency (CIA) in cooperation with the army of the Shah would succeed in orchestrating a coup against the government and the parliament and in restoring the Shah to power in Iran[1] and overthrowing the representative-constitutional epoch in the country. The general climate surrounding this major reversal would generate in Iran increasing numbers of factions predisposed towards progressive, radical political thoughts of the sort that Dr 'Alī Sharī'atī would express in his writings; except that his popularity – drawn from his ability to benefit from the symbols of revolution in Islam (especially Abū Dharr al-Ghifārī)[2] was not sufficient to eclipse, in the conceptual and political scene, the primacy of the role of the traditional *fiqh* establishment as represented by the Shī'ite *ḥawzāt 'ilmīyah* in Qom, Iran and Najaf, Iraq and the ideas of the imamate with deep roots in the mass culture of Iran ever since the Safavid period and the official conversion to Shī'ism.

The government of Mosaddeq had hardly fallen, when it became incumbent upon the men of religion to reclaim the control of matters – whether they were among those who were aligned with the 'National Front' and with Dr Mosaddeq such as Ayatollah al-Kāshānī[3] or those who supported it to one degree or another such as Grand Ayatollah al-Brūjerdī, who assumed the leadership of *al-marja'īyah* after the death of Grand Ayatollah al-Ḥā'irī – the teacher of Imam al-Khomeini.[4] In every case, the decade of the 1950s did not conclude before the Shī'ite *ḥawzāt* had reclaimed their leading role in political work, and the men of the *ulamā'* of the religion had established themselves in the leading role as the conceptual and political *marja'īyah* in Iran. And possibly, the most important of these who signed the '*Bayān al-Tis'ah*' – the 'Communiqué of the Nine'[5] which defied the 'White Revolution' initiative declared by the Shah in 1963,[6] and among those who would come to have the definitive word in matters of the world and religion, was Ayatollah Rūh-Allāh al-Mūsawī al-Khomeini.

This interesting transformation in the position of political leadership in Iraq was not only a political transformation in which the men of religion would come to take the central position in politics among the parties and politicians alone, but rather along with that, it was a tremendous *conceptual* transformation of significant dimensions. It was a restoration of political theory to the domain of creed and the *madhab* of *Imāmī-Ja'farī* Shī'ism in Iran. Thus, it was not only a revolution against the constitutional idea of the 1950s in Iran, but it was a revolution against the entire modern, Shī'ite political heritage which had served as an operational basis since the beginning of the twentieth century, including the constitutional political *fiqh* of al-'allāmah Muḥammad Ḥussayn al-Nā'īnī and his pioneering treatise: *Tanbīh al-Ummah wa Tanzīh al-Millah*.[7]

The reader of the '*al-imāmah*' and '*wilāyạt al-faqīh*' texts distributed in Iran, Iraq and Lebanon in the middle of the 1960s, finds a complete conceptual reversal from the *Tanwīrī* (illuminationist) legacy as conveyed by Shī'ite political *fiqh* in the early days of the twentieth century – the axis of which were questions of the nation state, the constitution, parliamentary representation, and the trusteeship of the *ummah* to rule itself. It is a reversal, for those who advocated it among the Shī'ite *fuqahā'* of the traditional subjects of *Imāmī fiqh* in the phase after the theories of '*al-intiẓār*' ('waiting') and '*al-idhn*' ('permission') that had come into prominence at the beginning of the Medieval period with the beginnings of the 'age of occultation'.[8] It is almost possible to view this turnaround in its sharpness and enormity in conjunction with that which obtained in Sunni Islamic political thought: the casting aside of the Islamic Reformist subjects of the *Nahḍah* concerning the nation state and the constitution and democracy and the subsequent erection upon the debris of its demolished skeleton, the new subjects of the 'Islamic state' possessed of an Islamic legal, *religious marja'īyah* as opposed to a *civil* one and subsequently the theocratic state of '*al-ḥākimīyah*' as conceived for the '*Jāhilī*' society. Just as Shī'ite *fuqahā'* returned to *Ja'farī* political *fiqh* concerning the 'imamate', the 'Revivalists' would return to many of the subjects of the *fiqh* of Islamic legal politics. In both of these two returns, Islamic political consciousness cut a path for itself to interact with the age and its questions, electing to rely on axioms that were exposed to some examination in a renaissance moment which came to appear, in the end, as though they were a departure from principle!

It is possible to assert that the distance between al-Nā'īnī's *Tanbīh al-Ummah wa Tanzīh al-Millah*, and Khomeini's *Ḥukūmah al-Islāmīyah* is precisely the same conceptual distance between the *Ṭabā'i' al-Istibdād* of al-Kawākibī and the *Ma'ālim fī al-Ṭarīq* of Sayyid Quṭb. This inclines us, following on that, to infer that the Islamic Revivalist discourse knew an internal unity – between its movements and *madhabs* (both Shī'ite and Sunni) that resembled or approached that which had founded the Islamic Reformist discourse almost a century before and which bridged the chasm between the texts of the Shī'ite thinkers. This is the matter that indicates, on another level, that the catalyst of these types of unity was not always creedal or one which pertains to *madhab*, but rather that it was, in some aspects, a *historical political* catalyst.

On the Renewal of Subjects of the *Fiqh* of the Imamate

The return to the subjects of the imamate represent, in Shī'ite political *fiqh*, and since the middle of the nineteenth century, a victory of the *fiqh* tradition of the *ḥawzah* over *ijtihād* open to modern thought and Sunni theory of the *khilāfah* and its subjects (*al-shūrā, ahl al-ḥal wa al-'aqd, al-ijmā'*, etc.) which might have begun from the time of al-Mīrzā al-Shīrāzī and the support of the *fuqahā'* for the Tobacco Rebellion at the end of the nineteenth century to the joining of the *ḥawzah 'ilmīyah* of the city of Qom in the constitutional battle in the first decade of the twentieth century. It is the *ijtihād* that reached its peak in the treatise of al-Nā'īnī, as previously indicated. The reader of contemporary Shī'ite political texts about the state and the system of rule does not perceive a major difference between what that *ijtihād* concluded in regard to conceptions and rules and between the givens of *Ja'farī* Shī'ite *fiqh* of the Middle Ages about the imamate! This is the matter that suggests that the knowledge continuum that governs the relation between modern and contemporary Shī'ite political *fiqh* and between the traditional *Imāmī fiqh* resembles that which governs the relation between the modern *fiqh* of the *khilāfah* – with Rāshid Riḍā – and between the legitimate traditional political order. However, it also suggests that the 'break' which occurred at the beginning of the twentieth century with the rise of the Modern constitutional idea is a transitional break which did not precipitate a major effect on previous conceptual development exactly as occurred with the Sunni Reformist discourse of the 'Awakening', taking into account differences in divisions and the degree of conceptual accumulations which cannot be overlooked.

The Imamate and its Designation

Sunni and Shīʿite *fuqahā'* are in consensus about the principle of the imamate and its necessity for systematizing Islamic society, even if they do not attribute the same meaning to it. The imam or *khalīfah* for the Sunnis is not the designated imam of the Shīʿah.[9] The appointment of the first reverts to choice (the selection of the people of authority – *ahl al-ḥal wa al-ʿaqd*), and thus he may be withdrawn if the *bayʿah* is revoked. As for the Shīʿah, it is said that the 'appointment' is divine, and the station of the imam is tantamount to that of the station of the Prophet in its affirmation, and therefore, it is *impossible* to remove him. Thus for the Shīʿah, the imamate is a source among the *uṣūl* of the religion, and for the Sunnis it is a branch among the branches (*furūʿ*).[10] The meaning of '*aṣl*' here is 'the basis and upon which other than it is built' and thus 'the *uṣūl* of the religion are that upon which the religion is constructed'. That is, these refer to 'the *ḥadīth*, *fiqh*, and *tafsīr* which rest upon the trustworthiness of the Messenger, and the trustworthiness of the Messenger rests upon confirmation of his being sent, and his characteristics, and his justice and the impossibility of attributing anything despicable (of any sort) to him.' Thus, it is built 'upon the trustworthiness of the imam as protector of the law *(ḥāfiẓan li-l-sharʿ)*'.[11] Similarly, Islamic legal texts specify the principle of the imamate, and thus reason and logic confirm the proof of it.[12]

Therefore, for the Shīʿah, there is no role for the *ummah* in the order of the imamate or the appointment of the imam because the imamate is nothing other than 'a form of divine trusteeship', or it is 'a divine contract as is prophethood'.[13] And, if prophethood is a message to convey and teach the religion and a system for governing the administration of the affairs of the Muslims, then the imamate – in Shīʿite *fiqh* – signifies the *khilāfah* and the *imāmah* at the same time, and in a form that does not permit separation, wherein Islam is both political and religious and 'neither permits dissociation from the other'.[14] Thus, there is in Shīʿite reasoning, the interspersion of the significance of the imamate with the significance of prophethood which clarifies the reasons that are carried along with the assertion that the imamate is among the *uṣūl* of the religion and not of its branches.

The blurring between the imamate and prophethood carries with its assertion implications for Shīʿite understanding of the religious message itself. That is, this blurring does not mesh with the assertion of the completion of prophethood with the message of Muḥammad as decreed by the *fuqahā'* of the Shī'ah along with the rest of the *fuqahā'* of Islam.[15] The upshot of that blurring is to make the imamate something of a renewal of prophethood so as not to say a renewed prophethood. The like of this formulation leads us to two issues: the first is the preservation of the imamate in the thesis of Shī'ite *fiqh* – of the same functions as prophethood: conveying the message, and leading the *ummah* and so on, as well as the same particulars and nature – *al-'iṣmah* (infallibility); and the second, which is its being established, like prophethood, according to the dictates of divine 'appointment'. In both cases, this imamate is utterly removed from the human sphere – socially and politically – and belongs to the domain of the transcendent. This, also, is among the reasons for which it is counted among the *uṣūl* of the religion. In any case, if we temporarily leave aside the subject of the functions of the imamate and the 'infallibility' of the imam and we deal with the matter of divine 'appointment', we must give pause before the major political results towards which the concepts of 'designation' (*al-waṣīyah*) drives the belief of the Ja'farī Imāmīyah. It clarifies for us the clear and obvious features of the idea of the state of the imamate in its description as a religious or theocratic state: in the Medieval past, where its matter was inconceivable to the modern present which has found a place for it since the Islamic Revolution in Iran more than twenty years ago.

Muḥammad Ḥussayn al-Anṣārī exonerates the assertion of the Shī'ah that the imamate is not confirmed except by appointment through a complete transmission of proofs of the harm that obtains in the absence of that appointment – along the lines of an inverse proof – and he mentions seven proofs: the impossibility of the Messenger leaving the *Anṣār* in opposition to *Quraysh* without appointing a successor; the impossibility of his leaving his people and his descendants to the aspirations of any who harbored them; the impossibility of leaving Imam 'Alī to face the spite of *Quraysh*; the pledging of the *khilāfah* by Abū Bakr to 'Umar; the appointment by the Messenger of a deputy for him in Medina who would act as a guardian trustee – *walī* – for him any time he left it and the people, leaders and chieftains being accustomed to this deputyship; and finally, the impossibility of the Messenger leaving the matters of the Arabian peninsula to Persian and Byzantine machinations and their aspirations.[16] These are all clear signs that the succession (*istikhlāf*) of 'Alī was among the primary concerns in the thinking of the Prophet in regard to the future of the *da'wah* (call) and the state. Bearing witness to this is that the Messenger 'clearly realized that his *ummah* would differ after him' and that tribal spirit had not ceased to dominate the social relations of the *ummah*, and accordingly, that it was not possible 'to ignore a matter that threatened its future with danger.'[17]

Despite this, the Shī'ite *fuqahā'* do not find this proof of 'reason' sufficient for the necessity of the naming and appointment (of the imam), but rather they embellish it with textual proofs – especially from Prophetic *ḥadīth*, such as in the case of the *ḥadīth al-thaqalayn,*[18] or the *ḥadīth al-manzilah,*[19] or the *ḥadīth al-Ghadīr,*[20] or others[21] which fall under the rubric of conferring religious legitimacy – after the rational – upon the matter of the 'appointment' of the imam. Given the multiplicity of these *ḥadīth*, one of them remains, and the event to which it refers – that of *al-Ghadīr* – the most often pressed into service for this goal – both in ancient and modern times. What is interesting is that this utilization – from the standpoint of producing the concept of 'appointment' (*al-ta'yīn*) – is that its advocates do not stop at the limits of the assertion that it is a Prophetic 'appointment' of 'Alī bin Abī Ṭalib, but rather they take the position that it is a *divine* 'appointment'. The *fuqahā'* of the Shī'ah asserted this in the Middle Ages, but they have not ceased to repeat it up to the present day. That, for example, is what we read in the text transmitted of a discussion of it by Ayatollah Khomeini:

> ...when it was possible that differences within the *ummah* might obtain after his death, and then Allah obliged the noblest Messenger to stop immediately in the middle of the desert to convey the command of the *khilāfah*. The most noble Messenger engaged in the rule of law and following the law in appointing ['Alī] the Commander of the Faithful, upon him be peace, to the *khalīfah*, not on account of his being his son-in-law or due to the fact that he had performed a number of services, but rather because he was *commanded* and he was following the rule of Allah, and executing the command of Allah.[22]

The imamate, then, obtains through divine appointment. There is no connection to the desire of people or their choice. The meaning of that is the matter is not rectified, for the Shī'ah, except in rejection of the subject of *shūrā* and choice (*al-ikhtīyār*), as espoused by the Sunnis, and in the demonstration of its invalidity. This is precisely that about which Shī'ite writings – both ancient and contemporary – concur. If we intend to clarify the relation between the assertion of 'appointment' and the invalidity of *shūrā*, then it is not for the purpose of examining the sources of Shī'ite political thought only but in order to clarify the type of political system which they envision today.

The Invalidation of al-Shūrā

Shīʿite political *fiqh* rejects the subjects of the imamate in the order of Islamic legal politics (*al-sīyāsah al-sharʿīyah*) of the Sunnis, and especially in what pertains to the appointment of the imam. As we have seen, the appointment for the Shīʿah is 'divine' whereas for the Sunnis it is according to the constraints of consensus (*al-ijmāʿ*), *al-shūrā* (consultation), and the pledge of allegiance (*al-bayʿah*). That is, it obtains through *choice*, and it is expressive on some form of 'will' (*irādah*) of the *ummah*. This difference, in itself, is perhaps sufficient to explain the defining by the *Shīʿah* of the imamate as being among the *uṣūl* of the religion while the Sunnis describe it as a branch (*farʿ*) belonging to the creed, or, more so *fiqh*.[23]

The Shīʿah deny the Sunni assertion that consensus – *ijmāʿ* – can be a basis for selection of the imam, given their consideration that *ijmāʿ* is an indication without proof or supporting basis from the standpoint of the *sharīʿah* because it is an indication of numerical majority, and this carries no argumentative weight neither according to the constraints of reason nor the *sharīʿah*. Rather, the noble Qur'ān casts blame on the majority in a number of instances: 'And few of My slaves are thankful'[24] and so on. Perhaps among the strongest of issues arguing against the majority is the frankness of the Qur'ān as to its benefit along with the existence of a comprehending minority when Allah says: 'How many has a group of a few overcome a group of many by leave of Allah? And Allah is with those who are patient.'[25] On the basis of this, it is not possible to reckon according to the principle of *ijmāʿ* or majority which might result in a negative decision as it is not infallible.[26]

The first result of invalidation of the principle of *ijmāʿ* or majority, or the principle of choice according to these constraints, is – in contemporary terms – to bring down the principle of elections expressive of the will of the *ummah*[27] on the account of its being a 'conceptual principle' and on account of its being unsuitable as a criterion of truth or falsity in the matters of rule.[28]

Along the same lines, Shīʿite *fiqh* denies the Sunni political assertion of *al-shūrā* as a means to choose the imam and the administration of politics and rule, considering that *shūrā* was an occurrence which had no legitimate right or connection to the *uṣūl* and texts of the *sharīʿah*. It finds in the contexts of history examples for the stance taken: the *khilāfah* of Abū Bakr did not rest on *shūrā*, nor did the *khilāfah* of ʿUmar; as for the third, whatever happened in regard to it was not, according to the Shīʿah, an instance of *shūrā*. Thus, instances of *shūrā* are not decisive here even along the lines of those who assert its decisiveness. Rather this *shūrā* is conceptual or fictitious; it has no form and no content.[29]

Probably, ayatollah Muḥammad Bāqir al-Ṣadr was the most outspoken of all contemporary Shī'ite thinkers in his criticism of the concept of *al-shūrā* and the explication of its nature as extraneous to the sources of rule in Islam. He proceeded in his rejection of it from the remark that:

> the nature of things and the general fixed situation for the Messenger and the *da'wah* as well as the one calling to it, rejects this supposition and denies that the Prophet could have operated according to this method and oriented towards tying the leadership of the *da'wah* after him directly to the *ummah* as represented in its upcoming generation of Muhājirīn and Anṣār, on the basis of the system of *shūrā*.[30]

He supports his opinion with the assertion that if the Prophet had actually meant to command the appending of political power and leadership to an elite after him on the basis of the system of *shūrā* that:

> he would have engendered the elements that were demanded by this position...that the leader – the Messenger – would have engaged in an operation of bringing the *ummah* to an awareness of this and would have called for the system of *al-shūrā* and clearly defined its limits and its details...and he would have engaged in preparing the Islamic *ummah* conceptually and spiritually to accept this system; and this is a society which originated from a group of tribes which had never before Islam lived in a political situation based on *shūrā*.[31]

Thus, the state of affairs is one for which we do not find indication in the Prophetic *ḥadīth* or experience, and not even in the mindset of the *ummah* or in the mindset of its upcoming generation; rather, it is the experience of the *khalīfah* resting on an indication of the opposite of this supposition.[32] The crux of the matter – according to al-Ṣadr – is that *al-shūrā* is not transmitted in the annals of Prophetic *ḥadīth* and, moreover, there is nothing that can justify its assertion.

Thus, the second result of negating the principle of *al-shūrā* is to sanction two ideas: the first is that the imamate is by 'appointment' and not by choice; and the second is that *shūrā* is nothing more than a usurpation of the legitimate political authority of the imam. These two ideas, together, have not ceased to be, until today, formative in the Shī'ite consciousness of political authority and rule despite the fact that the *wilāyat al-faqīh*, as we shall see, necessitates a new interpretation of the theory of the imamate, even if that interpretation rides on the principle of passing on the majority of the functions of the imamate!

If we leave aside the subject of infallibility (*ʿiṣmah*) of the imamate – as it pertains to the characteristics of the designated imam – and we deal with the matter of political authority in the 'age of occultation' where the infallible imam is absent, we find that the two ideas of 'appointment' and the invalidity of *shūrā* have not ceased to penetrate into contemporary Shīʿite political consciousness in some of its need for legitimacy and to justify its conception of political authority and the state – especially in the scope of the theory of the '*wilāyat al-faqīh*'. That is, a trusteeship – *wilāyah* – of qualified *fuqahāʾ* who possess the necessary qualifications of *ijtihād* and *al-marjaʿīyah*, which inheres as a derivative of the *wilāyah* of the imam through the description of them as his being his representative 'deputies', and thus, wherein there is something of that (divine) 'appointment'! Similarly, it occurs without *shūrā* or choice of the *ummah*, and is rather, an agreement between the *fuqahāʾ*. This means that the system of rule – from the viewpoint of the '*wilāyat al-faqīh*' – belongs to the *religious* field and it is not a matter among those of the political or social fields.

On the '*Wilāyat al-Faqīh*'

We will not repeat, in this section, what has been previously detailed (in Chapter Three) with regard to the historical and *fiqh* context in which the theory of the '*wilāyat al-faqīh*' originated. It only concerns us to recall that this theory engendered a solution for the question of trusteeship – *al-wilāyah* – for the Shīʿah whose consciousness had adapted from the assertion that there is no *wilāyah* except for the infallible imam – the *ṣāḥib al-zamān* (i.e., the awaited Mahdī), to the assertion of the possibility of cooperating with deviant rulers without acknowledging the legitimacy of their political authority, and to the assertion of the necessity of establishing a *wilāyah* for the deputies of the imam – that is for the *fuqahāʾ* who possessed all the necessary qualifications. Precisely this question, however, split the Shīʿite position into two opinions: the view which maintained a lack of legitimacy for establishing Islamic rule in the age of the 'major occultation' as that would dictate implementing a 'general trusteeship' – *wilāyah ʿāmah* and that is the exclusive domain of the Prophet and the infallible imam; as for the *faqih* who possesses requisite qualifications, he cannot hold anything other than a *particular* and limited trusteeship – *wilāyah khāṣah* – which does not reach the limit of the *wilāyah al-ʿāmah* This, in the main, was the position of the senior Shīʿah who did not seek rule,[33] on the consideration that the vacuum in political authority does not transpire due to the non-existence of the Imam, but rather from his *absence*; whereas, the second opinion goes to the assertion that there is a *wilāyah 'āmah* for the *fuqahā'*, and the necessity of establishing Islamic rule according to the rulings (*aḥkām*) of the religion.

The theory of the '*wilāyat al-faqīh*' obviously belongs to the second of these opinions and that of Imam Khomeini about which he originally theorized at the end of the 1960s and which became, after the Revolution, a basis for the system of rule in Iran. While it is true that this theory was not new in the Shī'ite political *fiqh* – as many had asserted it decades before – Khomeini resurrected it anew along with others such as Ayatollah Muntaẓirī,[34] and he succeeded in recruiting the *ḥawzāt* in al-Najaf and Qom in the political initiative which he established according to its constraints. More important than all of that is that he gave a place to this political-religious theory in a realistic material realization – transporting Shī'ite group consciousness through a jump from the doctrine of 'waiting' (*al-intiẓār*)[35] to what had previously been deemed to be of the realm of the prohibited and the impossible – the establishment of a religious state or a state of the men of religion.

In the theory of the '*wilāyat al-faqīh*', there are three determining factors: the need of Muslims for a government; the significance of a *wilāyah* of the *fuqahā'* and the limits of that *wilāyah*, and the significance of Islamic government.

On the Need for Government

The assertion of the necessity of government among Shī'ite *fuqahā'* belongs to those taking the position of the idea of the '*wilāyat al-faqīh*', to the necessity of *al-wilāyah*[36] and its being among the *uṣūl* of their *madhab*. The *wilāyah* from the standpoint of Allah in regard to his slaves: as sheikh Aḥmad al-Narāqī[37] asserts:

> It is confirmed of the Messenger and his infallible designates...and they are the sultans of the human race...that in their hands are the most important matters and that the rest of people are their flock and their charges. As for the Messenger and his designees, there is no doubt the fundamental principle (*uṣūl*) is the absence of confirmation of trusteeship (*wilāyah*) of anyone for another except whom Allah, glory be to Him, has appointed as a trustee or His messenger or one whom he has designated in this matter;[38] and at that point, he is the *wālī* of him who appointed him with what he was entrusted.[39]

Aside from the Messenger and his designated appointees,[40] none has the right of the *wilāyah al-'āmah*; and, its essence is the *political wilāyah*. The meaning of this is that the remainder of all those who have governed in the history of Islam, after the Prophet and the imam, do not possess the requisite legitimacy for this *wilāyah* due to the impossibility of their attaining to the constraints of 'divine appointment' and 'designation' (*al-waṣīyah*), and these altogether are among those to whom Shī'ite political *fiqh* has referred with the term '*wulāt al-jawr*' ('trusteeships of deviance'). When it is the case that the *wilāyah* is confirmed for the Prophet and his designated appointees, then this calls for him as well as his designated appointees after him, legally, to promote the establishment of a government, and this is exactly what He engaged in when He formed a government and when He 'appointed a ruler (*ḥākim*) after him by command of Allah the Most Exalted'[41] because that is what is commensurate with the command of the message of Islam in its distinction as being not only a conveyance of and legislation for the rulings (*al-aḥkām*) of the *sharī'ah*, but also the *execution* of them.

This basis is the point of departure for Khomeini's call, at the end of the 1960s, for the necessity of forming an Islamic government in the present. When it is the case that 'it is obvious that the necessity of executing rule requires the formation of the government of the most noble Messenger, upon him be peace, is not restricted or limited to his era...but rather this requirement continues after his passing' – due to the need to prevent chaos and corruption:

> If so, then there is no escape from the formation of a government [because] what was obligatory in the way of establishing government and executive and administrative political authority at the time of the Messenger and the Commander of the Faithful is, according to the dictates of both the reason and Islamic law, obligatory after them and in our time as well.[42]

This poses the question of the legitimacy of establishing a government by those who do not possess complete qualifications for the *wilāyah* – that is, by those who are not among the ranks of the Prophet and the infallible imams. This matter, however, is justified according to the Shī'ah in one case: in the case where the designation of the Prophet is constrained to only the infallible imams. This case was in conformity with the position taken by the ancient Shī'ite *fuqahā'* who imposed obstacles before this on the account of it being considered a usurpation of the station of the imam. As for contemporary Shī'ite *political fiqh*, the matter is markedly different, as competent *fuqahā'* who possessed the requisite qualifications in *ijtihād* came to be counted among those 'designated';[43] and moreover, it came to be supposed that they ought to promote the necessity of forming this government in the 'age of occultation'.[44]

Khomeini pushes the question about the legitimacy of forming a government in the era of the occultation much farther when he writes:

> Should the Islamic rulings, during the period from after the lesser occultation until today – more than a thousand years, and possibly for another hundred thousand years, await the appearance of the Mahdī without regulating the public good? Should they remain simply put forth without any implementation so that everyone can do whatever he wills? So that chaos may become general? Were the laws that the most noble Messenger struggled to clearly communicate and convey and spread and implement for twenty-three years, were they only for a limited time? Was Islam and all it connoted to be abandoned after the lesser occultation? Conviction of the veracity of all such matters or their appearance is worse than the belief in or declaration of the abrogation of Islam itself.'[45]

That is unacceptable for Khomeini because the rulings of Islam are permanent and directed towards Muslims in every time and place; it is not possible to execute them except through a political authority. Therefore, culpability (*al-taklīf*) in the time of the Prophet and the imams is the same culpability in the period of the occultation.

However, the problem is that the government of the Prophet was established through divinely ordained culpability and subsequently the Prophet 'designated' 'Alī bin Abī Ṭālib, according to the 'command of Allah' sent down, and in sum, both of them engaged in the 'divine appointment'. So, how should Islamic government be established today without a basis for 'appointment' – realizing that the asserters of this today reject such an establishment on the basis of consensus *ijmā'* (consensus) or *shūrā* (consultation) by which the Sunnis abide?

Khomeini does not experience great difficulty in responding to the like of this question: the thesis depends upon the capacity to occupy the position of the *wilāyah* and the extent of integration with the requisite conditions of the imamate and does not pertain to the *means* of 'attribution' (*naṣb*). Thus, we read:

> ...even if Allah the Most Exalted did not appoint a particular person for rule in the time of the occultation, the characteristics of the conditions for rule – from the rise of Islam to the time of the Imam al-Mahdī, are the same for the time of the occultation as well. These are the characteristics that are an expression of the knowledge of the law and equity, which are extant beyond count in the *fuqahā'* of our age; and if they were to gather together, they would be able to establish the government of complete justice in the world.[46]

If we go beyond noticing the transition, in the discourse of Khomeini, from discussion of the essence of the Prophet and the infallible imams to discussion of the characteristics of 'knowledge of the law and equity', we find – from the givens of the text – that plunging into the subject of the obligation to form a government dictates, objectively, research into the nature of this group upon whom Khomeini and others confer divine culpability and the function as deputy of the imam in the age of the occultation – namely, the *fuqahā'*. Who are these and what are the limits of their functions from the viewpoint of the '*wilāyat al-faqīh*'?

On the Functions of the Fuqahā'

In a text of Ayatollah Muḥammad Mahdī Shams al-Dīn,[47] he examines the supporting basis of those taking the position of advocating the '*wilāyat al-faqīh*':

> Those who take this position and advocate it see that the indication for it is that the infallible Imam deputized a *faqīh* possessing all the requisite qualifications in the age of the major occultation; a general trustee (*walīy 'ām*), and a trusteeship (*wilāyah*) over the Muslims. Confirmed for the *faqīh*, according to the dictates of this trusteeship were all that which were confirmed for the infallible imam and the *wilāyah*. This *faqīh*, possessing all the qualifications, is the appointed Islamic ruler – by general attribution (*bi-l-naṣb al-'ām*), as ruler over the Muslims. This is the basis of the term '*wilāyat al-faqīh*'.[48]

The '*wilāyat al-faqīh*', then, connotes conferral of the remainder of powers of the 'infallible imam' to the *fuqahā'*, and attributes to them the status of his representative deputies – transferring executive authority to them according to the dictates of this deputyship. If this conferral is mandated in the period of occultation by the needs of the Muslims (the Shī'ah) for one who will direct their matters according to the constraints of religion and the *madhab*, then it does not obtain in an *absolute* fashion, but rather is *conditional*. The basic condition is that the *fuqahā'* meet the necessary prerequisites of *ijtihād* for qualified jurists; and, as we have seen, the fitness of the *faqīh* ultimately reduces (according to Khomeini) to 'knowledge of the law and equity' – the conditional basis in the matter of *al-wilāyah*.

However, when the *faqīh*, in Khomeini's view, is the designee of the Messenger, it can be inferred that his powers are not only those of the Imam, but are rather those of the Prophet also. The significance of this, moreover, is that there is no difference between the Prophet and the imam or the *faqīh* from the standpoint of the function of the *wilāyah* and the practice of rule! This is not simply a matter of inference, but rather the result of that to which the texts of Khomeini bear witness directly[49] that, frankly stated, the qualified *fuqahā'* 'are charged and commanded to engage in all the matters that existed in the era of the prophets.'[50]

What are these functions that the '*wilāyat al-faqīh*' confers upon the *fuqahā'* and which render from among them designees and deputies and rulers?

Sheikh Aḥmad al-Narāqī advanced a thesis about these, and Khomeini took these from him part and parcel, with an albeit wider use of *ijtihād* to expand the bases and the arguments for them through transmitted reports of the imams and the *fuqahā'* and in extending the background of this assertion[51] '*wilāyat* al-*faqīh* is among the matters of rational consideration (that demand consideration by sages or wise men.)'[52] Al-Narāqī breaks these functions down into eight which are: judgeship (*al-qaḍā'*)[53] where 'they have the trusteeship of judgeship, and they are to be sought for legal opinion and those who are under their supervision have recourse to them and are to accept their judgments;[54] engaging in *ijtihād*[55] and among these are the *ḥudūd* [penalties] and punishments (*al-ta'zīrāt*);[56] the preservation of the wealth of orphans;[57] the preservation of the wealth of the insane and the mentally infirm;[58] trusteeship of marriage;[59] the trusteeship of orphans and the mentally infirm in providing for them and their physical wellbeing;[60] and preservation of the wealth of the absentee person;[61] and finally spending the wealth of the absent Imam from a half of the funds of *al-khums*'.[62] This group of functions which belonged to the Imam becomes the comprehensive work of the qualified *fuqahā'* via the obligation of the '*wilāyat al-faqīh*'. In sum, it also accords to them the right to exercise the *wilāyah al-'āmah* over the *ummah*, and grapple with the task of administering rule.

Khomeini wrote what he did about the '*wilāyat al-faqīh*' and the necessity of government and functions of *al-wilāyah* before the Iranian Revolution by more than a decade while in exile.[63] Naturally, he was obliged to put forth a picture of the nature of this Islamic government for which he was calling and heralding. In spite of the fact that, in our estimation, he traces the broad contours of this government in the context of his criticism of '*ḥukūmāt al-jawr*' ('deviant governments') or in the context of his defense of Islamic government in the period of the Prophet and Imam 'Alī, or in the context of his discussion of the role of the *fuqahā'* in handing down rule, he does not escape some of the problems of clarification and definition about the model of this government in various excerpts that he has written as we shall see.

On the Model of Islamic Government

Despite the fact that Khomeini defines the government for which he strives – he and the *fuqahā'* and the *ḥawzah* movement – as 'the government which the people desire',[64] this does not mean that this is a *civil* government. Rather, it means that it is a religious government for which it is not possible that a people – on the consideration of their being Muslim – should choose other than it from among the remainder of types of government. Khomeini, himself, did not leave any large scope for ambiguity in this matter as he described it as 'a divine government' (*ḥukūmah ilāhīyah*), 'in accordance with the rule of Allah',[65] and that the state towards which he hastened was 'a state ruled by the righteous'.[66] And when he called, in the context of the Revolution, for the establishment of 'an Islamic Republic', and heard those who were perplexed by the expression such as Shahpour Bakhtiar (the last Prime Minister under the Shah) or those who inquired as to its meaning, he responded: 'The meaning of "republic" is clear to you all and it implies the necessity of abiding by the position of public opinion; and "Islamic" means respecting the foundation principles of Islam...do you see yourselves as amenable to it being a "republic" and refusing that it be "Islamic"?!'[67] Thus, as long as public opinion remains *Islamic*, then there is nothing in its nature as a republic that is in conflict with its being Islamic.

Islamic government – in its context – is not like the rest of governments. It is not absolutely despotic, but rather conditionally so, however not according to the meaning understood or discussed by *al-ʿallāmah* al-Nā'īnī, but rather according to the meaning that it is conditioned by the rules of Islam and its laws. From here it is 'the government of the divine law over the people'.[68] And, from another angle, the basic difference between Islamic government and governments of 'conditional monarchy' and 'republics', in the view of Khomeini, pertains to legislation. In other systems of government, representatives of the people or the king engage in legislation 'whereas in Islamic government, legislation is the restricted domain of Allah the Most Exalted. The holy law in Islam is the single legislative authority';[69] and this is the very essence of the position taken by Ayatollah al-Sayyid Muḥammd al-Shīrāzī when he wrote that: 'legislative authority...is the sole right of Allah, glory be to Him, alone'.[70] Thus, this Islamic government – that is, the Islamic state – cannot possibly contain legislative institutions or legislative councils[71] because the representatives do not have the right to legislate.

What is to be done in that case?

Khomeini does not find anything better than positing a 'planning council' to set plans for the rest of the ministries on the basis of the rules of Islam.[72] And despite whatever might be said in that regard about placing the authority of law in the hands of a group not chosen by the people in an election indicative of its popular will, Khomeini does not find in that a definitive reason to object to this proposition because 'the Islamic laws transmitted in the Qur'ān and the *sunnah* are met by the Muslims with acceptance and obedience, and this is among that which facilitates the work of the government and makes it connected to the people.'[73]

This, in sum, is the model of Islamic government of which Khomeini conceives and expresses as 'divine government' ruled by 'the righteous', the system of which operates according to the dictates of the rules (*aḥkām*) of Islam where legislation is attributed to the (divine) legislator, and where the elite of the *fuqahā'* engages in planning its politics according to the constraints of the rules of the *sharī'ah*. It is the religious government wherein an elite among the *fuqahā'* is entrusted – according to the concept of '*wilāyat al-faqīh*' – a matter of a 'general trusteeship' – *wilāyah 'āmah* – over the *ummah*. It is exactly the same government that has persisted in Iran since its Revolution more than twenty years ago: the form of government wherein political authority is concentrated in the hand of the *walīy al-faqīh* (the guardian/trustee jurist) – the Guide of the Revolution and Leader of the Republic, where the *elected* President of the Republic is not about to retain anything of the powers normally accorded to presidents of other republics. The government is one where the *fuqahā'* stand alone – in the 'Council of Experts' – in powers of decision and where the 'Shūrā Council' does not possess any powers worthy of consideration. The representatives of the *ummah* are not – in this theory – at a higher rank than the 'deputies of the Imam' or the 'designees of the Prophet'.

The theory of the '*wilāyat al-faqīh*' established a model for the theocratic state in two regards: in regard to the assertion of the 'divine right' and in regard to according a place to the Shī'ite clergy (the qualified *fuqahā'*) at the top of the political system. In regard to the first aspect, political authority does not represent a general, political civic duty but rather a religious one (restricted to those who have the right to the *wilāyah* – according to the constraints of the theory – and these are the designees of the Prophet and the Imam during the period of occultation). Furthermore, this is among the *uṣūl* of the religion and the pillars (*arkān*) of Islam, that is, it is a creedal matter. As for the second aspect, the political authority of the *fuqahā'* – the 'designees' – is not derivative from the *ummah*, but rather from the 'designation' (*al-waṣīyah*), and thus, it rests on the rules of the religion in the consideration of them as the official representatives wherein the *ummah* does not engage in joint participation, censorship or holding them accountable. None of the modern apparatus of the state or techniques of political administration are appropriate analogs as instruments to describe the model of this system: the system of the ruling *fuqahā'* in the 'divine state'.

The theory of the '*wilāyat al-faqīh*' inherited the theory of the imamate in the blurring of the distinction between the Prophet and the 'infallible' imam. It adds to it, however, a new dimension in the blurring between the *faqīh mujtahid* possessing the requisite qualifications (and according to Khomeini there are many who do) and between the Prophet and the Imam. Thus, the state of the *fuqahā'* and 'Islamic government' is erected by means of this blurring to a level of holiness, and that is the hallmark of every religious state; furthermore, it is not the *ummah* which is its authoritative point of reference but rather the *faqīh* who is the deputy of the Imam[74] (and the Prophet). There is no trusteeship of the people over itself, but rather that of the *faqīh* over the *ummah*. It is not possible for the state to be other than a religious one like its Sunni counterpart – the state of '*al-ḥākimīyah*'.

With the *wilāyat al-faqīh*, we have transitioned to the religious trusteeship that was prevalent in traditional Medieval *Imāmī fiqh* – to a joint religious and political *wilāyah* – from the *faqīh* to the ruler *faqīh* (or the '*walīy al-faqīh*'). More than that, we have transitioned from the 'infallibility' of the imam who does not err to the 'infallibility' of the state that is not taken to account by its people and their representatives (because it, likewise, does not err). From here, we comprehend why it is that *shūrā* and the replacement of it with the principle of 'appointment' continues to rule the consciousness of the Shī'ite *fuqahā'* up until today despite the fact that the '*wilāyat al-faqīh*' liberated them considerably from the fetters of the 'major occultation'; and that is that a system persisting on the basis of *shūrā* will not be, of a necessity, a system of rule by the *fuqahā'*.

Notes

1. Abrahamian, Ervand, *Iran between Two Revolutions* (Princeton, NJ: Princeton University Press, 1982), pp. 267–80.
2. Yavari-D'Hellencourt, Nouchine, 'Le Radicalisme Shi'ite de Ali Shariati' in: Carré and Dumont, *Radicalisme Islamiques* (Paris: L'Harmattan, 1985), vol. 1.
3. 'One of its results was to have Mosaddeq gain power, and, no sooner than he had done so, he was at odds with the President of the government over the latter's suggestion to pay indemnities to the British as a reimbursement for nationalization of the

oil, on the consideration that it was Britain that ought pay reparations to Iran for stealing oil for half a century.' Available in: Al-Anṣārī, Ḥamīd, *Ḥadīth al-Inṭilāq: Naẓrah fī al-Ḥayāt al-'Ilmīyah wa al-Siyāsīyah lil-Imām al-Khomeini: (min al-Wilādah wa ḥattā al-'Urūj)*, 2nd edn (Tehran: Mu'asasat Tanẓīm wa Nashr Turāth al-Imām Al-Khomeini, 1996), pp. 54–6.

4. He was close to the radical organization 'Fidā'īī al-Islām', he was a member in the coordination process that led to the accord between the organization and its wing and 'al-Jabhah al-Waṭanīyah', Al-Anṣārī, *Ḥadīth al-Inṭilāq,* pp. 19–21.

5. The signatories were: Muḥammad Ḥussayn al-Ṭabāṭibā'ī, Muḥammad al-Mūsawī al-Yazdī, Muḥammad Riḍā al-Mūsawī al-Kalbāyakānī, Kāẓim al-Sharī'atmadārī, Rūḥu Allāh al-Mūsawī al-Khomeini, Hāshim al-Amalī, Murtaḍā al-Ḥā'irī. Available in: Al-Anṣārī, *Ḥadīth al-Inṭilāq.*

6. Al-Anṣārī, *Ḥadīth al-Inṭilāq,* pp. 71–7.

7. See Chapter 3 of this book.

8. We addressed this in detail in Chapter 3 of this book.

9. Arkoun, Mohammed, *L'Islam, Morale et Politique* (Paris: Desclée de Brouwer, 1986), pp. 135–41.

10. Al-Anṣārī, Muḥammad Ḥussayn, *al-Imāmah wa al-Ḥukūmah fī al-Islām* (Tehran: Maṭbū'āt Maktabat al-Najāḥ, 1998), p. 25.

11. Al-Anṣārī, *al-Imāmah,* p. 102.

12. 'If the *imāmah* was not a duty, and an imam did not exist, then the Islamic message would not have been the *khātimat al-risālāt* (the final message of God to humanity), as the revelation to receive these messages did not change or alter. And since it is a constant necessity to believe that Islam is undoubtedly the final divine message to humanity, then it is necessary to believe that the *imāmah* is a duty and that the Imam exists.' Available in: Al-Anṣārī, *al-Imāmah,* p. 114.

13. Al-Lārī, Mujtabā al-Mūsawī, *Dirāsah fī Usus al-Islām*, translated by Kamāl al-Sayyid (Qom: Markaz Nashr al-Thaqāfah al-Islāmīyah fī al-'Ālam, 1998), p. 257.

14. Al-Lārī, *Dirāsah,* p. 258.

15. In every major *madhab* of Islam, it is uniformly agreed that prophethood came to an end with the death of Muhammad in 632CE [if not with the third verse *sūrat al-ma'idah* in the Qur'ān (5:3)] and that he is understood to be the 'seal of the prophets' – *khātam al-anbiyā'* – where no prophet will come after him. – Translator.

16. Al-Anṣārī, *al-Imāmah,* pp. 59–65.

17. Al-Lārī, *Dirāsah,* p. 316.

18. 'I left you with two significant sources, each is greater than the other, Qur'ān and my family, so behold how will you succeed me by means of them, the twain will not diverge when...', as cited in: *Mustadrak al-Ṣaḥīḥayn*, or in other words (as cited in *Musnad Aḥmad, Sunnan al-Bayhaqī* and *Sunnan al-Dārmī*): 'I left you with two significant sources: the first is Qur'ān wherein God's guiding light lies, so cling to it and follow it...and my family.' Available in: Al-Anṣārī, *al-Imāmah,* p. 83.

19. Al-Bukhārī cited that the Prophet addressed 'Alī in front of people by saying: 'Don't you want to be to me as Hārūn (Aaron) was to Mūsā (Moses)?'. Available in: Al-Andalusī, 'Aydūs al-'Alawī [Ibn Darwīsh], *Shawāhid al-Tanzīl li-man Khuṣṣa bil-Tafḍīl* (Qom: al-Mujama' al-'Ālamī li-Ahl al-Bayt, 1996), p. 367.

20. 'God is my Patron (*walīy*), and I am the patron of believers and closer to them than their own selves, hence, whoever is under my patronage, then 'Alī is in turn his/her patron, O God, may You be the Patron of those who support him, and may You be the Enemy of those who hate him,' cited in tens of texts. Available in: Al-Ṣadr, Muḥammad Bāqir, *Baḥth Ḥawl al-Wilāyah*, 3rd edn (Beirut: Dār al-Ta'āruf, 1981), p. 85.

21. Al-Andalusī, *Shawāhid al-Tanzīl*, pp. 496–8.

22. Al-Khomeini, Rūḥ-Allāh al-Mūsawī, *al-Ḥukūmah al-Islāmīyah,* 2nd edn (Beirut: Markaz Baqīyat Allāh al-A'ẓam, 1999), pp. 83–4.

23. It is noteworthy to mention that contemporary 'Revivalist Islam' rejected this basis since the subjects addressed about the Islamic state by al-Bannā, who, scrutinized in rejecting them, the idea of '*ḥākimīyah*'. This is precisely what engendered the inclusive reconciliation between the Shī'ite 'Imamate' thought and the Sunni '*ḥākimīyah*' thought.

24. Qur'ān, *sūrat Saba',* (34:13).

25. Qur'ān, *sūrat al-baqarah,* (2:249).

26. Al-Anṣārī, *al-Imāmah,* p. 27.

27. 'One might say that the Islamic Republic of Iran which was established on the *Ja'farī/Imamī* sect and the concept of the *'wilāyat al-faqīh'*, is implementing the principle of elections to form the Majlis al-Shūrā and elect the President of the Republic, this is true. However, who can deny that the Majlis al-Shūrā and the President of the Republic do not possess much of authority before the '*wilāyat al-faqīh*' or the Supreme Guide of the Revolution who can dissolve the Parliament and depose the President; he also possesses the command of the military "Republican Guard", institutions of security and media...', in fact the latter's authority is not even comparable to that of the Majlis al-Khubarā' (which is supposed to be the council of experts) and the Majlis Tashkhīṣ Maṣlaḥat al-Niẓām. See: the Constitution of the Islamic Republic.

28. 'Does right go with the majority always? If the majority votes in favor of an opinion that contradicts reason, ethics or the *sharī'ah*, does it imply that its opinion is correct?...Logically, elections do not result in choosing the fittest person, in addition, the majority is not a measure for determining right and wrong.' Available in: Al-Lārī, *Dirāsah,* p. 260.

29. Al-Anṣārī, *al-Imāmah,* p. 49.

30. Al-Ṣadr, *Baḥth*, pp. 27–8.

31. Al-Ṣadr, *Baḥth*, p. 28.

32. Al-Ṣadr, *Baḥth*, pp. 30–5.

33. This urged al-Ash'arī to write: '*al-Rawāfiḍ* (the 'Rejectors') agreed to prohibit uprising and throw away the sword until the Imam appears again and orders them to take it up'. Available in: Al-Ash'arī, *Maqālāt al-Islāmīyīn*, p. 123.

34. Muntaẓirī, Ḥussayn, *Dirāsāt fī Wilāyat al-Faqīh wa Fiqh al-Dawlah al-Islāmīyah,* 2nd edn (Beirut: al-Dār al-Islāmīyah, 1988).

35. 'Khomeini served the Islamic nation greatly upon removing the hurdle (meaning the doctrine of "the waiting"), as he put "the waiting" in its historical context, that is, in some place along the extension of the line of the future that only God knows, so that "the waiting" becomes an impetus to work hard and not an obstacle.' Available in: Yāsīn, *al-Islām wa al-Qawmīyah*, p. 93.

36. 'The belief in the necessity of establishment of government and executive and administrative authority is part of the *wilāyah*, moreover, the perseverance and pursuit for achieving them is an integral part of the belief in it.' Available in: Al-Khomeini, *al-Ḥukūmah*, p. 56.

37. A prominent Iranian Shī'ite researcher who lived in the eighteenth century (1185–1245 AH); he founded an important *ḥawzah* in his town Narāq, in which many distinguished Shī'ite jurists (among his pupils) studied and graduated such as sheikh Murtaḍā al-Anṣārī. He is considered to be the first to formulate the concept of the '*wilāyat al-faqīh*', which would later be adopted by Khomeini.

38. Here, it is referring to the types of *al-wilāyah al-khāṣṣah* such as trusteeship over children, or the husband's trusteeship over his wife and so on.

39. Al-Narāqī, Aḥmad, *Wilāyat al-Faqīh*, edited by Yāsīn al-Mūsawī (Beirut: Dār al-Ta'āruf, 1990), p. 29.

40. We shall expound on the meaning of *waṣṣī al-nabī*, the sense of that idiom had been extended by modern Shi'ite jurists.

41. Al-Khomeini, *al-Ḥukūmah*, p. 62.

42. Al-Khomeini, *al-Ḥukūmah*, pp. 62–3.

43. Al-Khomeini, *al-Ḥukūmah*, p. 121.

44. Shī'ites distinguish two types of *ghaybah* (occultation): major and minor. The *Ghaybat al-Ṣughrā* (minor occultation) occurred when Muḥammad Ḥasan al-Mahdī (the 12th Imam in the Shī'ite Imamate chain) disappeared in 260 *Hijri* (aged five then). During this occultation, communication between the occulted Imam and the Shī'ites took place through four mediators (messengers): 'Uthmān bin Sa'īd al-'Umarī, Muḥammad bin 'Uthmān al-'Umarī, al-Ḥussayn bin Rūḥ-Allāh al-Nawbakhtī, and 'Alī bin Muḥammad al-Sammarī). This minor occultation extended until 329 *Hijri* upon the death of the last mediators, thence *al-Ghaybat al-Kubrā* (the major occultation) began. Available in: Al-Shīrāzī, Ḥasan, *Kalimat al-Imām al-Mahdī ('alayh al-salām)* (Beirut: Mu'asasat al-Wafā', 1983), p. 27.

45. Al-Khomeini, *al-Ḥukūmah*, pp. 63–4.

46. Al-Khomeini, *al-Ḥukūmah*, p. 90.

47. Former President of the Higher Islamic Shi'ite Council in Lebanon (died in 2001).

48. Shams al-Dīn, Muḥammad Mahdī, *fī al-Ijtimā' al-Siyāsī al-Islāmī: al-Mujtama' al-Siyāsī al-Islāmī Muḥāwalat Ta'ṣīl Fiqhī wa Tārīkhī* (Qom: Dār al-Thaqāfah, 1994).

49. '...the misconception that the Prophet has more authority than 'Alī, and that the latter has more authority than the *faqīh*, is indeed wrong and false. Sure, virtues of the Prophet outweigh those of all mankind, however, the abundance of moral virtues does not confer more authority in rule...'. Available in: Al-Khomeini, *al-Ḥukūmah*, p. 90.

50. Al-Khomeini, *al-Ḥukūmah*, p. 115.

51. Al-Khomeini, *al-Ḥukūmah*, p. 91.

52. 'The legal matters of the scholars – according to the Shī'ite *fiqh* – are those found in "*al-ja'l* (to make)" and "*al-waḍ'* (to set out)", and they are affiliated to the one who put them into place: whether he was a legislator (the legal consideration) or a scholar (the scholar's consideration).' Available in: Muẓaffar, Muḥammad Riḍā, *Uṣūl al-Fiqh* (Qom: Markaz al-Nashr, 1995), vol. 2, and Al-Khomeini, *al-Ijtihād wa al-Taqlīd* (Tehran: Mu'asasat Tanẓīm wa Nashr Turāth al-Imām Al-Khomeini, 1997), pp. 81–7.

53. Al-Khomeini, *al-Ijtihād,* pp. 22–30, and Al-Khomeini, *al-Ḥukūmah*, pp. 119–23.

54. Al-Narāqī, *Wilāyat al-Faqīh,* p. 103.

55. Al-Narāqī, *Wilāyat al-Faqīh,* p. 107.

56. Reprimand is: discipline without punishment, the root is *'uzr*, i.e. to prohibit. Available in: Al-Jarjānī, 'Alī bin Muḥammad al-Sharīf, *Kitāb al-Ta'rīfāt,* 3rd edn (Beirut: Dār al-Kitāb al-'Arabī, 1996), p. 85.

57. Al-Narāqī, *Wilāyat al-Faqīh,* p. 115.

58. Al-Narāqī, *Wilāyat al-Faqīh,* p. 127.

59. Al-Narāqī, *Wilāyat al-Faqīh,* p. 137.

60. Al-Narāqī, *Wilāyat al-Faqīh,* p. 161.

61. Al-Narāqī, *Wilāyat al-Faqīh,* p. 133.

62. Al-Narāqī, *Wilāyat al-Faqīh,* p. 163.

63. In Iraq, he lectured in Najaf about the '*wilāyah al-faqīh*', the series of these lectures were compiled in one book that was entitled *al-Ḥukūmah al-Islāmīyah*, which we cited here.

64. Al-Khomeini, *al-Kawthar* (Tehran: Mu'asasat Tanẓīm wa Nashr Turāth al-Imām Al-Khomeini, 1996), vol. 3, p. 12.

65. Al-Khomeini, *al-Kawthar*, p. 13.

66. Al-Khomeini, *al-Kawthar*, p. 339.

67. Al-Khomeini, *al-Kawthar*, p. 431.

68. Al-Khomeini, *al-Ḥukūmah*, p. 82.

69. Al-Khomeini, *al-Ḥukūmah*, p. 82.

70. Al-Shīrāzī, Muḥammad, *al-Ḥukm fī al-Islām*, cited by 'Abd al-Jabbār, Fāliḥ, *al-Māddīyah wa al-Fikr al-Dīnī al-Mu'āṣir* ([n.p.]: Markaz al-Abḥāth wa al-Dirāsāt al-Ishtirākīyah,1985), p. 47.

71. The Parliament in the Islamic Republic of Iran is not deemed a legislative council (it is called 'Majlis al-Shūrā'), in fact, the authority of the 'Majlis al-Khubarā'' far outweighs that of the 'Majlis al-Shūrā' in matters of legislation.

72. Al-Khomeini, *al-Ḥukūmah*, p. 83.

73. Al-Khomeini, *al-Ḥukūmah*, p. 83.

74. 'The *marja'* (religious authority) in the question of *al-wilāyah* is the *faqīh* (jurist) as he is the deputy of Imam, not of the *ummah*. This explains the theoretical basis for how the concept of '*wilāyat al-faqīh*' banned the *ummah* from running the issues of the Islamic government...the latent danger of this concept lies – for this reason – in having the *faqīh al-walīy*' responsible before God and the *ummah*.' Available in: Bārūt, *Yathrib al-Jadīdah*, p. 85.

Chapter 11

On the Criticism of 'Divine Right'

> We are absolutely certain that the utterance of '*al-ḥākimīyah*' was not transmitted in any verse of the Qur'ān, and we...have not found...a *ḥadīth* with the import of this utterance...we have no need beyond the book of Allah and the *ḥadīth* of the Messenger, upon him be peace, for any terminology put forth by a human being who is not infallible.
>
> Ḥasan al-Huḍaybī

> To consider the formulation of the *wilāyat al-faqīh* as an expression of the formulation of the 'infallible imamate'...is not correct either from the standpoint of *fiqh* or the *kalām* (Islamic theology)...even if some have attempted that or called for taking it into consideration and asserted that it is a matter of *fiqh*. The truth of the matter is that these are *political* matters without support in *fiqh* worth considering.
>
> Mahdī Shams al-Dīn

We indicated previously that the emergence of the *jihadist* and *takfīrī* revivalist discourse – that of Sayyid Quṭb from the womb of Muslim Brotherhood discourse – that of Ḥasan al-Bannā – is not grounds for considering it to be a natural extension of that even if it draws from it some essential subject matter such as the theme of 'Islam is a religion and state'; but rather, it 'forms a framework for a theory and movement *independent* of the theoretical framework and movement of the discourse of the "Brotherhood". The relation between them does not obtain as a "textual intervention" as much as it does as a device of "severance"'[1] when it is the case that both are established according to different authoritative political referents: the first resting for support on the idea of an Islamic state ruled by the *sharīʿah* where its political system persists in accordance with the dictates of the principle of consultative constitutionalism where the *ummah* has the right of decision and to censure the ruler; and the second resting for support on the idea of '*al-ḥākimīyah*' where the *ummah* has no opinion in affairs about its trusteeship and no right in it.

The discourse of '*al-ḥākimīyah*' then is analogous, in this sense, to the discourse of the '*wilāyat al-faqīh*', and rather to the Shīʿite Imāmī discourse in general, from the standpoint that both of them share in a unified political conception of a religious state established on the basis of 'divine right' – that is, a state where the ruler in it is Allah and Islamic *sharīʿah* and those engaging in the matter of the *wilāyah* are the men of religion. If the '*wilāyat al-faqīh*' is connected to its legacy in Shīʿite Imāmī *fiqh* in much of its bases and sources, '*al-ḥākimīyah*' is *disconnected* to a large degree from its Sunni *fiqh* heritage – both ancient and modern. The one connection which obtains is that which it has with ideas of the Shīʿah about the imamate and political authority, and it is the connection that justifies their shared view of a single model of political authority which, in effect, ordains an 'Islamic priesthood'.[2]

In reality, the discourse of '*al-ḥākimīyah*' and that of the '*wilāyat al-faqīh*', despite what there was of a resonance for them amidst the ranks of the Islamist movement since the 1960s, has been subject to fierce criticism directed towards elucidating the causes for its extremism and the modes of emergence from the 'Mecca' of moderate Islam. Not all of this criticism has come from un-Islamic conceptual movements or secular ones, but much of it has, in fact, come out of the Islamist movement itself – especially from intellectual forces adversely affected by these ideas. We shall attempt, in this chapter, to assess samples of this criticism which we deem emblematic, even if we shall preference samples of other criticism from outside the Islamist trend – whether or not they happen to be, of a necessity, from outside Islamist ideas.

On the Criticism of Religious Authority

'*Al-ḥākimīyah*' leads to an unfamiliar conception in the political order of Islam – unrecorded in the annals of those who had come before among the *fuqahāʾ* or the transmitters of *ḥadīth*. It portended a theocratic system of unknown origins in Islamic political culture, and this is what has impelled many contemporary Islamic researchers to criticize the concept of religious political authority and to demonstrate its strange character, alien to

Islamic thought and the experience of Muslim civilization. The subject matter of this criticism was not new as Islamic Reformist thinkers had contemplated it for a century – especially Muḥammad 'Abdūh and 'Abd al-Raḥmān al-Kawākibī[3] – even if the most significant and necessary criticism had yet to wait until the contemporary period, that is, until after the subject of religious political authority had reappeared anew in the guise of '*al-ḥākimīyah*' and what pertained to its meaning and provenance. It is a criticism that moved – like its Reformist precursor – from Islamic positions in the context of the defense of what it conceived of as an authentic position of Islam with regard to politics and rule.

Muḥammad 'Amārah, one of the most prominent contemporary critics of religious authority, defines it as follows:

> ...It means...that a human being claims to be the interlocutor in the name of Allah and to have the exclusive right to the opinion of Heaven and its exegesis. This is what pertains to the affairs of the religion or the matters of the world...and regardless of whether this claim is made by an individual occupying a religious or political position, or whether this claim is propagated by an individual or an institution...[4]

The upshot of this is that this authority derives from a claim of agency from Allah in the earthly or political *wilāyah* and, thus, rule in His name. This is precisely what the doctrine of 'Divine Right' dictates in its Christian Constantinian expression that served as a basis for the construction of a religious state predicated on the rule of the men of religion who 'represented' Heaven on earth!

Muḥammad 'Amārah rejects that Islam legitimized the like of this religious authority, or that the various *madhāhib* and movements in *fiqh* and thought, with the exception of the Shī'ah, ever advocated or accorded anything of divine sanctity to rules (*aḥkām*) of rulers because that is what might afford a place to the idea of infallibility (*al-'iṣmah*); that is, the 'infallibility' of the ruler. This is what 'Islam negates for human beings altogether, and it is not acknowledged for any except the Messenger.'[5] If 'Amārah acknowledges that the Shī'ah have taken the position of this *madhab*, unlike the rest of the Muslims, he does find in their assertion of that which justifies it or legitimizes it in Islam. He inclines towards the conviction that the source of this theory precedes Islam, and that it goes back, specifically, to the Persian emperors when Khusrau was ruling according to 'divine right' – 'rendering decisions and his injunctions divine revelation of the god "Ahura Mazda"', just as was the case with 'the Roman Caesars' before their embracing Christianity 'when the attributes of the emperor were of "divine sanctity"...'[6] This justification, however, does not nullify, in any case, questioning the Islamic experience in politics and the state, which embodied – to a certain extent – an entanglement between the religious and the temporal – between religious authority and political authority, which is the experience of the 'state of Medina' in the era of the Prophet. Did not this experience serve as a precedent or a foundation for presumptions of *al-tawḥīd* and the blurring between the two types of authority subsequently built upon in succeeding eras?

Muḥammad 'Amārah rejects that infallibility (*al-'iṣmah*) extends to the political or temporal aspect of the Prophetic practice – within the 'state of Medina' – as it extends to the religious; that is, in relation to the conveying of the message. This rejection is predicated on the decisive distinction between the *message* (*al-risālah*) and *politics* – between religion and the state.[7] In regard to the first, there exists a Prophet who is infallible and the recipient of revelation who conveys this revelation to people; in regard to the second, there is a political leader endeavoring, with consultation, to interpret the law in instances where there is no (specific) text provided.[8] However, this posits a question about the nature of Prophetic action: the *sunnah*, and specifically if it should be understood – from 'Amārah's discussion – whether or not it is exclusively human, temporal action. In this, he decides that the Prophetic *sunnah* has 'what is religion, and what is politics' and concludes that 'all of what may be subsumed of the Prophetic *sunnah* under political matters and the affairs of the world is *not* religion.'[9] Accordingly, it falls in the scope of human action which is determined by opinion and interpretation (*al-ijtihād*).[10]

If we were to be more precise, and we pushed this critical avenue to its logical ends, we would be obliged to assert the extraneousness of the idea of religious authority to Islam which not only does not entertain questions about excessive ideas such as '*al-ḥākimīyah*' and '*wilāyat al-faqīh*', but rather, even harbors reserve and questions with regard to the 'moderate' concept of the Islamic state; the state of the *sharī'ah* and *shūrā* for which al-Bannā and his followers called. That is, this state carries a religious connotation that is 'Islamic', and it, by this characteristic, sets modest limits for many Islamic attempts (such as those of al-Bannā, al-Qaraḍāwī, al-Turābī and al-Ghanūshī) to formulate a decisive proof and demonstrate the nature and correspondence between it and that of the religious state – on the basis of the assertion that it is a *constitutional*, *civil* state and so on. This is because Islam, here, is not an external characteristic or an addendum, rather it pertains to the matter in its vital content. Similarly, its description as 'Islamic' is not due to its being the state of Muslims –

contrary to what Burhān Ghalyūn is arguing[11] – because Muslims can establish a civil state without abandoning their Islam when they make a distinction between what is religious and what is political. Also, it is not sufficient here to say that those who describe it as religious are excused for their ignorance;[12] but rather its issue will remain in need of clarification and explication – where obfuscation of semantics – which is almost, until the present moment, the only technique being employed to escape from the problematic of the relation between the two concepts – does not suffice.

The Islamic writer and *mujtahid* Fahmī Hūwaydī attempts to draw the precise delineations between the two concepts and typologies, writing:

> the basic difference between the religious state and the Islamic state is that the first is based on the idea that Allah is the source of *authority* whereas in the second...Allah is the source of *law*, but the *ummah* is the source of authority. From this standpoint, there is no immunity and no infallibility for the ruler and the law is supreme over all, and, moreover, the ruler is first among them [under the law].[13]

This distinction does not contribute anything new to the concept of the Islamic state among its advocates. It asserts, in other words, the same primary concept about this state in its distinction as a state based on the *marja'īyah* (authoritative referent) of the *sharī'ah* in its political and legal system, and this is the meaning of the expression 'Allah is the source of *law*'. As for the *ummah* being the source of authority, this is a given when the *sharī'ah* is the authoritative referent (*marja'īyah*) of this authority. This, as previously mentioned, is what justifies the correlation between *shūrā* and the *sharī'ah,* on consideration of the best way to express this, that *shūrā,* is the political system in congruity with the state where the *sharī'ah* represents the authoritative referent for the law.

Criticism of religious authority, by contemporary Islamist researchers, stops at limits which it cannot transcend: confirmation of the Islamic content of the state. True, it is a bold criticism – not lacking in courage, and it aims clearly to bring down the concept of 'infallibility' and the idea of the subject of politics and the imamate belonging to the *uṣūl* of the religion. It takes the position from the standpoint of assessing the differences between religious authority and 'the civil [basis of] authority' (*madanīyāt al-sulṭah*);[14] but it is not able to deny the affinity of the state to Islam[15] or to deny the need of Islam for the state,[16] so it finds itself, in the end, responding to the foundational ideas themselves – the ideas of al-Bannā and 'Awdah and al-Qaraḍāwī – in new terms inclining towards co-opting the significations of the modern political lexicon. Perhaps, the causes that commended the founders of the idea of the Islamic state to stress the centrality of the political issue in Islam are the same ones that, today, push this new generation of Islamic researchers to go back to the production of that emphasis in less vehement language. Perhaps, Muḥammad Fatḥī ʿUthmān – one of the most prominent Islamist symbols previously and one of the brightest among their researchers presently – was correct when he noticed that

> If the Muslims in the Modern era neglect to estimate the place of the 'state' and the importance of 'the ruling authority' (*al-sulṭah al-ḥākimah*) in the religion of Islam...then it is feared that there will be a reaction in the political experience of contemporary Islamist movements that might push towards the neglect of estimating the place of 'authority' (*sulṭah*) in the religion of Islam.[17]

The truth is that this neglect – in some sense – was a result of that negligence.

The function of this critical digression is not a demonstration of the 'inconsistency' of the criticism of contemporary Islamists of religious authority; but rather, it is a demonstration of the limitedness of that criticism and its stopping at the threshold of the 'Islamic state'.[18] As for what is external to this question, we do not have any doubt that its rebuttal of the concept of '*al-ḥākimīyah*' and what resembles it was superfluous from the standpoint that there was no way to assail it, especially as it was a rebuttal which occurred within the Islamic conceptual *marjaʿīyah* and not from without, and it was a necessary Islamic conceptual realization in order to check the conceptual slippage in Islamic political thought.

On the Criticism of '*al-Ḥākimīyah*'

When thoughts of '*al-ḥākimīyah*' and '*jihad*' spilled over into the Islamic arena creating a wave of ideological and political extremist movements (especially among Arab circles), many apologists and intellectuals stood against the copious influx of such thoughts in order to restore legitimacy of matters that had become loose and uncontrollable. In considering themselves to be an injured party amid such intellectual relinquishment wherein they were accused wrongly – the Muslim Brotherhood took part in this stance as some of those involved in this intellectual relinquishment were once members of the Brotherhood's organizational hierarchy. In the vanguard, was Ḥasan al-Huḍaybī, who has 'demarcated' the lines of divorce between the Brotherhood's discourse and *takfīrī* discourse,[19] and who fiercely defended the Brotherhood's authentic thought against the distortion and violation that had plagued the consciousnesses of one of its generations since the birth of the concept of '*al-ḥākimīyah*' and up until production of new *takfīrī* ideology such as that espoused by Shukrī Aḥmad Muṣṭafā, emir of 'Jamā'at al-Muslimīn' ('Jamā'at al-Takfīr wa al-Jihād'),[20] or Ṣāliḥ Sarīyah in 'Wathīqat Risālat al-Imān 1973' ('The Document of the Letter of Faith of 1973').[21]

If we put aside al-Huḍaybī's criticism of *takfīrī* groups on many issues such as the declaration of the two professions of faith (the *shahādah*) which *takfīrīs* no longer recognize in acknowledging one's conversion to, or declaration of, Islam;[22] in regard to the issue of '*al-ḥākimīyah*', he denies that this utterance is derived from texts (*nuṣūṣ*) of Islam, maintaining that:[23] 'We are certain that the utterance "*ḥākimīyah*" has never been cited in any verse (*āyah*) of the Qur'ān. Moreover, in our diligent study of the Prophet's *aḥādīth*, we did not find any single *ḥadīth* that included such an utterance if contexts of its being appended to the name Allah are overlooked.'[24] Consequently, this term does not have a modicum of legitimacy even though the one who asserted it has won the trust of his supporters and remains an authoritative source of argument in their view, the problem, here, is one of a posited proposition that is not acceptable in the *uṣūl*, especially when use of the expression and believing in it resulted in repercussions that adversely affect Islam's position toward issues of the state and rule. Thus he decisively pronounces that 'there is absolutely no need for us to cling to anything except the Qur'ān and the Prophet's *aḥādīth*, rather than any terminology posited by human beings who are not infallible'[25] since such idioms – as others – are likely to be subject to argument even if they are among the terms of *fiqh*,[26] as they are not a revelation sent down (*waḥīy munazal*).

Where does the expression '*al-ḥākimīyah*' come from then?

It came from an improper derivation of the (Qur'ānic) encomia 'Verily, rule (*al-ḥukm*) belongs not except to Allah' or 'There is no rule (*al-ḥukm*) but that of Allah'. The two assertions were raised by the Kharijites against Imam 'Alī bin Abī Ṭālib after he conceded to arbitration in his struggle with Mu'āwīyah, and they were subsequently adopted by the Umayyads thereafter[27] in their pursuit of consolidating a despotic rule.[28] However, this linguistic Islamic origin is not possessed of great significance vis-à-vis the cultural non-Islamic one, or say, the Persian pre-Islamic one, which had been expounded by many who studied the origins of despotic political ideology hidden behind religion. It implanted its theocratic inference inside the consciousness of its proponents among the Kharijites. Contemporary apologists for *al-ḥākimīyah* reproduced the same concept on the basis of pre-Islamic bases of origin with some addenda derived from Kharijite and Rawāfid ideas, and numerous theses of Shī'ite Imāmī *fiqh*, along with some comprehensive modern perceptions of politics prevalent in the twentieth century.[29]

Muḥammad 'Amārah devotes much space in his texts to the criticism of the concept of '*al-ḥākimīyah*' of Sayyid Quṭb. We are not in the least doubt that he produced one of the deepest and boldest critical exposés in this regard from the standpoint of contemporary Islamic thought. 'Amārah proceeds in this criticism from a series of integrated assertions which suggest that '*al-ḥākimīyah*' is a new phenomenon in the Sunni Islamic concept of politics and political authority and that it represents a complete upset of that understanding.[30] We read:

> [Those asserting '*al-ḥākimīyah*'] assume that politics and the system of government in Islam are among the *uṣūl* (primary sources) of the religion...and thus that they are a religion...and a revelation (*waḥīyy*) wherein human will does not obtain...they claim that their evidence for their assertions is the mention of political theses and the system of government in the books of the *uṣūl al-dīn*...however, we say that this is a confusion [of issues]...which is not viable...and this 'doubtful matter' lacks proof...the *uṣūl* of faith in religion are three: divinity, prophethood and the Last Day...there is no category of the imamate or the *khilāfah* which is subsumed under political thought in the legacy of Islam.

The Sunni *madhāhib* – including the 'Ash'arīyah, al-Māturīdīyah and al-Ẓāhirīyah have all concurred about this...there is no exception to this except the Shī'ah who assert that the imamate belongs to the *uṣūl* of the religion. This criticism is shared equally by another Islamic researcher who asserts, in turn, that those who assert '*al-ḥākimīyah*':

> confuse between the *uṣūl* of the religion and its fundamentals and acts of worship; that is, between the matters to which pertain penalty or reward which will be judged by Allah the Most Exalted...and between the affairs of the world, and among these are the politics of the *ummah* and society – in times of peace and war and development.[31]

The first thing which derives from the assertion of '*al-ḥākimīyah*' is that the holder of political power becomes an entrusted agent (*wakīl*) of Allah, and over and above that, the consideration that the ruler is – in this sense – nothing more than the implementer of the law of the original holder of power who is Allah. Thus, 'If we say that political power belongs to Allah, then it is a religion and a revelation, and – from there – a religious political authority, and its steward is a ruler by "divine right" as well as a representative of Allah and his *khalīfah* as well as his shadow.'[32] Among the implications of the thesis are assertions that political power belongs to Allah and not to the human being. There is no function for him other than to practice a deputyship over the *ummah* in the name of the religion, and its right to trusteeship over itself is forfeited and it is prohibited from being a source of political power. It is natural that whoever asserts other than this – in the view of those asserting *al-ḥākimīyah* – is to be counted among the forces 'outside of the straight path of Allah, and hostile to its limits (*ḥudūd*), and transgressing the exclusive province of the Almighty Guardian (al-Mawlā; i.e., Allah)'.[33] The fact of the matter is that authority was always – for the remainder of societies – in the hands of human beings: it is they who propound the laws, and adjudicate and rule. This does not change the assertion of a segment of people that rule (*al-ḥukm*) belongs to Allah. They, with this assertion – that who rules and legislates does so in the name of Allah – bring nothing new to the matter except that we 'shall at that point have turned back the hands of time to the philosophy of "divine right"'.[34]

There is a second result obtaining from the assertion of *al-ḥākimīyah* in the view of its critics, and that is a distortion of the Qur'ānic meaning of the term *ḥukm* (rule) from which the utterance of '*al-ḥākimīyah*' was derived according to the assumption that it is indicative of, or signifying, the political order or political authority. The situation is that most of the Qur'ānic uses of the term '*al-ḥukm*' signify adjudication (*al-qaḍā'*) and resolution of disputes, or imply *al-ḥikmah* (wisdom) and rectitude of opinion; and furthermore, there is no connection for it to the *khilāfah* or the political order. Thus, when Qur'ānic verses describe Allah as *al-ḥākim* (the ruler), it is not in the connotation of the king or holder of political authority, but rather in the connotation of the one who judges and distinguishes between people about that in which they differ in regard to his command.[35] It is this meaning which is transmitted explicitly and without ambiguity in the Qur'ān: 'If you judge (*wa in ḥakamta*) [between people], then judge justly'.[36] For this reason, all that which those asserting *al-ḥākimīyah* call into evidence on the basis of derivations from the Qur'ānic concept of '*al-ḥukm*' is invalid in the view of those who take issue with it.

The fact is that these critical observations pertain to the relation of a phenomenon that merits attention, and that is the fluidity of calling the Qur'ān into evidence in Islamist Revival discourse in a haphazard fashion that ignores the context of the text, or rather takes the text out of its context and grants it an *absolute* character that violates its original meaning. This technique of interacting with the Qur'ānic text, which ignores the *asbāb al-nuzūl* (occasions of revelation) is responsible for much of the prevailing extraneous thought and opinion today among the ranks of the Islamists and especially in what pertains to matters of politics, state and civil society.

Raḍwān al-Sayyid notes correctly[37] that the Islamists:

> use the Qur'ānic texts in general and most often, and this is what pertains to matters of unbelief and faith in particular. These are most often verses that were transmitted in the context of the struggle between the Muslims in Medina and the hostile *Quraysh* in Mecca. They do not employ these as having transmitted for the struggle of Islam with the hostile *outside*, but for confrontation of the unbelieving *jāhilīyah within* the domain of Islam.[38]

The derived result of this poor usage of these texts is the transformation of the '*dār al-Islām*' into the '*dār al-hārb*' (lit., 'the house of war') and the instigation of *fitnah* and civil war in national society.

What Raḍwān al-Sayyid notices in regard to verses possessed of a relation to matters of unbelief and faith applies to the verses pertaining to *al-ḥukm* upon which are advocated the assertion that '*al-ḥākimīyah* belongs to Allah'. These verses, and many of them are to be found in *sūrat al-mā'idah*[39] – were taken out of their context in order to support a different function, alien to their original meaning, and that is to vindicate the idea of '*al-ḥākimīyah*' and the theocratic political initiative upon which it rests. Thus, interaction with these verses transpires as though they connote the divine command of the necessity of the Qur'ān governing in affairs of political management, just as the meaning of *al-ḥukm* was adapted to suggest a *political* connotation other than its restrictive connotation of adjudication (*al-qaḍā'*). In both instances, the use of these verses occurs as though they are unconcerned with the circumstances of revelation – '*asbāb al-nuzūl*', and thus, negligent of their original intent. In this direction Muḥammad 'Amārah takes a position in regard to the interpretation of the attribution of '*al-ḥākimīyah*' to the verses of *al-ḥukm* in *sūrat al-mā'idah* arguing:

> The 'book' to which these [verses] refer wherein *al-ḥukm* is demanded...is *not* the Qur'ān as the advocates of the theory of '*al-ḥākimīyah* belongs to Allah' whimsically imagine, but rather it is the *Torah* or the *Gospels* (*al-injīl*)...the desired meaning of '*al-ḥukm*' in these verses is 'adjudication'

> (*al-qaḍā'*) because the occasion for the revelation of the verses decisively confirms that they came and referred to the occurrence of a 'case' (*qaḍā'īyah*) in reality wherein a group of Jews applied to the Messenger for adjudication, and he ruled and judged in it according to what Allah had sent down in *their* book, the Torah...We are not face-to-face with discussion of political systems or political legislation of society, even if it were correct to extract the theory of 'divine political *ḥākimīyah*' from these verses; but rather we are confronting a 'case' brought by a group from amongst the people of the Book (*ahl al-kitāb*) before the Messenger 'in order that he adjudicate and judge' for them in it, so he adjudicated for them [in the matter] in accordance with their book...subsequently most of the communities and Qur'ānic exegetes (*mufasirīn*) – according to al-Qurṭubī – agree that these verses pertained to these people of the Book.[40]

What can be said about the original significance of the Qur'ānic expression of '*al-ḥukm*' can likewise be said about Prophetic *ḥadīth* where it is also transmitted that it is analogous to the meaning of adjudication (*al-qaḍā'*)[41] and dispute resolution between claimants. However, does this imply that there is an absence in the Qur'ān and the *ḥadīth* of a concept specifying authority and the system of rule? Many researchers are in consensus that this concept exists and that it is '*al-amr*'.[42] This meaning has been translated in a number of verses such as: 'O you who believe, obey Allah and obey the Messenger and those who have been given command/the matter [*al-amr*] among you';[43] and elsewhere as in the two verses pertaining to *al-shūrā* : 'Their matter [*amruhum*] is [one of] *shūrā* between them';[44] and 'consult them in the matter [*al-amr*]'.[45] And '*al-amr*' as 'Amārah notes is in relation to '*al-i'timār*' (deliberation/council), that is, *al-tashāwur* (consultation); and from this comes reference to the ruler (*al-ḥākim*) as '*al-amīr*' (the emir).[46] Most importantly, for what concerns us, is that the concept of *al-ḥukm* does not pertain in its Qur'ānic meaning to the political field and the system of rule, but rather to adjudication (*al-qaḍā'*), and consequently, positing '*al-ḥākimīyah*' according to its constraints of indication is without any argumentative weight in the critical view of '*al-ḥākimīyah*'.

In sum, despite whatever may have been the ambiguities of the relation between the idea of '*al-ḥākimīyah*' for al-Mawdūdī and Quṭb[47] and the idea of the 'Islamic state' according to al-Bannā, there is no doubt that '*al-ḥākimīyah*' is entirely cut off from any form of connection with the concept of the modern state along with what was attempted to bridge between it and '*al-shūrā*', the '*ahl al-ḥal wa al-'aqd*', the constitution, and so forth.

Furthermore, it effects a conspicuous separation from their (conceptual) order and comes from a context of a different model of the state and authority possessed of theocratic dimensions impossible to be observed or analyzed! Regardless, any endeavor to make a criticism of '*al-ḥākimīyah*' into a criticism of thought will ultimately be constrained to revert to its subject matter and the precursors of this thought, searching for the points of deficiency that produced the assertion of it. Additionally, among that which cannot be ignored in examination of its understanding and its explication is the political environment from which emerged thoughts of extremism that subsisted according to its givens. The environment was undemocratic in political reality as well as in thought. Moreover, it had the most tremendous of effects on the type of political thinking of the Islamists.[48] That is what matched reality and was in conformity with its open hostility to democracy, freedom and openness.

On the Criticism of the '*Wilāyat al-Faqīh*'

The '*wilāyat al-faqīh*' is the Shī'ite conceptual analog of '*al-ḥākimīyah*' as we clarified previously. And, if there are aspects of correspondence between them, then they are not among those that imply or lead to results on the side of conception of the political field only, but rather they also inhere in the precursors from which it springs where the most important of these is the consideration that politics is a source (*aṣl*) among the *uṣūl* of the religion. The one difference between the characteristics of both of them, so to speak, is that the theory of the '*wilāyat al-faqīh*' has a place in the *uṣūl* of the *madhāhib* (the 'theory of the imamate' in the *madhab* of Twelver Shī'ism) whereas '*al-ḥākimīyah*' is unconnected to the Sunni *fiqh* legacy and drawn from the idea of the imamate itself! Thus, if recourse for the concept of '*al-ḥākimīyah*' to the Sunni *uṣūl* is not to be found, then the matter is different in regard to the case of the '*wilāyat al-faqīh*' which represents a return to building on the idea of the imamate in the age of the 'occultation'.

Most of those who have confronted the theory of the '*wilāyat al-faqīh*' among contemporary Islamic researchers – both Sunni and Shī'ite – have proceeded from the supposition of the link between it and the concept of the imamate. It has not ceased, in their critical view, to consistently remain among the most important theoretical subjects of Shī'ite *fiqh* on the imamate; especially the assertion that the imamate is a *creedal* matter of the *uṣūl*, and the assertion of 'designation' (*al-waṣīy*) – that is 'appointment' (*al-ta'yīn*), and infallibility (*al-'iṣmah*). And, these are constant or basic issues which have continued to be operative in this theory even after they became a political system in Iran. Thus, if no one is able to extract this theory from the order of the imamate, even from the standpoint of a methodological extraction, then this is what leads to any criticism of the '*wilāyat al-faqīh*' becoming a criticism of the 'imamate' just as an objective criticism of the caliphate – for Rashīd Riḍā – was tantamount to a criticism of the Islamic-legal political order itself at the level of its foundational theoretical sources.

The effectiveness of the criticism – from the Sunni standpoint initially – was oriented towards the concept of the imamate in Shī'ite theory on the basis of its being a source (*aṣl*) among the *uṣūl* of the religion where 'faith is not complete except through the belief in it.'[49] This supposition has been the essence of Sunni criticism since ancient times,[50] and it has not ceased to be representative of the supposition in the view of its contemporary critics because the assertion of its being among the *uṣūl* implies – for the Sunni *fuqahā'* – a denigration of the order of the *khilāfah* – *al-bay'ah* (the pledge of allegiance), *al-shūrā* (consultation), and *al-ijmā'* (consensus), and an affirmation of Shī'ite transmitted accounts of the usurpation by the two sheikhs of the authority of the *āl al-bayt* (i.e., Abū Bakr and 'Umar bin al-Khaṭṭāb in Medina on the day of the Prophet's death).[51] It also implies for Islamic researchers and *mujtahidūn* the formation of a political system of clergy – expropriating the right of the *ummah* to power and placing it in the hands of a class of men of religion. From another angle, what is more pernicious in considering it to be among the *uṣūl* of the religion is that – according to their criticism – the correlation of the Message [of Islam] and politics turns politics into a revelation and a religion,[52] and also effects a correlation between the imamate and prophethood.

We read in this regard, sheikh Rāshid al-Ghanūshī criticizing contemporary Shī'ite thought in this matter:

> Twelver Shī'ite thought is not about to move away so much as a fingertip from its creedal point of departure in regard to reading history in the scope of a political opinion of leadership and its relation to the *ummah*, excepting the assertion of the '*wilāyat al-faqīh*' in a temporary fashion while waiting for the absent infallible imam. This deputy, if he is not infallible, resembles him in his powers, his relation to the *ummah* and in his position in the religion and state...Shī'ite theory has not ceased in this regard to proceed from a principle of an analogy between the imamate and prophethood...and, thus, rejection of the imamate is tantamount to disbelief just as is rejection of

> prophethood, given that ignorance of both is at the same threshold...so what has developed in this heritage?[53]

Nothing has developed except that the clear assertion of infallibility for the imam is not equivalent to comparable infallibility for the '*walīy al-faqīh*' even if the 'facts on the ground' – the ground of *politics* – go against this. We mean that he is 'unimpeachable' in the opinion of the Shī'ah, and if not, what would be the significance of the authority of the '*walīy al-faqīh*' being outside any popular or constitutional censure, and outside of accountability to any apparatus of state in the country wherein the political system persists on the constraints of this system – namely, Iran? Thus, contrary to what is apparent about the relation between the Imam and the *ummah* from the standpoint of a modification to the benefit of the latter in the age of occultation, 'the shadow of infallibility (*al-'iṣmah*) and designation (*al-waṣīyah*) will remain weighing heavily on the image of the Imam...so the holder of real power will remain absent, but the one standing in his place will speak for him,' that is, the one for whom the *ummah* has no means of intervention – whose legitimacy is derivative of his status as a deputy of the infallible Imam. So, how is it that this Imam – absent from the *ummah* – is not absent for his deputies? According to al-Ghanūshī, 'rather, he is present meeting the needs of them and advising them; and he has meetings with them at special times!'[54]

The *ummah* has no means of intervening with the sultan – '*al-walīy al-faqīh*' – just as it does not have any in regard to the power of the Imam; the matter of the imamate and the *wilāyah* does *not* proceed according to the constraints of *al-shūrā* and election when 'there is not doubt that we must know that *shūrā* and elections – and choice on the basis of elections – are among the innovations which have come to us from the West and from the culture of those differing with the Shī'ah in regard to the *wilāyah*,' says one of Khomeini's students[55] who adds that it is a 'Sunni innovation (*bid'ah*)' and its goal is the justification of 'the usurpation' of the authority of the Imams. For that reason this approach to power is not to the benefit of comprehending the legitimacy of the '*wilāyat al-faqīh*', where this is 'a part of the *wilāyah* of the pure Imams...and extending to their *wilāyah* which was created (*maj'ūlah*) before them, and it is not permissible for any to doubt that.'[56]

The truth in the matter of the connection between the '*walīyy al-faqīh*' and this 'sacrosanct truth' of the *wilāyah* is larger than what Maḥmūd al-Hāshimī expresses in the '*wilāyat al-faqīh*' that was 'created (*maj'ūlah*)' for the *faqīh* from the Imams, but actually persists at a much more exalted level: at the level of the relation between Allah and the Imam! It is Allah who appointed him for the *wilāyah* over the Muslims, in order to complete the prophetic message;[57] and it is not moot for Muslims to do other than to accept what he says and engages in doing. Al-Ghanūshī is not far off the mark when he criticizes this exaggeration and notices that:

> Even the leader of the revolution and the institution of state Imam Khomeini (may Allah have mercy on him) is not safe from this extremism as he wrote in his book *Islamic Government* a section that I initially thought was a slip of the pen of the scholar and that it would be realized (and corrected) in later editions of the book, but so far as I know that has not occurred. That is, he wrote that the *ḥujjat* Allah (lit. the 'argument of Allah', but, in Iran, a title) is the one whom *Allah* appoints to engage in commanding the Muslims; and his actions and sayings are an authoritative argument (*ḥujjah*) binding on the Muslims and they must execute these.[58]

When the imam is infallible, his infallibility is among that which indicates that the *wilāyat al-'āmah* over the Muslims and the engaging by the designee of the imam in the functions of this general *wilāyah* – representing him – cannot be reconciled with the assertion that he has a portion or share of infallibility, if it is not possible to promote the matter of the imamate by the deputies – and it is a 'divinely-ordained position' – without the support of a measure of this infallibility; wherefore yielding to him and submission is a yielding and submission to Allah.[59]

It is natural for a political theory that is based on the idea of the imamate, the essence of which is infallibility, to meet with rejection by its critics among traditional Sunni *fuqahā'*[60] and among Islamist Revivalist advocates who proceed from the position that 'there is no legitimacy in an Islamic system derived from inheritance or infallibility (*iṣmah*) or through succession or coup', on the basis of the belief that rule (*al-ḥukm*) in Islam is '*civil* rule' and 'consultative leadership/presidency' (*ri'āsah shawrīyah*).[61] On these grounds, the state of the imamate, according to the way it is presented in the theory of the *wilāyat al-faqīh* is a religious state *par excellence* because 'there is no religious state without infallibility or knowledge springing from revelation (*waḥīy*), and if not, then every decision is a *human* decision; and accordingly, derived from rational *al-ijtihād* even if it is engaged in by a man of religion.'[62] When the state of the '*wilāyat al-faqīh*' is among that which is textually specified and among that which is decided by the charging of the infallible imams, it is confirmed that in politics, actions are above the human being.

There are those who say that such criticism of the '*wilāyat al-faqīh*' is well understood and that the reasons that necessitate it are clear because it proceeds from a Sunni perspective; therefore, it inherits the tradition of the *madhab* that is opposed to the idea of the imamate and its political theory. Further, when any such individuals deal with the '*wilāyat al-faqīh*' today in debate or criticism, they do not perceive in it more than a branch of the root of the imamate. The truth is that this is correct to a certain degree: those who approach it critically – from Sunni conceptual positions – *do* differentiate between it and the imamate in their perception, but rather account it as a modern form of the assertion of the imamate and whatever is subsumed under it – designation and infallibility and so on. And, if this is not sufficient justification to assert that what governs their opinion and criticism is the Sunni *fiqh marja'*,[63] it is sufficient justification to acknowledge that their criticism could not, objectively speaking, do more than intersect or conjoin with the traditional Sunni thesis about the imamate. More importantly, those who object to this criticism because it is *Sunni* and that it does not contribute anything to its treatment of the '*wilāyat al-faqīh*' other than a repetition of what has been said before about the imamate on account of its being the origin, forget that they also did not create that distinction between the imamate and the '*wilāyat al-faqīh*'. Rather, contrary to that, they established the legitimacy of the '*wilāyat al-faqīh*' from within the imamate wherein it would not have gained what it did of argumentative weight – among the Shī'ah – except in its being presented as being the contemporary legitimate realization of the infallible imamate in the period of the occultation of the Imam al-Mahdī.

The truth of the matter is that, in this exposition, whatever criticism is directed towards the theory of the '*wilāyat al-faqīh*' from Shī'ite '*ulamā'* – the Arab and Iranian among them – is not any less valuable than the first, even if we do not say that it is more important. Perhaps, its value in a number of aspects might be is that among it is rich, objective criticism and not simply discursive debate between competitors for the *marja'īyah* within the *madhab*. It might be so because it proceeds from a position of the *madhab* that this criticism is rendered Islamic and, accordingly, it removes from Sunni criticism, accusations of sectarianism. Similarly, it might be among that which transpired in the transformation of this theory into the political ideology for the state in Iran. Therefore, it reveals that the authority of this theory is derivative from politics and the state and *not* from the *madhab* and *al-ijtihād*.

Muḥammad Ḥussayn al-Nā'īnī represents the first, modern Shī'ite Islamic thinker to produce a critical notion of the traditional Shī'ite theory of the imamate[64] at the beginning of the twentieth century. It is a thesis wherein he goes so far as to legitimize the establishment of the modern constitutional state because of the intractability or impossibility of leaving the position of the imam vacant during the period of the occultation. Al-Nā'īnī was not ignorant of the theory of the '*wilāyat al-faqīh*' as he acknowledges partially, its relative limits in the domain of personal comport as well as that of religious praxis; however, he does not proceed from it to think about the political question – the matter of the state and authority, but rather he proceeds from the standpoint of the '*wilāyah* of the *ummah* over itself'. Thus, there is no significance to the thesis of the existence of a conceptual continuity between the discourse of Khomeini and the discourse of al-Nā'īnī in asserting that both of their assertions pertain to the '*wilāyat al-faqīh*'[65] because al-Nā'īnī posits this theory outside the consultative political sphere, to erect – on its debris – a modern theory of state predicated on the idea that the *ummah* is entrusted with its affairs, that *it* is the source of authority, that the *marja'īyah* (authoritative reference) for this authority is the *constitution*, and that *shūrā* is the basis of the political system and so on. We have no doubt that many have drawn from it their criticism – in what followed – of the '*wilāyat al-faqīh*'; there is not a single Shī'ite thinker who did not reach a certain degree of radicalism and theoretical clarity in that, even Ayatollah Muntaẓirī himself![66]

However, the like of this criticism has transpired in recent years, from the standpoint of academic Shī'ite reviews after the theory was transformed into an ideology for the Iranian state. It is a criticism which runs from the fierce to the forbearing (indulgent); except that it is *fiqh* criticism for the most part, even if it is not removed from its underlying political basis. Ayatollah Muḥammad Mahdī Shams al-Dīn, and to a certain extent Ayatollah Muḥammad Ḥussayn Faḍlallah,[67] may be among the most prominent of those who have expressed, with certain dissimilarities, critical positions with regard to the theory of the '*wilāyat al-faqīh*' of all Shī'ite '*ulamā*' today.

Al-'allāmah Muḥammad Ḥussayn Faḍlallah proceeds from the theory of the '*wilāyat al-faqīh*', but he narrows its field of application to the extent that its comprehensiveness does not exceed the scope of religious praxis and the scope of probate cases (*al-qaḍāyā al-ḥasbīyah*).[68] Even though he has often spoken clearly about his position with regard to a number of matters pertaining to the relation between the premise of '*wilāyat al-faqīh*' and the premise of *al-shūrā* and democracy[69] as well as the right of the *ummah* in the administration of its own affairs, he attempts to establish – with difficulty – the responsibility of the *ummah* in the state from within the theory of the '*wilāyat al-faqīh*'. Among that which justifies the legitimacy of this *wilāyah* is the contention that the *ummah* 'cannot possibly be without leadership to rule it and that this leadership cannot possibly submit to the whims of people in selection.'[70] The matter which imposes – in his view – what he terms 'forced implementation' (*al-taṭbīq al-qasrī*)[71] is that any rule through the use of apparatuses of state ends in solicitation of some legitimacy from 'the *wilāyah* of the *ummah* over itself' proceeding from the standpoint that divinely-imposed culpability (*al-taklīf al-ilāhī*) on the Prophet and his designees among the imams to bear the burden of the *wilāyah* is culpability in the case of their actual presence, and the *ummah*, here, 'bears its responsibility through them'. As for anything 'outside this scope,[72] the verses do not charge the *ummah* with the responsibility of that'.[73] In this case, the question of authority and the state becomes the special domain of the *ummah* where 'there is no sphere for any single person to tyrannize it, even if he is a qualified *faqīh*';[74] and this is the matter that opens the door, then, before the question of *al-shūrā*.

It is not possible to understand this deduction except by returning to the (Shī'ite) Imāmī *fiqh* concept of 'the primary principle' (*al-aṣl al-awallī*), and that is for the relation of this concept to the matter of the *wilāyah* and the state. Faḍlallah iterates:

> the fundamental principle is the absence of the confirmation (*thubūt*) of the *wilāyah* of any person over another in anything among the things for which obedience is Islamically confirmed, or – in other words – confirmation of the obligation to obey does not give any particular human being the authority to execute this far outside the bounds of 'commanding what is just and forbidding what is unjust' (*al-amr bi-l-ma'rūf wa al-nahīy 'an al-munkar*).[75]

The 'fundamental principle' then is the impermissibility of a *wilāyah* of one person over another. However, how can this principle be reconciled with the premise of the necessity of the state and the *wilāyah* in order to preserve order? In this is what might suggest that the dominance of the state over the people is a revocation or rejection of the 'fundamental principle'. The solution is to enter authority into 'indication of the restriction of the fundamental principle'; that is, if authority is a branch of the original source (the 'fundamental principle'), then it ought to be governed by that principle; and the significance of this is that its legitimacy rests on the 'relative measure' of the necessity of its authority to preserve the system. It is *not* an *original* source (*aṣl*) in itself, but rather the need for it, *when it exists*, is what makes it conditional or restricted.

Muḥammad Mahdī Shams al-Dīn is perhaps the closest to being entirely explicit in a critical position vis-à-vis the '*wilāyat al-faqīh*' and the knowledge of this basis: the 'fundamental principle'. He asserts that the basic constraint of this principle pertains to the illegitimacy of the domination of anyone over anyone else. If he acknowledges the existence of indications for the necessity of establishing an authority to preserve order, he finds a way out of this conundrum through the assertion that the execution of this is in need of this authority to dictate rules that restrain it according to the dictates of that fundamental principle so as not to deviate from it. This is what impels him to the consideration that the state or authority is in the region of the 'legislative vacuum'. Thus, 'the empty legislative region here is governed by the fundamental principle, and there is no doubt that any deviation from it must be in accordance with the minimal and relative measure of society's need for it.' As for other than that: 'whatever for which the need of it is doubtful is constrained by the fundamental principle as illegitimate';[76] that is, the illegitimacy of the domination of one over another.

Is this a formula for the legitimacy of authority?

Yes, it is such. However, it is a *conditional* formula where there is no contradiction of the authority of the fundamental principle of the impermissibility of the *wilāyah* of one person over another. So, how is it that authority cannot contradict the fundamental principle which itself presupposes the impermissibility of authority: is there not in this something of a *non sequitur*?

Escape from this vicious circle is potentially to be found in the establishment of this authority on bases that remove the authoritative nature from it and render it nearer to the people and more expressive of their need in order to detach its contradiction of this fundamental principle; this is:

> whenever ruling political authority – organized and administrative or other – is nearer to the practicing of the human being of authority over himself, it is nearer to the fundamental principle, and the criterion of its legitimacy from the standpoint of its entrance into the indication of the restriction of the fundamental principle.[77]

However, how can this authority be 'nearer to the practicing of the human being of authority over himself' when it enters into that restriction? That cannot come except with democracy, or say, with the establishment of it according to democratic principles which guarantee people the right of political participation; that is, the right to practice authority for themselves over themselves, or to engage in *wilāyah* over themselves in *fiqh* terminology.

Democracy guarantees for people that the choice of whoever will engage in the functions of the *wilāyah* will do so on the basis of obedience and good pleasure *without* compulsion; and that is by means of elections which are practiced freely, as this way is:

> nearer to what the fundamental principle dictates in regard to authority, and nearer to the indication of the restriction than if the government exercises its authority in appointing responsible persons and administrative employees in isolation from the opinion of the people and their choice as that is farther removed from what the fundamental principle dictates; and there might not be any entrance into the indication of restriction. As for its being removed from what the fundamental dictates, it is from the standpoint that the government exercises its sovereignty and its authority in constructing and imposing a new authority upon people and enacting domination over them without any choice from them...[78]

Thus, democracy not only solves the dilemma of the contradiction of *fiqh* between the basis of the fundamental principle and the principle of the necessity of maintaining the system, but it also solves the dilemma of theocratic domination over the *ummah* in the name of the '*wilāyat al-faqīh*' through the *fiqh* defense of the restoring to the *ummah* its *wilāyah* over itself which modern political Shī'ite *fiqh* institutions have divested from it in the name of this theory. Thus, this criticism, open to the Sunni legacy – ancient and modern – also goes back to consideration of the principle of *al-shūrā* in building the political system – and accounts it among the principles which must be respected[79] after the Shī'ah rejected it and the Sunnis had dispensed with it.

If we leave aside the foundational critical thesis of al-'allāmah Muḥammad Ḥussayn al-Nā'īnī, which represented a minute fraction of what Shī'ite political discourse would attain in openness to and probing the frontiers, we realize that contemporary Shī'ite criticism of the '*wilāyat al-faqīh*', and the theocratic concept which commends the assertion of this theory, does not return the sphere of this theory to the theory of the 'imamate' along the lines of the matter as it is in Sunni criticism of it. Perhaps, that is not much cause for celebration for a simple reason, which is that this criticism operates from a Shī'ite *fiqh* position. Regardless of the fact, there is tremendous importance in any case when those who argue the legitimacy of the '*wilāyat al-faqīh*' are among the researchers and advocates of the Shī'ah who, thereby, confirm that Shī'ite political reasoning is not a prisoner to this theory despite what it has become today as a state ideology worthy of consideration, or moreover, that political benefits and the state are wider – for the Shīʿah – than the choice to foist the '*wilāyat al-faqīh*' upon the Shīʿite masses and thereby arrest them through it. Similarly, those who have endeavored to undo the connection between the '*wilāyat al-faqīh*' and the 'infallible imams', pulverized the legitimacy of the first in terms of *fiqh* and uncovered its political precursors[80] but were, at the same time, *not* deterred in their support of the 'infallible imams' in the triumph of a non-theocratic political system persisting on the basis of *al-shūrā* and on the right of the *ummah* to the *wilāyah* over itself. These much resemble the critics of the concept of '*al-ḥākimīyah*' as understood by al-Mawdūdī and Quṭb; as they attempted to break the connection between it and the consideration of it as an expression of the ideal of the religious state or the 'Islamic state'; and the triumph of the latter over the former did not prevent them from defending the state of *al-shūrā*, democracy and the constitution and so on.

There is no doubt that the idea of the 'imamate' (the mythology of the imams as al-Jabri terms it),[81] did not stand as an obstacle in the way of the development of Shīʿite political theory. In the shadow of its *marjaʿī fiqh* authority, there persisted the possibility of the legitimacy of cooperating with the deviant sultan, and in its shade a *fiqh* escape was provided from the crisis of authority in the 'period of occultation' from the *fiqh* formulation of 'permission' (*al-idhn*); and in its shade some of the powers of the absent Imam were delegated to his deputies possessing the requisite qualifications in *al-ijtihād*; rather in its shadow horizons of establishing the conditional state (the constitutional state) suddenly opened up with the *mujtahid al-ʿallāmah* Muḥammad Ḥussayn al-Nāʾīnī. These possibilities were only feasible because the Imam was absent, and moreover, the sphere of *ijtihād* is *open*. As for the '*wilāyat al-faqīh*', the doors have been completely slammed shut, and the *wilāyah* of the *ummah* has been expropriated and monopolized by the *fuqahāʾ*. The '*walīy al-faqīh*' is present, and his presence shall persist so long as the absent Imam is absent! Thus, the *ummah* will not ever be able to obtain its right in this *wilāyah* which has become – in the final analysis – the *wilāyah* of the *fuqahāʾ*!

The problem of the ancient Shīʿah was that deviant rule had usurped the *wilāyah* from its people: the 'pure imams' of the *āl al-bayt*. As for their problem today, perhaps it is that the '*wilāyat al-faqīh*' has usurped from the *ummah* its right to the *wilāyah* over itself.

Notes

1. Bārūt, *Yathrib al-Jadīdah*, p. 15.
2. ʿAlī, Ḥaydar Ibrāhīm, *al-Tayārāt al-Islāmīyah wa Qaḍīyat al-Dīmūqrāṭīyah* (Beirut: Centre for Arab Unity Studies, 1996), p. 136.
3. See Chapter Three of this book.
4. ʿAmārah, Muḥammad, *al-Dawlah al-Islāmīyah- Bayn al-ʿIlmānīyah wa al-Sulṭah al-Dīnīyah* (Cairo; Beirut: Dār al-Shurūq, 1988), p. 14.
5. ʿAmārah, *al-Dawlah al-Islāmīyah,* p. 14.
6. ʿAmārah, *al-Dawlah al-Islāmīyah,* pp. 80–1.
7. ʿAmārah, *al-Dawlah al-Islāmīyah,* p. 219.
8. 'The mundane aspect that the Prophet addressed, for the sake of propagating his fundamental message and religious mission, upon his establishment of the state, leading the *ummah*, organizing a community, and fostering development, he was indeed a diligent ordinary human being when no plain Qur'ānic text was available at the time; moreover, his *ijtihād* and opinions were subject to *shūrā,* that is, subject to exploration, give and take, acceptance, amendment and addendum, because infallibility is not applicable to him in this aspect of reasoning and practice…his own saying bears witness to this fact, in which he states: "What is relevant to your religion I will answer, and of what is relevant to your lives you are more aware".' Available in: ʿAmārah, *al-Dawlah al-Islāmīyah,* p. 14.
9. ʿAmārah, *al-Dawlah al-Islāmīyah,* p. 69.
10. ʿAmārah, *al-Dawlah al-Islāmīyah,* pp. 16–17.
11. The Islamic state is 'not Islamic in the context of being a political system and entity that was brought about by Islam as many other nations had established states long before Islam and were not that different in the means of organization, administration, military training and instatement of rulers. They were not Islamic in the sense that authority – for them – was conceived as being infallible or inspired by God...and they were not Islamic for the fact that they implemented laws of divine justice…not Islamic in the sense of having a structure, goals and means of governorship that are congruent to a model recommended – or approved by religion…so it was Islamic merely in the sense of being a state of Muslims as a *political* group…'. Available in: Ghalyūn, Burhān, *Naqd al-Sīyāsah: al-Dawlah wa al-Dīn* (Beirut: al-Mu'asasah al-ʿArabīyah lil-Dirāsāt wa al-Nashr, 1991), pp. 84–5.
12. 'If we want to clear doubt from those who described the Islamic state as being a religious state, which is – according to them – contradictory to the civil state, we shall find only one exit, that is: to pardon them as they do not know the inference of these expressions, and that is what made them fall into misunderstanding and go astray, unawares.' Available in: Hūwaydī, Fahmī, *al-Islām wa al-Dīmūqrāṭīyah* (Cairo, Markaz al-Ahrām, 1993), p. 184.
13. Hūwaydī, *al-Islām*, p. 185.
14. ʿAmārah, *al-Dawlah al-Islāmīyah,* p. 25.
15. 'Someone once told me: "You want a religious state," and my response to him was simultaneously negative and positive, for I did not deem it "religious" in a way analogous to the common concept of the idiom, however, it is "religious" in the sense that it is established on a basis of adherence to the principles of Islam.' Available in: Hūwaydī, *al-Islām*, p. 185.
16. 'The necessity of the state, for Islam, stems from the impossibility of fulfilling the religious obligation(s) without it…here its relation, and the relation of "politics" to "religion" emerge in the approach of Islam!...it is a "civil duty" determined and required by "religious duty" which God demands from the believers in Islam.'

Available in: 'Amārah, *al-Dawlah al-Islāmīyah*, p. 210.

17. 'Uthmān, Muḥammad Fatḥī, *al-Tajrubah al-Sīyāsah lil-Ḥarakah al-Islāmīyah al-Muʻāṣirah: Durūs al-Māḍī wa Āfāq al-Mustaqbal*, publications of Markaz Dirāsāt al-Mustaqbal al-Islāmī (Algiers: Dār al-Mustaqbal, 1991), p. 55.

18. We do not mean that the Islamic state in the discourses of the Brotherhood and that of other contemporary Islamists is the same Islamic state as it is in the discourse of '*al-ḥākimīyah*', but rather, we meant that attempts of its apologists to distinguish it from the theocratic state did not succeed in removing questions about its appellation as being 'Islamic' given that many other forms of *al-ḥākimīyah* may emerge from within such religious identification of the state, just as Quṭb's *ḥākimīyah* which emerged from al-Bannā and ʻAwdah's conceptual confusion about the Islamic state!... Evidently, lines of demarcation between the two concepts and models are still loose in the absence of clear delineation of them in the contemporary Islamic discourse.

19. Bārūt, *Yathrib al-Jadīdah*, p. 185.

20. Text of Shukrī Aḥmad Muṣṭafā's confessions before the military court of the Supreme State Security in Egypt in the case of Tanẓīm (it is the only text in which we clearly find the ideology of 'Jamāʻat al-Takfīr wa al-Hijrah'). Available in: Aḥmad, Rifʻat al-Sayyid, *al-Nabī al-Musallaḥ*. (London: Riyad al-Raies for Printing and Publishing, 1991), p. 40.

21. Aḥmad, Rifʻat al-Sayyid, *al-Nabī al-Musallaḥ*, p. 41.

22. Aḥmad, Rifʻat al-Sayyid, *al-Nabī al-Musallaḥ*, p. 41.

23. Al-Huḍaybī, Ḥasan Ismāʻīl, *Duʻāt...Lā Quḍāt: Abḥāth fī al-ʻAqīdah al-Islāmīyah wa Manhaj al-Daʻwah ilā Allāh*, 2nd edn (Cairo: Dār al-Ṭibāʻah wa al-Nashr al-Islāmīyah, 1977), p. 91.

24. Here, adding the phrase '*ḥākimīyat Allāh*' is intended.

25. Al-Huḍaybī, *Duʻāt...Lā Quḍāt*, p. 93.

26. Al-Huḍaybī argued *Takfīrīs* (jihādists) in their interpretation for the jurisprudential rule: 'whatever a duty is not to be fulfilled without is a duty', by considering it – also – an idiom formulated by fallible humans and which possesses no Qurʼānic text or *sunnah* reciting it. Available at: Al-Huḍaybī, *Duʻāt...Lā Quḍāt*, p. 197.

27. Al-ʻAshmāwī, Muḥammad Saʻīd, *al-Islām al-Sīyāsī*, 2nd edn (Algiers: Mūfam; Casablanca: Tansīft, 1991), pp. 38–9.

28. Al-Jabri, *al-ʻAql al-Sīyāsī al-ʻArabī*, pp. 323–6.

29. We cannot totally exclude the influence of Bolshevik political ideologies in the subconscious of Sayyid Quṭb, who was a good reader of Lenin's writings, especially before his enrollment in the Muslim Brotherhood. His own writings are replete with profuse implementations of concepts of material class analysis in social and economic aspects; that is, in addition to his conception for a model of a *vanguard* political organization that oftentimes almost approaches that of Lenin.

30. 'Amārah, *al-Dawlah al-Islāmīyah*, p. 51.

31. Al-Fanjarī, Aḥmad Shawqī, *Kayfa Naḥkum bil-Islām fī Dawlah ʻAṣrīyah* (Cairo: al-Hayʼah al-Miṣrīyah al-ʻĀmmah lil-Kitāb, 1990), p. 24.

32. 'Amārah, *al-Dawlah al-Islāmīyah*, p. 32.

33. 'Amārah, *al-Dawlah al-Islāmīyah*, p. 31.

34. 'Amārah, *al-Dawlah al-Islāmīyah*, p. 33.

35. 'Amārah, *al-Dawlah al-Islāmīyah*, pp. 35–6.

36. Qurʼān, *surat al-māʼidah*, (5:42).

37. Al-Sayyid, *Sīyāsāt al-Islām*, p. 189.

38. This is also true in how they treated Ibn Taymīyah's *fatwās* (especially, Shukrī Aḥmad Muṣṭafā, ʻAbd al-Salām Faraj, ʻAbbūd al-Zamur...etc), in that they detached

them from their contexts and particular historical circumstances. Available in: Al-Sayyid, *Siyāsāt al-Islām*, pp. 187–8.

39. O Messenger, do not let those who are hastening to unbelief grieve you from among those who say 'We believe' with their mouths but their hearts do not believe; and among the Jews are those who listen in order to lie and listen for others who have not come to you; they distort the words after they were put in place and say, 'If you are given this then take it, but if you are not given it, then beware'. And for whom Allah desires *fitnah*, you will be able to do nothing for him against Allah. These are those whom Allah has not desired to purify their hearts for them. In the life of the world there is grief for them and in the hereafter, there is a mighty punishment. They listen in order to lie and they eat what is illicit. If they come to you, then judge between them or turn away from them; and if you turn away from them, they will not harm you in aught, but if you judge, then judge between them in justice. Verily, Allah loves the just. And how can they ask you to judge when they have the Torah and in it is the rule (*ḥukm*) of Allah; and they turn away after that – these are not believers. It is We Who sent down the Torah and in it is guidance and light whereby the Prophets judged those who judged those who had submitted among the Jews and rabbis and monks according to what they had preserved of the Book of Allah and to which they were witnesses. So, do not fear people but rather fear Me and do not purchase with My verses trifling gains. And whoever does not judge by what Allah has sent down, then these are unbelievers. And We wrote for them: a soul for a soul, an eye for an eye, a nose for a nose, an ear for an ear, a tooth for a tooth, and the equivalent of an injury for an injury; but whoever forgives one of these it is a recompense for him (i.e., for his own sins). And, those who do not judge by what Allah has sent down, they are the wrongdoers. After them we sent Jesus, son of Mary, confirming what was with them of the Torah and We gave him the Gospels in which is guidance and truth confirming what was with them of the Torah and guidance and good preaching for the pious. So, let the people of the Gospels judge by what Allah has sent down and whoever does not judge by what Allah has sent down, verily they are the corrupt. And, We sent down upon you (Muhammad) the book in truth confirming what was sent before of the Book and superseding it, so judge between them according to what Allah has sent down and do not follow their whims in preference to what has come to you of the truth. For each we have made for you a law (*shir'ah*) and a method; and if Allah had so willed, he could have made you a single *ummah*, but he tests you according to what he has given you. So, race to do good deeds. Unto Allah is your return and he will inform you about that which you differ. So judge (Muhammad) between them according to what Allah sent down and do not follow their whims and warn them lest they cause you *fitnah* over some of that which Allah sent down upon you. If they turn away, know that Allah to afflict them with some of their sins; and many among people are corruptors. Do they desire the rule of (i.e., to judge according to) the *Jahiliyyah*? But, who is a better judge than Allah for people who are pious?' (*sūrat al-mā'idah*, 5: 41–50)

40. 'Amārah, *al-Dawlah al-Islāmīyah,* pp. 44–5.

41. 'Amārah, *al-Dawlah al-Islāmīyah,* pp. 45–7.

42. Al-Jabri, *al-'Aql al-Sīyāsī al-'Arabī.*

43. Qur'ān, *sūrat al-nisā'*, (4:59).

44. Qur'ān, *sūrat al-shūrā,* (42:38).

45. Qur'ān, *sūrat Āl 'Umrān,* (3:159).

46. 'Amārah, *al-Dawlah al-Islāmīyah,* p. 47.

47. 'Uthmān, *al-Tajrubah al-Sīyāsah,* p. 57.

48. 'The most troublesome problem associated with the striving Islamism is that it emerged, and then was consolidated within environments that were devoid of culture and politics since the late 1960s…whenever I read for Quṭb or Sheikh al-Qaraḍāwī or 'Alī Bil-Ḥajāj as they address the inevitability of having the Islamic solution, I recall the historical inevitability and that of having the socialist solution instantaneously. It is a recycled monolithic thought. So it is not a jape to say that the Islamic inevitability is, in fact, the Marxist inevitability itself, however, with an Islamic Turban. And when we hear Islamists arguing the absolute authority of the caliph or *sharī'ah*, neither the models of 'Umar bin al-Khaṭṭāb nor 'Alī bin Abī Ṭālib come to my mind, rather those of contemporary Arab rulers. It is the youth raised by those Islamists whose ages may not even reach the mid-40s now; where were they raised? Where did they learn? From what cultural sources they derived their knowledge? On what basis al-Qaraḍāwī criticizes democracy and he never knew it? Why would 'Umar 'Abd al-Raḥmān choose the orientations of *al-da'wah* and partisan pluralism when he knew nothing but imprisonment, apprehension, and the oppression of the sultan?' Al-Sayyid, *Siyāsāt al-Islām*, pp. 187–8.

49. Al-Muẓaffar, Muḥammad Riḍā, *'aqā'id al-imāmīyah*, edited by *Ḥamid Ḥafnī Dāwūd* (Najaf: Dār al-Nu'mān, [n.d]), p. 65.

50. In this concern, al-Shahristānī states in regard to *al-imāmah* which is venerated by Shī'ites and considered as a religious duty both in the eyes of reason and *sharī'ah*: 'one ought to know that *al-imāmah* is not taken amongst *uṣūl al-i'tiqād* (fundamentals of belief)'. Al-Shahristānī, *Nihāyat al-Aqdām fī 'Ilm al-Kalām*, edited by Alfred Guillaume (Baghdad: Maktabat al-Muthannā, [n.d.]), p. 484.

51. Ḥawwā, *Jund Allāh*, p. 365.

52. Fanaticism reached its zenith when a contemporary Sunni *dā'yah* (apologist) launched a *fatwa* in which he legalized killing whomever execrates the two sheikhs (Abū Bakr and 'Umar bin al-Khaṭṭāb), claiming: 'undoubtedly, the imam has the full right to kill anyone who curses the two sheikhs without needing any excuse!', this means that this *fatwa* is applicable to most Imāmī (Twelver) Shī'ites! Ḥawwā, *Jund Allāh*, p. 365.

53. Al-Ghanūshī, *al-Ḥurīyāt al-'Āmmah*, p. 142.

54. Al-Ghanūshī, *al-Ḥurīyāt al-'Āmmah*, p. 145.

55. Al-Hāshimī, *Naẓrah Jadīdah fī Wilāyat al-Faqīh*, pp. 22–3.

56. Al-Hāshimī, *Naẓrah Jadīdah fī Wilāyat al-Faqīh*, p. 22.

57. Arkoun, *Pour une Critique de la Raison Islamique*, Islam d'hier et d'aujourd'hui (Paris: Maisonneuve et Larose, 1984), p. 181.

58. Al-Ghanūshī, *al-Ḥurīyāt al-'Āmmah*, p. 143.

59. The Shī'ite hypothesis refuses to take the idea of *'aqd al-bay'ah* (the pledge of allegiance) as a foundation for the establishment of authority (on the consideration that the imamate [*imāmah*] is a divine position and anyone who belittles the rule of the designee [*al-waṣīy*] belittles God). Al-Ghanūshī, *al-Ḥurīyāt al-'Āmmah*, p. 145.

60. Some *'ulamā'* in Morocco went too far in considering al-Khomeini a *kafir* as did the Wahhābīs before them.

61. Al-Ghanūshī, *al-Ḥurīyāt al-'Āmmah*, p. 147.

62. Ghalyūn, *Naqd al-Siyāsah*, p. 89

63. One can refute *al-imāmah* or the *'wilāyat al-faqīh'* due to non-Sunni considerations as well: for example Shī'ite or modern political ideological ones.

64. See Chapter 3 of this book, p. 52.

65. An Islamic scholar maintains: 'There is no rupture between al-Nā'īnī's political discourse and that of al-Khomeini for they belong to one school and one

orientation especially regarding the concept of '*wilāyat al-faqīh*'.' Bārūt, *Yathrib al-Jadīdah,* p. 87.

66. Muntaẓirī, who was a deputy of Khomeini and who resigned after an argument with the latter, disavowed the '*wilāyat al-faqīh*' during the last three years of his academic lectures and speeches. In fact, this upset 'Alī Khāmina'ī (*murshid al-thawrah*-- Spiritual Guide of the Revolution) and other conservatives; consequently, house-arrest was imposed on him and he was libeled in all accounts. This can be attributed to two reasons: the first is a *political* one, since Muntaẓirī was counting on the reformist movement led by Muḥammad Khātamī – former President of the Islamic Republic of Iran; the second pertaining to*fiqh*, as Muntaẓirī was considered the *actual* contemporary theorizer for the '*wilāyat al-faqīh*' – three decades ago – and not Khomeini who merely implemented it for political purposes. In this sense, undermining the theorizer over his own theory will eventually erode its *fiqh* legitimacy; this – in turn – will succor no one but Reformists.

67. He was previously known as the 'spiritual guide' (*murshid rūḥī*) for Hezbollah in Lebanon, however this contention is often doubted.

68. Faḍlallah, Muḥammad Ḥussayn, 'al-Qīyādah al-Islāmīyah fī Dākhil al-Dawlah', *al-Thaqāfah al-Islāmīyah,* 37th issue (May–June 1991), p. 41.

69. Faḍlallah, *al-Ḥarakah al-Islāmīyah- Ḥumūm wa Qaḍāyā*, 3rd edn (Beirut: Dār al-Malāk, 1993), pp. 50–1.

70. Faḍlallah, 'al-Qīyādah al-Islāmīyah', p. 53.

71. Faḍlallah, 'al-Qīyādah al-Islāmīyah', p. 40.

72. It is meant in the age of occultation.

73. Faḍlallah, 'al-Qīyādah al-Islāmīyah', p. 43.

74. Faḍlallah, 'al-Qīyādah al-Islāmīyah', p. 44.

75. Faḍlallah, 'al-Qīyādah al-Islāmīyah', p. 49.

76. Shams al-Dīn, *Niẓām al-Ḥukm wa al-Idārah fi al-Islām,* 2nd edn (Beirut: al-Mu'asasah al-Dawlīyah, 1991), p. 448.

77. Shams al-Dīn, *Niẓām al-Ḥukm*, p. 452.

78. Shams al-Dīn, *Niẓām al-Ḥukm*, p. 454.

79. Mūḥammad Mahdī Shams al-Dīn clearly states that *shūrā*- in the era of *ghaybah* according to Imamite Shī'ites and since the death of the Prophet according to the rest of Muslims, is a religious duty of both *ummah* and the ruler, and they are both obliged to fulfill it, so that *ummah* runs its own affairs via *shūrā*, the ruler too, has to rule with *shūrā*, and he is legally obliged to fulfill any decision reached by it. Shams al-Dīn, *fī al-Ijtimā' al-Sīyāsī al-Islāmī: al-Mujtama' al-Sīyāsī al-Islāmī Muḥāwalat Ta'ṣīl Fiqhī wa Tārīkhī* (Qom: Dār al-Thaqāfah, 1994), pp. 107–8.

80. 'Rendering the expression of *wilayat al-faqīh al-'āmmah* analogous to that of *al-imāmah al-ma'ṣūmah* (the infallible imamate)...is far from the truth both in terms of *fiqh* and *kalām* (scholastic theology); it is rather an idiom that is discrete and independent from *al-imāmah al-ma'ṣūmah*...it does not meet the general comprehensiveness of the infallible imam's *wilayah* even though some are alleging – or even attempting to do that for so-called *fiqh* motives while in reality, they are sheer *political* ones that are remote from any *fiqh* basis. Shams al-Dīn, 'al-Mashrū' al-Sīyāsī al-Islāmī wa Āfāq al-Mustaqbal', *al-Ghadīr,* no. 14 and no. 16 (June 1991), p. 40.

81. Al-Jabri, *al-'Aql al-Sīyāsī al-'Arabī*, Chapter 8.

Chapter 12

Is there a Contemporary Islamic Thought?

On the Application of the Term 'Islamic' to 'Islamic Thought'

This tour of the texts of Islamists – modern and contemporary – has posed a legitimate natural problematic question: is there in these theses of various quantity and type what merits the assertion that there is a modern or contemporary Islamic thought, along the lines of what we are able to say is in fact an Islamic thought – or what is until today an authoritative thought?

The answer to that depends upon elucidating the desired meaning that the term 'Islamic thought' carried in or excluded from these theses. What is intended by it? Does it accrue from what Muslims have produced in thoughts about this or that matter, or does it pertain to what is commensurate with the dictates of the principles of Islam? In other words: does it draw its distinction from those who have endeavored in thought and writing about it among those affiliated with the Islamic *millet* (denomination), or does this descriptive come from respect for the creedal foundations which is the absolute essence of its employment?

The question is not, however, as simple as such a dichotomy, and that is for at least two reasons: the first is that we are not able to remove Islam from the Muslims and realize it as being descriptive of an absolute essence over and above its historical usage and its human affiliation because there is no Islam without Muslims – or say, if you will, in the language of the sociologists – there is no concept without an attack of the historians upon it (no idea propagates without historicists' campaign to support it). An assertion without this stipulation causes us to fall into the ahistorical organic *salafī* view that sheds history and change and dynamism with impunity and creates for thought an absolute beginning – which in the scheme of things – is also its end! It is a thought which we have attempted in the experience of working with the salafī method and the duality of authoritative Islam (*al-Islām al-miʿyārī* / *al-marjaʿī*) and historical Islam (that is 'rejected'), which did not produce anything except a precipitate of prematurity, projection and standard imperativeness. The second of them is that Islamic thought is not Islam which is divine revelation (*waḥīy*) or an exalted text but rather is in sum what (Muslim) human beings have attempted in understanding the teachings of their religion and the questions of their environment and their history, and is subsequently a human action not commensurate with the criteria (*aḥkām*) of an essence that transcends every historical identification.

What can be gleaned from this cautious critical realization is that the question about the meaning of Islamic thought is not to be found within the lines of a ready-made answer safe from conceptual dichotomies of varying degree surrounding Islam and Muslims. Thus, there is not contained in the scope of the assertion that Islamic thought is – exclusively – what conforms to the creedal affirmations of Islam because that conformity is relative in the view of others – the Shīʿah as opposed to the Sunnis or vice versa – anything is better in the end than the assertion that it is an act of interpretation.

Imam al-Ghazālī, for example, accused the philosophers of error in twenty matters of philosophy and accused them of unbelief in three (the assertion of the eternity of the world; the assertion of the non-existence of divine knowledge of particulars; and the lack of an assertion of a return [after death]);[1] and he advocated the assertion that their view of existence (that is, the theory of *al-fayḍ*), was taken from the precursors of Greek philosophy and propounded in essence in Islamic ontological guise (creation from pure absolute nothingness – *ex nihilo*). However, the defense of Ibn Rushd against the *takfīr* of al-Ghazālī brought back the connection of the relation between philosophy and Islam on the basis of the assertion that the reconciliation between (the certainty) their marriage cannot be dissolved.[2] Thus we witnessed, in Islamic thought, a rivalry between a supposition inclined towards extremism of creedal absolutism and another which goes back to the consideration of the participation of human invention in enriching the creed. No success was recorded for this other than that it enjoyed a minor existence in the history of Islamic thought to which some consideration returns today.

Before al-Ghazālī and after him, the matter of questioning and argument between the Muslims the major theme of contention revolved around the axis of attribution of the *uṣūl* (sources) and the *furū'* (branches), and it was one which was shared among Muslims – especially after the dissolution of their group with spread of the fierce internecine struggle over power. Perhaps, the *madhab* polarization – the Sunni–Shī'ite – was the highest form of expression of this contention. It did not persist merely as differences in interpretation of the text alone or only as a matter of argument over which should take precedent or was most efficacious in comprehending revelation: the reason (*al-'aql*) or the text (*al-naṣṣ*) as had been the matter of theological contention with the Mu'tazilah and the Ash'arīyah or a difference over the *uṣūl* with regard to the school of opinion (*madrasat al-ra'y*) or the textualist school – between the champions of *fiqh* and those of the *ḥadīth* and so on. Rather, it persisted, more than that, in the essential difference about the attribution and constraint of the *uṣūl*. It is sufficient that what was counted by the Shī'ah as a source (*aṣl*) among the *uṣūl* of the religion – namely, the imamate – was for the Sunnis only among the branches (*al-furū'*) and interpretations of *fiqh* which were not determinative in matters of creed. It goes without saying that this difference was not an ordinary detail which might characterize a practical point of view or an ideological rivalry, but rather it was an essential difference in the *uṣūl* of the religion!

The Sunnis did not take the position, and they are the majority of the *ummah* and the group, of excommunicating the Shī'ah from the *millet*. They described them as al-Rāfiḍūn ('rejectors') and al-Baṭinīyah ('occultists'), but they did not stone them for unbelief and remained counting them among the *madhāhib* of Islam, or as proponents of an assertion in Islam[3] and these are among the sum total of assertions of the Islamists[4] according to most historians of thought. Perhaps in that is provided an indication that the attribution of Shī'ite thought to Islam is not among that which was possible to challenge – even among the most extreme defenders of the group among the Sunnis. This is the matter that means that the concept of Islamic thought was extended among the thinkers of Islam in the Medieval period to the rest of Islamic groups and *madhāhib*, overlooking the divisions and distinctions between them which surpassed the *furū'* and extended to the *uṣūl*. Sufficient indication of that is that the historians of Islamic thought did not hesitate in history to include these *madhāhib* and groups, on this account, as belonging to the wider locus of Islamic thought.

We conclude from that the assertion that the meaning of 'Islamic thought' was wider of scope in the Medieval period – according to the assertion that dictated that the Islamic character of this thought was to be determined according to the extent of conformity with the confirmed aspects of Islam and its *uṣūl*; and that is, that these confirmed aspects and *uṣūl* were not the province of consensus between the currents in Islamic consciousness not to mention that many among the Muslims – and the Sunni among them in particular – did not take a position against its opponents in the *uṣūl* to the extent of excommunicating them from the *millah* (denomination). If this confirmed the position of the Sunni thinkers, then it also confirms, to a lesser degree, the position of the thinkers and *fuqahā'* of the Shī'ah. True, the Shī'ah were excessive in their vilification of the Sunnis, and in pulverizing their opinion in regard to *al-shūrā*, *al-ijmā'* and *al-bay'ah*, considering it to be absent from the *uṣūl* of the *imāmah* and its seriousness; thus with that the Shī'ites (the Imāmīyah among them, at least) did not go to the extent of accusing the Sunnis of unbelief (*al-takfīr*) or expelling them from the locus of the *millah*. They considered its position a deviation from the *uṣūl* and the fundamental principles and attributing to the usurping authority the right of the *imāmah*, the '*walīy al-amr*'; and the Sunnis did similarly when they accounted the Shī'ite thought as innovation and being extraneous to the province of the *uṣūl*: along the lines of what the Sunnis understood the *uṣūl* to be.

Has anything changed today in this relation between mutual inclusive recognition that was knitted together in the Medieval period between Sunni and Shī'ite thought? Or has anyone diverged from these two groups to critique along the lines of reconsidering the attribution and relative affiliation of the thought of his opponent to the locus of Islam?

We tend towards the belief that nothing of that sort has occurred during the Modern period. The relation has remained open between the two systems of *fiqh* and the two ideas to a large extent despite what there is between them among distinctions and clarifications. True, the distinction continues to prevail in this relation, especially at the level of individuals (thinkers) or that of institutions; the affiliation of Sunni and Shī'ite thinkers has remained strong with their respective points of authoritative reference; and the *ḥawzah 'ilmīyah* in al-Najaf and in Qom have remained independent of the system of religious and *fiqh* education from what was established in al-Azhar and al-Zaytūnah or al-Qayrawān. In other words, the Sunni has remained Sunni, and the Shī'ite has remained Shī'ite: whether in regard to the *uṣūl* of the *madhab* or its *al-furū'*. However the new change in their contention does not go back to concept but rather is ultimately a change of political reality and it is, in some sense, what has lessened the excesses of the conceptual and *madhāhib* differences and accorded to them a stamp of relative objectivity.

The divergence over what came to pass – that is in the Medieval period – occurring between the stronger of the two groups and *madhāhib* in the *ummah* managing its affairs by itself, even if opposition to the existing power in them was an unbearable matter for this side or that. The point of contention – in other words – was internal and political; even it presented itself as conceptual or pertaining to *madhāhib*. If we did not employ the lexicon of modern politics, it is possible for us to use it in the ongoing contention which still continues between a political power which is in its majority Sunni and an opposition which is, primarily in the general sense, Shīʿite. For that reason the like of this contention fell back on its nebulous internal factors naturally between a conceptual difference and a political one – except there occurred a prime polarizing separation of the internal forces; and, moreover, it could not have only but created the impression that the unity of Islam is difficult or intractable in light of the polarized dichotomy and the fierce mutual ostracism between the Sunnis and the Shīʿah. What added to the sharpness of that contention and polarization is that the masses of the Sunnis and Shīʿah understood it as such: that is, difficult to resolve, and a gap that is difficult to bridge.

The matter of that contention as such has not yet returned today, new and tremendous changes have transpired in the social-political scene – since the beginning of the nineteenth century – the rearrangement of the relation between the two groups in the context demands a review of the borders of the positions between them. The Muslims have yet to rule the *dār al-Islām* (domains of Islam) for two centuries since the surprise attack of the colonizing West upon them when their domains fell into its grip militarily initially and subsequently came under the power of its legislative and cultural apparatuses thereafter. The import of that is the legitimacy of the internal contention was lifted or, at least, suspended until it becomes legitimate. The foreign danger remained threatening and consequently the call for unity became clamorous and echoed louder than did the call for separation and division.

Our talk does not belong in this matter to discussion of a theoretical 'consolation'; but rather it has justifications of reality and support. It suffices us to indicate – by way of example – three conceptual and political events which provide proof for the position we have taken: the first is that the Islamic reformism of the nineteenth century transcended the bounds of the traditional Shīʿite–Sunni duality in order to defend the idea of Islamic unity; and the harbinger of that flood is what al-sayyid Jamāl al-Afghānī penned on the subject.[5] The second of these is what the Iranian Revolution evinced of respect and praise in the Sunni milieu not as a Shīʿite revolution but as an Islamic revolution. And the third is confrontation by the armed Lebanese resistance in the South against the Zionist occupation from the standpoint that it is an Islamic resistance and not a Shīʿite resistance.

The matter does not pertain in this to politics alone but rather goes back to religion: the Shīʿah have moved much closer to the Sunni *fiqh* order, especially the *fiqh* of politics; and they have reconciled with the central Sunni principle of *al-shūrā* which they had rejected for so long for its contradiction of the principles of appointment (*al-waṣīyah*) and infallibility (*al-ʿiṣmah*) whereby the order of the imamate does not persist except on the basis of them. True, they do not retreat from the concept of the imamate, and it is not possible for them to do so, just as they take *al-shūrā* according to the limits that attach to management of the deputy of the imam to the affairs, and they did not make it a condition for the choice of the imam as had the Sunni political *fiqh* tradition. However, that does not change – in the end – the fact of that openness that they had towards an idea that was always accounted as incompatible with the logic of the imamate. Correspondingly, some Sunni movements opened up to the ideas of the Shīʿah and in establishing the idea of political issue and rule belonging to the *uṣūl* of the religion and not to the branches as Sunni *fiqh* had been inclined since ancient times. Despite the fact that these movements asserting the *uṣūlī* character of politics and the imamate did not represent the official Sunni position, and this position did not enjoy the good graces or favor of the religious *fiqh* institutions (such as al-Azhar, *fiqh* groups, knowledge councils or institutions for official *fatwas*), it did represent, in the Shīʿite view of things – a perceptible conceptual rapprochement with the subjects of Shīʿite *fiqh* about the centrality of the matter of the imamate (that is, rule) inside the creedal order of Islam.

We draw from this context the following result: the attribute 'Islamic' for substantive thought in Islamic thought does not guarantee that it will be respective of foundations of creed and a shared agreed upon *uṣūl*. That is because these foundations and *uṣūl* are not the subject of consensus between the *fuqahā'* of Islam as we have seen, just as the contention between them has not been a justification for casting a group out of the confines of the *millet* and the creed from the point of view of another group. And even if we consider the phenomenon of 'political Islam' or 'confrontational Islam' a limbo between the Sunni position and the Shīʿite in regard to the matter of the *uṣūl* of the religion (in its entrance of politics and the imamate into its ranks); the matter which is not open to argument is that the position of this Sunni 'political Islam' remains – in the end – Sunni, and is not easily subsumable into the Shī'ite order because it, simply, rejects the Shī'ite principle of the imamate. The same situation coincides with the Shī'ite position in regard to *al-shūrā* which does not cause them to lose their *madhāhib* identity centered on the infallibility of the imam and the assertion of the divine nature of his position. Thus, criterion for the Islamic character of thought is against the backdrop of its relative creedal and *uṣūlī* affiliation and is thus only a relative measure. However that opens the door before us to the assertion that this Islamic characteristic comes from two factors: from a common denominator among the *madhāhib* of Islam (that is a common denominator other than *al-ijmā'* – consensus), and from the standpoint that those who produce Islamic thought are Muslims.

There is a certain correspondence between the two factors: the assertion that there is a common denominator between the *madhāhib* of Islam – which does not reach the level of consensus – is not among the aberrations of discourse on the history of Islam, that is when consensus has been precluded within the ranks of the Sunnis – where it is a source among the *uṣūl* of the *fiqh* – why should it be considered strange if it is precluded between the Sunnis and the Shī'ah between whom are divisions and distinctions in both the *uṣūl* as in the branches? Subsequently, that permits the belief that the absence of consensus is tantamount to a legitimate call for *ijtihād*. This is clear for the Sunnis in the *uṣūl* of their *fiqh*, so how is it that it is not used – in a general way – to be implemented in 'ameliorating' the absence of consensus between the Sunnis and the Shī'ah? Most important in this is that when we decide upon the legitimacy of the principle of *ijtihād* – ordained by consensus of both the Sunnis and the Shī'ah – we acknowledge a priori that the matter of religion has gone out, to a degree, from being the responsibility of the text to the responsibility of the reason; that is ultimately it has become in the rule of assessment a human action for Muslims. This, in the end, is tantamount to the assertion that there is no Islam without Muslims because Muslims, when they believe in Islam as a creed, represent it in a web of ideal and consciousness that is changing with their changing and which varies with their time and place. If this puts the meaning of the relativity in place for us in the consciousness of Islam, it also puts in place a concept of Islam which transcends it as a text – to extend the circle of those believing in it and belonging to it – that is, to people. Thus, Islam no longer remains only a text and teachings but rather becomes a combination of what the *fuqahā'* and scholars of the *uṣūl* and thinkers have produced against the backdrop of the supreme authority of the principle of *ijtihād* which accords to them that status.

The Sunnis have long been absorbed in the text–*ijtihād* dichotomy; and some of them have taken the position of ruling that the connection between *ijtihād* and the text is on the basis of the assertion that 'there is no *ijtihād* where there is a text', whereas others have gone to the assertion of the permissibility of *ijtihād* along with a text. Like them, the Shī'ah have been absorbed in the dichotomy of the manifest (*al-ẓāhir*) and the hidden (*al-bāṭin*), *al-tanzīl* and *al-ta'wīl* (interpretation), and most of them have taken the position of asserting that the spiritual truth (*al-ḥaqīqah al-rūḥīyah*) is other than the literally apparent meaning of the text,[6] legitimizing recourse to *ijtihād*. Given this reality, there is nothing for us to do except acknowledge that this *ijtihād* is a part of the heritage of Islam and that Islamic thought is all that which has been produced by those affiliated with the creed and culture of Islam whatever their conceptual points of departure or ideological predilections. However, that pertains to an aspect of the equation which is the Islamic character of the thought – that which is termed 'Islamic thought'; as for the second aspect which is primary in study and analysis, it is the connection to the connotation of the term 'thought' of that Islamic production: have we come to the point where we may describe the Islamic production – modern and contemporary – as conceptual production or as belonging, theoretically, to the locus of thought?

On the Conceptual Affiliation to Contemporary 'Islamic Literature'

The methodological point of entry into the approach to this subject is to assign the concept of thought towards which we direct this research into its presence or absence in this Islamic production. In the first sense, we mean by 'thought' the sum total of knowledges and conceptions constructed about a particular subject that present as theoretical conception, that is, in the form of the theoretical context and from the conceptual, theoretical framework. As for the second connotation, we intend by it the sum of all instruments of knowledge that are used in the production of these knowledges and conceptions that subsumes method and conceptual system (or theoretical language), and the referential knowledge system from which these conceptions and suppositions are produced. Thought is not thought if it is not manifest in a tangible theoretical framework, and if it does not present itself in intelligible conceptual language. Neither is it thought if it does not roam in thinking or fails to engage the instruments of knowledge production. We might add to all of this that thought is analysis and criticism and construction (or reconstruction) and it is not ready-made opinions.

Some might say that we are blurring – in this definition – between thought and between the concept of scientific knowledge (in the field of anthropology of course, and that we are reproducing the decisive Althusserian theoretical distinction between knowledge and ideology).[7] The truth is other than that as thought might be ideological whereas ideology might possibly be presented in an organized conceptual fashion; this, for example, is what correlates to the Liberal ideological case or the Socialist or, now the ideology of Globalization coming into prominence today. That is ideology is not fabrications and trivialities, but rather it is an order of thoughts and a universal world-view,[8] and it is, for that reason, a conceptual concept. Here we digress and say, the distance is wide between ideological discourse and propagandist discourse: the first relies for support on an order of knowledges and concepts that might be at variance with its content without us doubting the abundance or strength of its conceptual theoretical or external framework. As for the second, it cannot be claimed that it is a literal discourse, entreating slogans and ready-made opinions and value judgments and trying unsuccessfully to present itself as being a kind of thought or knowledge! It might be difficult for the research to derive the ideological in a certain discourse, but there is no doubt that propagandist can be clearly denoted in a given discourse without much effort.

The preceding pertains to our discussion of the attempt to define the concept of thought theoretically and that – if necessary – does not suffice our essential task: delimiting the meaning of Islamic thought – the absence or presence for which we search in Islamic (political) literature, both modern and contemporary. Thus, in light of the givens of the preceding analysis – we are able to define Islamic thought as the thought that strives to produce knowledge in the religious text and in the social reality on the principle of the connection to the universal Islamic *marja'īyah* order.

We confronted in this definition three components: knowledge (*al-ma'rifah*); its subject; and scope of *marja'īyah*.

It was previously emphasized that 'thought' does not attain to this identity (as such) except when it connotes knowledge. Knowledge is a complicated operation, it transpires in regard to a subject and the thought itself rests on the same framework and it does not proffer any ready given(s). When it operates on that subject, it engages in the transformation of it and it reforms its nature through its use of means of operation (or tools of production) and these are: method, concept, hypothesis and the remainder of theoretical techniques and approaches. The result of this operation of the relation between thought and the tools of knowledge production and between the subject of thought is a knowledge termed a product (*Produit*). And if we borrow theoretical concepts of historical dialectical materialism in economic analysis (*L'Economique*) in the social structure – as Karl Marx formulated them in *Das Kapital*,[9] and as theorized by Louis Althusser[10] and Charles Bettelheim[11] and Nicos Poulantzas,[12] we find that the context for the realization of the operation of material-economic production is the selfsame context for knowledge production: labor, the equivalent of thought, is acting upon the material substrate (for example, the subject of knowledge) which might be the earth or the raw material. It uses the tools of labor such as the harvester or tractor or the industrial machine or the human implement (and its equivalents are method and concepts and suppositions in thought). As for the result of that, it is precisely a material product: agricultural or manufactured (it is – in thought – the knowledge radiating from the operation of thinking as exemplified in new thoughts and conceptions building on initial thoughts or suppositions...)

Islamic thought, however, has subjects which might be particular to it, attaining to its uniqueness through them, or general ones shared with other than it in thinking about these; and it is what has come textually to be defined as: the religious text and social reality. The truth is that this text is not haphazard; rather, it brings into prominence the importance of these two subjects in the consciousness of Muslims, both ancient and modern.

The attention of Islamic thinkers, modern and contemporary, to the question of religious text was not an innovation or invention of them, rather it was imposed upon them by two matters: the first is the ancient Islamic tradition in consideration of the text and the continual recourse to it in order to understand it more or to grasp answers from it for the occurrences of change; and the second is their need for that text to confront the recurring problems of their age, and especially in conditions where religion no longer possesses a monopoly of response to the world, but rather the number of sources for answer to that have multiplied where religion has become only one among these sources. This is the matter that laid the foundation for some to refuse to acknowledge this reality; and imposed on some others acknowledgment of it without hardship and an attempt to listen to other sources of knowledge, and perhaps endeavoring to reconcile it with religious knowledge. In any case, the connection of the modern and contemporary Islamic thinkers to the question of the religious text remained strong, and it produced in their consciousness two theses: a Reformist *ijtihād* thesis which attempted to represent the text as contemporary through a web of hermeneutics and interpretation, and in horizons that enabled it to renew its ideational mastery in a changing contemporary world; and a regressive Salafī thesis emphasizing the closed, textualist view of Islam, taking it as a protective fence against the march of facts of wasteful transformation in thought as well as in human society.

The attention of modern and contemporary thinkers to reality was not any less than their attention to the text. It might have appeared to them, *in toto*, that reality was full of symbols of interesting transformation that shook everything in human civilization. It was incumbent upon them, and they were defending progress (the Reformists in particular) and they were dedicated to fathoming the reasons for the delay of the Muslims and to critique autocracy, and to attempt to understand the essence of modern European civilization. They endeavored to understand this reality that engaged them in frequent consultation of the texts, after reality itself had become a text. Similarly it was incumbent upon others among them when they were defending identity (the Revivalists in particular) to be busied greatly by the operation of '*al-istikbār al-ʿālamī*' (arrogant world oppression) and in the matter of how it was able to realize superiority and ascendancy and to impose '*al-istiḍʿāf*' (oppressed weakness) on Muslims, just as they were engaged in searching for the means of extricating society and the *ummah* from the abyss of civilizational collapse. And to be just, not all of the Revivalists were adamantly holding to the religious text, rather there were those among them who tried to understand the new reality with a reason open to *ijtihād* and they were more inclined to pay heed to reality and its facts.

Lastly, the thought of modern and contemporary thinkers of Islam would not have been 'Islamic' thought except in the sense that it retained its intense connection to a *marjaʿīyah* (authoritatively referential) order which is Islam. We reiterate what we said previously and emphasize that Islam, understood in a comprehensive sense – as a creed and a civilization and a culture – is far remote from contentions and differences of *madhab* and group that reached the *uṣūl* as well as the *furūʿ* (branches) without losing track of the common denominator. Whoever believes that this *marjaʿīyah* order is homogeneous is mistaken; rather it is, like all authoritative referential orders, multiple/heterogeneous[13] because of its being conceived and formed in the womb of multiplicity. Some might ask why they should be concerned with this multiplicity. This order in the first instance is the Qur'ānic text. We reply by saying that comprehending this text was never unified among all groups and *madhāhib* of Islam, and accordingly, it is not possible for us to bring down the principle of hermeneutical interpretation (*al-ta'wīl*)[14] which has been affirmed by all.

If the frontiers between thought and the road to formulating opinion are clarified in definition, as we have sought, and if defining Islamic thought, theoretically, has delimited a scope, then it is within our capacity now to ask the extent to which Arab political writing – modern and contemporary – belongs to the locus of thought.

Islamic thought – modern and contemporary – is not one in nature and structure, and it is not permissible to judge it absolutely or to generalize; that is because it is multiple in aspect: from the standpoint of its times that imposed the view of it on the basis of its being distinct moments of knowledge; and from the standpoint of its problematic being changed with the changing of every conceptual moment of its moments; then subsequently from the standpoint of its dissimilar and contradictory knowledge value, the extent and importance in contradictoriness or dissimilarity in its place in time and its problematic. We are able to distinguish, in this demonstration, between three moments in the modern and contemporary history of Islamic thought: the moment of classical Islamic Reformism of the nineteenth century and the beginning of the twentieth; the moment of renewed Islamic Reformism – and narrow fringe groups in the twentieth century; then the moment of Islamic Revivalism (*al-iḥyā'īyah/al-ṣaḥwah*) from the dawn of the 1930s. Perhaps the separations between them are not always sharp or decisive; however, they trace clear borders of symbols that cannot be mistaken in analysis.

It is no longer a subject of doubt or contention among historians of modern Islamic thought and those who study it, that classical Islamic Reformism, in the nineteenth century and the early years of the twentieth, formed a complete conceptual order, intertwining bonds of proximity and theory between its major texts, and it realized an organic unity between its different problematics and carved out a theoretical dictionary shared among its various theses. This resulted in Reformist preoccupation, general among the circle of thinkers of the *Nahḍah* expressing itself in two regards: in regard to the conceptual problematic amalgam (the question of the *Nahḍah* or advancement or civilization or progress), and in regard to the conceptual goal (production of a modern ideational order that Muslims might consult to answer the questions of their new age).

Al-Ṭahṭāwī and Khayr al-Dīn al-Tūnsī heralded the state and the modern political system, as they viewed in Europe and as they represented texts of the Liberal thinkers defending it. Ibn Abī al-Ḍayyāf and al-Afghānī assailed the sultanate system which did not implement the operation of reform from within. Muḥammad ʻAbdūh criticized religious authority and considered it contradictory to the understanding of Islam of rule and the political system, which was, in his view, a civil system. Al-Kawākibī and al-Nā'īnī fiercely vilified the system of political autocracy and considered it responsible for the underdevelopment of the societies of Islam and so on.[15] All of these, on the basis of the dissimilarities of the contexts of their assertions and the variations in their points of departure, represented nothing more than multiple conceptual modalities in expressing the Reformist thesis itself that was ordered by a system which is the problematic of progress, and which manifested in their political thought about the subject of the modern nation state.

The value of Islamic Reformism is, however, not here: we mean not in its being possessed of a theoretical problematic which is the problematic of progress (or renaissance) and possessed of an initiative which is the nation state (whereas with the Revivalists it is else – the problematic being that of identity and the initiative being that of the Islamic state). Its value, rather, is in that it produced a political thought or an order among the knowledges about the sultanate state and the political question which drew its principles and its sources from modern Liberal political thought just as from the order of Islamic legal politics according to the *fuqahā'* of the Islamic state in the Medieval period. The Reformists were particular in their being supplied with a congruous ideational dictionary (or a theoretical language) and the nature of the subject of their view was conceptual. More important than that is that they dealt with the matter from the standpoint of their being thinkers or possessors of a conceptual initiative (reformist or renaissance) and not as their being politicians or partisans of political parties, impelled by the call of 'political necessity' to improvise a political opinion on the question of the state. The reader of their texts is able to notice – with little duress – the conceptual preoccupation in them, and what came to represent in time a cultural revolution in the ideational consciousness of Islam on the matter of political power. We are able, today, to say without hesitation or trepidation that the one modern Islamic political thought in our *ḥawzah* is, by definition, the classical Reformist Islamic political thought that expresses itself in the texts of the *Nahḍah* and that was authored in the intervening period between the 1830s and the middle of the first decade of the twentieth century. Everything other than it is either one of two types: a late and difficult continuum of the thoughts of Reformism – in either centrifugal or centripetal circumstances – or a complete break from it, in terms of problematic and knowledge.

Among the examples of that continuum are what late- and neo-Islamic Reformism attempted in the intervening period between the 1920s and the 1960s represented, with discrepancies, by ʿAlī ʿAbd al-Rāziq and ʿAbd al-Razāq al-Sanhūrī in Egypt; ʿAbd al-Ḥamīd bin Bādīs in Algeria, and then ʿAllāl al-Fāsī in Morocco. It is neo-Islamic Reformism because it does not go out of the scope of the Reformist conceptual order of the nineteenth century; rather, it reproduced much of its concepts and conceptions about the state, politics and reform, even if some of its texts – especially with ʿAbd al-Razāq al-Sanhūrī and ʿAllāl al-Fāsī – venture far from the openness to the order of modern political thought and outshine, to a degree, the previous tradition of Islamic Reformism.

The return of Reformist thought to Egypt anew was somewhat 'surprising' after the end of the period of Muḥammad ʿAbdūh, and the success of 'al-Azhar' in re-spreading its 'sovereignty' over the religious (after it had lost this in a relative sense in the Reformist period), and the rise of the Islamist movement in political dispensation. There was no surprise in the cases of Algeria and Morocco whose *fuqahāʾ* and intellectuals came to know the thought of Muḥammad ʿAbdūh and Rashīd Riḍā late (after the First World War),[16] and those who would find in the Salafī thought material for the ideology of the national movement in Morocco[17] and perhaps the Jamʿīyat ʿulamāʾ al-Muslimīn (Association of Muslim *ʿulamāʾ*) in Algeria.[18] And, just as in the past, when the end of philosophy and *ijtihād* were announced in the East, they were born in the Maghreb and al-Andalus (Muslim Spain), the end of Reformism in the East would be the date of its rebirth in Morocco.

Perhaps, the circumstances of the inception of this (continued, or) neo-Islamic Reformism were difficult for a number of reasons: from the standpoint of this Reformism remaining, in its general orientation, a faint and delayed echo of Reformism of the *marjaʿīyah* – thirsty for and very delayed in regard to its authoritative referent of the original Reformism; and from the standpoint of its being unsuccessful in producing a true Islamic school of thought, like its predecessor, with an impact but rather it continued to represent radiating flashes cut off in time; and finally for its being conceived – especially in the East and Egypt – in the shadow of a state of conceptual siege represented by the violent sweeping trend of the Revivalist Movement with the Muslim Brotherhood and its offshoots in Arab and Islamic countries. With all of that, what can be said decisively, is that we are not able to acknowledge for it except two merits which it inherited from the mother Reformism: the first is its boldness in express Reformist thoughts which lacked a context or for which there was not a general religious mood – and it is a boldness which cost its proponents dearly[19] in excessive personal and psychological terms. The second is the same clear and strong conceptual expression in representing the political question: the question of the state and authority and exposing it to an approach to the subject in raw political language. Perhaps a book of the standing of *al-Islam wa uṣūl al-Hukm* (*Islam and the Origin of Rule*) of ʿAlī ʿAbd al-Rāziq or *al-Naqd al-Dhātī wa Maqāṣid al-Sharīʿah al-Islāmīyah wa Makārimuhā* (*Self Criticism and the Intents of Islamic Sharīʿah and Its Excellences*) of ʿAllāl al-Fāsī or other than these is the example par-excellence of that conceptual spirit in the literary output of these late Reformers.

As for examples of disjuncture with Islamic Reformism – and the strongest of these examples is the contemporary Islamic Revivalism that came into existence as a political conceptual movement since the beginning of the second quarter of the twentieth century with the rise of the Muslim Brotherhood movement in Egypt in order to wander about the edifice of modern Reformist heritage and return the consciousness of the Muslims to the state and rule to what it had been before the age of the Modern Arab Nahḍah ('Awakening')! The Revivalism won independence for its problematic from Reformism, where the import of thought was no longer directed towards the matter of progress (or advancement) but was rather employed as a segue into the problematic of identity in the contemporary Islamic consciousness – viewing it exclusively from a religious angle.[20] Similarly, it was separated from the political heritage radiating from around the initiative of the nation state to establish on its debris the edifice of the idea of the Islamic state and what informed it of theocratic ideas about authority and the system of rule and about the relation of the political to the religious. There is no problem – in what concerns us here – in this formal and conceptual demonstration, it has its context that explains it; rather the problem is that the contemporary Revivalist heritage was not, from its inception more than three quarters of a century ago – a conceptual heritage. It is not permissible for us, knowingly, to account it as thought and to read its givens according to this principle or on this basis; it is not only because in that we will do it disservice and demand of it that of which it is not able, but rather because to do so would debase the meaning of 'thought'; but contribution in this debasement has not ceased until today to be practices under the rubric that it is 'new' and 'unified' Islamic thought!

If the contemporary Islamic Revivalist heritage is not a conceptual heritage or an accumulation that belongs to knowledge and thought, as we have surmised, then what may we describe it as being, and to what extent are we able to attain to that?

We do not exaggerate when we say that what the contemporary Islamic Revivalists produced for half a century at least (even if we do not say since the end of the 1920s) are not about to be counted among the ranks of 'political movement literature' – we mean in the locus of political party organizations and their production of communiqués and positions and daily programs of work! Though some of it tried and still tries to attribute to itself a conceptual or *fiqh* anointment, removing it somewhat from direct politicization, and according to itself religious legitimacy; if this paint is removed from the discourse of some, its naked political propagandist nature is exposed, and unmasks the game of ideological masquerade that restores it to its genuine nature as being a propagandist discourse aimed at inciting and militarizing and mobilizing followers and partisans. It attains to that through literal sermonizing that appeals to the instincts and the emotions, and to feelings of inequity and deprivation for those who have been crushed by the conditions of life and from whom nothing remains to support them except their threatened dignity.[21] How many indications have there been of the social force that this Revivalist discourse has succeeded in inflaming in the midst of marginal groups and those excluded from the field of production, or some of the strata of the world among the middle class whose interests were harmed after the collapse of the state initiative and who ultimately came to feel unequal and downtrodden, as well as some of the intermediate groups such as university students fearful of their destinies and a future with unclear horizons.

There are two reasons, at least, to explain why the Revivalist discourse succeeded in this propagandist declivity incompatible with the logic of conceptual construction: the first is the triumph of the objective of politicization (or the politicization objective) of it. And it is a natural triumph from the perspective that it was a propagandist discourse with a message of struggle and resistance in the first instance: the heralding of the initiative of the Islamic state. And thus, what is not surprising is that this politicizing-propagandist discourse itself radiates from political party institutions conceived for this objective; rather what is surprising is that translation of this into material terms goes to the farthest possible limit: construction of fighting institutions charged with the goal of effecting a takeover of authority in order to build the 'Islamic state'! The second of these reasons is that those who disseminate the 'Revivalist' or 'Political

Islamic' outlook charge themselves with the task of authoring and writing: writing movement literature, and the vast majority of them are not researchers, nor thinkers, nor intellectuals in general, but rather they are either preachers, or men of a particular politics or organization, or categories of educated people. What calls for amazement is that they who trust them and believe in their 'thoughts' and transform them into a material force are not aided by their 'Islamic culture/education' in anything more than a knowledge of the literature of *al-wuḍū'* (ritual ablutions) and what contravenes it; the vast majority of them do not have a clear idea about the 'Islamic legal obligations' in which they ought to culpably engage![22]

What is most deplorable is that the Islamic reason that engaged in dialog with Western Orientalists in the nineteenth century devolved to the point where it became an ideological (propagandist) shouting and debased jingoist yelling, transitioning from the defense of the *ummah* and the group and the future to defense of the political party and the militia…and the past.

Notes

1. Al-Ghazālī, Abū Ḥamid Muḥammad bin Muḥammad, *Tahāfut al-Falāsifah*, edited by Sulaymān Dunyā, Dhakhā'ir al-'Arab, 3rd edn (Cairo: Dār al-Ma'ārif, 1958).

2. Ibn Rushd, *Faṣl al-Maqāl.*

3. Al-Shahristānī categorized Islamic thought on the basis of its theses, in which he implements strict rules to classify such opinions, he writes: '…it is well-known, that not everyone who becomes distinguished for writing about a certain issue, is considered to be a textualist, otherwise we shall have myriads of theses, whereas he who becomes unique in addressing essential issues, definitely he is considered one, so there must be disciplines for one to be a textualist. I saw not a single one amongst pioneers of the textualists who was concerned about this discipline, they instead, went on citing *madhāhib* of the *ummah* haphazardly, not depending on any constant law or *aṣl*, I worked hard to clarify them in four bases, which are the major ones'.

After he provides a definition in detail for each of these bases (the Shī''ah in the fourth base), he concludes by stating: 'If we see one of the imams of the *ummah* addresses one of these bases, we deem his thesis a *madhab* and his group a faction, and if we see that one of them addresses any given issue, we deem not his thesis a *madhab,* nor his group is to be a faction'. Al-Shahristānī, *al-Milal wa al-Niḥal,* pp. 14–15.

4. Al-Ash'arī, *Maqālāt al-Islāmīyīn.*

5. Al-Afghānī, *al-A'māl al-Kāmilah.*

6. See Chapter Three in: Corbin, Henry, *En Islam Iranien: Aspects Spirituels et Philosophiques* (Paris: Gallimard, 1971–2), vol. 1: Le Shi'isme duodécimain.

7. Althusser, Louis, *Pour Marx*, Théorie (Paris: Maspéro, 1965).

8. Al-'Arawī, *Mafhūm al-Īdyulujīyā- al-Adlajah* (Casablanca: al-Markaz al-Thaqāfī al-'Arabī, 1980).

9. Marx, Karl, *Le Capital* (Paris: Editions sociales, [n.d]).

10. Althusser, *Lire 'le capital',* Théorie (Paris: Maspéro, 1965).

11. Bettelheim, Charles, *Les Luttes de classes en URSS* (Paris: Maspéro; Seuil, 1979).

12. Poulantzas, Nicos, *Les Classes Socials dans le Capitalisme aujourd'hui*, collection sociologie politique (Paris: Seuil, 1974).

13. The liberal ideological apparatus is not one entity, so is the Marxist apparatus. And the supposition of homogeneity in such ideologies stems from metaphysical comprehension for them.

14. See Chapter Two in: Corbin, *En Islam Iranien.*

15. We amply discussed this issue in the first three chapters of this book.

16. Muḥammad bin al-Ḥasan al-Ḥajawī was the first one among them although he may have been preceded by Muḥammad al-Makkī al-Nāṣirī and Abdul Salām Banūnah.

17. Belkeziz, *al-Khiṭāb al-Iṣlāḥī fī al-Maghrib: al-Takwīn wa al-Maṣādir 1844–1918*, Fikr ʿArabī Muʿāṣir (Beirut: Dār al-Muntakhab al-ʿArabī, 1997).

18. Merad, Ali, *Le Réformisme Musulman en Algérie de 1925 à 1940: Essai d'Histoire Religieuse et Sociale,* Recherches Méditerranéennes (Paris: Mouton, 1967).

19. Among these was the aggressive campaign against ʿAlī ʿAbd al-Rāziq and his book: *al-Islam wa Uṣūl al-Hukm*, and against al-Ḥajawī and his paradigm to enter reforms to al-Qurawiyīn, and against Muḥammad BilʿArabī, al-Dakkālī and ʿAllāl al-Fāsī...Al-Ḥajawī, Muḥammad Bin al-Ḥasan, *al-Fikr al-Sāmī fī Tārīkh al-Fiqh al-Islāmī* (Medina: al-Maktabah al-ʿIlmīyah, 1977), vol. 2, pp. 195–7.

20. The Pan-Arab discourse concentrated on the same issue, however confined to identity in its national context, so that *ummah* is united in its cultural, historic and social aspects, and diverse in its religious affiliations.

21. The same thing was tried by al-Bannā, ʿAwdah, Sayyid Quṭb, al-Qaraḍāwī and al-Turābī.

22. Those who assassinated Ḥussayn Marwah and Mahdī ʿĀmil, and those who attempted to assassinate Najīb Maḥfūẓ, never read any work of those great writers.

Epilogue

In this research we have attempted to trace – through exposition, analysis and criticism – the different elements of conceptual formation and development which have impacted the Islamic consciousness both modern and contemporary; and, it has dealt with the mother of all questions in political thought; the question of state. In this operation of tracing we have gathered a number of conclusions that pertain to the degree of theoretical and conceptual knowledge in that thought and in the mode of its relations with its political and theoretical authoritative references, as well as constants and variables in its problematics and concepts, and factors of the declining curve of its intellectual performance, as well as to the inclination towards correction and review that is apparent today, especially after wandering for so long within trackless desolation.

– 1 –

Perhaps what will attract the interest of researchers in texts of Islamic thinkers from the 1830s to the end of the twentieth century is the absence of any theoretical epistemological construction. In general, it does not present itself in the image of knowledge with solid and uniform structure. As for the texts which incorporate a small measure of that, and these are rare in any case, it is almost rote repetition of previous knowledge: whether in its introduction, conceptual framework, or in patterns of derivation, inference or explication. The reader of these may not find in them an indication for the theory of state, but may find myriad political essays rife with ideological tensions. Thus, Islamic thought failed to produce a theory of state at the same time it succeeded in producing a political ideology quenched and nurtured by chauvinism.

Possibly, Islamic Reformism in the nineteenth century was more qualified scientifically to produce knowledge and order of thoughts than Islamic Revivalism could ever achieve in the twentieth century. However, the modern political agenda produced by this Reformism did not enjoy sufficient capacity in logical contexts or theoretical depth: it was mostly selective and superficial; it was preoccupied primarily by functionalism: addressing pressing objective needs, knowledge was never among its interests. Although it was beneficial in cultivating general interest in the scope of development and prerequisites for this development, as well as drawing attention to realities of modern political society, knowledge paid the highest price. Reformism left behind a legacy replete with generalizations, poor in theoretical content, and confused due to impurities and misconceptions that disturbed its theses; chief among these was the provocative combination of modern subjects of politics and state with traditional ones. For this reason, they were easily expunged – by the end of 1920s – from positions of authoritative central knowledge, and its legacy was dissolved. Some of those who participated in this intellectual liquidation were already protégés of Reformism itself; some others rode it as a vessel to reach other problematic shores!

As for Islamic Revivalism in its two major tributaries: the Muslim Brotherhood and the *Ṣaḥwah*, it was intellectually impoverished *vis-à-vis* Reformism; although, it was not less coherent in its topics than the latter, especially in its Muslim Brotherhood intellectual manifestation.[1] However, this relative uniformity or intellectual conformity was not a good indicator of its stamina or intellectual fecundity; rather it was nothing more than reiteration of ancient Islamic intellectual problematics in questions of state and the ruling system, in addition to its addiction to Revivalism in its practices, especially in *fiqh* topics of 'Islamic legal politics'. We may affirm that the ideology of contemporary Revivalism did not add anything new to the texts of al-Mawardī, al-Ghazālī, Ibn Taymīyah, and Ibn al-Qayyim; it was, in fact, confined to its intellectual orbit even in addressing topics such as the constitution, parliamentary representation, and so on. One reason for such intellectual deficiency in the thought of Revivalism[2] is its propensity towards politicizing its own discourse, that is, shifting it from the level of thought to one of politics, due to the casting of the Islamic idea into the framework of the political party and its eventual recruitment for active political purposes. Thus, the questions of Islam are no longer theoretical in its consciousness; rather they were transformed to questions of practice, or say, questions posed by practice!

Many political conditions played a role in this process, in addition to the entrance of Reformists and Revivalists into their battle against developing Islamic knowledge – whether modern or contemporary – in the issues of politics and the problem of state specifically. It conferred upon them a pragmatic aspect that justified for them selectivity and ready-made repetition, neglecting – in this way – all the needs of knowledge. Thus ideology dominated the scene in this thought along with decreasing indications of knowledge and theoretical production, this process continued with the passage of time and came to be exacerbated by political pressures, the needs of reality and the demands of practice!

– 2 –

The reader may notice another phenomenon in this thought and that pertains to the tendency of selectivity we mentioned above; that is, the unstable relation between it and other systems of religious authoritative references from which the former benefited through exploitation of some of its subjects, specifically the relation between both Reformism and Revivalism with the order of modern Liberal political concepts and the conceptual *fiqh* order of 'Islamic legal politics'. They were prone to borrow these concepts in a selective fashion, then re-interpret them along the lines of the conceptual assumptions and precursors of the one doing the interpretation. We can detect these very concepts whether modern or legal in the texts of Reformists and Revivalists in varying degrees of intensity in usage and presence. However, the outcome of this process of borrowing did not obtain the same inferences or results due to the difference in the methods utilized for each in discourse, and the result corresponded to the type of operation of interpretation to which it had been submitted.

Reformists utilized expressions such as: 'freedom', 'constitution', 'parliament' (or parliamentary representation), 'public opinion', side-by-side with concepts of: *al-shūrā, al-bay'ah, ahl al-ḥal wa al-'aqd, al-ijmā'*. This was also true for Revivalists. They all, both Reformists and Revivalists, compared concepts of the first system with those of the second one due to their belief that they are analogous in inferences. However, no mutual understanding for these inferences took place due to differences in aspects and purposes of interpretation. So, while Islamic Reformism embarked on implementing concepts of traditional political thought to reflect those of modern political thought, Revivalism, on the other hand, went on to implement modern concepts in reflecting the order of 'Islamic legal politics'. And, the result was to drive the point of departure towards contradictory conceptual results.

Undoubtedly, one of the goals of Reformism was educational; to approach the meaning of modern terminology through the implementation of ancient terminology, and especially given the difficulty of the translation and Arabicization of these. The most important goal, however, was soliciting a cultural and religious legitimacy for concepts of modern political thought using the nuance that the concepts of the *sharī'ah* lead to a meaning that is identical. As for Revivalism, the goal of using modern concepts to express the concepts of *al-sharī'ah*, was nothing but to give the general impression that the two are cognates, to remove the fingerprints of 'Secularism' from the thought, and to assert that Islam presaged it in the specification of concepts such as democracy (*al-shūrā*), political contract (*al-bay'ah*), and representation (*ahl al-ḥal wa al-'aqd*) in spite of all the obstacles associated with the process of comparison and interfacing, among which was the difficulty in constructing the two concepts of *al-shūrā* and representation remote from the idea of *ahl al-ḥal wa al-'aqd*![3] Thus, the two sides engaged in a battle to consolidate their own ideas about state – using elusive tactics and cunning wits sometimes – as they navigated between selectivity and utilitarianism in the relation of the two authoritative referential orders.

– 3 –

The Islamic Reformist–Revivalist thesis about the state was characterized by a jumbled theoretical or conceptual admixture arising, in turn, from an epistemological poverty that we have indicated. This tendency towards confused intermixing likely reached an apex with Revivalism, almost to the extent that the political identity of the state was lost and it became enveloped in cultural and creedal obscurity, and accordingly, came to be viewed from a *fiqh* 'philosophical' perspective. This confused theoretical amalgam which nullified boundaries in Islamic thought between the state and authority (or the political system) and the discussion of them as being analogs. The like of this is exactly what transpired with its salient implication – bringing down political identity – in the absence of viewing the state in a socio-political context but rather as an analog of the *ummah* and the group.

What is certain is that the thinkers of Islam – both modern and contemporary – did not deal with the state as a theoretical problematic, and they did not inquire into its political identity in national society; but rather they turned away from that completely as though its theoretical definition were at the level of axiom. In contrast, they endeavored to discuss two relations from it: its relation to the religion and its relation to the *ummah* from the standpoint of it being an axiom. This was among the reasons for the poverty of their approach, especially among the thinkers of the twentieth century, where what dominated their approach were appeals to cultural questions – extrinsic to the question of state – such as the question of identity and bringing down from on high into the field of thinking about the state! However this complete absence of dealing theoretically and independently with the question of the state did not even so much as drive towards a reductive concept of the two relations; rather, it drove to thinking about the state from the perspective of authority (*sulṭah*), or rather say, from the supposition that the state was an authority – only an authority!

The Islamists did not consider the state as being only an entity suspended above the field of political, social and cultural practice only; rather, they reduced it to a device amenable to possession as an object, ownership and use; or in other words, to an authority where there was a struggle to control it in order to realize a goal or political initiative. Thus, to some extent, they endeavored to think about the Islamic political system on account of that being thinking about the Islamic state, reproducing a conceptual instrumentalism (Conception instrumentaliste) for the state in which Bolshevik-Marxism had preceded them.[4] Thus, rather than connect the state to society – on account of its being a condensation of its contradictions and the relations of force within it[5] – they tethered it to the concept 'the religion' and the elite of the *ahl al-ḥal wa al-ʿaqd*, and the qualified *fuqahāʾ* – in the case of the *Shīʿah*, just as the Marxists had done when they connected it to the concept of 'Socialism' and a social class – the 'Proletariat'.

The tendency was magnified to the extent that it abandoned the boundaries and separations between the state and authority for the turning of Islamic thought towards the Revivalist idea ever since the end of the 1920s. However it took on a new form in constructing a creedal perspective for the state and for politics and authority and forsaking its political conception. The state would never be in this view possessed of a political dimension representing the national context and solidifying its contradictions; rather it would become a cultural identity analogous to the meaning of the *ummah* itself! The clearest expression of that is the thesis being expressed as being 'religious' – an Islamic state. That is, the state would no longer be a transcendent entity and a principle for regulating the political and the social, but rather it became an essence delimited by a principle higher than itself and its function – where there would no longer be an identity or existence for it except through it. In the expansion of this apolitical 'creedal' view of the state, the Revivalist thinkers produced, in reality, a thought about the *ummah* and the group and not about the state!

That does not mean that the state does not derive from the *ummah* or that it has no connection to it when this connection is extant and fixed in the entity of the state; however, the *ummah* to which this connection is made – from the standpoint of the state – is not a cultural or religious entity, but rather a dual social-political entity in the first instance and the state is not correlated to the *ummah* except according to this meaning; and if not, it transforms into another analog for the religious message: into a state that resembles the religious state of the Christian Church in the Middle Ages – containing within it the concept that, for the state, the point of departure is not to think about it as national society (or civil political society), but rather is to conceive of it from within religious society. And, the reason for that is that it will inevitably be transformed into a cultural problematic and into a branch of the original problematic which is the problematic of identity![6]

– 4 –

The history of modern and contemporary Islamic thought is a history of disjuncture; every intellectual moment is severed from the previous one: Reformism – for instance – represented a split from the *fiqh* of 'Islamic legal politics'; the Salafism of Rāshid Riḍā effected an initial split from Reformism, the Revivalism of Ḥasan al-Bannā even effected a dual split from both Reformism and Riḍā's Salafism; the discourse of '*al-ḥākimīyah*' and *al-takfīr* – again – represented a split from Muslim Brotherhood discourse; the '*wilāyat al-faqīh*' – on the other hand – was a breakaway from Reformist Shī'ite discourse: that of *al-mashrūṭah*. However, the degrees of disjuncture varied among all of these, depending on the extent and geography each one of these splits has delineated: so, while Riḍā's split was once without limits, his split from Reformism became limited to one thesis (*al-khilāfah* or *al-imāmah al-'uẓmā*), and as for al-Bannā's split from Riḍā and Reformism it had certain limits revolving around his defense of a constitutional and parliamentary system; we may find Quṭb's 'Revivalist' split from Reformism, and what emanated from its essence later, was so limitless and complete that it left no doubt or confusion for anyone that there is a total divorce between the two. This is also true with the splitting of the '*wilāyat al-faqīh*'[7] from the '*wilāyat al-ummah 'alā nafsihā*': which was espoused in al-Nā'īnī's constitutional Shī'ite *fiqh*. Thus, the most decisive intellectual separation that occurred in the history of modern Islamic thought that really merits description as a 'split', was the split engendered by '*al-ṣaḥwah*' – the split of the movement of Revivalism from that of Reformism, which ultimately precipitated the demolition and destruction of the Islamic legacy of the Arab *Nahḍah*' (Renaissance) from the 1830s up to the early 1920s.[8]

The split of the Revivalist discourse of the *Ṣaḥwah* from the Reformist was clearly manifested in the total departure from the idea of the nation state and the legacy of modern political human thought, and in the re-interpretation of the concept of the Islamic state – '*al-dawlah al-islāmīyah*' – in which it was transformed to a theocratic state. This departure was not merely a superficial conceptual substitution; in fact, it was a total intellectual coup against foundations and preliminary conditions that produced the discourse of Islamic *Ṣaḥwah*. Thus, the Revivalist movement of the *Ṣaḥwah* reconsidered politics in the Islamic consciousness: in regard to an Islamic creedal position with regard to politics and state, and the position of clerics in authoritative power! Politics – for this movement – is no longer among the tangential derivations of *al-fiqhīyyāt* or *al-furū'*, but rather among the original sources of the *uṣūl* of the religion. Also, functions of *fuqahā'* are no longer religious, but rather are political. In short, the Sunni conceptualization, itself, for politics and state, was entirely reconsidered when it had been a subject of study by Muslims and *fuqahā'* throughout all times!

The departure took place – thus – from the general Sunni *fiqh* legacy as a whole and not merely the Reformist legacy, the clue to this, is the openness of the Revivalist movement to ideas of the *imāmah* and the 'Rawāfiḍ' – as the Sunni *fuqahā'* prefer to call them – and arraying their thoughts with concepts of 'Islamic legal politics'! Simply by noticing who the referential authorities – *marāji'* – of modern Revivalist movement were, one can infer the kind of Islam they were spreading: the Islam of al-Mawdūdī and al-Nadawī that defended the Muslim group (*jamā'at al-muslimīn*) in the '*dār al-kufr*' (India), and had ambitions to render it among the '*dār al-Islām*' after migration to it (Pakistan). What formulated that was the factor of the creedal-theological dichotomies such the 'ignorant society' verses the 'Muslim society' ('*al-mujtama' al-jāhilī*'/'*al-mujtama' al-islāmī*'), or the 'domain of war' and the 'domain of Islam' ('*dār al-ḥarb*'/'*dār al-Islām*'); the utilization of such dichotomies facilitated, in turn, further linguistic and dogmatic dichotomies such as: unbelief/faith, unbelief/jihad (*al-kufr/al-imān*, *al-kufr/al-jihād*) and so on, to end in the preparation of volatile political and intellectual *milieu* that is liable to explode into strife!

The Reformist movement attempted to implement Islam for the purpose of progress and integration in the new world, whereas the Revivalist movement endeavored to achieve a full withdrawal from history[9] and to restrict Islam to defensive positions whenever the balance of civilizational force was taken into consideration! The result was that Reformism drew a positive role for Islam in modern universal history, as a creed and a culture, meanwhile Revivalism – at best – transformed it into political ideology that is incompatible with modernization and history! Thus its splitting from Reformism was also a split with modern times given that the Reformist *Nahḍah* emerged as the result of the first intellectual attempt by Muslims to achieve a balanced and constructive interaction with the changes of the world after the collapse of their civilization. In this sense, if the Reformist movement was a cry of appeal, the Revivalist was a death rattle!

– 5 –

Again, history of Islamic political thought tends to be diminishing and declining in nature as we advance onwards in time, rates of production and diligence dropped to frightening levels. The distance – today – between Muḥammad ʿAbdūh or al-Kawākibī and ʿAbd al-Salām Faraj or ʿAlī Bilḥajāj is astronomical, it is the same distance – in Iran – between al-Nāʾīnī and Taskhīrī; in fact, it is the same distance – all over the Islamic world – between al-Afghānī and the ʿArab Afghans': the lords of war and *fatwas* in (permitting) the spilling of the blood of Muslims! Contemporary Islam embarked on a cumbersome task – although audacious – to breath life into reason, *ijtihād*, and *al-shūrā* and openness to all the fruits of human thought; then its determination faltered and feebleness crept into its depth to end up today as nothing more than thoughts that reject civilization under the pretext that civilization is a product of atheism. Now, it calls for resurrecting the dead and killing the living; it consecrates illiteracy on the pretext that the Prophet was illiterate! Indeed, we shifted hastily from the age of intellects (Reformists) to the age of (political) apologists, and most recently to the age of warlords within *dār al-Islām* and authors writing on the punishment of the grave and the Day of Resurrection! History is no longer a history, Islamic thought is no longer a history, today, it has become ahistorical!

The issue of culture and education alone cannot explain such a retrograde and devolving path, even though it is one of its primary causes;[10] events of political transformation – through the last century – also cast light on other explanations. Many international political factors combined with modern universal variables (the massive triumph of Western civilization and its material and intellectual apparatus); and other regional political factors with their flagrant realities (the emergence and rooting of positive political systems in Islamic countries); this resulted in making Islam: as a creed, culture and communities take up a defensive position against such a victory. The problem is that this defensive position was not only political, or say, was not confined to this limit, but also ultimately became a defensive position culturally-speaking! Due to this, one of the most rampant manifestations of contemporary Islam to the continuous onslaught of realities from the outside world is opposition and resistance of political-party Islam; this trend drifted towards introversion, constriction and introversion of the Islamic consciousness. The equation became most manifest and clear: whenever the attack of modernity (social, political and intellectual) against Islam escalated, rates of decline and constriction increased proportionally!

This might explain the grave intellectual hemorrhaging – unprecedented in its acuteness even in comparison to the darkest moments in Medieval history – that has beset contemporary Islamic reason, in which it has lost many of its brain cells and vital elements rendering it so weak and emaciated that it is poignant to behold.

– 6 –

This decline in Islamic political reason unleashed – during the last quarter of the century – a correctional backlash by diligent intellects; they could not tolerate witnessing such tragic results of partisanship in Islamic thought, that transform it from a unifying idea into an ideology that tears apart and fragments entities of community and *ummah*, they also could not bear how obstacles and walls – in front of creativity and diligence in understanding variables of reality and dealing with them accordingly – were thrown up in the consciousness of the Islamists. This backlash resulted in criticism of varying degrees of the contemporary Islamic intellectual legacy, from the Muslim Brotherhood's foundational moment up to this day, although most of this criticism was directed against the last period which began in the first half of the 1960s, during which concepts of '*al-jāhilīyah*', '*al-ḥākimīyah*' and '*wilāyat al-faqīh*' emerged. Many Islamic scholars unaffiliated with Islamist movements enrolled in this intellectual workshop of criticism: a workshop of theoretical review of dominant concepts and hypotheses in contemporary Islam's arena. Others who participated in this workshop are those writers who withdrew from Islamic organizational frameworks and those who are trying to accomplish this review from political organizational positions or from new positions achieved after departure from other frameworks or the dissolution of others.

Maybe the most important outcome of such criticism and review is the return to modern Islamic intellectual fundamentals: their theoretical antecedents, concepts, problematics, and preoccupations, in this way; overcoming all the subsequent legacy produced by the second and third generations of the Muslim Brotherhood since the second half of the twentieth century by considering that it had departed from these fundamentals, established different assumptions of its own, and produced an idea within its closed structure. The reader of this new movement of critical review will notice that 'this return to modern fundamentals' took two forms: the form of returning back to 'fundamentals' which is close in definition to the thought of Ḥasan al-Bannā, and the other form is the return to 'fundamentals' that are remote from Islamic Reformist thought.

Those who returned Islamic thought to its Muslim Brotherhood origins: realistic and open, are mostly Muslim Brothers who are loyal to al-Bannā's thought and others who are – up to this day – operating within the framework of Islamic politics. Writings of al-Ghazālī, Yūsuf al-Qaraḍāwī, and some of his pupils, about Islam, state, the Islamic *Ṣaḥwah* and other related topics are good examples of this return. And, if this return was total in the instances mentioned above, it was partial in instances where Islamist apologists found in al-Bannā's writings a moderately acceptable foundation to build upon with various political inferences. This was true – with preservation of themes – between 'Abd al-Salām Yāsīn – the mystic – and Rāshid al-Ghanūshī – the rational, and 'Alī Abdullah al-Nafīsī – the chauvinist. Again, this was true with Islamist writers who maintained a distance within political fields such as: Fahmī Huwaydī, Muḥammad Salīm al-'Awā, Țāriq al-Bishrī, Aḥmad Kamāl Abū al-Majd, Mūnir Shafīq and others. However, they see in al-Bannā's theses in politics a realistic text that supports an Islamic model in politics and state that does not conflict with modernization or progress.

As for those who returned Islamic thought to its Reformist fundamentals, they were mostly independent scholars[11] who held belief that Islamist partisanship had a sabotaging role in considering Islamist thought a cliché, and they restored consideration to methods of scientific research and Islamist Reformism itself. Fahmī Jad'ān, Raḍwān al-Sayyid, Muḥammad 'Amārah, Wajīh Kawtharānī (in an earlier stage) and to some degree Aḥmad Mousalli and Muḥammad Fatḥī 'Uthmān were the most prominent examples in this context, restoring Islamic Reformism to its position in thought. Even those who returned to al-Bannā's thought did a great favor to Islamic politics by reshaping what is possible, however, those who returned to Reformism provided an even greater intellectual service to Arab and Islamic thought, and they opened wider horizons for studying its problems concerning the nexus between what is religious and what is political.

Is it enough to return to Reformism to put it as a realistic authoritatively referential conceptual rubric for the review of the contemporary Islamic intellectual legacy?

For many, this seemed to be a new Salafism. However, it is only a false impression, because the Reformist paradigm of the nineteenth century did not achieve anything to permit it to be described as *salafist*! It was aborted 75 years ago, and we do not think that this abortion resulted in killing historical legitimacy. Indeed, Reformism might not be beneficial in its previous form, however – undoubtedly – it is the only Islamic legacy in this age upon which to build.

Notes

1. 'Brotherhood' here – is not meant as the modern Islamic intellectual legacy which was produced by the movement of 'Muslim Brotherhood' (texts of its intellects specifically), we meant rather the legacy which was established on the basis of al-Bannā's thought and 'the Brotherhood', many participated in the process of its production, however not all were affiliates or became prominent figures among the movement.

2. It is a double deficiency: in regard to the *fiqh* of 'Islamic legal politics' and in regard to the discourse of modern Islamic Reformism.

3. This beset *fuqahā'* in the Medieval ages: they did the very same thing. So that the *fuqahā'* did not reach the idea of representation or the possibility of having the majority represent the whole. They kept on pursuing this in the group and *ijmā'* and they continued to hold the concept of *ahl al-ḥal wa-'aqd* which undermines the meaning of the *wilāyat al-ummah 'alā nafsihā* . Available at: Al-Sayyid, *Sīyāsāt al-Islām*, p. 272.

4. Poulantzas, *L'Etat, le Pouvoir et le Socialisme,* politiques (Paris: Presses Universitaires de France, 1978).

5. Poulantzas, *Pouvoir Politique et le Classes Socialisme* (Paris: Maspéro, 1980), vol. 1, pp. 51–2.

6. Al-Sayyid was quite right when he considered Islamic movements as revivalist; religious and cultural at their core and that they tend towards politics nowadays is due

to subsequent social and political crises. Available in: Al-Sayyid, *Sīyāsāt al-Islām*, pp. 190–1.

7. We shall include in this context and the one that follows the idea of *wilāyat al-faqīh* within '*al-ṣaḥwah*' movement.

8. There is no doubt that al-Bannā and the Muslim Brotherhood's thought was leading the thought of *ṣaḥwah*. However, the legacy of '*al-ḥākimīyah*', *al-takfīr, jihad* and '*wilāyat al-faqīh*' widened the chasm between the two in an irreparable fashion. It is necessary, thus, to consider al-Bannā's discourse, as it is a transitional moment in the discourse of *ṣaḥwah* more than being part of its legacy; similarly the writings of al-Bannā's pupils, today, compel us to consider them being an attempt to return this *ṣaḥwah* to its Brotherhood point of departure, which is clearly described by al-Qaraḍāwī and others in the concept of '*tarshīd al-ṣaḥwah*'!

9. '...Reformists want to be involved in the world and participate in civilization, with their Islam of course, not to confront modernization or the world, but rather to live within values shared by all religions and civilizations...whereas Revivalists seek separation and distinction from the world.' Available in: Al-Sayyid, *Sīyāsāt al-Islām*, p. 182.

10. The Islamist movement transformed Islam from a creed which was the particular concern of a part of the society: the '*ulamā*', *fuqahā*' and scholars, to a general or generalized culture joined by whoever utters the two professions of faith in Islam. For this reason, there has been huge damage as everyone who has superficial (partisan) knowledge has a say in it. Naturally, the new converts or latecomers would probably choose bullets, axes, swords and verbal abuse as their approach since they have no other weapons of dialogue with their opponents!

11. al-Ghanūshī is unique among his fellow apologists and politicians in that he returns to Reformist fundamentals.

References

'Abd al-Fattāḥ, Nabīl, *al-Muṣḥaf wa al-Sayf: Ṣirā' al-Dīn wa al-Dawlah fī Miṣr* (Cairo: Maktabat Madbūlī, 1984).
'Abd al-Jabbār, Fāliḥ, *al-Māddīyah wa al-Fikr al-Dīnī al-Mu'āṣir* ([n.p.]: Markaz al-Abḥāth wa al-Dirāsāt al-Ishtirākīyah,1985).
'Abd al-Laṭīf, Kamāl, *fī Tashrīḥ Uṣūl al-Istibdād: Qirā'ah fī Niẓām al-Ādāb al-Sulṭānīyah* (Beirut: Dār al-Ṭalī'ah, 1999).
'Abd al-Laṭīf, *al-Ta'wīl wa al-Mufāraqah: Naḥwa Ta'ṣīl Falsafī li-l-Naẓar al-Sīyāsī al-'Arabī* (Beirut; Casablanca: al-Markaz al-Thaqāfī al-'Arabī, 1987).
'Abd al-Rāziq, 'Alī, *al-Islām wa Uṣūl al-Ḥukm* (Beirut: Dār Maktabat al-Ḥayyāh, 1978).
'Abdūh, Muḥammad, *al-A'māl al-Kāmilah*, edited by Muḥammad 'Amārah (Beirut: al-Mu'asasah al-'Arabīyah li-al-Dirāsāt wa al-Nashr, 1972–3).
Volume 1: *al-kitābāt al-Sīyāsīyah.*
Volume 2: *al-kitābāt al-Ijtimā'īyah.*
Volume 3: *al-Iṣlāḥ al-Fikrī wa al-Tarbawī wa al-Ilāhīyāt.*
Volume 4: *fī Tafsīr al-Qur'ān.*
Volume 5: *fī Tafsīr al-Qur'ān.*
Abrahamian, Ervand, *Iran between Two Revolutions* (Princeton, NJ: Princeton University Press, 1982).
Al-Afghānī, Jamāl al-Dīn, *al-A'māl al-Kāmilah*, edited by Muḥammad 'Amārah (Beirut: al-Mu'asasah al-'Arabīyah li-al-Dirāsāt wa al-Nashr, 1981).
Al-'Alawī, Sa'īd bin-Sa'īd, *Dawlat al-Khilāfah: Dirāsah fī al-Tafkīr al-*

Sīyāsī 'inda al-Mawardī, Silsilat al-Uṭrūḥāt wa al-Rasā'il, no. 6 (Rabat: Kullīyat al-Ādāb wa al-'Ulūm al-Insānīyah, [n.d.]).

Al-'Alawī, *al-Īdyulujīyā wa al-Ḥadāthah: Qirā'āt fī al-Fikr al-'Ārabī al-Mu'āṣir* (Beirut; Casablanca: al-Markaz al-Thaqāfī al-'Arabī, 1987),

Al-'Alawī, *al-Ijtihād wa al-Taḥdīth: Dirāsah fī Uṣūl al-Fikr al-Salafī fī al-Maghrib*, Silsilat al-Fikr al-Islāmī al-Mu'āṣir, no. 3 (Malta: Centre for Muslim World Studies, 1992).

Al-'Alawī, *Uruppa fī Mir'āt al-Riḥlah: Ṣūrat al-Ākhar fī Adab al-Riḥlah al-Maghribīyah al-Mu'āṣirah*, Silsilat Buḥūth wa Dirāsāt, no.12 (Rabat: Kullīyat al-Ādāb wa al-'Ulūm al-Insānīyah, 1995).

'Alī, Ḥaydar Ibrāhīm, *al-Tayārāt al-Islāmīyah wa Qaḍīyat al-Dīmūqrāṭīyah* (Beirut: Centre for Arab Unity Studies, 1996).

Althusser, Louis, *Lire 'le capital'* (Paris: Maspéro, 1965).

Althusser, *Positions, 1964–1975* (Paris: Editions Sociales, 1976).

Althusser, *Pour Marx* (Paris: Maspéro, 1965).

'Amārah, Muḥammad, *al-Dawlah al-Islāmīyah- Bayn al-'Ilmānīyah wa al-Sulṭah al-Dīnīyah* (Cairo; Beirut: Dār al-Shurūq, 1988).

Amīn, Aḥmad, *Ḍuḥā al-Islām*, 10th ed. (Beirut: Dār al-Kitāb al-'Arabī, [n.d.]).

Amīn, *Zu'amā' al-Iṣlaḥ fī al-'Aṣr al-Ḥadīth* (Cairo: Maktabat al-Nahḍah al-Miṣrīyah, [n.d.]).

Al-Andalusī, 'Aydūs al-'Alawī [Ibn Darwīsh], *Shawāhid al-Tanzīl li-man Khuṣṣa bil-Tafḍīl* (Qom: al-Mujama' al-'Ālamī li-Ahl al-Bayt, 1996).

Al-Anṣārī, Ḥamīd, *Ḥadīth al-Inṭilāq: Naẓrah fī al-Ḥayāt al-'Ilmīyah wa al-Sīyāsīyah lil-Imām al-Khumaynī: (min al-Wilādah wa ḥattā al-'Urūj)*, 2nd ed. (Tehran: Mu'asasat Tanẓīm wa Nashr Turāth al-Imām al-Khumaynī, 1996).

Al-Anṣārī, Muḥammad Ḥussayn, *al-Imāmah wa al-Ḥukūmah fī al-Islām* (Tehran: Maṭbū'āt Maktabat al-Najāḥ, 1998).

Al-Anṣārī, Murtaḍā, *al-makāsib*, edited by al-Sayyid Muḥammad klāntir (Beirut: Mu'asasat al-Nūr, 1990).

Al-'Arawī, 'Abdullah, *Mafhūm al-'Aql: Maqālah fī al-Mufāraqāt* (Beirut; Casablanca: al-Markaz al-Thaqāfī al-'Arabī, 1997).

Al-'Arawī, *Mafhūm al-Dawlah* (Casablanca: al-Markaz al-Thaqāfī al-'Arabī, 1983).

Al-'Arawī, *Mafhūm al-Īdyulujīyā- al-Adlajah* (Casablanca: al-Markaz al-Thaqāfī al-'Arabī, 1980).

Al-'Arawī, *Mafhūm al-Ḥurīyah* (Casablanca: al-Markaz al-Thaqāfī al-'Arabī, 1981).

Arkoun, Mohammed, *L'Islam, Morale et Politique* (Paris: Desclée de Brouwer, 1986).

Arkoun, *Pour une Critique de la Raison Islamique,* Islam d'hier et d'aujourd'hui, no. 24 (Paris: Maisonneuve et Larose, 1984).

Al-Ash'arī, Abū al-Ḥasan 'Alī bin Ismā'īl, *Maqālāt al-Islāmīyīn wa Ikhtilāf al-Muṣalīn*, edited by Muḥammad Muḥyī al-Dīn 'Abd al-Ḥamīd, 2nd ed. (Cairo: Maktabat al-Nahḍah al-Miṣrīyah, 1969).

Al-'Ashmāwī, Muḥammad Sa'īd, *al-Islām al-Sīyāsī,* 2nd ed. (Algiers: Mūfam; Casablanca: Tansīft, 1991).

'Awdah, 'Abd al-Qādir, *al-Tashrī' al-Jinā'ī al-Islāmī Muqāranan bil-Qānūn al-Waḍ'ī,* Silsilat al-Thaqāfah al-'Āmmah (Cairo: Maktabat Dār al-'Urūbah, 1960).

Al-'Aẓmah, 'Azīz, *Al-'Ilmānīyah min Manẓūr Mukhtalif* (Beirut: Center of Arab Unity Studies, 1992).

Badie, Bertrand, *Culture et Politique,* collection politique comparée (Paris: Economica, 1983).

Badie, *Les Deux Etats: Pouvoir et Société en Occident et en Terre d'Islam,* l'Espace du Politique (Paris: Fayard, 1986).

Al-Bannā, Ḥasan, *Majmū'at Rasā'il al-Imām al-Shahīd Ḥasan al-Bannā* (Beirut: al-Mu'asasah al-Islāmīyah, [n.d]).

Bārūt, Muḥammad Jamāl, *Yathrib al-Jadīdah: al-Ḥarakāt al-Islāmīyah al-Rāhinah* (London: Rīyaḍ al-Rayyis, 1994).

Belkeziz, Abdelilah, *Fī al-Bad' kanat al-Thaqāfah: Naḥwa Wa'ī 'Arabī Mutajadid bi-l-Mas'alah al-Thaqāfīyah* (Casablance; Beirut: Dār Afrīqīyah al-Sharq, 1998).

Belkeziz, *Ishkālīyat al-Marja' fī al-Fikr al-'Arabī al-Mu'āṣir* (Beirut: Dār al-Muntakhab al-'Arabī, 1992).

Belkeziz, *Al-Islām wa al-Sīyāsah: Dawr al-Ḥarakah al-Islāmīyah fi Ṣawgh al-Majāl al-Sīyāsī* (Beirut: al-Markaz al-Thaqāfī al-'Arabī, 2001).

Belkeziz, *al-Khiṭāb al-Iṣlāḥī fī al-Maghrib: al-Takwīn wa al-Maṣādir 1844–1918*, Fikr 'Arabī Mu'āṣir (Beirut: Dār al-Muntakhab al-'Arabī, 1997)

Belkeziz, *Al-'Unf wa al-Dīmuqraṭīyah*, 2nd ed. (Beirut: Dār al-Kunūz al-Adabīyah, 2000).

Bettelheim, Charles, *Les Luttes de classes en URSS* (Paris: Maspéro; Seuil, 1974).

Al-Bishrī, Ṭāriq, *Al-Ḥiwār al-Islāmī al-'Ilmānī, fī al-Mas'alah al-Islāmīyah al-Mu'āṣirah* (Cairo; Beirut: Dār al-Shurūq, 1996).

Al-Bishrī, *Al-Malāmiḥ al-'Āmah li-al-Fikr al-Sīyāsī al-Islāmī fī al-Tārīkh al-Mu'āṣir, fī al-Mas'alah al-Islāmīyah al-Mu'āṣirah* (Cairo; Beirut: Dār al-Shurūq, 1996).

Carré, Olivier, *Mystique et Politique: Lecture Révolutionnairre du Coran par Sayyid Qutub, Frère Musulman radical,* Patrimoines Islam (Paris: Cerf; Presses de la Fondation Nationale des Sciences Politique, 1984).

Carré and Dumont, Paul, *Radicalisme Islamiques* (Paris: L'Harmattan, 1985).

Corbin, Henry, *En Islam Iranien: Aspects Spirituels et Philosophiques* (Paris: Gallimard, 1971–2).
Volume 1: *Le Shi'isme duodécimain.*

Corm, Georges, *Ta'addud al-Adyān wa Anẓimat al-Ḥukm: Dirāsah Susīyulujīyah wa Qānūnīyah Muqāranah*, 2nd edn (Beirut: : Dār al-Nahār li-al-Nashr, 1992).

Darwīsh, Ṣāliḥ Q., 'Rāshid al-Ghanūshī', *Silsilat al-Ḥiwār* (Casablanca: Manshūrat al-Furqān, 1993).

Al-Dawlah wa al-Khilāfah fī al-Khiṭāb al-'Arabī ibbān al-Thawrah al-Kamālīyah fī Turkīyah, Rashīd Riḍā- 'Alī 'Abd al-Rāziq- 'Abd al-Raḥmān al-Shāhbandar: Dirāsah wa nuṣūṣ, Study and preface by Wajīh Kawtharānī, Silsilat al-Turāth al-'Arabī (Beirut: Dār al-Ṭalī'ah, 1996).

Djaît, Hichem, *L'Europe et l'Islam,* collections esprit (Paris: Seuil, 1978).

Djaît, *La Grande Discorde: Religion et Politique dans l'Islam des Origines,* Bibliothèque des Histoires (Paris: Gallimard, 1989).

Djaît, *La Personnalité et le Devenir Arabo-Islamique,* collection esprit (Paris: Seuil, 1974).

Dyāb, Muḥammad Ḥāfiẓ, *Sayyid Quṭb: al-Khiṭāb wa al-Īdyulujīyā*, 2nd edn (Beirut: Dār al-Ṭalī'ah, 1988).

Faḍl Allah, Muḥammad Ḥussayn, *al-Ḥarakah al-Islāmīyah- Ḥumūm wa Qaḍāyā*, 3rd edn (Beirut: Dār al-Malāk, 1993).

Faḍl Allah, 'al-Qīyādah al-Islāmīyah fī Dākhil al-Dawlah', *al-Thaqāfah al-Islāmīyah,* no. 37 (May/June 1991).

Al-Fanjarī, Aḥmad Shawqī, *Kayfa Naḥkum bil-Islām fī Dawlah 'Aṣrīyah* (Cairo: al-Hay'ah al-Miṣrīyah al-'Āmmah lil-Kitāb, 1990).

Al-Fāsī, 'Allāl, *Difā' 'an al-Sharī'ah* (Rabat: [n.pb.], 1966).

Al-Fāsī, *al-Ḥarakāt al-Istiqlālīyah fi al-Maghrib al-'Arabī* (Tangier, 'Abd al-Salām Jasūs, 1948).

Al-Fāsī, *Maqāṣid al-sharī'ah al-Islāmīyah wa Makārimuhā* (Casablanca: Maktabat al-Wiḥdah al-'Arabīyah, 1963).

Al-Fāsī, *al-Naqd al-Dhātī,* 2nd edn (Tiṭwān, Morocco: Dār al-Fikr al-Maghribī, [n.d]).

Gardet, Louis, *La Cité Musulmane: Vie Sociale et Politique* (Paris: Vrin, 1961).
Ghalyūn, Burhān, *Ightīyāl al-'Aql: Miḥnat al-Thaqāfah al-'Arabīyah bayn al-Salafīyah wa al-Taba'īyah* (Beirut: Dār al-Tanwīr, 1985).
Ghalyūn, *Naqd al-Sīyāsah: al-Dawlah wa al-Dīn* (Beirut: al-Mu'asasah al-'Arabīyah lil-Dirāsāt wa al-Nashr, 1991).
Al-Ghanūshī, Rāshid, *Ḥuqūq al-Mūwāṭanah: Ḥuqūq Ghayr al-Muslim fī al-Mujtama' al-Islāmī* (Tunis: [n.pb.], 1989).
Al-Ghanūshī, *al-Ḥurīyāt al-'Āmmah fī al-Dawlah al-Islāmīyah* (Beirut: Centre for Arab Unity Studies, 1992–3).
Al-Ghazālī, Abū Ḥamid Muḥammad bin Muḥammad, *Tahāfut al-Falāsifah*, edited by Sulaymān Dunyā, Dhakhā'ir al-'Arab, 3rd edn (Cairo: Dār al-Ma'ārif, 1958).
Al-Ghazālī, Muḥammad, *al-Sunnah al-Nabawīyah bayn Ahl al-Fiqh... wa Ahl al-Ḥadīth* (Beirut: Dār al-Shurūq, 1989).
Al-Ḥajawī, Muḥammad Bin al-Ḥasan, *al-Fikr al-Sāmī fī Tārīkh al-Fiqh al-Islāmī* (Medina: al-Maktabah al-'ilmīyah, 1977).
Al-Hāshimī, Maḥmūd, *Naẓrah Jadīdah fī Wilāyat al-Faqīh*.
Ḥawwā, Sa'īd, *Jund Allāh: Thaqāfatan wa Akhlāqan*, 2nd ed. (Cairo: Dār al-Ṭibā'ah al-Ḥadīthah, 1977).
Haykal, Muḥammad Ḥasanayn, *Kharīf al-Ghaḍab: Qiṣṣat Bidāyat wa Nihāyat 'Aṣr Anwar al-Sādāt*, 2nd edn (Beirut: Sharikat al-Maṭbū'āt, 1983).
Al-Huḍaybī, Ḥasan Ismā'īl, *Du'āt.....Lā Quḍāt: Abḥāth fī al-'Aqīdah al-Islāmīyah wa Manhaj al-Da'wah ilā Allāh*, 2nd edn (Cairo: Dār al-Ṭibā'ah wa al-Nashr al-Islāmīyah, 1977).
Al-Ḥusaynī, Muḥammad, 'al-Lutharīyah al-Mukhtalifah wa Mashrū' al-'Almanah al-Maz'ūmah', *al-Hadaf*, no. 22 (November 1992).
Hūwaydī, Fahmī, *al-Islām wa al-Dīmūqrāṭīyah* (Cairo: Markaz al-Ahrām, 1993).
Ibn Abī al-Ḍayyāf, Abū Zayd Aḥmad, *Itḥāf Ahl al-Zamān bi-Akhbār Mulūk Tūnis wa 'Ahd al-Amān* (Tunis: Kitābat al-Duwal li-al-Thaqāfah wa al-Akhbār, 1966).
Ibn Bādīs, 'Abd al-Ḥamīd, *Āthār Ibn Bādīs*, edited and compiled by 'Amār al-Ṭālibī (Algiers: Dār wa Maktabat al-Sharikah al-Jazā'irīyah, 1986).
Ibn Khaldūn, *al-Muqadimah* (Beirut: Dār al-Kitāb al-'Arabī, 1996).
Ibn Rushd, Abū al-Walīd Muḥammad bin Aḥmad, *Faṣl al-Maqāl fī Taqrīr mā bayn al-Sharī'ah wa al-Ḥikmah min Itiṣāl aw Wujūb al-Naẓar al-'Aqlī wa Ḥudūd al-Ta'wīl (al-Dīn wa al-Mujtama')*, preface by

Mohammed Abed al-Jabri, Silsilat al-Turāth al-Falsafī al-ʿArabī, Mu'alafāt Ibn Rushd (Beirut: Centre for Arab Unity Studies, 1997).

Ibn Taymīyah, Taqqī al-Dīn Aḥmad Bin ʿAbd al-Ḥalīm. *Iqtiḍā' al-Ṣirāṭ al-Mustaqīm Mukhālafat Aṣḥāb al-Jaḥīm.* Edited by ʿIṣām Fāris al-Ḥarastānī and Muḥammed Ibrāhīm al-Zaghlī (Beirut: Dār al-Jīl, 1993).

Ibn Taymīyah, *al-Sīyāsah al-Sharʿīyah fī Iṣlāḥ al-Rāʿī wa al-Raʿīyah* (Beirut: Dār al-Kutub al-ʿIlmīyah, 1988).

Al-Jabri, Mohammed Abed, *al-ʿAql al-Sīyāsī al-ʿArabī: Muḥadidātih wa Tajallīyātih* (Casablanca: al-Markaz al-Thaqāfī al-ʿArabī, 1990).

Al-Jabri, *Bunyat al-ʿAql al-ʿArabī: Dirāsah Taḥlīlīyah Naqdīyah li-Nuẓum al-Maʿrifah fī al-Thaqāfah al-ʿArabīyah.* 6th edn (Beirut: Centre for Arab Unity Studies, 2000).

Al-Jabri, *al-Khiṭāb al-ʿArabī al-Muʿāṣir: Dirāsah Taḥlīlīyah Naqdīyah* (Beirut: al-Markaz al-Thaqāfī al-ʿArabī; Dār al-Ṭalīʿah, 1982).

Jadʿān, Fahmī, *al-Māḍī fī al-Ḥāḍir: Dirāsah fī Tashakkulat wa Masālik al-Tajrubah al-Fikrīyah al-ʿArabīyah* (Beirut: al-Mu'asasah al-ʿArabīyah li-al-Dirāsāt wa al-Nashr, 1997).

Jadʿān, *Usus al-Taqqadum ʿinda Muffakirī al-Islām fī al-ʿĀlam al-ʿArabī al-Ḥadīth* (Beirut: al-Mu'asasah al-ʿArabīyah li-al-Dirāsāt wa al-Nashr, 1979).

Al-Jarjānī, ʿAlī bin Muḥammad al-Sharīf, *Kitāb al-Taʿrīfāt,* 3rd edn (Beirut: Dār al-Kitāb al-ʿArabī, 1996).

Al-Kawākibī,ʿAbd al-Raḥmān, *al-Aʿmal al-Kāmilah li-al-Kawākibī,* Silsilat al-Turāth al-Qawmī (Beirut: Centre for Arab Unity Studies, 1995).

Keppel, Gilles, *La Revanche de Dieu: Chrétiens, Juifs et Musulmans à la reconquête du monde* (Paris: Seuil, 1991).

Khālid, Khālid Muḥammad, *al-Dawlah fī al-Islām* (Cairo: Dār Thābit, 1981).

Khālid, *min Hunā Nabda',* 4th ed. (Cairo: Dār al-Nīl, 1950).

Khālidī, Ṣalāḥ ʿAbd al-Fattāḥ, *Sayyid Quṭb al-Shahīd al-Ḥay* (Amman: Maktabat al-Aqṣā, 1981).

Al-Khalīlī, Jaʿfar, *Madkhal ilā Mawsūʿat al-ʿAtabāt al-Muqadasah*, 2nd edn (Beirut: Mu'asasat al-Aʿlamī, 1987).

Khallāf, ʿAbd al-Wahhāb, *al-Sīyāsah al-Sharʿīyah aw Niẓām al-Dawlah al-Islāmīyah fī al-Shu'ūn al-Dustūrīyah wa al-Khārijīyah wa al-Mālīyah* (Cairo: al-Maṭbaʿah al-Salafīyah, 1931).

Al-Khomeini, Rūḥu Allāh al-Mūsawī, *al-Ḥukūmah al-Islāmīyah,* 2nd edn (Beirut: Markaz Baqīyat Allāh al-Aʿẓam, 1999).

Al-Khomeini, *al-Ijtihād wa al-Taqlīd* (Tehran: Mu'asasat Tanẓīm wa Nashr Turāth al-Imām al-Khumaynī, 1997),

Al-Khomeini, *al-Kawthar* (Tehran: Mu'asasat Tanẓīm wa Nashr Turāth al-Imām al-Khumaynī, 1996).
Al-Lārī, Mujtabā al-Mūsawī, *Dirāsah fī Usus al-Islām*, translated by Kamāl al-Sayyid (Qom: Markaz Nashr al-Thaqāfah al-Islāmīyah fī al-ʿĀlam, 1998).
Laroui, Abdallah, *La Crise des Intellectuels Arabes, Traditionalisme ou Historicisme?*, textes à l'appui'. Série Philosophie (Paris: Maspéro, 1978).
Laroui, *L'idéologie Arabe contemporaine,* preface by Maxime Rodinson, Fondations (Paris: Maspéro, 1982).
Laroui, *Islamisme, Modernisme, Libéralisme: Esquisses Critiques* (Casablanca: Centre Culturel Arabe, 1997).
Laroui, *Les Origines Sociales et Culturelles du Nationalisme Marocain, 1830–1912,* textes à l'appui' (Paris: Maspéro, 1980).
Laroui, *Les Origines Sociales*, 2nd ed. (Casablanca: Centre Culturel Arabe, 2001).
Lewis, Bernard, *The Emergence of Modern Turkey,* Oxford Paperbacks; no. 135, 2nd ed. (London: Oxford University Press, 1968).
Mabrūk, Muḥammad Ibrāhīm, *Mūwājahat al-Mūwājahah* (Cairo: Dār Thābit, 1994).
Maḥmūd, Zakī Najīb, *Tajdīd al-Fikr al-ʿArabī* (Beirut: Dār al-Shurūq, 1971).
Mantran, Robert, ed., *Histoire de l'Empire Ottoman,* translated by Bashīr al-Sibāʿī (Cairo: Dār al-Fikr, 1992–3).
Marx, Karl, *Le Capital* (Paris: Editions sociales, [n.d.]).
Al-Mawardī, Abū al-Ḥasan ʿAlī bin Muḥammad, *al-Aḥkām al-Sulṭānīyah wa al-Wilāyāt al-Dīnīyah* (Beirut: Dār al-Kutub al-ʿIlmīyah, [n.d.])
Al-Mawdūdī, Abū al-Aʿlā, *Naẓarīyat al-Islām wa Hadyih fī al-Sīyāsah wa al-Qānūn wa al-Dustūr* (Beirut: Mu'asasat al-Risālah, 1980).
Merad, Ali, *Le Réformisme Musulman en Algérie de 1925 à 1940: Essai d'Histoire Religieuse et Sociale,* Recherches Méditerranéennes (Paris: Mouton, 1967).
Merad, *Le Réformisme Musulman en Algérie*, 2nd ed. (Algiers: Editions el Hikma, 1999).
Mitchell, Richard P., *The Society of Muslim Brothers,* translated by ʿAbd al-Salām Raḍwān & Munā Anīs (Cairo: Maktabat Madbūlī, 1977).
Mousalli, Aḥmad, *al-Uṣūlīyah al-Islāmīyah: Dirāsah fī al-Khiṭāb al-Īdyulujī wa al-Sīyāsī ʿinda Sayyid Quṭb (Baḥth Muqāran li-Mabādiʾ al-Uṣūlīyīn wa al-Iṣlāḥīyīn* (Beirut: al-Nāshir, 1993).

Al-Mubārak, Muḥammad, *Niẓām al-Islām: al-Ḥukm wa al-Dawlah*, 4th edn (Beirut: Dār al-Fikr, 1981).

Muntaẓirī, Ḥussayn, *Dirāsāt fī Wilāyat al-Faqīh wa Fiqh al-Dawlah al-Islāmīyah,* 2nd edn (Beirut: al-Dār al-Islāmīyah, 1988).

Mūsā, Salāmah, *ma Hiya al-Nahḍah* (Cairo: Al-Hay'ah al-Miṣrīyah al-'Āmmah li-l-Kitāb, [n.d]).

Mūsā, *al-Tathqīf al-Dhātī aw kayfa Narā Anfusinā* (Cairo: Maṭba'at al-Taqaddum, [n.d]).

Al-Muẓaffar, Muḥammad Riḍā, *'Aqā'id al-imāmīyah,* edited by Ḥamid Ḥafnī Dāwūd (Tehran: Kitāb-khana Bazrak Islāmī, 1961).

Al-Muẓaffar, *Uṣūl al-Fiqh*, 3rd edn (Najaf: Maktabat al-Muẓaffar, 1971).

Al-Nadawī, Abū al-Ḥasan 'Alī al-Ḥasanī, *Mādhā Khasira al-'Ālam bi-Inḥiṭāṭ al-Muslimīn* (Kuwait: al-Markaz al-'Ālamī lil-Kitāb al-Islāmī, [n.d]).

Al-Narāqī, Aḥmad, *'Awā'id al-Ayām*, 3rd edn (Qom: Maktabat Baṣīratī, 1988).

Al-Narāqī, *Wilāyat al-Faqīh*, edited by Yāsīn al-Mūsawī (Beirut: Dār al-Ta'āruf, 1990).

Al-Nāṣirī, Abū al-'Abbās Aḥmad bin Khālid, *Al-Istiqṣā' li-Akhbār Duwal al-Maghrib al-'Arabī*, edited by Ja'far al-Nāṣirī and Muḥammad al-Nāṣirī (Casablanca: Dār al-Kitāb, 1954–6).

Omlīl, 'Alī, *Al-Iṣlāḥīyah al-'Arabīyah wa al-Dawlah al-Waṭanīyah* (Casablanca: al-Markaz al-Thaqāfī al-'Arabī; Beirut: Dār al-Tanwīr, 1985).

Poulantzas, Nicos, *Les Classes Socials dans le Capitalisme aujourd'hui*, collection sociologie politique (Paris: Seuil, 1974).

Poulantzas, *L'Etat, le Pouvoir et le Socialisme,* politiques (Paris: Presses Universitaires de France, 1978).

Poulantzas, *Pouvoir Politique et Classes Sociales* (Paris: Maspéro, 1980).

Al-Qaraḍāwī, Yūsuf, *al-Ḥal al-Islāmī: Farīḍah wa Ḍarūrah* ([n.p.]: [n.pb.], [n.d]).

Al-Qaraḍāwī, *al-Ḥilūl al-Mustawradah wa kayfa janat 'alā Ummatinā*, Silsilat Ḥatmīyat al-Ḥal al-Islāmī; (Beirut: Mu'asasah al-Risālah, 1971).

Al-Qaraḍāwī, *min Ajl Ṣaḥwah Islāmīyah Rāshidah* (Casablanca: Dār al-Ma'rifah, [n.d]).

Al-Qaraḍāwī, *min Fiqh al-Dawlah fī al-Islām* (Cairo; Beirut: Dār al-Shurūq, 1997).

Al-Qaraḍāwī, *al-Ṣaḥwah al-Islāmīyah* (Cairo: Dār al al-Ṣaḥwah, 1988).

Al-Qaraḍāwī, *al-Sīyāsah al-Shar'īyah fī Ḍaw' Nuṣūṣ al-Sharī'ah al-Islāmīyah wa Maqaṣiduhā* (Cairo: Maktabat Wahbah, 1998).

Quṭb, Muḥammad, *al-ʿIlmānyūn wa al-Islām* (Cairo; Beirut: Dār al-Shurūq, 1994).

Quṭb, Muḥammad, *Jāhilīyat al-Qarn al-ʿIshrīn* (Cairo: Dār al-Shurūq, 1980).

Quṭb, Sayyid, *Dirāsāt Islāmīyah*, 9th edn (Cairo; Beirut: Dār al-Shurūq, 1993).

Quṭb, Sayyid, *al-Islām wa Mushkilāt al-Ḥaḍārah*, 11th edn (Cairo; Beirut: Dār al-Shurūq, 1992).

Quṭb, Sayyid, *Maʿālim fī al-Ṭarīq*, 10th edn (Cairo; Beirut: Dār al-Shurūq, 1983).

Quṭb, Sayyid, *Maʿrakat al-Islām wa al-Raʾsmālīyah*, 13th edn (Cairo; Beirut: Dār al-Shurūq, 1993).

Quṭb, Sayyid, *al-Mustaqbal li-Hādhā al-Dīn*, 12th edn (Cairo; Beirut: Dār al-Shurūq, 1992).

Quṭb, Sayyid, *Naḥwa Mujtamaʿ Islāmī*, 10th edn (Cairo; Beirut: Dār al-Shurūq, 1993).

Redissi, Hamadi, *L'Exception Islamique, La Couleur des Idées* (Paris: Seuil, 2004).

Riḍā, Muḥammad Rashīd, *al-Khilāfah aw al-Imāmah al-ʿUẓmā: Mabāḥith Sharʿīyah Sīyāsīyah Ijtimāʿīyah Iṣlāḥīyah* (Cairo: Maṭbaʿat al-Manār, 1922).

Riḍā, *Mukhtārāt Sīyāsīyah min Majalat al-Manār*, Silsilat al-Turāth al-ʿArabī al-Muʿāṣir (Beirut: Dār al-Ṭalīʿah, 1980).

Roy, Olivier, *Les Illusions du 11 Septembre: Le Débat Stratégique Face au Terrorisme* (Paris: Seuil, 2002).

Al-Ṣadr, Muḥammad Bāqir, *Baḥth Ḥawl al-Wilāyah*, 3rd edn (Beirut: Dār al-Taʿāruf, 1981).

Al-Sayf, Tawfīq, *Ḍid al-Istibdād* (Beirut; Casablanca: al-Markaz al-Thaqāfī al-ʿArabī, 1999).

Al-Sayf and al-Nāʾīnī, Muḥammad Ḥussayn, 'Tanbīh al-Ummah wa tanzīh al-millah', in: *Ḍid al-Istibdād*: *al-Fiqh al-Sīyāsī al-Shīʿī fī ʿAṣr al-Ghaybah* (Beirut; Casablanca: al-Markaz al-Thaqāfī al-ʿArabī, 1999).

Sayyid Aḥmad, Rifʿat, *al-Nabī al-Musallaḥ*, (London/Beirut: Rīyaḍ al-Rayyis, 1991).
Volume 1: *al-Rāfiḍūn*.
Volume 2: *al-Thāʾirūn*.

Al-Sayyid, Raḍwān, *al-Jamāʿah wa al-Mujtamaʿ wa al-Dawlah* (Beirut: Dār al-Kitāb al-ʿArabī, 1997).

Al-Sayyid, *al-Ṣirāʿ ʿalā al-Islām: al-ʾUṣūlīyah wa al-Iṣlāḥ wa al-Sīyāsāt al-Dawlīyah* (Beirut: Dār al-Kitāb al-ʿArabī, 2004).

Al-Sayyid, *Sīyāsāt al-Islām al-Mu'āṣir: Murāja'āt wa Mutāba'āt* (Beirut: Dār al-Kitāb al-'Arabī, 1997).

Al-Sayyid, *al-Ummah wa al-Jamā'ah wa al-Sulṭah* (Beirut: Dār Iqra', 1984).

Shafīq, Munīr, *al-Islām wa Mūwājahat al-Dawlah al-Ḥadīthah*, 3rd ed. (Tunis: al-Nāshir; Dār al-Bayraq, 1992).

Al-Shahristānī, Abū al-Fatḥ Muḥammad bin 'Abd al-Karīm, *al-Milal wa al-Niḥal*, edited by Muḥammad Sayyid Gaylānī (Beirut: Dār al-Ma'rifah, 2000/1980).

Al-Shahristānī, *Nihāyat al-Aqdām fī 'Ilm al-Kalām,* edited by Alfred Guillaume (Baghdad: Maktabat al-Muthannā, [n.d.]).

Shams al-Dīn, Muḥammad Mahdī, *fī al-Ijtimā' al-Sīyāsī al-Islāmī: al-Mujtama' al-Sīyāsī al-Islāmī Muḥāwalat Ta'ṣīl Fiqhī wa Tārīkhī* (Qom: Dār al-Thaqāfah, 1994).

Shams al-Dīn, *Niẓām al-Ḥukm wa al-Idārah fī al-Islām,* 2nd ed. (Beirut: al-Mu'asasah al-Dawlīyah, 1991).

Shams al-Dīn, 'al-Mashrū' al-Sīyāsī al-Islāmī wa Āfāq al-Mustaqbal', *al-Ghadīr*, no. 14 and no. 16 (June 1991).

Al-Shāṭibī, Abū Isḥāq Ibrāhīm bin Mūsā, *al-Muwāfaqāt fī Uṣūl al-Aḥkām* (Beirut: Dār al-Fikr, [n.d.]).

Al-Shāṭibī and Riḍā, Muḥammad Rashīd, *al-I'tiṣām* (Cairo: al-Maktabah al-Tijārīyah al-Kubrā, 1913).

Al-Shīrāzī, Ḥasan, *Kalimat al-Imām al-Mahdī ('alayh al-salām)* (Beirut: Mu'asasat al-Wafā', 1983).

Al-Shīrāzī, Muḥammad, *al-Ḥukm fī al-Islām* ([n.p.]: [n.pb.], [n.d]).

Al-Sibā'ī, Muṣṭafā, *Ishtirākīyat al-Islām*, 2nd ed. (Damascus: Mu'asasat al-Maṭbū'āt al-'Arabīyah, 1960) (Cairo: al-Dār al-Qawmīyah li-l-Ṭibā'ah wa al-Nashr, 1960).

Stewart, Desmond, *The Middle East: Temple of Janus*, Translated to Arabic by Zuhdī Jār-Allah (Beirut: Dār al-Nahār li-l-Nashr, 1974).

Al-Sulaymānī, Abū 'Abdullah [al-A'raj], *al-Lisān al-Mu'rib 'an Tahāfut al-Ajnabī ḥawla al-Maghrib* ([n.p.]: [n.pb], [n.d.]).

Al-Ṭahṭāwī, Rufā'ah Rāfi', *al-A'māl al-Kāmilah li-Rufā'ah Rāfi al-Ṭahṭāwī,* edited by Muḥammad 'Amārah (Beirut: al-Mu'asasah al-'Arabīyah li-al-Dirāsāt wa al-Nashr, [1973–7]).
volume 1: *al-Tamaddun wa al-Ḥaḍārah wa al-'Umrān.*

Tozy, Mohamed, *Monarchie et Islam Politique au Maroc* (Paris: Presses de la Fondation Nationale des Sciences Politiques, 1999).

Al-Tūnisī, Khayr al-Dīn, *Aqwam al-Masālik fī Ma'rifat Aḥwāl al-Mamalik*, edited by Munṣif al-Shūfī, 2nd edn (Tunis: Al-Dār al-Tūnisīyah li-l-Nashr; Algeria: al-Mu'asasah al-Waṭanīyah li-al-Kitāb, 1972).

Al-Turābī, Ḥasan 'Abdullah, *Naẓarāt fī al-Fiqh al-Sīyāsī* (Khartoum: al-Sharikah al-'Ālamīyah li-Khadamāt al-I'lām, 1988).

'Uthmān, Muḥammad Fatḥī, *al-Tajrubah al-Sīyāsah lil-Ḥarakah al-Islāmīyah al-Mu'āṣirah: Durūs al-Māḍī wa Āfāq al-Mustaqbal*, publications of Markaz Dirāsāt al-Mustaqbal al-Islāmī (Algiers: Dār al-Mustaqbal, 1991).

Various, *Al-Mu'jam al-Fiqhī* (Qom: Markaz Al-Mu'jam al-Fiqhī fī Al-Ḥawzah al-'Ilmīyah, [n.d.]).

Various, papers presented at: *al-ḥarakāt al-Islāmīyah al-mu'āṣirah fī al-waṭan al-'Arabī,* 4th ed. (Beirut: Centre for Arab Unity Studies, 1998) (Maktabat al-Mustaqbalāt al-'Arabīyah al-Badīlah)

Various, papers presented at: *al-ḥiwār al-qawmī-al-dīnī*, conducted by Centre for Arab Unity Studies (Beirut: Centre for Arab Unity Studies, 1989),

Various, papers presented at: *al-'ilāqāt al-'arabīyah-al-īrānīyah: al-itijāhāt al-rāhinah wa āfāq al-mustaqbal: buḥūth wa munāqashāt al-nadwah al-fifrīyah,* conducted by Centre for Arab Unity Studies in cooperation with the University of Qatar (Beirut: Centre for Arab Unity Studies, 1996).

Yakan, Fatḥī, *Mushkilāt al-Da'wah wa al-Dā'īyah*, 3rd ed. (Beirut: Mu'asasat al-Risālah, 1974).

Yāsīn, 'Abd al-Salām, *Ḥiwār ma'a al-Fuḍalā' al-Dīmuqrāṭīyin* (Casablanca: al-Mu'alif, 1994).

Yāsīn, *al-Islām wa al-Qawmīyah al-'Ilmānīyah*, 2nd ed. (Ṭanṭā: Dār al-Bashīr li-al-Thaqāfah wa al-'Ilūm al-Islāmīyah, 1985).

Yāsīn, *al-Minhāj al-Nabawī: Tarbīyatan wa Tanẓīman wa Zaḥfan* ([n.p]: [n.pb.], [n.d.]).

Yāsīn, *al-Shūrā wa al-Dīmuqrāṭīyah* (Casablanca: Maṭbū'āt al-Ufuq, 1996).

Yassine, Abdessalam, *Islamiser la Modernité* (Rabat: Al-Ofok impressions, 1998).

Index

'Abd al-Ḥamīd II 29, 30, 72, 74
'Abd al-Raḥmān, 'Umar 16, 95
'Abd al-Rāziq, 'Ali 100–1, 106–7, 280
Islam and the Origin of Rule 98–9, 281
khilāfah 88, 95, 99–108
nation state 196
'Abdūh, Muḥammad
Cairo 43n9
civil authority 35–6, 39
education and culture 40
fiqh 18
khilāfah 107
Lighthouse, The 72
opposed to sultanate 28–9
Reformism 280
religious authority 27, 32–4, 243, 279
secularism 145
Absent Duty, The 211
absolute rulers 14
Abū Bakr al-Ṣiddīq 82, 106, 224, 226
accountability 19, 39, 55–6, 99–100, 127
Afghanistan xvi
Age of Occultation 49–53
ahl al-ḥal wa al-'aqd 82–4, 102–3, 108, 178, 179
Al-Afghānī, Jamāl al-Dīn xiii, 31–2
criticisms of sultanate 41–2
Islamic unity 29, 30, 271–2
Muslim unity 43n8
opposed to sultanate 28–9
reforms 279
revolution 41
secularism 145
Al-Anṣārī, Muḥammad Ḥussayn 224
Al-'Arawī, 'Abdullah 196
Al-Bannā, Ḥasan
constitution 129
Egyptian constitution 129–31
Islamic rule 122–3
Islamic state 121, 128–37, 143–5, 195–7
khilāfah 87–8
Muslim Brotherhood 119
partisanship 133–4, 136
political participation 132–3
political realism 198–9
politics and religion 125
Reformism 294
Revivalism 290
rule 119
sharī'ah 162
Al-Bishrī, Ṭāriq 198
Al-Brūjerdī (Ayatollah) 220
Al-Fāsī, 'Allāl
citizenship 183–4

constitution 154
ijtihād 159
Islam 155–6
Islamic state 145
Morocco 280
political representation 182
Self Criticism and the Intents of Islamic Sharī'ah and Its Excellences 281
sharī'ah 162–3
ummah 177
Al-Ghanūshī, Rāshid 171, 174, 180–1, 182, 253–4, 255
Al-Ghazālī, Muḥammad 83, 176, 179–80, 184–5, 268
Al-Ḥa'irī, 'Abd al-Karīm (Ayatollah) 220
al-ḥākimīyah
ascendancy 213
concept 205–13
criticisms 246–52
derivation 247–9
Islamic Discourse 290
political thought 215n40
theocracy 207
Al-Hāshimī, Maḥmūd 254–5
Al-Huḍaybī, Ḥasan 241, 246–7
Al-Jabri, Mohammed Abed 149
Al-Kāshānī (Ayatollah) 220
Al-Kawākibī, 'Abd al-Raḥmān
autocracy 38–40
freedom 27
Hallmarks of Autocracy and the Struggles of Enslavement, The 37, 49
khilāfah 107
opposed to sultanate 28–9
political autocracy 37, 279
Reformism 72
religious authority 243
ummah 46n49
al-Khilāfah aw al-Imāmah al-'Uẓmā 76, 78, 79, 84, 98
Al-Khomeini, Rūḥ-Allah al-Mūsawī (Ayatollah)
Al-Ghanūshī, Rāshid 255
faqīh 232–3
fuqahā' 219
leadership 221
legitimacy 231
ummah 225
Al-Khurāsānī, al-Ākhūnd Muḥammad Kāẓim (Ayatollah) 48, 63
al-Manār 89n15
Al-Mawardī, Abū al-Ḥasan 'Alī bin Muḥammad
bay'ah (pledge of allegiance) 81
governorship 90n25
imamate 71, 85–6
khilāfah 73, 80
Riḍā, Muḥammad Rashīd 87
Sultanate Rules 79
Al-Mawdūdī, Abū al-A'lā 205–7
Al-Māzindarānī (Ayatollah) 48
Al-Mubārak, Muḥammad 122
Al-Nabahānī, Taqqī al-Dīn 123
Al-Nadawī, Abū al-Ḥasan 'Alī al-Ḥasanī 203–4
Al-Nā'īnī, Muḥammad Ḥussayn
citizenship 61–2
constitution 56
ijtihād 222
imamate 256–7
infallibility 55
Islamic legal politics 57–8
political autocracy 37, 279
Tanbīh al-Ummah 53, 59
ummah 47
Warning to the Ummah and Admonition to the Denomination 48–9, 62–3
Al-Narāqī, Aḥmad 229, 233
Al-Qaraḍāwī, Yūsuf
al-sharī'ah 153–4
al-shūrā 178–9
citizenship 183–4
ijtihād 157–9
Islamic state 126–7, 144, 157, 162
khilāfah 123–4
Liberalism 191n30
secularism 150, 167n35

sharī'ah 86, 156
spiritual Islam 146
Western philosophy 150
Al-Ṣadr, Muḥammad Bāqir (Ayatollah) 227
Al-Sanhūrī, 'Abd al-Razzāq 280
Al-Sayyid Marsot, Lutfi 71, 91n33
Al-Sayyid, Raḍwān 4, 211–12, 250
al-sharī'ah 15
al-sharī'ah
ijtihād 155–61
implementation 152–63
khilāfah 96–7
meaning 154–5
political system 7
Tanẓīmāt (reforms) 28
Al-Sharīf al-Murtaḍā, Abū al-Qāsim
Matter of Dealing with the Sultan, A 52
Al-Shāṭibī, Abū Isḥāq Ibrāhīm bin Mūsā 159
al-shūrā
citizenship 183
civil authority 177
democracy 186–7
divine rule 187
invalidation 226–8
Islamic law 108
Islamic rule 175–6
meaning 173–5
nation state 38
political authority 188
political realms 171–3
priority 61
religious authority 185–9
Shī'ah 270
Al-Sibā'ī, Muṣṭafā 160, 161
Al-Sīyāsah al-Shar'īyah fī Iṣlāḥ al-Rā'ī wa al-Ra'īyah 79
Al-Ṭahṭāwī, Rufā'ah Rāfi'
Egypt 27–8
Europe 278
freedom 3, 13, 43n2
French constitution 18
French law 12
intelligentsia x
nation state 11
observations 9
Takhlīṣ al-Ibrīz 12
Tanẓīmāt (reforms) 17, 21
Al-Ṭāliqānī (Ayatollah) 48–9
Al-Tūnsī , Khayr al-Dīn 28
caliphate 43n7
Europe 278
European civilization 10–11, 13–14
freedom 23n26
khilāfah 107
Ottoman state 27
religion 3
Surest Means for Knowledge of the Conditions of Kingdoms, The 17
Tanẓīmāt (reforms) 18–20, 21, 41
Al-Turābī, Ḥassan 'Abdullah 172, 174–5, 193n60
Algeria 108–11, 115n51, 212, 280
Alī bin Abī Ṭālib 49, 184–5, 225
Althusser, Louis 274, 276
'Amārah, Muḥammad
al-ḥākimīyah 248, 250–1
Al-Ṭahṭāwī, Rufā'ah Rāfi' 43n4
infallibility 244
Islamic state 123
religious authority 243–4
Amīn, Qāsim 72
analysis xxvi
Anthon, Faraḥ 107, 145
Arkoun, Muḥammad 149
authoritative referents 75
authority
administration 32
autocracy 40
categorization 138n7
conception xi
delegation 14
justice 56
khilāfah 99
legitimacy 53, 64, 259
occultation 60
parliamentary representation 140n39
temporal and spiritual 32

theocracy 281
tyranny 67n34
ummah 35–6
autocracy
civilization 37–42, 57
constitution 37
crisis 31
criticisms 31–42
defined 45n45
fiqh 48
Iran 48
Islamic law 57
Reformism 38
sultanate 29
awareness xii
'Awdah, 'Abd al-Qādir 156–7, 161, 195

Badie, Bertrand 86
bay'ah (pledge of allegiance) 16, 81, 84–5, 103, xxiii
Bettelheim, Charles 276

caliphate *see also khilāfah*
defense 37
Islamic law 15
Islamic state ix
modern state 28
renewal 71
revival 114n25
Riḍā, Muḥammad Rashīd 73–8
state xi
Tanẓīmāt (reforms) 28
'ulamā' 84
caliphate state 71–2
caliphs 91n32, 96, 99–100, 101–2, 114n19
censorship 56
citizenship 61–2, 68n58, 129, 183, 184, 187
civil authority 32–3, 34, 39, 80–1
civil society 147
civil state 127
civil war 146
civilization 12, 17, 19, 277, 292
colonialism 9, 147, 149, 154
constitution
Al-Bannā, Ḥasan 129
al-sharī'ah 178
autocracy 37
France 18
justice 12, 13, 56
legitimacy 39, 257
organization 68n56
political authority 54–6
political system 47
quest 63
respect 15
sharī'ah 129, 137
status 58–9
theorizing 62
constitutional *fiqh* 57–62
constitutional state 127
consultation 21
context 9, 10
criticisms 293–4, xxvi
culpability 59, 183–4, 231
culture 40

Das Kapital 275
democracy
al-shūrā 173, 179–85, 257
choice 260
citizenship 183, 191n28
divergence from *al-shūrā* 188
Islamic state 164
natural rule 187
rationalization 192n49
reservations 180–1
Riḍā, Muḥammad Rashīd 89n2
secularism 185–9
deputy representatives 50–3, 60
despotism 56
dialogue xxiv
divine right 243
draconian rule 14–15

education 40
education and culture 283, 293
Egypt

constitution 129–30
constitutional obscurities 131
Islamic state 120
multiple court systems 166n25
Muslim Brotherhood 88, 119
Napoleonic invasion 4
nation state 71
partisanship 133–4
Quṭb, Sayyid 212
reconciliation xvi
Reformism 280
reforms 9–10
Special Apparatus 129, 198
Tanẓīmāt (reforms) 27
Tawfīq, the Khedive of Egypt 30
equality 184
Europe
advancement 8
al-shūrā 179
Egyptian reforms 10
influence 17, 21, 64
Jāhilī Society 204
nation state 9
parliamentary representation 132
secularism 151
study of 37
Tanẓīmāt (reforms) 11

Faḍlallah, Muḥammad Ḥussayn 257, 258
faith 34
fanaticism 265n52
faqīh 52, 85
Faraj, ʻAbd al-Salām
Absent Duty, The 211
fiqh
autocracy 48
heritage 52–3, 63–4
imamate 222–36
Islamic legal politics 290
primacy 220
principles 58–9
reconciliation 272
relationship 270
Shīʻah 223
Shīʻite 47
Shīʻite thesis xxiv
Tanẓīmāt (reforms) 18
waiting 50
France 18
freedom
Al-Ṭahṭāwī, Rufāʻah Rāfiʻ 43n2
Al-Tūnsī, Khayr al-Dīn 24n30
censorship 56
justice 12–13
Laroui, Abdullah 23n22
of opinion 135
political 175
sharīʻah 58
fuqahāʼ
divine state 236
functions 232–3
ijtihād 230
imamate 223
Islamic legal authority 50
Islamic legal politics 3–4, 79, 80
jihadism xv
land ownership 160–1
political authority 291
political thought xx
sharīʻah 167n37
supervision 56
Tanẓīmāt (reforms) 20

Ghalyūn, Burhān 245
governance 54
governments
accountability 39
autocracy 40
executive powers 14
formation 230
Islamic Discourse 80
necessity 229–32
political nature 99
political rule 105–8
religious authority 234
governorship 113n8

Hallmarks of Autocracy and the Struggles of Enslavement, The 37, 49

Ḥanafī, Ḥasan 149
Ḥawwā, Saʿīd 201–2
heritage 32, 281
Ḥizb al-Wafd 135
Ḥussayn, Ṭāhā 112
  Poetry of the Jāhilīyah 146
Hūwaydī, Fahmī 245

Ibn Abī al-Ḍayyāf, Abū Zayd Aḥmad 14–15, 16, 21, 279
Ibn al-Qayyim al-Jawzī 79, 87
Ibn Bādīs, ʿAbd al-Ḥamīd 108–11, 280
Ibn Khaldūn 14, 44n22, 81, 91n34, 97, 103
Ibn Rushd, Abū al-Walīd Muḥammad bin Aḥmad 16, 24n45
Ibn Taymīyah, Taqqī al-Dīn Aḥmad Bin ʿAbd al-Ḥalīm 73, 83, 87
  Al-Sīyāsah al-Sharʿīyyah fi Iṣlāḥ al-Rāʿī wa al-Raʿīyah 79, 113n11
identity 54, 149, 287, 289, xii
ideology 172, 263n29, 274, 286
ijtihād 152, 155–61, 176, 222, 273–4
imamate
  absence 228–9
  Age of Occultation 49–53
  constitution 219–22
  criticisms 253
  deputy representatives 61
  designation 223–5
  divine appointment 225
  divine right 255
  fiqh 226
  infallibility 55, 68n60, 80, 232, 236, 254, 272
  Islamic law 15
  justice 66n22
  legitimacy 59, 97
  political authority 50, 228
  political theory 261
  religious authority 35
  unity 86
  Wilāyat al-Faqīh 252
Independence Party 163
India 29, 145, 208
infallibility 245, 255
innovation 58
intellectual elites xix
intelligentsia xiii
interpretation 287
Iran
  autocracy 48
  constitution 62, 65n13, 219–20
  constitutional battle 47
  ideology 257
  Islamic state 238n27
  Islamic unity 30
  oppression 31
  Parliament 240n71
  religious government 234
  revolution 213, 272
  wilāyat al-faqīh xvi
Isḥāq, Adīb 107
Islam
  ahl al-ḥal wa al-ʿaqd 82
  authority 267–8
  civil authority 34–5
  compatibility 15
  comprehensiveness 146
  conception 273
  constitutional government 48–9
  culture 277
  defensive position 293
  government 105–6
  heritage 274
  parliamentary representation 133
  political order 111
  politics 144
  politics and religion 126
  purity 54
  religion and state 196–7
  religious authority 243–4
  religious state 244–5
  rules 140n34
  social and political system 122
  social system 209
  textualist view 277
  unity 271
Islam and the Origin of Rule 98–9, 146, 281
Islamic culture xv

Islamic Discourse
al-shūrā 172, 189
consciousness 71
Reformism 41
religion xix
religious authority 32
secularism 148, 150
Islamic Fundamentalism xiv
Islamic government 165n9, 234–6
Islamic group 29
Islamic heritage 13
Islamic knowledge 287
Islamic Law 18–21
Islamic law 57, 97, 100–2, 108, 235
Islamic legal causes 73–6
Islamic legal obligation 20, 57, 85, 86
Islamic legal politics
ahl al-ḥal wa al-'aqd 82
Al-Nā'īnī, Muḥammad Ḥussayn 57
caliph 81
civil authority 39
culpability 33
fuqahā' 3–4, 80, 178–9
ijtihād 152
imamate 226
Islamic Discourse 87
khilāfah 78
parliamentary representation 36
partisanship 135
political concepts 287–8
renewal 71, 78–84
ummah 82
Islamic legal rights 49, 159
Islamic legal state 49–50
Islamic legal system 209
Islamic literature 274–83
Islamic political thought 221, 292
Islamic Reformism 6, 281
Islamic rule 228
Islamic societies 6
Islamic state
Al-Bannā, Ḥasan 137, 157
al-Ḥākimīyah 213
birth 120–8
boundaries 164n6
civil state 127
constitutional system 130
defense 206
democracy 181, 187
destinies 195–200
divergence in understanding 128–37
Islamic Discourse xi
Islamic theology 124
Muslim Brotherhood xxii
necessity 143, 262n16
need 121–4
Pakistan 219
political system 262n11, 289
politics and religion 126
Religious State 124–8
secularism 150
sharī'ah 119, 162
Sunnis 221
Islamic system 16, 132–3
Islamic theology 124
Islamic thought
application of the term 267–74
defined 274
history 269–70, 290
intellectual separation 291
lack of theory 285–6
multiplicity 278
religious text 276–7
Islamic unity 29, 30, 74
Islamism xi
isolation xiv

Jad'ān, Fahmī 30, 109, 111, 120
Jāhilī society 200–5
Jamā'at al-'Adl wa al-Iḥsān (Morocco) 186
jihadism xi, xii, xiv, xvi
jurisprudence 163
justice 12, 16, 21, 54–5

Kemal, Mustafa (Atatürk) 72, 77, 83, 90n18, 148
Khālid, Khālid Muḥammad 112
Kharijites 7

khilāfah see also caliphate
al-shar'īyah 96–7
collapse 6
corruption 102
criticisms 106–7, 112
defense 83
defined 95–6
force 102–5
foundations 99
Islamic law 101
Islamic state 121
meaning 80–2
necessity 84–8
Ottoman state 75, 85, 86
political causes 76–8
power 114n32
Riḍā, Muḥammad Rashīd 73–8
symbolism 77, 109
Khilafah or the Grand Imamah, The 6, 72
knowledge 274–5, 285, 286

Laroui, Abdullah 16, 23n22, 96, 97
law 111
leadership 227
Lebanon 272
legislation 35, 91n26, 176, 234
legitimacy
authority 258
caliphate 81
caliphs 101
constitution 39
deputy representatives 60
imamate 254
Islamic rule 228
Islamic state 128
khilāfah 99
political authority 53–64, 180
political thought 288
political *wilāyah* 230
religious authority 51
rulers 156
sultanate 32, 41, 53
Lighthouse, The 72

Mabrūk, Muḥammad Ibrāhīm 123
Maḥmūd II 27
Maḥmūd , Zakī Najīb 148
Marx, Karl
Das Kapital 275
Matter of Dealing with the Sultan, A 52
Medina 106, 122
Milestones 199, 208, 211
modern state 21, 28
Morocco 186, 280
Mosaddeq, Dr Muḥammad 220, 236n3
Mu'āwīyah bin Abī Sufyān 97
Muntaẓirī, Ḥussayn (Ayatollah) 229, 266n66
Mūsā, Salāmah 43n9, 148
Muslim Brotherhood xxi
Al-Bannā, Ḥasan 119, 137
al-ḥākimīyah 246–7
constitution 130
Egyptian constitution 130–1
Islamic state 213n7
Islamic State xxii
Islamic thought 294
khilāfah 87–8, 138n3
leadership 219
parliamentary representation 140n46
partisanship 134
political participation 129, 132
political thesis 126
politics and religion 124–5
Quṭb, Sayyid 198
Revivalists 281, 286
sharī'ah 162
Muslim Society 201, 203
Muslims 8, 29, 76, 105, 122, 184, 268
Muẓaffar al-Dīn (Shah of Iran) 48

Nāṣir al-Dīn (Shah of Iran) 30, 48
nation state
accountability 55
Al-Fāsī, 'Allāl 163
al-shūrā 179
autocracy 41
concept 27
context 9–11

defense 28
departure from 291
Egypt 71, 212
government 111
as an idea 11
justice 42
preservation 54
problematics xxii
Reformism 4, 5, 78
secularism 196
theocracy 281
unity 129
National Front (Iran) 220
National Movement (Morocco) 186
National Shūrā Council 61, 62, 67n43, 68n63
Nationalist Assembly (Turkey) 77
Nationalist Movement (Iran) 220
natural rule 24n43

occultation 60, 239n44
Omlīl, ʻAlī 208
Ottoman state
democracy 72
Egypt 10
khilāfah 75, 85, 86
Republican System 77
Tanẓīmāt (reforms) 27, 30
unity 89n3

Pahlavi, Muḥammad Rezza (Shah of Iran) 220
Pakistan 208, 212
parliamentary representation 14, 131–3
partisanship 134, 135, 294–5
Poetry of the Jāhilīyah 146
polarization 271
political authority
al-shūrā 188
Al-Tūnsī, Khayr al-Dīn 28
co-operation 52, 60
defense 53
imamate 50, 228
Iran 221
khilāfah 104
lack of unity 272–3
legitimacy 53–64, 180
religious authority 235
restraints 59
state 256
trusteeship 55
political autocracy 36, 39, 51
political freedom 13, 23n27, 23n28, 175
political geography 121
political order 111
political participation 180
political parties 133–7
political power 85, 197
political rights 61–2
political system 8, 16, 36, 37, 47, 133
political thesis 32
political thought 19, 121, xxiii
politicians 55
politics
conception xi
fiqh 50
resistance 87
Revivalist Discourse x
separated from religion 76, 77, 121–2
uṣūl 252
Poulantzas, Nicos 276
power 14, 104
problematics 6, xxii
propaganda 282–3, 286, x
prophethood 80, 224

Qurʾān 158, 172, 226, 249–50, 278
Quṭb, Muḥammad
Europe 139n16
Islamic state 123, 144–5, 195
Jāhilī Society 214n19
religion and state 197
rule 195
sharīʻah 151–2, 156
Quṭb, Sayyid
al-ḥākimīyah 205, 209
executed 210
government 195
Islamic state 123, 195–6, 208–9
Jāhilī Society 200–3, 204–5

Milestones 199, 211
Muslim Brotherhood 198, 214n9, 241

rational laws 20
Reformism
autocracy 38
caliphate state 71–2
colonialism 29
criticism of autocracy 32
education and culture 286
goals 288
ijtihād 277
Islamic thought 278, 295
Islamic unity 271
justice 12, 42
legitimacy of Tanẓīmāt 19
nation state 5, 78, xxii
neo-reformism 280
political reform 41
political threats 8
politics and religion 145
progress 292
renaissance 22n5
state 3
Sunnis 223
Tanẓīmāt (reforms) 10
thought xv
ummah 290
underdevelopment 7
value 279
Reformists x, xxii
reforms 3, 18
religion
Islamism xi
safeguarding 80
separated from politics 76, 77, 121–2, 147
and state 119
state 289
religious authority
autocracy 34
civil authority 32–3
criticisms 242–6
divine right 32
Islamic thought 276–7
legitimacy 51
references 287
religious government 235
religious legitimacy 10, 96
religious obligations 73, 123
religious power 85
Religious State 124–8
religious state 196, 242
renaissance 72
representatives 15
Revivalism 286, 292, xv
Revivalists
heritage 282
identity 277, xii
Islamic Discourse x
khilāfah 87
sharī'ah 157
revolution 60
Riḍā, Muḥammad Rashīd
ahl al-ḥal wa al-'aqd 82
Al-Khilāfah aw al-Imāmah al-'Uẓmā 76, 78, 84, 98
al-Manār 89n15
imamate 86
Islamic Discourse 87
Islamic legal politics 78–84
Islamic state 137
khilāfah 71, 73–8, 80, 107
Khilāfah or the Grand Imāmah, The 6, 72
retrograde discourse 87
Salafism 290
utopian discourse 97–8
rights 111, 180
rule 15, 16, 79, 110
rule of compulsion 85

Salafism xiii, xiv–xv, xxii
Salīm III 27
Saudi Arabia xvi
science 150
secularism 145–53
Self Criticism and the Intents of Islamic Sharī'ah and Its Excellences 281
Shafiq, Mūnīr 145

Shams al-Dīn, Muḥammad Mahdī (Ayatollah) 232, 241, 257, 259
sharī'ah
  Al-Bannā, Ḥasan 136–7
  al-ḥākimīyah 208
  Al-Mawdūdī, Abū al-A'lā 207
  authenticity 148
  authoritative referents 147
  defense 147, 149
  deviation 37
  execution 150
  freedom 58
  implementation 157, 162
  Islamic state 127–8, 131, 151
  khilāfah 86
  legitimacy 84
  opposition to Tanẓīmāt 19
  Riḍā, Muḥammad Rashīd 74–5
  rulers 35
  rulings 161–4
  separated from politics 139n15
  state 143–5
  system for life 210
  Tanẓīmāt (reforms) 18
Sharī'atī, Dr 'Alī 220
Shī'ah 7, 123–4, 223–4, 269–70
Shī'ite
  fiqh 47, 49, 60
  Islamic Discourse xxiii
  Islamic state 122
  Reformism 42
Shī'ite *fiqh* 62, 65n8
Shī'ite *uṣūl* 58
socio-political system 7
sovereignty 22n2, 180
Spark, The 110
Special Apparatus 129, 198
state
  al-ḥākimīyah 251
  conception xi
  constitution 129–33
  formation 82
  Isamic necessity 143–5
  necessity 53–4
  political identity 288
  political thought 3, 9, 285
  and religion 119
  religion 289
  separated from religion 147
  theoretical problematic 288
sultanate
  abolished 77, 98
  absolute rule 99–100
  despotism 56
  illegitimacy 7
  infallibility 55
  legitimacy 32, 35, 41, 53
  permission 52
  subservience 34
  trial 76
  tyranny 57
  unity 74
Sultanate Rules 79
Sunnis
  al-sharī'ah 155
  constitution 219
  fuqahā' 81
  Islamic Discourse xxiii
  Islamic political thought 221
  khilāfah 123–4
  political authority 123
  Reformism 42
  ummah 269–70
  uṣūl 168n53
  wilāyat al-faqīh 256
Surest Means for Knowledge of the Conditions of Kingdoms, The 17
Sykes Picot Agreement 98
system of rule 150–1
systems 122, 175–9

Takhlīṣ al-Ibrīz 12
Taliban xvi
Tanbīh al-Ummah 53
  Al-Nā'īnī, Muḥammad Ḥussayn 59
Tanẓīmāt (reforms)
  al-sharī'ah 28
  Al-Ṭahṭāwī, Rufā'ah Rāfi' 17
  autocracy 41
  conflict with *sharī'ah* 18

defense 42
Europe 11
intervention 24n51
Islamic legal obligation 20
Ottoman state 10, 27
political objections 19
Tawfīq, Khedive of Egypt 30
theocracy 207, 210, 235, 281, xxii
theocratic state 197, xi
theory 72
thought 274, xxii
transformation 221
trusteeship
ahl al-ḥal wa al-ʿaqd 103
al-sharīʿah 154
caliphs 99–100
endorsement 177
fuqahāʾ 51, 228
imamate 236
political authority 55
religious obligations 73
rights 110–11
ummah 59, 61
Turkey 76, 77, 109, 148, 149
tyranny 57

ʿulamā 20, 82–3, 125
ʿUmar bin ʿAbd al-ʿAzīz 97
ummah
al-shūrā 174
authority 35–6, 45n30
central elite 82
future 225
identity 54, 289
ijtihād 156
intervention 254
political power 197
representatives 61
responsibility 257–8
rule 190n11
Shīʿah 223
supervision 110–11
system of rule 136
trusteeship 59, 61
unity 41
wilāyat al-faqīh 261
ʿUmar bin al-Khaṭṭāb 82
uṣūl 5, 175, 223, 269–70
uṣūlī 21
ʿUthmān, Muḥammad Fatḥī 246

Warning to the Ummah and Admonition to the Denomination 48–9, 62–3
Western philosophy 150
wilāyat al-faqīh
criticisms 252–61
legitimacy 260–1
political wilayah 229
split 291
trusteeship 228
ummah 257–8

Yakan, Fatḥī 171, 188, 190n5, 201
Yāsīn, ʿAbd al-Salām 119, 143, 149, 153–4, 166n34, 185–9
Yazīd bin Muʿāwīyah 49

Zaghlūl, Saʿd Pāshā 83

www.ingramcontent.com/pod-product-compliance
Ingram Content Group UK Ltd.
Pitfield, Milton Keynes, MK11 3LW, UK
UKHW021904220326
469204UK00008B/175

9 781780 766492